Essays On Otherness

Jean Laplanche is one of the most trenchant psychoanalytic thinkers of our time. These essays in particular clarify a number of themes that have not yet been adequately introduced to an English-speaking audience.

Judith Butler, University of California, Berkeley

Essays On Otherness offers the most original, philosophically sophisticated, and far-reaching critical reading of Freud's metapsychology since Lacan. Exegetically scrupulous and rigorously argued, these essays go straight to the heart of the psychoanalytical enterprise.

Peter Osborne, Professor of Modern European Philosophy, Middlesex University

Essays On Otherness presents, for the first time in English, a key selection from the recent work of Jean Laplanche. He is one of the most important theorists of contemporary psychoanalysis. His work takes the decentering of the subject beyond the familiar parameters of post-structuralist theory towards a new understanding of otherness in the formation of human subjectivity.

The central theme of Essays On Otherness is the role of the other in psychic life. Since Freud's newly controversial abandonment of his seduction theory in 1897, psychoanalysis has given priority to the innate development program of the individual over the intersubjective relation to the other person. Laplanche returns to and reformulates Freud's abandoned seduction theory as a general theory of primal seduction: a seduction intrinsic to the everyday relations of childcare and nurturing.

Essays On Otherness reformulates some of the central categories of psychoanalysis leading to a new understanding of the analytic situation, of the role of seduction and transference in cultural production, and a new psychoanalytic theory of human time. Its implications will transform the current controversies over recovered memory and the after-effects of trauma and sexual abuse. The essays gathered together here for the first time are indispensable reading for all those concerned with the implications of contemporary developments in psychoanalysis.

Jean Laplanche is Professor Emeritus of Psychoanalysis at the University of Paris, (VII).

Warwick Studies in European Philosophy

Edited by Andrew Benjamin
Professor of Philosophy, University of Warwick

This series presents the best and most original work being done within the European philosophical tradition. The books included in the series seek not merely to reflect what is taking place within European philosophy, but also to contribute to the growth and development of that plural tradition. Work written in the English language as well as translations into English are to be included, engaging the tradition at all levels – whether by introductions that show the contemporary philosophical force of certain works, or by collections that explore an important thinker or topic, or by significant contributions that call for their own critical evaluation.

Titles already published in the series

Walter Benjamin's Philosophy
Edited by Andrew Benjamin and Peter Osborne

Bataille: Writing the Sacred
Edited by Carolyn Bailey Gill

Emmanuel Levinas: The Genealogy of Ethics
John Llewelyn

Maurice Blanchot: The Demand of Writing
Edited by Carolyn Bailey Gill

Body- and Image-Space: Re-reading Walter Benjamin
Sigrid Weigel (*trans.* Georgina Paul)

Passion in Theory: Conceptions of Freud and Lacan
Robyn Ferrell

Hegel After Derrida
Edited by Stuart Barnett

Retreating the Political
Philippe Lacoue-Labarthe and Jean-Luc Nancy

On Jean-Luc Nancy: The Sense of Philosophy
Edited by Darren Sheppard, Simon Sparks and Colin Thomas

Deleuze and Philosophy: The Difference Engineer
Edited by Keith Ansell Pearson

Very Little . . . Almost Nothing: Death, Philosophy, Literature
Simon Critchley

Blanchot: Extreme Contemporary
Leslie Hill

Textures of Light: Vision and Touch in Irigaray, Levinas and Merleau-Ponty
Cathryn Vasseleu

Essays On Otherness

Jean Laplanche

London and New York

First published 1999
by Routledge
2 Park Square, Milton Park, Abingdon, Oxon, OX14 4RN

Simultaneously published in the USA and Canada
by Routledge
270 Madison Ave, New York NY 10016

Transferred to Digital Printing 2005

Chapters 1, 3, 4, 5, 7, 8 and 9 originally published in French by Aubier in Jean
Laplanche, *La révolution copernicienne inachevée*, 1992.

Typeset in Perpetua by J&L Composition Ltd, Filey, North Yorkshire

British Library Cataloguing in Publication Data
A catalogue record for this book is available from the British Library

Library of Congress Cataloging in Publication Data
A catalogue record for this book has been requested

ISBN 0-415-13107-3 (hbk)
ISBN 0-415-13108-1 (pbk)

The publication of this book is supported
by the Cultural Service of the
French Embassy in London.

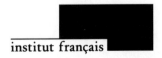

institut français

Contents

Acknowledgements

International Journal of Psychoanalysis for the use of 'Interpretation between Determinism and Hermeneutics: a Restatement of the Problem', *International Journal of Psychoanalysis* (1992) 73, 429–45; 'Seduction, Persecution, Revelation', *International Journal of Psychoanalysis* (1995) 75, 663–82. Copyright © Institute of Psycho-Analysis.

Jean Laplanche for the use of articles from *La révolution copernicienne inachevée,* © Aubier, 1992, and for the use of 'A Short Treatise on the Unconscious', *La Nouvelle Revue de Psychanalyse*, no. 48, Paris: Gallimard, 1993.

Editions Aubier/Flammarion for the use of articles from *La révolution copernicienne inachevée/The Unfinished Copernican Revolution*, © Aubier, Paris, 1992.

The Institute of Contemporary Arts for the use of 'Notes on Afterwardsness' which is an extensively revised version of a conversation with Martin Stanton which first appeared in John Fletcher and Martin Stanton, eds, *Jean Laplanche: Seduction, Translation and the Drives: A Dossier,* © Institute of Contemporary Arts, London, 1992.

Essays 1, 3, 4, 5, 7, 8 and 9 were previously published in *La révolution copernicienne inachevée*, Paris: Aubier, 1992. Essay 2 first appeared as 'Court traité de l'inconscient', *Nouvelle Revue de Psychanalyse*, no. 48, Autumn, 1993, pp. 69–96. Essay 6 first appeared as 'Séduction, Persécution, Révélation', in *Psychanalyse à l'Université*, vol. 18, no. 72, 1993, pp. 3–34.

Acknowledgements

Essays 1, 2, 4, 7, 8 and 9 were translated by Luke Thurston; Essay 3 was retranslated by Leslie Hill for this volume; Essays 5 and 6 first appeared in English in the *International Journal of Psychoanalysis* and were translated by Philip Slotkin, and revised by Professor Laplanche; Essay 10 is based on a conversation with Martin Stanton that appeared in *Jean Laplanche: Seduction, Translation and the Drives*, eds John Fletcher and Martin Stanton, Institute of Contemporary Arts, London, 1992, and has been extensively revised by Professor Laplanche for this volume.

I would like to thank both Professor Laplanche and Dr Leslie Hill, University of Warwick, for their extensive help with the laborious process of editing and revising the translations.

John Fletcher

Introduction:
Psychoanalysis and the Question
of the Other

The essays in this volume represent the most important theoretical develop-ments in the recent work of Jean Laplanche. Most of them are taken from the French collection *La révolution copernicienne inachevée*[1] whose title essay appears in this volume. They have been selected because they focus on the primacy of the other in the formation of subjectivity as conceived by Laplanche in his return to and reformulation of Freud's abandoned 'seduction theory'. This return and reformulation have been the basis for Laplanche's critique of traditional Freudian metapsychology and for his proposed 'new foundations' for the theory of psychoanalysis.[2] Over the last thirty years Laplanche has produced a critical archaeology of the Freudian conceptual field, of its contra-dictory logics and of the crucial role of certain 'lost' concepts within it – the primal fantasies, 'leaning-on' (*Anlehnung*, Strachey's 'anaclisis'), afterwardsness (*Nachträglichkeit*, Strachey's 'deferred action'). He is best known in the English language world as the co-author with Jean-Bertrand Pontalis of the great critical and theoretical dictionary *The Language of Psychoanalysis* (1967), and in literary and film studies as the co-author, also with Pontalis, of the classic essay on the primal fantasies translated as 'Fantasy and the Origins of Sexuality' (1964).[3] From this work of retrieval and critical reconstruction has emerged in

---

1 Paris: Aubier, 1992.

2 See *New Foundations for Psychoanalysis* (1987b), trans. David Macey, Oxford: Basil Blackwell, 1989.

3 'Fantasy and the Origins of Sexuality', *Formations of Fantasy*, eds Victor Burgin, James Donald and Cora Kaplan, London: Methuen, 1986; *The Language of Psychoanalysis* (1967), trans. Donald Nicholson-Smith, London: The Hogarth Press, 1973.

a series of published 'seminars' the five-volume *Problématiques* (1980–7), a reformulation of the conceptual grounds of psychoanalysis of which *New Foundations* (1987) provides a retrospective overview. This work continues with *Le fourvoiement biologisant de la sexualité chez Freud* (1993).[4]

The essays collected here present the constitutive role of the other in psychic life within Laplanche's generalised theory of primal or originary seduction and they work through its radical implications for certain key categories and concepts of traditional metapsychology: repression, the drives, primal fantasy, afterwardsness, paranoia, masochism, transference, mourning and, of course, the unconscious itself. They also draw out its implications for a new psycho-analytic understanding of human time.

In its opening essay 'The Unfinished Copernican Revolution', the present volume introduces Laplanche's reposing of Freudian metapsychology in relation to the question of the other through the theme of the decentering of the human subject, a theme that has been characteristic of post-structuralist thought especially in France, from the 1960s to the 1980s. Laplanche addresses this theme through Freud's famous positioning of his work as one of the three world-historic blows to human narcissism, each of which is said to have brought about a decentering of the human being – 'Man' – in relation to the cosmos (Copernicus), to the natural world and its evolution (Darwin), and to his own nature (Freud himself).[5] The conflicting traditions of astronomical speculation in western thought were divided between a dominant geocentric or earth-centered model of the universe (represented in the 'great synthesis' of Ptolemy in the second century A.D.) and a minority heliocentric or sun-centered one (from Aristarchus of Samos in the third century B.C. to Copernicus and Galileo at the beginning of the modern era, and beyond). At issue, as Laplanche suggests, was the question of 'centering': whether the stars and planets moved around a fixed point, the earth; or whether the earth moved around the sun, and the 'fixed' stars and constellations were at distances beyond the earth's solar system, thus opening up the possibility of a quasi-infinite universe without a single center.

In a rather different way from Freud, Laplanche proposes an illuminating analogy between metapsychology and the so-called Copernican Revolution. He

---

4 *Problématiques I–V*, Paris: Presses Universitaires de France, 1980–7. *Le fourvoiement biologisant de la sexualité chez Freud*, Paris: Synthélabo, 1993.
5 'A Difficulty in the Path of Psycho-Analysis' (1917a), *SE* XVII, pp. 137–44.

argues that, 'if Freud is his own Copernicus, he is also his own Ptolemy',[6] describing a constant oscillation in Freud's thought between a formulation of concepts and arguments that pose a radical decentering of the human psyche, Freud's 'Copernican Revolution', and a continually resurgent movement of Ptolemaic recentering, that either abandons those elements or draws them back into an endogenous model of psychic life. To this dialectic between a decentering to which Freud officially aligns himself and a recurrent recentering, Laplanche joins the diagnostic notion of a wandering or going-astray (*fourvoiement*) of Freudian thought. This characteristically manifests itself in the insistence of a metaphorical biology or metabiology (although it may take other forms), and as much as the initial discoveries is marked by a certain theoretical necessity (*exigence*) that is determined by its object: the human psyche and its formation (*Le fourvoiement biologisant . . .*, op. cit., pp. 5–10). These wanderings astray are magnetised and drawn by the object of inquiry even when they lead to an impasse. The covering over and occlusion of the discovery of the radical otherness of the unconscious and of sexuality in Freud's thought, Laplanche suggests, trace out the movements of just such a covering over in the human subject itself. In a formula parodying Haeckel's law of which Freud was so enamoured – 'ontogenesis [the development of the human being] reproduces the stages of phylogenesis [the development of the species]' – Laplanche formulates 'Laplanche's law' in which 'theoreticogenesis', the development of theory, reproduces ontogenesis, the fate of sexuality and the unconscious in the human being.

A number of Freud's central concepts – the ego, narcissism, the unconscious, the sexual 'instinct' – are marked by an oscillation between distinct and competing conceptualisations in which an original breakthrough is covered over by a revision that initiates a certain going-astray of the concept along a structurally determined path. So Jeffrey Mehlman in the introduction to his translation of Laplanche's *Life and Death in Psychoanalysis* (1970) notes that Laplanche's analyses locate a conflict inhabiting each of these terms, such that 'the entire body of Freud's *œuvre* is constituted by Laplanche as an elaborately structured polemical field in which two mutually exclusive conceptual schemes may be seen to be struggling, as it were, to dominate – or cathect – a single terminological apparatus'.[7] *Life and Death*, the *Problématiques* and the recent *Le*

6 'The Unfinished Copernican Revolution' in this volume, p. 60.
7 *Life and Death in Psychoanalysis* (1970), trans. Jeffrey Mehlman, Baltimore: The Johns Hopkins University Press, 1976, p. ix.

fourvoiement biologisant demonstrate the displacements, compensations and retrievals internal to the general economy of Freudian thought that are consequent upon such strayings. The most striking of these is the reappearance of an original conception of a sexual component drive pressing repetitively towards the unbinding that separates the libido from its unconscious representations, and tends towards absolute discharge. This conception had been lost in the absorption of sexuality into the totalising dynamic of 'Eros', the new 'life instinct'. However, the 'daemonic' sexual drive returns in displaced form, Laplanche argues, in Freud's deliriously speculative, metabiological elaboration of the 'death instinct'.

Laplanche sketches out three major strayings of Freudian thought which can be clearly defined, he suggests provocatively, by what they lead to, by their post-Freudian progeny (*Le fourvoiement biologisant*, op. cit., pp. 10–11). The first involves the biologising of sexuality and finds its direct descendants in Melanie Klein and her followers. The second, which finds its heirs in the structuralism of Lacan, consists of situating structure or the structural in the heart of the unconscious. A third going-astray is indicated by the theme of the Ptolemaic reconstruction or recentering of the human being on itself (the legacy of which one might see at work in classical ego-psychology).

The essays gathered here seek to use the analysis of a 'decentering' and a 'straying' to prolong the 'Copernican' dynamic of Freud's unfinished revolution, and to confront certain key metapsychological concepts with the constitutive action of the other that their 'excentric' but foreshortened movement opens onto. In doing so they elaborate an understanding of 'otherness' – of the external other and of the internal other, and of the relation between them – that amounts to a refoundation of psychoanalytic theory.

The Return to Freud's Special Theory of Seduction

In the current controversies over child sexual abuse and the recovered/false memory syndrome, Freud is attacked by polemicists on both sides but for opposite reasons. Jeffrey Masson in *The Assault on Truth* (1984), subtitled 'Freud's Suppression of the Seduction Theory', claims that Freud had not so much changed his mind as, through a failure of moral courage when faced with the consequences of his findings, 'suppressed' the truth of the extensiveness of child abuse. Frederick Crews in *The Memory Wars* (1997) claims that the scenes of child abuse cited by Freud were not directly recalled but were the result of interpretation and reconstruction, and consequently that

4

Freud had invented them and forced them on his patients.[8] However retrospectively simplified and sweeping Freud's later accounts of the abandoned seduction theory and its materials were, it is clear from the correspondence with Fliess that some patients did directly present conscious memories of incest and abuse, and that even after the abandonment of the theory Freud acknowledged both the occurrence and the destructive effects of such events.[9] The crucial question, however, is the significance to be attributed to such events and what they were being invoked to prove.

Freud had been attempting to explain and thereby cure hysterical and obsessional symptoms, by tracing them back to repressed memories of sexual scenes in early childhood. While his concern was to account for a range of adult symptoms, the theory of infantile sexuality with which he comes to replace the seduction theory is not so much an account of hysteria as a general theory of human sexual development, within which neurosis is repositioned as a particular vicissitude. What was involved was not just a change of causal explanations but a change in the object to be explained. Freud and Freudian orthodoxy have presented this as a necessary progress from the insufficiently explanatory power of 'seduction' to the universal biological stages of endogenous development,

8 Frederick Crews et al., The Memory Wars: Freud's Legacy in Dispute, London: Granta Books, 1997. J. M. Masson, The Assault on Truth: Freud's Suppression of the Seduction Theory with new Preface and Afterword, Harmondsworth: Penguin Books, 1995.
9 While the classic statement of the seduction theory, 'The Aetiology of Hysteria' (1896c, SE III), predominantly stresses cases where the sexual scenes were the outcome of a complex process of retrieval, not something the patients came into analysis conscious of, and so are open to the claim that Freud suggested them, they also contain references to cases where childhood sexual relations were sustained over a long period continuous with adult memory. The Emma case, from 'A Project for a Scientific Psychology' (1950a [1895], SE I), discussed below, deals with a case of remembered rather than reconstructed sexual molestation, although only recalled after the analysis had begun. An early retrospect such as 'My Views on the Part played by Sexuality in the Neuroses' (1906a, SE VII) cites cases Freud still regarded as cases of seduction 'not open to doubt' while going on to expound the new theory of infantile sexuality. Later retrospects such as 'On the History of the Psycho-Analytic Movement' (1914d, SE XIV) and An Autobiographical Study (1925d, SE XX), however, treat the earlier cases and the variety of different materials they presented rather reductively, as examples of clinical error, based on the analyst's naive belief in directly offered and remembered rather than reconstructed sexual scenes.

from the memory of supposedly real events to the power of fantasy and the universality of the Oedipus Complex. Laplanche has argued, however, that something was lost in this much celebrated and currently much vilified transition: a particular temporal model of psychic causality, *Nachträglichkeit*, translated by Strachey as 'deferred action' but for which Laplanche suggests the English neologism 'afterwardsness' (Fr. *après coup*), and an understanding of the origins of human sexuality as exogenous, traumatic and intrusive – an incursion from the other.

In 'A Project for a Scientific Psychology' (1950a [1895]), Freud presents the case of Emma as one where the hysterical phobia of a young woman – a compulsion not to go into shops *alone* – is traced back to a forgotten childhood scene of sexual molestation. The connection between the hysterical symptom and the sexual scene is governed by the logic of afterwardsness; as Freud says of hysterical repression in his conclusion to his presentation: 'We invariably find that a memory is repressed which has only become a trauma by deferred action [*Nachträglichkeit*]. The cause of this state of things is the retardation of puberty as compared with the rest of the individual's development' (*SE* I, p. 356). The second sentence indicates that Freud is as yet still operating with the pre-psychoanalytic assumption that sexuality only develops naturally with the maturation of the genitals at puberty and in ignorance of the infantile sexuality whose modes and organisations he was later to describe in the *Three Essays* (1905d). Nevertheless, the case presents a distinctive temporal model of psychic causality that instead of being developed and refined disappears underground with the shift to the new developmental framework. For the trauma of seduction takes place, not as the breaking in or flooding of the ego's defences by painful or unmasterable excitations, whose discharge is either immediate or delayed (as in the theory of abreaction), but in the interval between two events. Emma traces her hysterical outbreak back to the remembered scene of its first appearance, where at the age of twelve she fled in fright from a shop when she saw two shop assistants laughing together. She recalls that they seemed to be laughing at her clothes and that one of them pleased her sexually. Her phobic reaction, both then and in its persistence years afterwards, is unintelligible in its intensity, so disproportionate is it to the apparently untraumatic occasion. She seems hardly in need of protection, however, for on later occasions even the company of a small child is enough to make her feel safe. This reaction seems puzzlingly unconnected with either the laughter at her clothes or her pleasure in one of the assistants. The analysis then gives rise to a second

6

memory of an earlier scene which she denies having in mind at the moment of the first hysterical outbreak. On two occasions as a child of eight she had gone into a shop to buy sweets, when her genitals had been touched through her clothes by the shopkeeper. After the second occasion she stayed away. She reproached herself for her second visit and Freud claims that a state of 'oppressive bad conscience' could be traced back to this experience.

Freud traces the associative pathways between the two events and the role of certain symbolic elements – the shop as *mise en scène*, the shopkeeper in one and the assistants in the other, the laughter which she later associates with the grin of the shopkeeper as he perpetrated his assault, the reference to clothes – by means of which the second scene retroactively evokes the first, such that its sexual meaning for her is now precipitated. The memory of the first scene was operating in the second scene, however, with a different effect from when it happened as an event. Freud comments: 'The memory aroused what it was certainly not able to do at the time, a *sexual release*, which was transformed into anxiety. The fact that the sexual release too entered consciousness is proved by the otherwise incomprehensible idea that the laughing shop-assistant pleased her' (ibid., pp. 354–5). The anxiety that produces her flight and sustains her continuing phobia – the fear that the assault may be repeated – also blocks out any memory of the first scene, except for the element of the clothes. The reference to clothes, together with the elements of the second scene that rhyme with the first scene, as Freud points out, are subject to two false connections or displacements: that the laughter is at her clothes and that it is one of the assistants who excites sexual pleasure in her. Freud sees the release of sexual feeling as precipitating the pathological defence of hysterical repression with the formation of the overdetermined symbolic substitute, the clothes, and observes:

> . . . it is highly noteworthy that it [the sexual release] was not linked to the assault when it was experienced. Here we have a case of a memory arousing an affect which it did not arouse as an experience, because in the meantime the change [brought about] in puberty had made possible a different understanding of what was remembered.
>
> (p. 356)

In their commentary on this case Laplanche and Pontalis retrieve two emphases: first, 'sexuality literally breaks in from the outside . . . reaches the subject from *the other*' where its traces remain unintegrated and 'encysted';

second, after the events of puberty the traumatic anxiety 'is traced back to the recollection of the first event, an external event which has become an inner event, an inner "foreign body", which now breaks out from within the subject' ('Fantasy and the Origins of Sexuality', op. cit., p. 10). The status of the first scene in the interval between the two is not clearly specified, and Laplanche suggests that it is neither repressed nor integrated into the preconscious store of memories, but remains in a limbo, unworked over and isolated. Most strikingly it appears to have produced no phobic reaction or flight in the way that the later 'innocent' scene did. It undergoes repression, however, from the moment in the second scene when it is translated into the sexual understanding of puberty, produces a sexual release which is both displaced onto the laughing assistant of the second scene, and is transformed into anxiety and its phobic reaction. From then onwards it persists, and Laplanche in his more extended commentary on the case in *Life and Death in Psychoanalysis* cites a return by Freud to the same theme in another text of the same year, the *Studies on Hysteria* (1895d): 'We presume that the psychical trauma – or more precisely the memory of the trauma – acts like a foreign body which long after its entry must be continued to be regarded as an agent that is still at work' (*SE* II, p. 6). The ego's defences, oriented towards distressing perceptions coming in from the outside, as Freud points out, are caught unawares by the appearance of an internal representation, a memory that in the new context releases both a pleasure that is displaced and consequently anxiety. In the interplay between the two scenes, a moment of inscription and a later moment of reinscription or translation (a term that is to be central to Laplanche's reformulation of the seduction theory), there arises a sexual and traumatic representation of a scene that was for the subject neither fully sexual nor traumatic in its happening as an event. In the *Project* Freud labels this model 'The Hysterical *Proton Pseudos*', a term taken from Aristotle's theory of the syllogism as Strachey informs us (a false premise from which results a false conclusion). Laplanche interprets this as a 'primal deceit', 'a kind of objective lie inscribed in the facts . . . as though there existed in the facts themselves a kind of fundamental duplicity' (*Life and Death*, op. cit., p. 34). Freud restated this proposition as an anomaly in a text of the following year, 'The Aetiology of Hysteria' (1896c): '. . . we are not accustomed to the notion of powers emanating from a mnemic image which were absent from the real impression' (*SE* III, p. 213). The condition for this disjunction between the external event and its internal representation or derivative is attributed at this stage to the intervening force of a biological sexuality that comes with puberty. For this reason it has been ignored as

8

obsolete by orthodox Freudianism.[10] However, it is in this gap between the seductive intrusion of the other and the attack of the internal foreign body that Laplanche will install his theses of primal seduction, the enigmatic signifier and the translation model of primal repression.

As Laplanche has argued, the 'turning point' of 1897, the abandonment of the seduction theory, does not represent a clean or absolute break. Elements of the theory persist in different forms throughout Freud's work, and the acknowledgement of the traumatic power of actual events is a recurrent emphasis throughout the later period of the elaboration of infantile sexuality and the dominance of the two theories of the drives. In the case of the Wolf Man (1918b), Freud claims to trace his analysand's dream of the white wolves watching from the tree outside his window back to early memories of a scene of parental intercourse, which he attempts to establish in considerable detail: the parents dressed in white, the afternoon setting, the act of intercourse from behind repeated three times, etc. Throughout the case Freud wrestles with the Jungian objection that such scenes are mere back-projections from the present (*Zurückphantasien*), until the moment where he allows that such primal scenes may in fact be primal fantasies, albeit typical and quasi-universal structures, that he compares to Kant's transcendental categories as conditions for the possibility of particular experiences. Even then he sees them as attached to early perceptions, if not of parental intercourse then of the sight of animals coupling, that are only reactivated and given meaning at a later point. As Laplanche and Pontalis show in their classic essay on the primal fantasies, when the ground of the real traumatic event fails to materialise in individual biography, then Freud is driven to supplement this with his anthropological speculations from *Totem and Taboo* (1912–13, *SE* XIII), with its postulation of

10 In the retrospective light of the later developments in psychoanalytic theory with respect to infantile sexuality, Freud's assertion that the first scene of molestation produced no sexual excitation seems unlikely, especially given Emma's return to the shop a second time and her 'bad conscience' afterwards. What seems more relevant, however, is not the absence or presence of sexual excitation in the first scene, but the deferral of the trauma and its phobic reaction thereafter to the second scene, together with the appearance in displaced form of sexual feeling, in the new context of the sexual representations and understandings that come with puberty. This would make sense in terms of Laplanche's model of the blocking of a new 'translation' and the continuing attack from within of the untranslated. Laplanche returns to the case of Emma in the context of his 'translation' theory in *Problématiques IV: L'inconscient et le ça*, Paris: Presses Universitaires de France, 1981, pp. 124–6.

a phylogenetic heritage of collective memories and scenes of the *Urvater* and his dominance of the Darwinian primal horde from human prehistory, where the violent scenes of rape, castration and patricide were supposedly actual events. These two alternative explanatory paradigms, of the traumatic infantile event, prototypically incestuous, and of the phylogenetic heritage, in which ontogenesis or individual development repeats the stages of phylogenesis or the supposed development of the species, coexist alongside the dominant later model of the unfolding of an endogenous, libidinal development, through fixed oral, anal and genital stages. In their archaeological retrieval of the concept of the primal fantasies Laplanche and Pontalis interpret the three scenes of the castration of the son, the seduction of the daughter, the sadistic possession of the mother, all turning on the primal father with his reference back to phylogenesis and pre-history, as theoretical symptoms of an impasse in which Freud found himself in the wake of the break up of the conceptual complex of the seduction theory: an entrapment in a dualism of inherited constitution versus the traumatic event. The primal fantasies represent a false synthesis of the scenario of the event with the antecedent reality of hereditary givens ('Fantasy and the Origins of Sexuality', op. cit., p. 18).

Laplanche's reproach to Masson is that in his polemic against Freud he reduces the seduction *theory* to the mere observation or suppression of abusive events, and completely fails to grasp the presence of a distinctive if incompletely elaborated theoretical problematic. In returning to the seduction theory and Freud's failure with it, Laplanche is seeking to elaborate what he calls 'the general theory of seduction', one which will account, not just for specific pathological formations, but for the construction of the unconscious and the psychical apparatus in general. This will take place on the terrain of infantile sexuality and the drives as classically systematised in the *Three Essays on the Theory of Sexuality* (1905d), but will also involve the temporality of afterwardsness as the very temporality of seduction, and essentially the primacy of the adult other, the other of *personal* prehistory (to adapt Freud's formulation).[11]

The General Theory of Primal Seduction

Seduction for Laplanche characterises what he calls the foundational process of the human being, a primal or universal situation that is 'beyond even the most

---

11 'the father in his own personal prehistory', *The Ego and the Id* (1923b), *SE* XIX, p. 31.

general contingency'. He describes this and its ramifications extensively in the long third chapter of *New Foundations*:

> The *primal* situation is one in which a new born child, an infant in the etymological sense of the word (*in-fans*: speechless), is confronted with the adult world. This may even mean that what we call the Oedipus complex is in a sense subject to contingency.
>
> (pp. 89–90)

> I am, then, using the term *primal seduction* to describe a fundamental situation in which an adult proffers to a child verbal, non-verbal and even behavioural signifiers which are pregnant with unconscious sexual significations.
>
> (p. 126)

One of the key differences from Freud's specialised theory of seduction is the primacy and agency of the other as a fully constituted subject, i.e. one with an unconscious. Whatever the preformed or instinctual reflexes the infant as biological subject of need may *actively* engage in, such as suckling reflexes, crying and excretory functions (an *activity* with respect to the functions of self-preservation), the situation of primal seduction, that coincides in part with the adult's meeting of the infant's needs, is nevertheless distinguished from that reciprocal activity by a profound asymmetry: the infant's passivity and openness to the actions, gestures and words of the other. Laplanche continually insists that the mechanisms traditionally postulated by psychoanalytic theory, even the most primitive – projection, introjection, splitting, repression, forclosure, etc. – are all the work of the individual in question, 'auto-centered'. What this ignores is the action of the other on the subject, in particular the implantation, in some cases the violent intromission, of enigmatic signifiers from the other into the primitive body-ego or skin-ego of the infant. Seduction then is not reducible either to the memories or fantasies of the subject, nor to the brute reality or materiality of certain gestures: touching the child's penis or vagina might seem clearly sexual and therefore 'seductive', but as Laplanche remarks this is to regress to a pre-psychoanalytic *genital* conception of sexuality. What about touching the child's lips or anus? given the potential erogeneity of the entire body surface, Laplanche asks, what about touching the child's big toe? What kind of 'reality' is at stake?[12] The presence of sexual representations and unconscious

---

12 'Seduction, Persecution, Revelation' in this volume, p. 169.

fantasies in the adult are crucial, but these must be conceived in relation to the irreducible reality of transmission, of communication and of the message.

Taking the formulation from Lacan,[13] Laplanche establishes the 'enigmatic signifier' as a fully-fledged concept by invoking another Lacanian distinction between a signifier *of* – a specific meaning or signified – and a signifier *to* – addressed to and interpellating a specific subject, a subject who may not be able to attribute a specific signified to it but who knows that it is addressed to them. The enigmatic signifier is based on 'the possibility that the signifier may be *designified*, or lose what it signifies, without thereby losing its power to signify *to*' (*New Foundations*, p. 45). They are enigmatic, not just because the infant has no access to a code to determine their meaning, or because they outstrip its capacities for understanding, but because, compromised by the unconscious wishes of the other, they are opaque to the adult as well.

> In the primal situation we have, then, a child whose ability to adapt is real but limited, weak and waiting to be perverted, and a deviant adult (deviant with regard to any sexual norms . . . deviant or split with regard to himself) . . . given that the child lives on in the adult, an adult faced with a child is particularly likely to be deviant and inclined to perform bungled or even symbolic actions because he is involved in a relationship with his other self, with the other he once was. The child in front of him brings out the child within him . . . we have a 'Traviata', someone who has been led astray and 'seduced'.
>
> (p. 103)

While this may have the scandalous effect of building a structurally inescapable perversity into the adult–child relationship, what are in question are not abusive events. In Laplanche's sense seduction is ordinary. As he notes, 'The "attentions

13 'The agency of the letter in the unconscious or reason since Freud', *Écrits: A Selection*, trans. Alan Sheridan, London: Tavistock, 1977, p. 166. Lacan's 'enigmatic signifier of the sexual trauma' refers to the repressed term which is substituted for by a conscious representation in the metaphorical structure of the symptom. Laplanche, however, reserves the phrase for the gestures, actions or words of the other in the situation of primal seduction. For a discussion and genealogy of the concept in Laplanche's thought, see John Fletcher, 'The Letter in the Unconscious: the enigmatic signifier in the work of Jean Laplanche', in *Jean Laplanche: Seduction, Translation and the Drives*, Institute of Contemporary Arts, 1992, pp. 93–120. As the title of this essay unfortunately indicates the unwitting slippage between the Lacanian and Laplanchean usage is all too easy.

of a mother" or the "aggression of a father" are seductive only because they are not transparent . . . because they convey something enigmatic' (p. 128).

The notion of an enigma that poses a question and elicits various attempts at a solution was central to the retrieval and explication of the primal fantasies as subjective myths of origin by Laplanche and Pontalis in their 1964 paper. This parallels Freud's account of the sexual theories of children in his 1908 paper of that name, where children puzzle over answers to the two leading questions of the origins of babies and the difference between the sexes, on the basis of the predominance of a particular component drive and erogenous zone, and where the parental primal scene makes an early appearance as the infantile sadistic theory of intercourse. Similarly, Laplanche and Pontalis write of the primal fantasies: 'Like myths, they claim to provide a representation of, and a solution to, the major enigmas that confront the child'.[14] In a recent autocritique of this explication of the primal fantasies as enigma, Laplanche disposes of the idea of any 'objective' enigma, inscribed as it were in the facts. Why should the sight or fantasy of parental intercourse necessarily raise the question of fertilisation leading to childbirth, and hence of its own origin for the child? These questions, Laplanche notes, were associated by Freud not with the primal scene but with the arrival of the little brother or sister and the drama that comes with it. He asserts: '. . . there is no enigma . . . other than that whose components are to be found, not in the objectivity of the data, but within the person who proffers the enigma' ('Seduction, Persecution, Revelation' in this volume, p. 171).

This emphasis on the primacy of the other and the enigma of the other's desire differentiates Laplanche's conception of primal seduction from Freud's conceptions, whether of seduction, the primal fantasies or children's sexual theories. In a famous passage from the *Three Essays* Freud describes the ordinary seductions of maternal care:

> A child's intercourse with anyone responsible for his care affords him an unending source of sexual excitation and satisfaction from his erotogenic zones. This is especially so since the person in charge of him, who, after all, is as a rule his mother, herself regards him with feelings that are derived from her sexual life: she strokes him, kisses him, rocks him and quite clearly treats him as a substitute for a complete sexual object. A mother would probably be horrified if she were made aware that all her marks of

14 'Fantasy and the Origins of Sexuality', op. cit., p. 19; 'On the Sexual Theories of Children' (1908c), *SE* IX, pp. 205–26.

affection were rousing her child's sexual instinct and preparing for its later intensity. . . . She is only fulfilling her task in teaching the child to love.

(*SE* VII, p. 223)

The eroticism of the infant–mother couple is subsumed by Freud into a developmental framework in which the mother's activity is construed as the arousing of a pregiven 'instinct'. The brief glimpse of the other as a sexual subject disappears into the performance of a fore-ordained task and so remains uninterrogated and secondary. By contrast, Laplanche dramatises the primacy of the other's desire and its enigmatic provoking effect most memorably in his comedy of the child at the breast:

> Can analytic theory afford to go on ignoring the extent to which women unconsciously and sexually cathect the breast, which appears to be a natural organ for lactation? It is inconceivable that the infant does not notice this sexual cathexis, which might be said to be perverse in the sense that the term is defined in the *Three Essays*. It is impossible to imagine that the infant does not suspect that this cathexis is the source of a nagging question: what does the breast want from me, apart from wanting to suckle me, and, come to that, why does it want to suckle me?
>
> (*New Foundations*, p. 126)

The maternal breast, apart from satisfying the infant's needs and offering warmth and comfort, is itself an erogenous organ and agent of maternal fantasy, stimulating the infant's oral eroticism, transmitting a sexual excitation with a hidden or unconscious meaning, a lost signified, and so posing a question that the infant is constitutionally ill-equipped to answer. It is in this context that Laplanche re-interprets Melanie Klein's account of the earliest paranoid fantasies with their splitting of the breast into the good breast and the persecutory bad breast. The 'bad' breast is described by Klein as the projection of the infant's aggression and envy. This is experienced by the ego as attacking in the absence of the pacifying 'good' breast. Laplanche situates this in terms of primal seduction as the attacking internalised object that results from the exciting implantation of the other. Laplanche insists that 'this "bad" breast, this exciting breast, is a sexual breast', and that the attack of this excitation as an internal foreign body is the very attack of the death drive itself (*Problématiques IV*, op. cit., p. 254).

14

Afterwardsness, Translation and the Other

The above three concepts are complexly intricated in Laplanche's new theory of human foundations, of 'generalised seduction'. The fate of afterwardsness in the aftermath of the turn away from seduction, as the essay devoted to it in this volume indicates,[15] is to be split between two usages. The predominant one is a heavily determinist usage, in which early moments or stages determine later ones and often in conjunction with phylogenetic speculations, of which the recently discovered *Overview of the Transference Neuroses* (1915) with its invocation of the Ice Ages matches even the drama of the primal horde in its fantasmatic ambitiousness.[16] This determinist priority of the earlier moment over the later moment becomes caught up in the debate with Jung over the reality of the primal scene, which Freud sought to defend against Jung's notion of a retrospective fantasy that gives priority to the present over the past. A second usage reverses the temporal direction as events registered in a first moment are then understood retrospectively, an emphasis that can readily be absorbed into a Jungian or hermeneutic endowment or retrospective attribution of meaning. This polarisation can be seen in two alternative translations into English of Freud's *Nachträglichkeit*: the canonical 'deferred action' of Strachey that stresses a progressive causality that is merely delayed in its effects, and one arising from the recent criticism of Strachey by Helmut Thomä who emphasises the reverse direction of Freud's 'double-barrelled concept', suggesting 'retrospective attribution' which explicitly assimilates Freud's term to Jung's concept.[17] These different temporal perspectives in Freud's usage remain unrelated or unintegrated, as Laplanche observes, as the result of the absence of the other and seduction.

The tension between these two moments of the schema of afterwardsness, and the temptation to privilege one over the other, producing the binary opposition of either a determinism or a hermeneutics,[18] can only be avoided

---

15 'Notes on Afterwardsness' in this volume, pp. 260–65.

16 *A Phylogenetic Fantasy: Overview of the Transference Neuroses*, ed. Ilse Gubrich-Simitis, Cambridge, Mass.: The Belknap Press of Harvard University Press, 1987. For Laplanche's comments on this text and on the phylogenetic thesis generally, see *New Foundations*, op. cit., pp. 31–7.

17 Helmut Thomä and Neil Cheshire, 'Freud's *Nachträglichkeit* and Strachey's "Deferred Action": Trauma, Constructions and the Direction of Causality', *International Review of Psychoanalysis*, vol. 18, 1991, p. 407. For Laplanche's arguments against these translations see 'Notes on Afterwardsness' in this volume, p. 263.

18 For Laplanche's extended meditation on this binary, see 'Interpretation between Determinism and Hermeneutics: a Restatement of the Problem' in this volume, pp. 138–65.

by locating the schema in relation to the other's implantation of a compromised message (the message as compromise-formation), in the first moment, and the subject's activity of translation, binding and repression, in the second moment. Laplanche takes up an undeveloped aspect of Freud's theory of repression, repression-as-translation. In a letter to Fliess (6 December 1896), Freud lays out a model of the psyche as the stratification of memory traces and registrations from successive epochs of life, material that is at different times subject to rearrangement and retranscription. 'At the boundary between two such epochs', he writes, 'a translation of the psychic material must take place'. In the neuroses translation of certain material is unable to happen, and Freud adds: 'A failure of translation – this is what is known clinically as "repression"'.[19] Translation, Laplanche suggests, describes the child's attempts from infancy to transpose and bind the stimulating and intrusive intimacies of the other. These are attempts to translate into representations, fantasies, 'infantile sexual theories', the enigma of the other's desire and designs on the child. What does he or she want with me? However, the child's attempt to substitute a signifier or signifying sequence of its own, for the enigmatic signifier or message of the other, always leaves something untranslated; there is always a remainder, which Laplanche calls the *à traduire*, the yet-to-be-translated. Developing Freud's idea of repression as a failure of translation, Laplanche reconceptualises repression, not just as a substitution of signifiers in the manner of Lacan's model of metaphor, but as a fragmentation and dislocation of the enigmatic signifiers; the active production of a remainder that constitutes the unconscious as a separate mental system; the depositing of a residue or fallout from a translation process that is also a work of self-translation or primary self-representation.

Two reformulations are at work here. The two-phase schema of afterwardsness has been relocated within the theory of a generalised primal seduction, in the form of the two moments of implantation and translation, of inscription and reinscription. At the same time the concept of repression, and especially of primal repression as distinct from secondary repression, together with its

---

19 *The Complete Letters of Sigmund Freud to Wilhelm Fliess: 1887–1904*, ed. Jeffrey Moussaieff Masson, Cambridge, Mass.: The Belknap Press of Harvard University Press, 1985, p. 208. For a discussion of some of these issues in a philosophical context see Andrew Benjamin, 'Translating Origins: Psychoanalysis and Philosophy', in *Rethinking Translation*, ed. Lawrence Venturi, London: Routledge, 1990, and 'The Unconscious: Structuring as a Translation', in eds John Fletcher and Martin Stanton, *Jean Laplanche: Seduction, Translation and the Drives*, London: Institute of Contemporary Arts, 1992.

simultaneous production of the repressed unconscious and the formation of the ego as a distinct psychical agency, has also been relocated and reformulated within the matrix of primal seduction and its after-effects. Laplanche regularly adduces a differentiation within Freud's usage of the German term for the other, a differentiation between *der Andere*, the other person, and *das Andere*, the other thing, the psychical thing in the unconscious. These are located on either side of primal repression as a process of translation and self-representation, in the two-phase schema of afterwardsness: *der Andere*, the other person in the first moment of inscription and implantation, and *das Andere*, the other thing in the uncon-scious as the untranslated remainder, the by-product of the second moment of reinscription and translation.

The Unconscious: the Repressed versus the Id

Laplanche's thesis of the realism of the unconscious, first defended system-atically in the joint article written with Serge Leclaire and given as a paper at the Bonneval conference in 1959, affirms a quite specific conception of the unconscious that bears on its genesis and its mode of existence. It is a conception that derives the characteristics of the unconscious, classically described by Freud – its timelessness, its primary process characteristics, its exemption from the law of non-contradiction, hence its lack of coordination and negation – from the process of repression that is its genesis, in a way that Freud hesitated to do. It is in Freud's treatment of the unconscious as a system, both topographically and genetically, Laplanche argues, that ambiguity resides, an ambiguity which manifests the going-astray of Freudian thought in the wake of the abandonment of the seduction theory. Alongside the conception of an individual unconscious as the creation of a process of repression, systematised in the metapsychological papers of 1915, 'Repression' and 'The Unconscious', there is elaborated an alternative conception of an unconscious that is primordial. This unconscious may be primordial in terms of a psychological genesis – 'everything which is conscious was first unconscious'; or primordial in terms of individual biology – the id as 'the great reservoir of the instincts', pregiven rather than repressed, and opening directly onto the body; primordial, finally, in terms of the species and phylogenesis, the inherited schemata of the primal fantasies encoding collective memory traces of prehistory, or else the assimilation of the unconscious drives to an agonistic struggle of the great vital forces of the life and death instincts. The concept of a mechanism of repression is thus opposed to a dynamic of emergence from a primordial moment or level of functioning to which the unconscious is assimilated. Gradually from 1915 onwards, Laplanche argues, the point of view of repression is subordinated to that of emergence and, as a consequence, the distinction made in the 1915 texts between primal and secondary repression appears only sporadically.

In Freud's account repression requires the operation of two forces: one that expels an idea from consciousness, and one that draws it into the unconscious system operating from the already repressed. This implies the existence of a 'primal' repression (*Urverdrangen*) or first phase of repression which consists in a particular idea or 'instinctual representative' being denied entry into conscious-ness: 'with this a *fixation* is established; the representative in question persists unaltered from then onwards and the instinct remains attached to it'.[20] This primal repressed is the core of the unconscious and primal repression is in Laplanche's phrase the 'creator of the unconscious as a place',[21] i.e. as a separate topographical system. The force that effects this cleavage into different psychical systems Freud terms 'anti-cathexis' or counter-investment, which 'represents the permanent expenditure [of energy] of a primal repression and which also guarantees the permanence of that repression'.[22] This implies the formation of an irreducible, structural and 'normal' unconscious rather than a reducible, temporary and pathological one. Secondary repression or repression proper, acting on ideas that come into association with the repressed, is in Freud's phrase 'actually an after-pressure' (*Nachdrangen*).[23] However, with the increasing predominance of a biological conception of the unconscious or id, 'repression', as Laplanche notes, 'will be essentially secondary, that is, bearing on the drive impulses already present and welling up from the primordial, non-repressed unconscious' ('A Short Treatise', op. cit., p. 86). The drives (*Triebe*) lose their specificity as such and are assimilated to an instinctual functioning, pregiven in the biological system.

These two related emphases, on the primordial and on the tendential assimilation of the unconscious to a non-repressed, biologically based id, are the subject of strong criticism in the essays in this collection. The unconscious

20 'Repression' (1915d), *SE* XIV, p. 148.
21 'A Short Treatise on the Unconscious' in this volume, pp. 85–6.
22 'The Unconscious' (1915e), *SE* XIV, p. 181.
23 'Repression', op. cit., p. 148. Strachey's note tells us that in a late text of 1937, 'Analysis Terminable and Interminable' (1937c), *SE* XXIII, Freud uses the term *Nachverdrangen* or 'after-repression'. This might suggest a parallel with the two-phase schema of *Nachträglichkeit*.

in the first topography is said to be characterised by the primary process, i.e. a mobility of investments of libidinal energy operating through the mechanisms of condensation and displacement, and these characteristics are taken over by the id of the second topography. Laplanche draws out the problems this poses for the thesis of primordiality, and for the assimilation of the unconscious to the biological and the instinctual.

Laplanche's critique of the thesis of primordiality occurs in 'The Unfinished Copernican Revolution' (pp. 67–71) where the 'primary' is cited as a crucial instance of the domestication of the otherness of the unconscious. The primary process in its condensation of representations and displacement of intensities from one representation to another, governed only by relations of contiguity and analogy, is said to escape the rationality of conscious thought and its logical rules. As with the unconscious, Laplanche notes, the notion is haunted by the same ambiguity as to whether it is withdrawn from conscious rationality by a process of exclusion, or, being more primal than rational thought, was never subject to it in the first place. The very term 'primary', he goes on to argue, brings along with it a whole theory, systematised by the late nineteenth-century neurologist Hughlings Jackson and taken over by Freud, of a hierarchy of progressively more complex forms and the possibility of an entropy or regression by which the later, 'higher' can give way to the 'lower' and more primitive. Laplanche analyses the 'primary' in terms of a coalescence of three aspects: the temporal, the topographical and the formal. The primary is there before the secondary, with the latter coming into existence both after the primary and being dependent for its structure on it as a foundation. The notion of 'regression', so important for Freud, is simultaneously temporal regression – 'a return to a time before the subject's existence' – topographical regression – 'regression to the system from which the excitation derives, the unconscious' – and formal regression – 'return to a lower level of organisation . . . less structured than the "secondary" process'. These three dimensions coalesce in the 'primary': 'that which is least organised and from which excitation arises is also the most archaic' (p. 67).

The Jacksonian model of organisational progression or regression, Laplanche points out, is at work in a number of classic Freudian texts, such as chapter 7 of *The Interpretation of Dreams* (1900a), Part I of 'A Project for a Scientific Psychology' (1950a [1895]), and a text Laplanche designates as exemplary in the Freudian going-astray: the 'Formulations on the Two Principles of Mental Functioning' of 1911. The last two texts exemplify the building along Jacksonian lines of a model of the functioning of an ideally simplified organism. Beginning with the postulate of a free circulation of energy through the system in a purely associative mode and of its unhindered and rapid discharge, Freud describes a mode of functioning in the organism dominated by what he calls the pleasure principle. Only secondarily comes the acquisition of the reality principle, with its regulated mode of functioning in which energy is stabilised along fixed pathways, allowing the accumulation of a reserve of energy, inhibition of immediate discharge and the possibility of behaviour adapted to the exigencies of external reality. In other words, as Laplanche illustrates, the characteristics of vital functioning that meet the 'needs of life' necessary for survival, the general postulate of homeostasis and a constancy of energy level, are only secondarily introduced into what should from the beginning have been a living organism, but whose 'primary' functioning is presented as mechanical and non-organic. Against this Laplanche argues for a 'becoming-primary': 'if the primary is the unconscious, and the unconscious is the repressed, then this "primary" has "*become* primary", so to speak. It is neither prior nor primitive, but a sort of "reduced state" caused by something else' (p. 69). The primary process is a unique form of 'reduced' functioning as a result of the process of repression. Freud's Jacksonian model of primitive functioning, Laplanche argues, 'is rightly interpreted as a model not of the living being but of the process occurring in a preliminary living being *from the moment when an unconscious comes to exist*' (p. 69, n. 33).

The above contradiction, between the characteristics of the repressed psychical unconscious governed by the primary process and the functioning of any imaginable living organism, is further heightened by their restatement and reassertion within the context of the second topography, with its endogenous id that opens directly onto the body and its instincts. The denial in the id of organisation, of collective will, of the logical laws of thought, especially the law of non-contradiction and negation, conflicts strikingly with the new conception of the id as in Freud's words 'taking up into itself instinctual needs'.[24] As Laplanche argues: 'Nothing, indeed, in the observation of living *organisms* allows any such *disorganisation* of needs to be asserted – which would be incompatible with life' ('A Short Treatise', op. cit., p. 103). There is, then, an aporia in the assimilation of the unconscious into the biological id, a contradiction between the system of the repressed unconscious with its 'primary' process characteristics of non-coordination and

---

24 *New Introductory Lectures* (1933a), *SE* XXII, p. 73.

pressure towards discharge, on the one hand, and the vital functioning of biological organisms with their necessary constancy of energy level and their complex coordination of developmental patterns and behavioural reflexes, on the other. This is obscured and covered over by the second theory of the drives and by the introduction of the new concept of the 'life instinct'. This new conflation of the sexual drives with the functions of self-preservation, which had been opposed in the first theory of the drives, results in the disappearance of both the specificity of the sexual drive as such and the related concept of 'leaning on' that had been part of Freud's attempt to think the articulation of the biological dimension of needs and self-preservatory functions with the different dimension of sexuality. As Laplanche has enabled us to see, as an after-effect of the discovery of narcissism and ego-libido, sexuality in the guise of the life instinct, with its production of more complex and libidinally bound forms, had gradually passed over in Freud's thinking to the realm of the higher agencies and their organisation. The reaffirmation of the alienness and heterogeneity of the opposing forces were to be henceforth entrusted to the id as the site of the 'death instinct', through a massive recourse to the biological.

In his extended consideration of Freud's borrowing from Georg Groddeck of the term *das Es* (literally 'the it', but translated by Strachey like the other terms of the second topography in Latinised form as 'the id'), Laplanche locates what he calls certain theoretical 'requirements' or 'exigencies' that are at work in the renaming and reformulation of the psychical unconscious in the second topography (*Problématiques IV*, op. cit., p. 192). These include a reference to biology and to vital life-forces, central to Groddeck's vitalist metaphysics; a genetic concern with origins, with what is foundational and primordial; a renewed insistence on impersonal forces, in Groddeck's phrase, 'that live us', i.e. a paradoxical insistence on heteronomy and the dethroning or decentering of the conscious, autonomous subject, at the very moment in the 1920s, when the further development of the theory of the ego threatened a turn to the rationality, even autonomy, of the reality-testing, adaptational ego of later ego-psychology. Laplanche's systematic tracing of these paradoxical displacements and returns of Freudian thought has led him to challenge the predominance of the biological, and to reaffirm the priority of the other, the seduction of the other's message and its translation and repression, in the very formation of the unconscious and the drives.

The Freudian Drive

The rejection or critique of biologism within psychoanalytic thought might be assumed to entail a playing-down or rejection of the determining importance, even the very idea, of the instinct or drive. After all what could be more intractably 'biological' or of the body? more tied to a 'one-body' model of the psyche, to a monadic or solipsistic paradigm? Such a rejection is in fact common enough among contemporary psychoanalytic writers. It is striking, however, that the two theorists who elaborate a vehement and systematic critique of the false biologism of classical psychoanalytic theory, Jean Laplanche and Jacques Lacan, both retain a concept of the drive; indeed, both elaborate new theories of the drive, not as the expression of the body and its needs but as the by-product of the signifying relations between the subject and the other (however differently conceived these new theories may be).

Although Freud operates from the beginning with the notion of a constantly flowing excitation whose source is internal (as distinct from an external and episodic stimulus), an excitation that provokes or impels to action, it is only in the wake of the abandonment of the seduction theory that he elaborates a theory of the drives as the form taken by his account of human sexual development in general. The consequent biologism that haunts Freud's drive theory, without entirely absorbing it, is the result of an oscillation in thought constrained by the alternatives of a binary opposition of external event or inherited constitution. Freud retrospectively describes his theoretical shift thus: 'Accidental influences derived from experience having thus receded into the background, the factors of constitution and heredity necessarily gained the upper hand . . . the "sexual constitution" took the place of a "general neuropathic disposition"'. This echoes his private explanation to Fliess in what Laplanche calls his 'letter of the equinox' or turning-point, where he announces his abandonment of the seduction theory: '. . . and with this the factor of an hereditary disposition regains a sphere of influence from which I had made it my task to dislodge it'.[25] If the determining power of the traumatic event gives way to that of the sexual constitution, then Freud's epigrammatic summary in the above essay of the change – '"infantile sexual traumas' were in

---

25 'My Views on the Part Played by Sexuality in the Neuroses' (1906a), *SE* VII, pp. 275–6; 'Letter to Fliess, 21st September, 1897', in *The Complete Letters of Sigmund Freud to Wilhelm Fliess: 1887–1904*, trans. and ed. Jeffrey Moussaieff Masson, Cambridge, Mass.: The Belknap Press of Harvard University Press, 1985, p. 265.

22

a sense replaced by the 'infantilism of sexuality"' (p. 275) – signals clearly that the notion of the sexual constitution was to be rethought anew in a way that differentiates the sexual drive from the usual conceptions of the biological instinct. Indeed the famous opening paragraphs of the *Three Essays on the Theory of Sexuality* (1905d) pointedly set out the common biological conception of sexuality, both according to popular opinion and 'in biology', as an instinct by analogy with hunger or the instinct for nutrition. Freud then outlines the 'false picture' popularly entertained of such an instinct: absent in childhood, setting in at puberty with its processes of maturation, manifested as an attraction between the sexes, aiming at sexual union for the purposes of reproduction.[26] Pointedly devoting the first essay to homosexuality and the second to infantile sexuality, however, the *Three Essays* proceeds to give an account of human sexuality that is radically at odds with these traditional understandings of the functioning and the *functionality* of the biological instincts.

At stake here are two distinctions – one terminological and one conceptual – that are closely related but which by no means coincide. Both of these are lucidly set out by Laplanche and Pontalis in the entries on 'Instinct/Drive' and associated terms in *The Language of Psychoanalysis* (1967) and are returned to and further elaborated in *Le fourvoiement biologisant*. Freud uses two German terms, *Instinkt* (instinct) and *Trieb* (drive), in two systematically different senses, although there is no explicit reflection on these terms in his work. He uses *Instinkt* in the traditional sense, which designates a behavioural schema that is adapted to a particular end or aim, with a pregiven object; is more or less fixed and invariant for a particular individual or species; is hereditary and innate, so not acquired by the individual but by the species (*Le fourvoiement biologisant*, op. cit., pp. 18–19). Freud's standard reference is to instinct in animals; and significantly, as Laplanche and Pontalis point out, when he asks in 'The Unconscious' (1915e) whether 'inherited mental formations exist in the human being – something analogous to instinct [*Instinkt*] in animals', he does not cite what he designates as *Triebe*, the drives, but rather, here and in the Wolf Man case, he invokes the 'hereditary, [phylo]genetically acquired factor in mental life', the primal fantasies. Indeed, the latter case-study develops an extended comparison between 'the far-reaching *instinctive* [*instinktiv*] knowledge of animals' and 'phylogenetically inherited schemata . . .

26 *Three Essays on the Theory of Sexuality* (1905d), *SE* VII, pp. 135–6.

precipitates from the history of human civilization' rather than with the sexual drives.[27] In his discussion of infantile anxiety as libidinal rather than realistic Freud comments on the virtual absence of innate or inherited 'life preserving instincts' in small children (as distinct from animals) that would automatically keep them out of situations of danger.[28] By implication it is clear that *Triebe* are not the same as *Instinkts*. In the light of this crucial but under-theorised distinction it is all the more unfortunate that Strachey should have chosen in the canonical Standard Edition of Freud's *Complete Works* to have translated *Trieb* and *triebhaft* as 'instinct' and 'instinctual' rather than as 'drive', thus laying down the terminological preconditions in English for the reassimilation of the properly psychoanalytic concept of the drive back into the biological concept of the instinct.

This fragile and imperilled terminological difference points to a crucial conceptual distinction between the drive and the instinct, between in particular the sexual drives and the functions of self-preservation, with which it does not, however, consistently coincide in Freud's thought. Freud's two theories of the drives are both dualistic, each consisting of a distinction amounting to an opposition between the sexual drives (*Sexualtriebe*) and the self-preservatory drives (*Selbsterhaltungstriebe*) in the first theory, and beween the life-drives (*Lebenstriebe*) and death-drives (*Todestriebe*) in the second. Freud specifies the sexual drive through the four categories borrowed from traditional instinct theory, while differentiating it from the assumptions that go with them. The sexual drive like the instinct is said to be composed of a source, an aim, an object and an energy or pressure. The relations that obtain between the sexual drives and the functions of self-preservation are specified by Freud through the concept of *Anlehnung*, translated by Strachey as 'anaclisis' but for which

27 Jean Laplanche and J. B. Pontalis, op. cit., p. 214; 'The Unconscious' (1915e), *SE* XIV, p. 195; *From the History of an Infantile Neurosis* (1918b), *SE* XVII, pp. 120–1 (the citation in the English translation of Laplanche and Pontalis has 'genetically' rather than Freud's 'phylogenetically').

28 'Innately, children seem to have little true realistic anxiety. . . . . It would have been a good thing if they had inherited more of such life-preserving instincts. . . . When in the end realistic anxiety is awakened in them, that is wholly the result of education . . .', Lecture 25, *Introductory Lectures on Psychoanalysis* (1916–17), *SE* XVI, pp. 407–8. For Laplanche's commentary see *Le fourvoiement biologisant*, op. cit., pp. 14–18. For Laplanche's discussion of Freud's account of realistic and neurotic anxiety and their relation to instinct and the drives, see Jean Laplanche, 'A Metapsychology put to the test of Anxiety' (1979), *International Journal of Psychoanalysis*, vol. 62, 1981.

Laplanche suggests the more literal translation of 'leaning-on'. The sexual drive is said to lean on the instinctual function and its operation, deriving its form, i.e. its source, aim and object from it, before at a later moment deviating from it and becoming autonomous.[29]

This model of 'leaning-on' articulates the instinctual functions of self-preservation and the sexual drives, as related but distinct and differentiated dimensions of the human being. Freud's use of the same term *Trieb*, however, together with its compound words for both sexuality and self-preservation fails to register consistently at the level of terminology the conceptual distinction. When Freud attempts to produce a model of the drive in general, of the *Trieb* conceived as biologically based, he nevertheless attributes to it the variability of aim and contingency of object, not to mention the series of vicissitudes – reversal into its opposite, turning round upon the subject's own self, repression, sublimation – that characterise the sexual drives, and cannot apply to the so-called *Selbsterhaltungstriebe* or instincts for self-preservation with their fixed aims and pregiven objects.[30] Biological needs and instinctual functions such as hunger and feeding cannot be repressed, sublimated, reversed into their opposites, etc. The very notion of a vicissitude in the Freudian sense requires the indeterminacy (or *acquired* determinacy) of aim and object specific to the sexual drive. There can be no vicissitude of the *instinct* as such: Strachey's translation – 'Instincts and their Vicissitudes' (1915) – is a contradiction in terms (as indeed is Freud's *Selbsterhaltungstriebe*, i.e. the self-preservatory functions are instinctual schemas not *drives*). The terminological contradiction here is exactly parallel to that discussed above, between the primary process characteristics of the repressed (condensation and displacement as processes of substitution) and the biological id as repository of the instinctual needs.

29 Jeffrey Mehlman in his translation of Laplanche's *Life and Death in Psychoanalysis* (1976) translates *Anlehnung* (Fr. *étayage*) as 'propping'. Laplanche's objection has been that to say that the sexual drive 'is propped on' the instinct or function (or even more the instinct 'props up' the drive) is to reassign agency from the Freudian usage in which it is the sexual drive that actively 'leans on' the instinct or function. This objection might be met by putting Mehlman's term in reflexive form and saying that the sexual drive 'props itself' on the instinct.
30 See 'Instincts and their Vicissitudes' (1915c), *SE* XIV, pp. 109–40; and Laplanche and Pontalis's commentary on 'Instincts of Self-Preservation', *The Language of Psycho-analysis*, op. cit., pp. 220–2.

After the theoretical retrieval of the schema of 'leaning-on' in *The Language of Psychoanalysis* (1967) and in *Life and Death in Psychoanalysis* (1970), Laplanche in his later texts such as *New Foundations* (1987) and the recent *Le fourvoiement biologisant de la sexualité chez Freud* (1993) argues that by itself the schema is inadequate to deliver a non-reductive account of the sexual drive. The aporias of Freud's theory of the drives arise from the fact that the break from the biological concept of the instinct is incomplete, and the relations between the drives and the self-preservatory functions are described in different ways, thus putting under pressure if not into question their common conceptual framework (source, aim, object, pressure), while the 're-instinctualisation' of the drives is a perpetual temptation finally succumbed to in the grand dualism of the life and death instincts.[31] Laplanche has come to argue that different versions of *Anlehnung* in Freud describe either a bald 'parallel' of function and drive in which the biological description of the source, aim and object of the former dominates the descriptions of the latter, or alternatively, a spontaneous autogenesis of the sexual drives from the instinctual functions, an endogenous movement of emergence in which the source, aim and object of the drive are then displaced and transformed with respect to the function.

In contrast with the popular misconception of the sexual 'instinct' Freud conceives sexuality not as a single, heterosexually-oriented, genitally-centered 'instinct-to-reproduce', but as made up of a number of component drives with diverse sources, dispersed about the body at the sites of the major bodily functions on which they lean: mouth, anus, the eyes and even the musculature and skin surface, as well as the genitals. If the sexual component drives that arise at these sites take as their 'source' both the bodily site and its functioning, e.g. the mouth and lips and their predetermined suckling and feeding sequence, which thus becomes an erogenous zone (the mouth is the infant's first sexual organ and sucking its first sexual act), their multiplicity and initial fragmentation in the infant are nevertheless seen as expressions of a single drive-energy which Freud calls the libido. The component drives, however, are only coordinated and synthesised under the dominance of the genitals at later stages of development.

The differentiation between drive and instinctual function is most striking, however, with the aim and object. For if the instinctual aim is a specific act or

---

31 For an extensive commentary on these themes, see *Le fourvoiement biologisant*, op. cit., pp. 29–65.

sequence directed towards fulfilling a need that must be met to ensure the organism's survival (the sucking and digestion sequence), and the object is also a given object preadapted to the organism's needs (the mother's milk or a specifically designed substitute), by contrast, the sexual drive is characterised by an indeterminacy and contingency of both aim and object. The general aim of the sexual drive is conceived as the localised satisfaction achieved through the reduction of tension, and the removal of a localised stimulus ('organ-pleasure'), which might be achieved through a variety of acts (sucking, kissing, stroking and licking as well as the original acts of feeding). The sexual object is in principle an infinite series of objects that can produce that satisfaction (whatever might touch the lips or be put in the mouth). The first aim and object are in fact derived from the instinctual function, for the organ pleasure is first stimulated through the very performance of the function and its associated activities. If the infant's first sexual activity is the very sucking that brings it nourishment and its first sexual object is the mother's breast, the sexual drive emerges fully as such, independent of the function, when these first satisfying acts are repeated, seeking only a repetition of past pleasures in the absence of either need or of the object of need (the infant's sensual sucking of its own lips or substitute body part, e.g. the thumb or toe). This passage from the fulfilment of need with its external object to the auto-erotic self-pleasuring when the infant takes its own body as an object, Laplanche in his extensive commentaries[32] describes as a moment of 'auto-time', in which the drive turns round on the subject and appears as such, with both aim and object having become fantasmatic.

Laplanche describes this derivation and deviation of the aim and object, from 'leaning-on' to 'auto-time', through the classic structuralist polarities of metaphor and metonymy, derivation by analogy and derivation by contiguity.[33] The sexual *aim* of the oral drive, deriving by analogy from the act of feeding and in its absence, becomes a fantasy of incorporation, while the sexual *object* of the oral drive, deriving by contiguity from the object of need (the mother's milk) and in its absence, becomes the fantasy of the mother's breast (which may find its support in a series of later objects). However,

32 See *Life and Death in Psychoanalysis*, chapter 1, and 'Fantasy and the Origins of Sexuality', op. cit., pp. 24–6.
33 See his discussion of these principles of derivation in 'Derivation of Psycho-analytic Entities', reprinted as an appendix to *Life and Death in Psychoanalysis*, op. cit., pp. 127–39.

Freud's account of the auto-erotic turn, from the breast as object of both function and drive to the infant's own body, does not recognise the fantasmatic dimension of both aim and object for all their contingency. Equally, many of his general formulations of the drive as the mental representation of a somatic process tend to locate its origin in a purely organic source of which it is the necessary mental expression. This framework of an endogenous emergence from the organism and its functions tends theoretically to lock the component drives into an overall developmental trajectory in which they are gradually organised into a normative sequence. The oral stage, the anal stage, the phallic and, finally, the genital stage, all find their appointed place and time, and the sexual drives are returned to the functionality and the teleology of the organism and its vital needs (here the goal and norm of reproductive functioning, more properly a requirement for the survival of the species than of the individual). The future absorption of sexuality into the vital order of self-preservation in the 'life instinct' of the last theory of the drives is here anticipated.

Reformulating the Drive

Responding to the pragmatic questions – 'what use is the drive? what is it for?' – in the essay on the drive included in this volume, Laplanche outlines four requirements that clinical experience makes of any theory of the drive. All four requirements may be seen to proceed from the practical recognition of the fundamental decenteredness of the human subject and its consequences for psychic life. First, under the heading of a general psychic determinism, Laplanche argues that what is at issue is the description, not just of hidden or unconscious meanings but of 'another *content* and consequently a real cause'. Freud's *id*, a 'set of obscure causes' that act on or drive us from within and alienate us from ourselves making us strangers to our own actions, 'puts a virtually definitive seal on this recognition of our fundamental decenteredness'.[34] The second requirement is that these causes are of the order of representation – memories, fantasies, imagos – but they are representations with two distinctive features that are the result of repression. Most obviously, they are unconscious and a part of them can never be made conscious and directly experienced as such.

---

34 'The Drive and its Source-Object: its Fate in the Transference' in this volume, p. 120.

They can only be approached asymptotically, as it were, through successive constructions and approximations. But the most striking feature of Laplanche's description is his account of the reification of these representations and their reduction to an alien materiality. They are, he says, 'frozen, fixed beyond the meaning that may inhabit them . . . beyond all referentiality'. These congealed significations are accorded 'the generative power of schemas and the materiality of quasi-things' (ibid., p. 120). He presents this paradoxical status through a meditation on Freud's *Sachvorstellung*, translated by Strachey as 'thing-presentation' by contrast with *Wortvorstellung* or 'word-presentation'. Where the former are the perceptual traces, predominantly visual, of the object, the latter are acoustic traces of the word. The unconscious is said by Freud to contain thing-presentations cut off by repression from access to related word-presentations. Laplanche elaborates this distinction further in his discussion in *Problématiques IV*, making use of the ambiguity of both the German composite noun and its French translation (*représentation de chose*), both of which suggest the intentional object, the presentation-*of*-the-thing and as well the presentation-*as*-thing (*Problématiques IV*, op. cit., p. 96). He insists in both French and in English that the thing-presentation (*représentation de chose*) becomes in the unconscious a thing-like presentation (*représentation-chose*).

The third requirement is that these representations are tied to bodily functions and processes, whether to the body as a whole or to particular zones and activities and the fantasmatic organisations connected with them. This raises the problem of the *source* of the drive and Freud's conception of it as ultimately biological, thus making the drive for all its 'vicissitudes' an endogenous, ultimately somatic tension. The fourth requirement is the need to account for the various phenomena of displacement: affective reactions that separate from and appear to forget the circumstances of their genesis, becoming bound to very different representations; the somatisations of hysteria; the detachment of affect from any representation in the dequalified or degraded form of free-floating anxiety; the varieties of transference, from the dream with its previous day's residues to the dynamics of the analytic session; not to mention the varieties of displaced aggression or love in everyday experience. All these require a theory of the radical separation of affect and representation and of the separate 'vicissitudes' of each.

All four requirements – the action from within of unconscious representations as thing-like causes on the subject, connected to bodily processes but also potentially disconnected from the affective charge they carry – map out an area where a theory of the drives can be re-elaborated. It is also clear from the four requirements above that the drive is being reconceived by Laplanche in relation to primal repression. One could add further that the relation between drive and instinctual function, specified by Freud through the model of leaning-on, is being relocated in terms of the two-phase schema of afterwardsness, of primal seduction and translation. Laplanche's own theory of the drives could be said to begin with the assertion that 'the only truth of "leaning-on" is primal seduction';[35] and he goes on to pose the whole problematic of the drive afresh, from the point of view of primal seduction and in relation to the primacy of the other. Rather than *secondary* repression acting on the endogenous emergence from the body and its functions of the already constituted drives, Laplanche takes Freud's description of primal repression – the refusal of entry into consciousness to the 'instinctual representative' – as a *creation* of the drive in the form of the primal repressed. 'With this a *fixation* is established; the representative in question persists unaltered from then onwards and the instinct [*Trieb*] remains attached to it' ('Repression', op. cit., p. 148). This permanent *fixation* of the *Trieb* in a repressed representation from which successive derivatives are to arise is the very creation of what henceforth will act as the *source* of the drive. This representation or signifier as source is the result of the double activity of translation-repression described earlier, acting not on 'instinctual representatives' understood naturalistically as mental expressions of purely biological stimuli, but on the enigmatic signifiers implanted by the gestures of parental care that target the major zones and functions of the infant's body.

Laplanche's account of the nursling organism committed to homeostasis and self-preservation stresses the delays and deficiencies of the infant's adaptive mechanisms, its dependency on the other for the meeting of needs and its openness to an adult world saturated with unconscious sexual significations. If the schema of leaning-on describes the initial *coincidence* of self-preservation and the sexual drive in the same sites and activities, the consequent splitting and drifting of aim and object in the moment of auto-eroticism cannot be explained as a spontaneous process, but only as the infant's response to the seductive ministrations of the other: '[T]he obligatory vehicle of auto-eroticism, that which stimulates it and brings it into existence, is the intrusion and then

35 'The Drive and its Source-Object . . .', op. cit., pp. 128–9; *New Foundations*, op. cit., p. 144.

repression of the enigmatic signifiers supplied by the adult' ('The Drive and its Source-Object', op. cit., p. 129).

This embedding of the drives in the problematic of primal seduction and the other makes of the primal repressed the source of the drive, understood as the untranslated deposit, the internal foreign body that results from the afterwardsness, as it were, of seduction through the process of the infant's primal repression-translation. The effect is to shift, even to liquidate, the Freudian conceptual architecture of source, aim, object and pressure that twinned both instinct and drive so misleadingly together.[36] It transforms the very notion of the source from a biological stimulus to an exciting internal foreign body that attacks the ego from within. The erogenous zones as excitable breaks or turnings in the body's surface are sites of passage, stimulated by inputs and outflows – the warmth of the mother's milk on the lips in Freud's famous example.[37] These processes mark the boundaries between inside and outside as sites of exchange and targets of parental care. The source is thus, as much exogenous as endogenous, established and marked in relation to the outside and the intrusive intimacies of the other. Its distinction from the object, as in the case of the oral drive with the breast that is taken in from the outside as both satisfying and enigmatically exciting, is no longer so clear. Laplanche recognises this with his new portmanteau

36 In *Le fourvoiement biologisant* Laplanche questions the appropriateness of describing the anal and urinary functions of the infant in terms of an instinct with an object, unlike the hunger and the feeding sequence with its dependence on the other and the external object for the meeting of needs. See pp. 60–5 for a discussion of the notion of 'object' in relation to the functions of self-preservation.

37 Of the autoerotic pleasure in sensual sucking, Freud writes: 'It was the child's first and most vital activity, his sucking at his mother's breast, or at substitutes for it, that must have familiarised him with this pleasure. The child's lips, in our view, behave like an *erotogenic zone*, and no doubt stimulation by the warm flow of the milk is the cause of the pleasurable sensation. The satisfaction of the erotogenic zone is associated, in the first instance, with the satisfaction of the need for nourishment, *Three Essays on the Theory of Sexuality* (1905d), *SE* VII, p. 181. Freud goes on to generalise a notion of 'co-excitation' independent of the erogenous zones: '. . . in the case of a great number of internal processes sexual excitation arises as a concomitant effect, as soon as the intensity of those processes passes beyond certain limits. . . . It may well be that nothing of considerable importance can occur in the organism without contributing some component to the excitation of the sexual instinct' (ibid., p. 205). For Laplanche's comments on 'co-excitation', see 'Masochism and the General Theory of Seduction' in this volume, pp. 205–8.

term *objet-source*, the 'source-object': what is taken in and subjected to translating substitutions and binding symbolisations to produce the fantasy of the comforting, appeasing 'good' breast also leaves as deposit the untranslatable, traumatic and exciting elements that Laplanche suggestively correlates with the Kleinian fantasy of the persecutory and attacking 'bad' breast (*Problématiques IV*, op. cit., p. 254). The 'source-object' designates the external object and its enigmatic 'co-excitations' that, implanted, taken in and metabolised as an internal foreign body, come to function as a source.

The correlate of this process of the formation of the drives and their source-objects as the reified, unmasterable rejects of the process of primal repression-translation-symbolisation is the reverse formation of the ego. In *New Foundations* Laplanche sketches an outline of the topographical evolution that is the correlate of primal repression and the formation of the unconscious and its primal source-objects. In the first phase of implantation of the enigmatic signifiers in the peripheral surface of the body, and especially in the erogenous zones as sites of passage and exchange, the primitive body-ego (Freud) or skin-ego (Anzieu) is mapped or zoned and various thresholds marked. In the second phase, the ego as agency is formed through both a metonymic derivation as *part* of the whole and a metaphoric derivation as image of the whole (Freud's 'mental projection of the surface of the body').[38] The untranslated residue of the enigmatic signifier on the periphery or skin surface becomes the internal source-object in the unconscious. This remains nevertheless external to the ego as agency, embedded in its periphery and acting on it from outside, a liminal external-internal element. The fate of the auto-erotic drives with their source-objects tied to specific erogenous zones is to be precipitated in the moment of primary narcissism into a totalising form or *gestalt*.[39] Laplanche conceives this as a bound and binding narcissistic self-representation, a reflection in the mirror of the other. Through this totalising representation the drives and their fragmented source-objects are contained, the erogenous zones

38 Freud, *The Ego and the Id* (1923b), *SE* XIX, p. 26. See *New Foundations*, op. cit., pp. 133–6 and the entry on the ego in *The Language of Psychoanalysis*; Didier Anzieu, *The Skin Ego* (1985), trans. Chris Turner, New Haven: Yale University Press, 1989.
39 '. . . a unity comparable to the ego cannot exist in the individual from the start; the ego has to be developed. The auto-erotic instincts, however, are there from the very first; so there must be something added to auto-eroticism – a new psychical action – in order to bring about narcissism'. Freud, 'On Narcissism' (1914c), *SE* XIV, p. 77.

coordinated and the ego as regulator and 'reservoir of the libido' in Freud's formulation is constituted.[40]

Freud's classic statement about the drive at his most generalising and assimilationist, 'considering mental life from a biological point of view', defines it as: 'a concept on the frontier between the mental and the somatic, as the psychical representative of the stimuli originating from within the organism and reaching the mind, as a measure of the demand made upon the mind for work in consequence of its connection with the body'.[41] To this Laplanche counterposes his own summary statement: 'The drive is therefore neither a mythical entity, nor a biological force, nor a concept lying on the frontier between the mental and the physical. It is the impact on the individual and the ego of the constant stimulation exerted from the inside by the repressed thing-like presentations, which can be described as the source-objects of the drive' ('The Drive and its Source-Object', op. cit., p. 129). The drive's relation to the body is here a reversal of the biological model. Instead of the body acting as the primordial origin and motor of the drive, the drive is 'the action of the repressed source-objects on the body, taking place by way of the ego, which is initially a body-ego, and in which, naturally enough, the erogenous zones become the sites for the precipitation and organisation of fantasies' (p. 129). The economic aspect or 'pressure', which Freud describes as 'a measure of the demand made upon the mind for work', Laplanche relates not to a constant biological force but to 'the demand for work' made by the repressed, untranslated source-objects: 'the measure of the difference or disequilibrium between what is symbolisable and what is not in the enigmatic messages supplied to the infant . . . [i]f you will, the measure of the quantity of trauma' (p. 130).

A further point about Laplanche's reformulated theory of the drives is his reworking of Freud's final opposition between life and death drives. Noting that Freud refused to assign a separate energy to the death drive, a *destrudo* in parallel with the libido, Laplanche sees the death drive as a modality or regime of the only true drive which is the sexual drive. The distinction between life and death drives is a distinction within the field of sexuality. Laplanche's reading of the successive shifts in Freud's thinking about the drives traces what he calls a

40 See the extensive commentary in *Le fourvoiement biologisant*, pp. 67–119, on narcissism and its relation to the different levels of self-preservation, the auto-erotic sexual drives and the narcissistic libido.
41 'Instincts and their Vicissitudes' (1915c), *SE* XIV, pp. 121–2.

strange chiasmus in which sexuality, hitherto associated with the primary process, the tendency to unbinding and fragmentation in opposition to the ego, binding and the secondary process, passes over to its opposite, after the formulation of narcissism and of the life drive as Eros. At this point the concept of death drive also appears as the reaffirmation of unbinding, the repetition-compulsion, the discharge of all tensions in opposition to the bound and binding Eros. 'For the death drive does not possess its own energy. Its energy is libido. Or, better put, the death drive is the very soul, the constitutive principle of libidinal circulation' (*Life and Death*, op. cit., p. 124). Significantly, Lacan also reached a similar conclusion, stating 'that every drive is virtually a death drive' and that the life/death opposition references different aspects of the drive.[42] Laplanche locates this distinction, between a tendency towards fragmentation, unbinding and discharge as against a tendency towards the binding and synthesis of complex totalities, in the very source-objects of the drives. With the death drive 'they are diminished, pared down so to speak, reduced to indices of excitation', while with the life drive 'the tendency to unify and synthesise may be found in the very presentation of the source-object' ('The Drive and its Source-Object', op. cit., p. 130). This description of the source-objects of the life drives, with its emphasis on unification and synthesis, suggests a correlation with the narcissistic unification of the auto-erotic component drives, in the first totalising ego-representations that constitute the ego as love object and libidinal 'reservoir'.[43]

Translation and the Question of Unconscious Memory

Along with the rejected thesis of the unconscious as an original or primordial reality is the understanding of repression as a form of memorisation and of the unconscious as a store of more deeply inscribed memories. Although in some senses they function as alternatives – the unconscious consisting *either* of split-off representations of traumatic events *or* of 'instinctual representatives',

42 *Écrits*, p. 848, cited in Dylan Evans, *An Introductory Dictionary of Lacanian Psycho-analysis*, London: Routledge (1966), p. 33.
43 As noted above, Freud's *Todestrieb* is translated as 'Death instinct', which is unintendedly appropriate given the 're-instinctualisation' and biologising of the drives that *Beyond the Pleasure Principle* (1920g) effects. Laplanche's reading of the role of the Death drive as a retrieval of the 'demonic' in the field of sexuality restores it to its full status as *the* sexual drive.

representatives of somatic processes and their demands – they do so within the larger framework of an homogenising 'Ptolemaic' logic. In both cases the unconscious contents are to be recognised and reclaimed as either *my* instincts or *my* memories. For all the apparent other-centeredness of the *id* as the seat of the instincts, Laplanche argues, the biologising model 'ends up recentering the subject on the id – as that which is in him from the beginning and around which, so to speak, he grows' ('The Unfinished Copernican Revolution', op. cit., p. 60). Whether the unconscious is considered as my primordial and instinctual being or as my lost, authentic memories, in both these conceptions 'we can observe a return to centering: there is something in me which I've split off from, denied, but which I must re-assimilate' (p. 67).

One consequence of the notion of the unconscious as a store of inaccessible repressed memories, which having been mine can in principle come back into my possession again, as Laplanche points out, is that the unconscious becomes temporary, reducible and pathological. Hence Freud's first hubristic project of 'overcoming' and 'taming', in effect abolishing the resistances that keep consciousness and the unconscious as separate systems. As his letter to Fliess makes clear, in abandoning such aspirations and their assumptions, in accepting that the unconscious consists of fantasies and that unconscious fantasy is not simply the memory of lived scenes, Freud turns, however, to the retrospective use of childhood material in later fantasy (prior to Jung's *Zurückphantasien* and more in the spirit of his own analysis of screen memories) and to hereditary 'disposition'.[44] In response to this impasse in Freudian thought, Laplanche asks:

> Would it not be possible, then, to argue that the unconscious has a close link with the past of the individual, *while at the same time abandoning the psychological problematic of memory* with its intentionality aimed at *my* past, but also its retrospective illusions and its ultimately undecidable nature?
>
> (p. 71)

Asking the question – 'what is the relation of repression to memory?' – in the context of Freud's metapsychology, and specifically of the two contradictory hypotheses about repression that Freud advances, Laplanche proposes in answer the general thesis that the unconscious element or trace is not 'a stored memory or representation, but a waste-product of certain processes of memorisation' ('The Unconscious', 1915e, pp. 172–6; 'A Short Treatise' in this

---

44 *Complete Letters*, ed. Masson, op. cit., p. 265.

volume, p. 89). The functional hypothesis, that the same mental content changes from the preconscious to the unconscious system depending on which system invests it with psychic energy and draws it into itself, seems more readily to account for the initial act of repression as the laying down of a memory. The alternative hypothesis of the double inscription, that the repressed element involves a second, separate inscription in the unconscious, seems more able to account for the return of the repressed in symptoms and derivatives. The unconscious inscription, however, behaves quite differently from a simple memory or copy of what was once conscious: for making conscious the representation, merely confronting the subject with a clinical reconstruction of the event does not automatically abolish the unconscious inscription or its effects. The analytic work of overcoming repression entails a series of approaches through the specific pathways and associations of the repressed, through its derivatives and displaced repetitions.

Freud's solution to the question of the two hypotheses was to repose the problem of repression in terms of the distinction between thing-presentations, perceptual, especially visual traces of the object or event, and word-presentations, the acoustic traces of the related words ('The Unconscious', p. 201). The unconscious is said to consist of the former cut off from the latter by repression. The retrieval or bringing to consciousness of an unconscious sequence is said to depend on being able to make connections to the relevant series of word-presentations, thus enabling the conscious perception of the repressed non-verbal material. Laplanche's objection to this psychological theory is that it is more pertinent to normal processes of memory and recall than to the strange metabolising transformations that produce the unconscious. His proposition is that unconscious elements cannot be said to consist simply of 'mnemic images of things' with its mimetic assumption about 'thing-presentations'. The thing-presentation, presentation-of-the-object such as might properly inhabit our stock of preconscious memories, becomes, when subjected to repression, a thing-like presentation or presentation-as-thing. The postulate of reification, the second of Laplanche's four requirements of any theory of the drive discussed above, entails that the unconscious element cease to be 'a representation to be *referred* to an external thing whose trace it would be' for 'the passage to the unconscious is correlative with a loss of referentiality'. As the untranslated remainder of the process of primal translation-repression, it 'loses its status as representation (as signifier) in order to become a thing which no longer represents (signifies) anything other than itself' ('A Short Treatise' p. 90). A further consequence of the reifying effects of repression, which applies to *all* repressed material, is that the distinction between word-presentations and thing-presentations loses its relevance for unconscious processes: 'The presentation of the word (verbal representation) becomes in the unconscious, like the (visual) presentation of the thing, a thing-like presentation' (p. 92, n. 20).

The classical problematic of representation is thus overthrown or transformed by Laplanche's model of translation-repression, the situation of seduction and the enigmatic message on which repression operates. With it must go any simple analogy of clinical interpretation and construction with the work of historical reconstruction as practised by historians. The leading metaphor of psychoanalysis as an archaeological uncovering of deposits with consequent reconstructions, so favoured by Freud and such a stimulus to his thinking, can only be retained, Laplanche argues, if understood in a very specific sense. In particular the false binarism of a simple prospective determinism as against a retrospective hermeneutics, which Laplanche argues against at length in the essay included in this volume[45] – if unconscious material is not the record of determining events then it must be retrospective fantasy or construction – can be traced back to the privileging of one or other moment of the two-phase schema of afterwardsness, impoverished by the absence of the other and seduction. For if unconscious elements are remainders, 'waste-products' of translation, and not copies of past events – not memories in the ordinary sense – this is not only because of the reifying and dislocating process of translation-repression, but also because the material on which it operates is not the full range of perceptions, of adjacent experiential data that might be produced by an event, whether infantile trauma or the infantile experience of instinctual satisfaction (to take the canonical examples). For repression bears selectively *only* on those enigmatic and exciting elements that resist binding and symbolisation:

> . . . these elements are not mere side-effects of the situation or its concomitant details; rather, originating in the sender of the message, they *make a sign* in a double, linked sense – they acquire the force of signs and this is because, isolated by the sender, they are addressed to the subject.
>
> ('The Unfinished Copernican Revolution', p. 74)

45 'Interpretation between Determinism and Hermeneutics: a Restatement of the Problem' in this volume, pp. 138–65.

The presentation *of* the thing is of *no* interest to psychoanalysis; it is 'treated' by repression only to the extent that it transmits a message, or 'signifies to'.

('A Short Treatise', p. 92, n. 20)

In his criticism of the closely interrelated conceptions of unconscious elements as mimetic *representations*, of the unconscious as a more deeply buried store of repressed memories, of analysis as the historical reconstruction of forgotten events, Laplanche discusses two analyses of Freud's: the non-clinical analysis of Leonardo da Vinci based on historical records and the analysis of beating fantasies based on a number of patients. The former is mapped in terms of Laplanche's current reformulation of his earlier schema of signifying substitutions derived from Lacan's account of the metaphoric structure of the symptom and in particular the paternal metaphor.[46] It can be found in 'A Short Treatise on the Unconscious' included in the present volume. His commentary on Freud's classic essay, 'A Child is being Beaten' (1919e) – to be found in the essay cited above, 'Interpretation beween Determinism and Hermeneutics' – occurs in the context of a discussion of the pertinence of the archaeological metaphor and of the relation of psychoanalysis to the work of the historian that seeks to differentiate rather than assimilate them. It is the latter that I wish to consider here.

Laplanche's arguments about the nature of repression, and consequently of the repressed, undermine any notion of the unconscious as representation, as memory and as historical record. They make impossible a naive realism of the unconscious in something like a literary sense of that phrase (unconscious representations as 'realistic', as reliable if simply inaccessible records of external 'reality'). The replacement of this naive 'realism', however, by a broadly hermeneutic and relativist position – the past is simply the creation of the present, whether the retrospective projections of the analysand or the interpretative constructions of the analyst or the historian – is also opposed by Laplanche's claim to a 'realism of the unconscious' in a philosophical and more rigorous sense. In his early joint essay with Serge Leclaire, where the thesis of 'a realism of the unconscious' was first elaborated, Laplanche posed the question: 'Is the unconscious a meaning or a letter?',[47] as part of a critique of Georges

46 Jacques Lacan, 'On a question preliminary to any possible treatment of psychosis' (1955–6), in *Écrits: A Selection*, trans. Alan Sheridan, London: Tavistock, 1977.
47 Jean Laplanche and Serge Leclaire, 'The unconscious: A psychoanalytic study' (1966), trans. *Yale French Studies*, no. 48, 1972, pp. 118–202.

Politzer's phenomenological reduction of the unconscious to a meaning immanent within manifest phenomena, as in the relation of a theme to the play that
embodies it. Rather than being a question of an implicit or hidden meaning as
the truth of the manifest, Laplanche argues that what is at issue is an absent
letter or inscription, an excluded fragment of discourse. Laplanche's 'realism' is
a realism of the letter rather than a realism of the meanings or references that
might be ascribed to the letter, e.g. the true representation of causal or
traumatising events. But that very realism of the letter, of the thing-like
presentations in the unconscious, the reified fragments of enigmatic messages
that continue to interpellate and excite the subject from within, a realism of the
source-objects of the drive with their inscription in the very body image of the
ego, also contests the 'constructivism' and facile relativism of the hermeneutic
'invention' of the past by the present.

In differentiating psychoanalysis from the sophistications of the 'new history'
of the *Annales* historians, with its replacement of the old-fashioned 'event' with
its often singular 'cause', by a history of the *longue durée*, of mentalities,
institutions, daily practices, long-term conditions and relations, Laplanche
invokes Freud's definition of 'psychical reality' as 'unconscious wishes reduced
to their most fundamental and truest shape'.[48] In returning to Freud's
formulation of a 'psychical reality' that would be neither objective material
reality, nor the reality of the psychological field and of mental processes in
general (to which Freud too often reduces it), but a third reality, Laplanche also
returns to the archaeological metaphor. This archaeology, however, is not the
contemporary 'didacticised' service discipline to the ancient historians, but an
older archaeology of the found and fascinating object. This would involve the
reconstruction not of a minutely documented factual event but of a petrified
scene or scenario. He invokes Freud's extended analogy and contrast between
Ancient Rome as an archaeological site and, Laplanche would insist, the
hyperarchaeological site of the unconscious, where in Freud's words 'nothing
which has once been formed can perish'. For as the contrast makes clear, on a
physical site, such as Rome, successive layers and constructions destroy and
reduce to rubble those before and below them, whereas in Freud's hyperarchaeological site of a 'psychical entity with a similarly long and copious past . . .
all the earliest phases of development continue to exist alongside the latest one
. . . the same piece of ground would be supporting the church of Santa Maria

48 *The Interpretation of Dreams* (1900a), *SE* V, p. 620.

39

sopra Minerva and the ancient temple over which it was built'.[49] However, in Freud's four-dimensional hologram in which time features as a fourth dimension, Laplanche points out, there is not the endless succession of stages of construction, alteration, destruction, of everything that actually happened, an inchoate jumble of experience, but rather Freud presents a succession of isolated, finished, named and identified monuments or images, separate from each other, that 'exist side by side without being influenced by one another' as Freud says of the primally repressed prototypes of the unconscious ('The Unconscious', p. 186). The Christian church coexists with the ancient temple it replaced and which is memorialised in its very name: Santa Maria sopra Minerva. Laplanche gives his own example of Nero's Domus Aurea as an instance of the arresting of the temporal in a frozen scene: not the historian's three-year-long process of its construction but 'Nero's Domus Aurea that was built in three years'; like the 'three times repeated' act of parental intercourse in the Wolf Man's *single* primal scene (rather than three successive moments). The reification of thing-like presentations, their enchainment in determinate sequences as the fixed and fixating scenes of unconscious fantasy, are in Laplanche's hyperarchaeological metaphor 'at one and the same time a cataclysm (like the engulfment of Pompeii) and a permanent preservation (like the burial of Tutankhamen's objects in his tomb)'. Unlike history or memorisation, repression 'is as different from memorisation as the engulfment of Pompeii is from Joinville's *Chronicle of the Seventh Crusade of Louis IX*' ('Interpretation between Determinism and Hermeneutics', p. 151).

Unconscious Fantasy: Beating as an Enigmatic Signifier

Freud's analysis of a common beating fantasy in both childhood and adulthood can be seen to exemplify these propositions.[50] He begins with its final conscious form which can be summed up in the formulation 'a child is being beaten'. In adulthood this bare formula can be elaborated into quite complex narratives, but the final form in girls from whom most of Freud's material is taken involves a number of children, usually boys, being beaten by an adult authority figure. The fantasy is persistent and sexually charged, being usually accompanied by

49 *Civilisation and its Discontents* (1930a), *SE* XXI, p. 70.
50 '"A Child is being Beaten": A Contribution to the Study of the Origin of Sexual Perversions' (1919e), *SE* XVII, pp. 175–204.

masturbation. The fantasising child does not appear as such in the fantasy, and in reply to questions states: 'I am probably looking on' ('A Child is being Beaten', p. 186). Freud traces this back to a first stage that can be formulated as 'my father is beating a child (usually brother or sister)'. Both of these stages are consciously remembered or entertained. However, he explains the derivation of the final stage of the fantasy from the first stage via a second *unconscious* stage, formulated as 'I am being beaten by my father'. The first stage Freud describes as proto-fantasy barely to be distinguished from memory and the reactions to actual events: 'It is perhaps rather a question of recollections of events which have been witnessed, or desires which have arisen on various occasions' (p. 185). Of the second stage he observes that, while the person beating remains the father, the child being beaten has changed into the child producing the fantasy, which is accompanied by intense pleasure of a masochistic character. Most strikingly, he says of it: 'in a certain sense it has never had a real existence. It is never remembered, it has never succeeded in becoming conscious. It is a construction of analysis, but no less a necessity on that account' (p. 185).

Laplanche's commentary on Freud's analysis argues a double thesis. The material exemplifies the specificity of unconscious fantasy in that it is different from the memory from which it has arisen, as well as from the conscious masturbatory fantasy that derives in turn from it. The virtually permanent repression of the second stage is not a form of memorisation of the actual scene or scenes, but the production of a new and different 'psychical reality' which is not a copy of the events preceding it. Laplanche notes that Freud terms the second unconscious scene an 'original fantasy' (*ursprüngliche Phantasie*), partly because it is here that fantasy proper begins. Also such a formulation, as he puts it, 'competes with and even invalidates the conception of "primal fantasies" [*Urphantasien*] of phylogenetic origin, formulated two or three years earlier'. Despite Freud's allusion to man's 'archaic heritage' elsewhere in his paper, his analysis of the beating fantasy indicates, in Laplanche's words, that 'unconscious fantasy can be *"original" without ceasing to be the product of an individual process*' ('Interpretation' in this volume, p. 156). The status of the real event of the first stage is very different from that object of intense 'archaeological' detective work, the Wolf Man's 'primal scene'. Rather than a single traumatic event to be meticulously reconstructed, Freud refers to 'various occasions' and the desires they gave rise to. As Laplanche observes, 'different circumstances, we shall say, have been able to convey one and the same message, and it has been possible for this to be repeated in different ways' ('Interpretation', p.156).

The above comment leads us to Laplanche's main thesis which he sees exemplified in Freud's analysis of the transformations of the beating scene, without Freud having theorised it as such. '*[I]nfantile scenes — the ones with which psychoanalysis is concerned — are first and foremost messages*' ('Interpretation', p. 154), Laplanche argues, from the perspective of primal seduction-implantation, and he proceeds to demonstrate the transmission and translation-repression at work in the material Freud reports. The familial drama between father and siblings is not simply a material sequence of events, for they are *presented* to the child. As Laplanche dryly observes: '[i]f a little brother or sister is beaten in the presence of the child in question, it is not like beating an egg white in the kitchen' ('Interpretation', p. 156). This is clear from the addition Freud makes to the beating formula that locates it in the drama of sibling jealousy: 'My father is beating the child *whom I hate*' ('A Child is being Beaten', p. 185). In this emotionally loaded context the father's act is not innocent; it sends a message part of which has been translated by the child. This can be seen from the further transformations of the beating formula that Freud suggests. For what makes the scene so gratifying for the watching child, and a likely candidate for further elaboration in fantasy, is the translation of it that Freud's further addition makes: 'The idea of the father beating this hateful child is therefore an agreeable one . . . [i]t means: "My father does not love this other child. *He loves only me*"' ('A Child is being Beaten', p. 187).

Indeed Freud sets up the transformation of the material from the first stage into the unconscious fantasy of the second stage partly in terms of a dialogue between different translations of the father's implicit message:

> The fantasy of the first stage of incestuous love had said: 'He (my father) loves only me, and not the other child, for he is beating it.' The sense of guilt can discover no punishment more severe than the reversal of this triumph: 'No, he does not love you, for he is beating you.'
>
> ('A Child is being Beaten', p. 189)

If this punitive translation is driven by guilt, Freud sees it symptom-like as a compromise-formation that is also driven by the very incestuous wish being punished with repression. For repression brings with it a regression from the genital to the pre-genital, anal-sadistic organisation in which the wish to be loved by the father is transformed into a wish to be beaten by him. In Freud's account beating is both a punishment and the regressive substitute for the incestuous wish being punished.

Laplanche locates this split between beating-as-loving and beating-as-punishment (a kind of loving) in relation to the paternal other and the other's compromised message to the child. In other words, the equation between beating and loving inhabits the father's message before it structures the child's unconscious fantasy. Laplanche sets out a series of reconstructions of the father's presentation of the act of beating one child, as a seductive message to the other child. He may mean: 'Disobedient children must be punished . . .'; and to the child in question: 'so you see you are better behaved than he is . . . you do not deserve a spanking . . .'. As well Laplanche invokes the cultural context in the form of the old maxim 'spare the rod and spoil the child' (Fr. *qui aime bien chatie bien*: who loves well punishes well), a traditional rationale for the practice of beating, in which the opposites merge and punishment is claimed (an adult translation) to signify not hate but love ('Interpretation', p. 158). Beyond this traditional rationalisation, Laplanche suggests the unconscious fantasy that sustains it of an anal-sadistic primal scene involving an assault from the rear, in which the father positions himself as beater in relation to all the family members. If 'he loves only me' is the child's binding and only tolerable translation of the father's culturally and unconsciously loaded act of beating, it is precisely the obscure, violent aspects of the message in which loving involves such a beating that are excluded, but which form the unconscious scenario. This scenario Laplanche calls:

> a fixed and immutable fantasy, not historicized but de-signified, senseless and inaccessible directly – a truly original fantasy, which can only be identified by the perverse derivatives with which we are all familiar.
>
> ('Interpretation', p. 159)

The sado-masochistic significance of beating, and of beating a child, for Laplanche, is not so much generated spontaneously out of an internal drama of guilt and regression in the unconscious of the child, as always already present and at work in the parental other of the infantile scene with his already constituted unconscious. The unconscious fantasy – 'I am being beaten by my father' – marks the insertion of the little voyeur-recipient of the father's message into the scene he or she watches (the unconscious fantasy is common to both sexes). It can be conceived as something like a source-object, not only of a voyeuristic drive to view or imagine such a scene, as in the conscious masturbation fantasy of the third stage – 'I am probably looking on' – but of a

43

drive that marks the subject's own body, evident in Freud's further addition to the beating formula – 'a child is being beaten on its naked bottom' ('A Child is being Beaten', p. 181). It is the parental targeting of the beaten child's body and in particular the buttocks, rather than any ontogenetic developmental sequence of stages, that maps its 'anal-sadistic' significance and provokes the watching child's masochistic identification with its rival as the imagined object of the enigmatic love that beats from behind.

In 'Masochism and the General Theory of Seduction' Laplanche returns to the beating fantasy and takes the sequence there as exemplary of 'a second moment – masochist, unconscious, repressed – which *inaugurates sexuality*, the sexual drive in the subject' (this volume, p. 211). In this context the 'economic problem of masochism'[51] is revealed to be largely a false problem. The apparent paradox of 'the pleasure of unpleasure' is understood as the pleasure or *co-excitation* of pain, where 'pain' is not to be confused with 'unpleasure' (understood variously by Freud as the heightening or, again, as the discharge of tensions), but is rather the effraction or breach of the organism or psychic entity from the outside. The intervention of the other with the intrusions and co-excitations of his or her gestures is necessarily traumatic in that it occasions the breaking in characteristic of pain, the breaching of a limit or boundary, both in its initial impact and in its deposit, 'the internal foreign body'. Laplanche insists 'that the "drive" is to the ego what pain is to the body' for 'the source-object of the drive is "stuck" in the envelope of the ego like a splinter in the skin' (p. 209). So also with the question of passivity, rejecting Freud's confusions of activity/passivity with masculinity/femininity, Laplanche provides the criterion: 'of there being "more" of representation on the active side (the adult with his conscious *and* unconscious representations) than on the passive (the infant, in the beginning)' (p. 211).[52] This imbalance of representation together with the openness and dependency of the nursling are connected to both pain and passivity: 'for it is the breaking in of an "excess of message" emanating from the other, which functions like pain, originating first from the

51 Freud, 'The Economic Problem of Masochism' (1924c), *SE* XIX, pp. 155–70.
52 For a critical discussion of Freud's confusions around passivity and femininity and in relation to Laplanche's work, see Elizabeth Cowie, 'The Seductive Theories of Jean Laplanche: a new view of the drive, passivity and femininity' in Fletcher and Stanton, op. cit., also Jacques André, 'La sexualité féminine: retour aux sources', *Psychanalyse à l'Université*, vol. 16, no. 62, 1991, reprinted in *Aux origines féminines de la sexualité*, Paris: Presses Universitaires de France, 1995.

outside, then coming from that internal other which is repressed fantasy' (p. 211). In this sense the situation of primal seduction is 'objectively and originally, sado-masochistic' (p. 212). In relation to the other, to the other's fantasy intruding within us and consequently to the source-object of the drive, 'we are in an essentially passive position, a position of "originary masochism"' (p. 212). 'Perverse' masochism 'is merely an exacerbation and a fixation of a major dimension of human sexuality, *ab origine*' (p. 210).

Laplanche ends his commentary on Freud's analysis of the beating fantasy by insisting that, if the concepts of the enigmatic *message* and its correlative of *translation* entail the idea of a pre-existing structure of meaning that is offered to the child, a meaning 'of which, however, he is not the master and of which he can become the master only by submitting to it', thus attributing a certain determining power to the pregiven, nevertheless, 'with the concept of *enigma*, a break in determinism appears' ('Interpretation', p. 160). For the enigma also entails that the adult is not in possession of the unconscious dimension of the message that he addresses to the infant, just as the latter does not have the means to translate and make sense of what is communicated to him. From this Laplanche concludes that there can be no direct transmission of the parental unconscious and discourse to the infant, no direct determination by it of what the infant does with it in the process of primal repression-translation. The classical formulae of Lacan and his followers – 'the unconscious is the discourse of the Other', 'the child is the symptom of the parents' – Laplanche argues, 'disregard the break, the profound reshaping, which occurs between the two, which may be likened to a metabolism that breaks down food into its constituent parts and reassembles them into a completely different entity' (p. 160).

Something like the determining force of the other and the dependency of the subject implied by the Lacanian formulae appear, however, in Laplanche's reflections on intromission and psychosis. Laplanche proposes what he calls *intromission* as a 'violent variant' of the normal processes of implantation. Where the latter provokes and allows the ordinary process of primal translation-repression, the violence of parental intromission, by contrast, blocks or paralyses the active reworking of the parental messages, inserting aggressively into the subject 'an element resistant to all metabolisation'.[53] This notion of an untranslatable and unbound implantation, not susceptible to the schema of substitutions, of violently inscribed parental signifiers that cannot be transposed

---

53 'Implantation, Intromission' in this volume, p. 136.

or modified by primal translation-repression, is invoked by Laplanche in two related gestures towards a further project of reconceiving both psychosis and the superego. In relation to psychosis intromission produces a failure of primal repression that 'short-circuits the formation of the agencies' (p. 136), prevents the sealing of the unconscious and leads to what a formulation from an earlier, untranslated paper calls a fracture or fault in the formation and coherence of the ego as an intensely invested body image.[54] It is the violence of intromission in the first moment of afterwardsness that would present the necessary condition for that blockage of symbolisation in a second moment, described by previous psychoanalytic accounts of a specifically *psychotic* mechanism different from repression, Freud's *Verwerfung* or repudiation, and Lacan's *forclusion* or foreclosure. These mechanisms result in an attempted expulsion of a traumatic and intolerable element leading to hallucination: 'what was abolished internally returns from without' (Freud); 'whatever has been refused in the Symbolic order, in the sense of *Verwerfung*, reappears in the real' (Lacan).[55] Laplanche's reiterated critique of these earlier conceptions, however, is that they remain centered on the individual in question and that they require, and tacitly presuppose, a centripetal intervention from the other (rather than just a centrifugal process of expulsion into the exterior). For something to be repudiated or even foreclosed, it has first to be registered in some provisional form. Like translation-repression, what these psychotic mechanisms bear selectively on are those traumatising elements that 'make a sign' from the other, but in this case a violence of signification that blocks or paralyses translation. It would be possible to say that the 'excess of message' that the subject is unable to bind by translation-repression is then submitted to the more desperate measures of expulsion – repudiation, foreclosure, projection – with their hallucinatory consequences. Paradoxically, Laplanche also suggests

54 'Le traitement psychanalytique des états psychotiques' (1972), *La révolution copernicienne inachevée*, Paris: Aubier, 1992, p. 127. For a very productive elaboration of a theory of psychosis in relation to the theory of generalised seduction, see Dominique Scarfone, '"Ma mère, ce n'est pas elle". De la séduction à la négation', in Jean Laplanche et al., *Colloque internationale de psychanalyse: Montréal 3–5 juillet 1992*, Paris: Presses Universitaires de France, 1994.

55 Freud, *Psycho-Analytic Notes on an Autobiographical Account of a Case of Paranoia (Dementia Paranoides)* (1911c), *SE* XII, p. 71. Jacques Lacan, *Seminar III: The Psychoses* (1955–6), trans. Russell Grigg; London: Routledge, 1993, p. 13. See entries under 'Foreclosure', 'Disavowal' and 'Projection' in Laplanche and Pontalis 1967, op. cit.

that just such an unmetabolisable foreign body also plays a role not in the short-circuiting but in the very formation of the agency of the superego. In *New Foundations* he draws the two propositions together, suggesting the hypothesis that the superego, made up of parental messages, embodies a law and gives rise to categorical imperatives that 'cannot be diluted, and cannot be replaced by anything else'. 'Trapped between the two stages of primal repression', the categorical imperatives and unjustifiable injunctions of the superego should be seen as 'psychotic enclaves within the human personality as such' (*New Foundations*, p. 139).

Closures and Re-openings

Laplanche's insistence on the primacy of the other and of the other's implant-ations in the situation of primal seduction is a radical intervention within Freudian metapsychology and the ambiguities that inhabit its categories. His concern has been to retrieve the otherness of the unconscious and of the origins of sexuality, from both the 'Ptolemaic' recentering that is endemic to metapsychology and the narcissistic closure of the human 'psychical apparatus' that supports that recentering, with its formation of an ego and the sealing off and the sealing in of those enigmatic and traumatising elements that resist the ego's synthesising symbolisations. He writes this 'otherness' as a neologism in French – not just *étrangeté*, strangeness, foreignness, alienness, but *étrangèreté*, stranger-ness, foreigner-ness which we have attempted to translate as 'alien-ness' – in order to insist that it is only in relation to the other and the other's signifying and desiring actions that the alterity of the unconscious can be upheld. Given the connivance between theory and its object, the 'covering-up of truth inherent in the very thing to which thought conforms' ('The Unfinished Copernican Revo-lution', p. 81), that is to say the complicity between the going-astray of Freudian thought and the closing-in-on-itself of the human being in the very process of its constitution, Laplanche asks, 'can the psychoanalytic Copernican revolution be finished?' (p. 82).

The re-opening to the other introduced by the theory of general seduction would not be sustainable, and so a further Ptolemaic turn and recuperation would be inevitable, Laplanche argues 'if psychoanalysis were nothing but a theory confronted with an object' (p. 83). But, as he reminds us, psycho-analysis is a practice, a method of analysis, of decomposition, that is inseparable from the analytic situation, and the analytic situation *repeats* the originary situation of primal seduction. At this point the limitations of the astronomical analogy are obvious. For while the universe and its movements cannot be said to be at first Copernican and then afterwards Ptolemaic or vice-versa, both moments characterise the formation of the subject: 'the Ptolemaism of the human psyche, its narcissistic recentering, follows upon a "Copernican" stage as its presupposition, in which the nursling infant is caught up in the orbit of the other and has a passive relation to its messages' (p. 82). The analytic situation is characterised by both dynamics but in particular, Laplanche argues, its Copernican opening is manifest 'in that it finds its immediate centre of gravity in the other: both in the observation of the fundamental rule [of free association] . . . as well as in the transference' (p. 83).

The analytic situation is characterised by the combination of transference and analysis (the deconstruction or dismantling of the analysand's existing translations) with its correlative of free association. Laplanche argues that transference, as the repetition of the originary relation to the enigma of the other, gives the specifically *clinical* situation a kinship with certain privileged sites that are *extra*-clinical. For instead of defining transference as clinical only to export it thence as *applied* psychoanalysis, he suggests, very strikingly, that 'perhaps the principal site of transference, "ordinary" transference, before, beyond or after analysis, would be the multiple relation to the cultural, to creation, or more precisely, to the cultural message', always conceived 'from the relation to the enigma'.[56] While distinguishing three types of this relation to the originary enigma, that of the producer, the recipient and the recipient-analyst, he focuses in particular on the cultural producer's relation to the addressee or recipient. Beyond the standard model of communication as a pragmatics, with the aim to produce specific effects by a calculation of means to ends, is the address to an anonymous recipient who is essentially enigmatic: 'what can be isolated as characteristic of the cultural, is an address to an other who is out of reach, to others "scattered in the future", as the poet says[57] . . . the nameless crowd, addressees of the message in the bottle' (p. 224). This fundamental relation of poetics and of cultural production in general opens up the space of a transferential repetition of the situation of primal seduction and a renewal of its force; for such an address 'is a repercussion, which prolongs and echoes the enigmatic messages by which the [poet] himself, so to speak, was bombarded' (p. 224).

The unprecedented character of the practice Freud inaugurated lies, then,

56 'Transference: its Provocation by the Analyst' in this volume, p. 222.
57 From Mallarmé's poem, 'Le tombeau d'Edgar Poe'.

not in the phenomenon of the transference as such or in itself, for transference 'like our interpellation by the enigma, exists outside and beyond analysis . . . [and] is a fundamental dimension of the human being' (p. 230). By the same token such a fundamental dimension cannot end with the termination of the analysis. Very simply, what is new in the practice of analysis, Laplanche argues, is analysis itself, which he names from Freud as *Lösung*, the dissolution, untying or unweaving which, in a very suggestive meditation on the exemplary figure of Homer's Penelope, he connects with mourning and its processes of working through: 'mourning, as a work of unweaving, as much as it is the prototype of melancholy, can also be conceived as the very model of psychoanalysis: unweaving so that a new fabric can be woven, disentangling to *allow* the formation of new knots'.[58] However, Laplanche also connects this process of segmentation of the analysand's speech, of its symbolisations and translations of the originary enigmas, and the cross-referencing of its associations and contexts, guided by the condensations and displacements of the primary process, with the death drive: a process of decomposition and repetition 'which potentially leads to the dissolution of all formations – psychical, egoic, ideological, symptomatic' ('Transference' in this volume, p. 227). Such a dangerous unbinding of psychical energies and representations can only take place within a frame, an artificially maintained space, constituted by the fundamental rule and associated conventions, in which the utilitarian or functional realm of needs and worldly ends is bracketed out. However, it also can only take place in relation to the analyst, the analyst-as-other and the offer of analysis which, Laplanche insists, is what creates or provokes the transference, 'the re-opening of . . . the originary relation, in which the other was primary for the subject' (p. 226).

Laplanche attributes three functions to the analyst and the situation he institutes: the analyst as 'the guarantor of constancy', of holding and containment, 'the constancy of a presence, of a solicitude, the flexible but attentive constancy of a frame'; the analyst as 'the director of the method and the companion of the primary process', as 'the artisan of unbinding'; the analyst 'as the one who guards the enigma and provokes the transference' (pp. 226–7). If the analyst is, in a formulation Laplanche borrows from Lacan, *the subject supposed to know (le sujet supposé savoir)*,[59] the repetition for the analysand of

58 'Time and the Other' in this volume, pp. 253–4.
59 Jacques Lacan, *The Four Fundamental Concepts of Psychoanalysis* (1973), ed. J.-A. Miller, trans. Alan Sheridan, Harmondsworth: Penguin books, 1977, p. 230.

the originary other with his 'more' of representation, his 'excess of message', he is also other to himself, divided by his own unconscious and in relation to his own enigmatic significations and his own internal other. So Laplanche proposes of the analyst: 'It is the maintaining of the dimension of interior alterity which enables the setting up of alterity in the transference' (pp. 228–9).

If it is the analyst as other to himself and in his offer of analysis that provokes the transference, then it is by reference to analysis as unbinding, as the *de-translation* of existing translations, that Laplanche discriminates different modalities of the transference. In particular he distinguishes between what he calls the 'filled-in' transference – *transfert en plein* – and the 'hollowed-out' transference – *transfert en creux*. The former involves the repetition of childhood imagos, scenarios, behaviours and relationships, the positive translations of the past, which are deposited in the 'hollow' of the analyst's neutrality, his *refusal* to know, to translate and to bind in relation to his own and the analysand's enigmas, what Laplanche calls 'the maintenance of the analyst's interpellation by the enigma' (p. 229). It is only by working through and dismantling, *de-translating* the contents of this 'filled-in' transference that the 'hollowed-out' transference can come into play, the emergence of the analysand's originary relation to the enigmatic other of his personal prehistory. Laplanche gives a compelling account of the spiralling dynamics of the transference and its periodical returns to and passage through the same memories, fantasies, old translations, by which the analysand has lived, the derivatives of the primal repressed, so as to mourn, to unweave in order to re-translate, to produce less repressive, less exclusionary, less blindly defensive self-representations. The end of analysis cannot be the dissolution of transference as such, Laplanche insists, any more than it can mean the abolition of the unconscious as such. Both testify to the permanence of the internal other, the primal repressed, and the relation to the external other, which can only be transferred – what Laplanche calls the transference of the 'hollowed-out' transference – outside the clinical to other cultural sites of elaboration and working through. The possibility of sustaining Freud's unfinished Copernican revolution at the level of theory is inscribed in what Laplanche calls the drive to translate that arises from the pressure of the untranslated, the *à traduire*. This continually renewed opening towards the other thing in the unconscious and the other person, of which the practice of analysis itself is not the only or even perhaps the most important exemplar, is what gives rise to the theoretical exigency of the psychoanalytic field postulated by Laplanche, and so provides the condition of possibility for continuing Freud's unfinished Copernican revolution.

50

The work of Jean Laplanche has systematically retraced the trajectory of Freudian thought, its strayings, returns and displacements, seeking to intervene in its aporiae, and to confront its 'Ptolemaic' recenterings, whether biological or ego-psychological, with its own Copernican decenterings and openings to the other. He has inserted the categories of otherness and the 'module' of primal seduction – the other/implantation/enigma/translation/remainder – into a metapsychology from which it was virtually absent, and whose contradictions he has exposed and recast in relation to an exogenous as much as to an endogenous dynamic. This redescription of the foundational process of the human sexual being, in terms of the afterwardsness of seduction and trauma as 'ordinary' processes, constitutes a radical refoundation of psychoanalytic thought and a renewal of its inaugural provocation and exigency.

John Fletcher

1

The Unfinished Copernican Revolution

Copernicus: The Decentering of the Human Being

The fate of the word 'revolution' is linked in a curious manner to the name of Copernicus. Only the properly astronomical or geometrical meaning of the term existed in his time, and his treatise *De revolutionibus orbium caelestium*, published in 1543, discusses the cyclical and essentially repetitive motion of the heavenly spheres. [1]

The 'revolutionary' aspect of these 'revolutions' is therefore not yet reflected in the terminology, and it is not until sixteen years later, in 1559, that Amyot began to set in motion the evolution of the term with his immortal translations of Plutarch – an illustration, among so many others, of the creative role of translators in the evolution of language. The change in meaning is, moreover, a progressive one: for Amyot, 'revolution' admittedly indicates an abrupt transformation – although one which is still predetermined, signalled in advance by 'various heavenly signs'. [2] I do not have at my disposal sufficient documentation to trace in detail this metabolization of the word. Whatever its course, by the time of Kant, more than two hundred years later, our modern term 'revolution' [3] is well established. In 1787, in the second Preface to *The*

---

1 The work was published just after Copernicus' death, no doubt as a precaution – better to risk an *auto-da-fé* for his book than for himself.
2 Plutarch, *Les Vies des Hommes Illustres Grecs et Romains: Vie de Demosthenes*, trans. Jacques Amyot (1559), Édition Critique par Jean Normand, Paris: Société des Textes Français Modernes, Librairie Hachette, 1924, p. 26.
3 In German, *Revolution*. It is true that Kant did not invent the expression 'Copernican revolution' and, moreover, that Freud does not use it. From whom does it come?

Critique of Pure Reason, it seems that scientific and political revolutions go hand in hand: the thought of Copernicus constitutes a 'sudden revolution in natural science'. But at the price of what misunderstanding is Kant to take it up as a model for his own philosophy? We shall return to this later.

It is well known that the revolution of Copernicus in astronomy is invoked by Freud as the first humiliating blow, the first narcissistic wound inflicted on mankind by science. It is worth looking in more detail at what it consists of, without for the time being considering its relation to psychoanalysis.

The history of astronomy, which is known to go back to earliest antiquity (the Assyrians, the Babylonians and then the Greeks) is anything but linear as far as its major problem is concerned, which can be stated as follows: we observe movements of circular appearance in the universe – but what finally turns around what?

The opposition between Ptolemy and Copernicus, geocentrism and helio-centrism is a simple, pedagogical one; but let us remember that a revolution is never as revolutionary as it thinks – it has its forerunners in the past, and what it offers as a new opening also carries with it possibilities for potential relapses. Throughout the centuries, even the millennia, of astronomical theories, what ultimately emerges is the confrontation and alternation of two lines of thought – the one Ptolemaic, the other Copernican (or so called) – with equally remarkable thinkers on both sides. Ptolemy, who lived in the second century A.D., was only the culmination of a long, double tradition going back at least to the fourth or fifth century B.C.; with the philosophers (the Pythagoreans, Plato and Aristotle) on one side, and on the other scholars closer to observation – astronomers, geographers and mathematicians. Eudoxes of Cnidus (408–355 B.C.), who was the first to reconstruct the movements of the stars on the basis of their circular motion; Autolycus (fourth century B.C.), Hipparchus of Nicea (second century B.C.), to whom we owe the first great catalogue of stars, and finally Ptolemy himself (138–180 A.D.), who proposed his 'great synthesis' (Μεγάλη Σύνταξις).[4]

As for the Copernican lineage, it is well known that this was to continue its illustrious descent through Galileo, Kepler, Newton – then beyond – in the Einsteinian revolution. What is not generally known is that it goes back explicitly to the third century B.C., to the astonishing Aristarchus of Samos, whose works Copernicus knew. Of these we still have the *Treatise on the Sizes and*

4 Which in the Arabic tradition will be given the syncretic name of *Al-mageste*.

53

Distances of the Sun and the Moon, in which he has the daring to work out these measurements, in some cases with a surprising accuracy, due to observation and to innovative trigonometric calculations. But above all we know him as the first to propose a heliocentric system, thus incurring – even then, in the Greek world – the accusation of impiety. What is at stake in this Copernican revolution (which should therefore really be termed Aristarchan)? Here, a distinction might be made between the astronomical level and the philosophico-anthropological level.

From the point of view of astronomy, the aim is to explain the trajectories of the different heavenly bodies in relation to the earth. I leave to one side a number of issues which, though important, are nonetheless outside the Copernican shift of perspective. For instance, the privilege accorded to circular movement will not be questioned by Copernicus. Similarly, the rotundity of the earth, which was accepted in antiquity from the fourth century B.C. onwards. Not even the earth's rotation on its own axis, the cause of the alternation of day and night, is at issue. This last hypothesis, attributed to Heraclitus, is in itself nothing but a change of co-ordinates *vis-à-vis* something shown by everyday observation: the unchanging rotation of the astral sphere in relation to the earth.[5] Without going into details, we can note that the main obstacle to the notion of a simple rotation of the sphere said to be 'fixed' (let's say, the totality of distant stars) is the movement of different heavenly bodies – the sun, the moon, finally the 'planets' – *in relation to* that sphere. Above all, this is because the movements of these wandering, straying[6] stars in the end defy all straightforward explanation in a system where the earth remains the centre of reference.

The foremost issue in the whole of astronomy, up to and including the Ptolemaic synthesis, is thus located on the path of an initial going-astray.[7] Starting out from a basic hypothesis which is false, it becomes a question of finding – of inventing – 'those regular and ordered movements which must be

---

5 Plato is even supposed to have allowed this hypothesis, a sign that it was not deemed impious.

6 One cannot ignore the fact that the wandering stars, πλάνητες ἀστέρες [planetes asteres], derive their name from the verb πλανάω [planao], which means 'to lead astray, to seduce' and which is notably used in this sense in the Bible, to describe 'seduction' by God or by Christ (John VII, 47).

7 [*Fourvoiement*: literally, 'wandering off the path', hence 'straying into error'. To maintain the conceptual status of the metaphor – as a consistent term in Laplanche's theoretical vocabulary – it is translated throughout as 'going-astray'. Translator's note.]

assumed in order to save [i.e. take account of] the appearances observed in the movement of the planets'.[8]

Since the multiplication of 'spheres' centering on the earth is hardly enough to account for the movements of the sun and moon, a whole series of accidental movements must be called upon – movements which are always circular but displaced from the center, then displaced in relation to one another: 'excentrics', 'epicycles', 'deferents', etc. All these are highly mathematical hypotheses which mobilize the ingenuity, even the genius, of astronomers up to the Ptolemaic summation which will remain the Bible of astronomy for fourteen centuries. Given its complexity, it is almost impossible to add anything further to it. It is a system in which each unexplained detail, far from bringing the whole in question, was made the object of a supplementary *ad hoc* hypothesis. Overload, blockage – one thinks of what became of Freudian metapsychology at a certain level of complication, when it began to fill out certain inadequacies with new concepts, without bothering to determine whether they were congruent with the whole or whether it was not rather the whole which should have been reconstructed.[9]

What is at stake in what we neatly term 'the Copernican revolution' is a question of 'centering' which at the outset seems limited to a change of astronomical center (from the earth to the sun) but which actually opens onto far vaster consequences.

The immediate result of heliocentrism, the perspective adopted by Copernicus, is an immense simplification (at least, a potential one). The idea which seems banal to us today, that the earth is a planet in orbit like the others around the sun, does not make things simpler straight away: the circularity of the orbits means that a certain number of accidental hypotheses, epicycles and others, have to be retained. The way is open, however, to further progress towards unification; not only simplifications, but also an indefinite number of improvements: the system is no longer 'stuffed'; not only the physical closure of the world but also an epistemological closure has been surpassed.

The immensity or even infinity of the universe is a consequence of

8 Plato, quoted in *Histoire Générale des Sciences*, vol. I, ed. René Taton, Paris: Presses Universitaires de France, 1966, p. 243.
9 Is it possible to load the Freudian vessel with all this supplementary excess baggage – Kleinian positions, foreclosure, false self or omnipotent self, transitional space, etc., etc. – without the whole thing capsizing? Is there no place for moving from local questions to a re-problematization of the whole?

heliocentric theory — and was already perceived as such from the time of Aristarchus. This started with the following objection: if the earth was in motion and therefore, constantly changing its point of view, the positions of the 'fixed' stars in relation to one another, the 'constellations', would have to undergo modifications and deformations . . . which does not occur. This leads to two possible conclusions: either the Aristarchan-Copernican theory is false . . . or else the stars are at a distance from us incommensurable with the internal distances of the solar system. The specific idea of heliocentrism was thus only the first step: the Copernican revolution, to some extent, opened up the possibility of the absence of a center. In a world of quasi-infinite distances it becomes absurd to persist in trying to preserve one star among others — the sun or solar system — as center.

If the 'center' of the world can be everywhere, it follows correlatively that 'its circumference is nowhere'.[10] A decentered and infinite world — this double affirmation led, as surely in the time of Aristarchus as in the Renaissance, to the accusation of impiety. If man is no longer at the center of the universe, not only are all cosmogonies and creation myths contradicted, but all the pantheons forged in the image of man or centered on man are thereby devalorized.

But doubtless there are deeper roots to humanity's clinging to the Ptolemaic vision. When Freud speaks of narcissistic wounding in this connection, he is referring to the humiliation of man as *flesh and blood*, as an empirical individual. But one must go further: it is not only that man in his concrete existence is humbled to find himself nowhere, in the midst of the immensity of the universe; the Copernican revolution is perhaps still more radical in that it *suggests* that man, even as subject of knowledge, is not the central reference-point of what he knows. No more than they orbit around him do the stars

---

10 The formula 'a sphere whose center is everywhere and whose circumference is nowhere' is attributed to Hermes Trismegistus as an expression of divine infinity. It is again as a definition of God that it is quoted by Nicholas Mulerius (Müler, Muller or Muler of Bruges) in 1617, in his edition of Copernicus' *Révolutions*. Pascal, in his famous 'Pensée' on 'the two infinities' (*Pensées I*, Paris: Cluny, 1938, p. 112) takes up exactly the same terms but profoundly alters the meaning because he no longer applies them to God but to the 'infinite vastness of things'. Between Mulerius and Pascal, the Copernican revolution has had a double effect: it is accepted that the world is both decentered and infinite *but* these propositions are no longer deemed impious. The infinite universe is no longer in competition with divine infinity, which for Pascal is of another order.

recognize the primacy of man's knowledge. Conversely, if the Copernican revolution sets in motion an open-ended progress of knowledge (even through crises), it is no doubt because it affirms implicitly that man is in no way the measure of all things. Thus the decentering and the infinity of the universe would herald an infinity of knowledge, as well as an epistemological decentering much harder to accept.[11]

I find this potential link between astronomical decentering and the decentering of knowledge confirmed in three thinkers, whom I will consider briefly in their relation to Copernicus.

In the second Preface to the *Critique of Pure Reason*, Kant evokes the 'revolutions' in science that may provide a model that 'promises to metaphysics . . . the secure path of a science'. It is immediately Copernicus who is invoked, in that it was he who 'made the spectator to revolve and the stars to remain at rest'. According to Kant, metaphysics should make a similar attempt. . . . Yet far from offering us a Copernican decentering, it is quite clearly a Ptolemaic recentering that Kant wishes to effect – far from intuition on one side and concepts 'conforming to the object' on the other, he would rather turn things around and claim that it is the object which 'conforms' to the 'constitution of our faculty of intuition' and our '*a priori* concepts'.[12] I do not wish to discuss here the significance of Kantian idealism,[13] but I cannot fail to be troubled by the fact that a movement of radical decentering is being invoked to support a no less radical recentering. There is clearly only one way to save Kant – to recall that 'worldly', physical science has nothing in common with metaphysical knowledge, the conditions of possibility of which are prescribed by transcendental philosophy. The empirical subject accords with Copernicus: he is carried back and forth in the movement of the universe. The transcendental subject for his part remains faithful to Ptolemy: it is to him that the movements of heavenly bodies, which are only 'objects in general', conform. So be it! But in that case, why invoke the procedures of the one to found that of the other, and this against the grain?

However, two authors after Kant refuse this too easy dissociation of the

---

11 Our difficulties in accepting, other than in a purely abstract way, the theory of relativity or quantum theory, are doubtless reactions to the same epistemological decentering.

12 Kant, *The Critique of Pure Reason*, trans. Norman Kemp Smith, Macmillan: London, 1929/85, pp. 22–3.

13 Even if the anthropological interpretation of Kant cannot be so easily rejected.

empirical and the transcendental, and do so in diametrically opposed ways. Let us take Husserl first – the later Husserl whom the thought of Merleau-Ponty invokes as an authority. In the *Phenomenology of Perception* (1945), the latter was already quoting a text by Husserl of 1934, whose title alone is an entire programme: *Umsturz der kopernikanischen Lehre: die Erde als Ur-Arche bewegt sich nicht*; which can be translated, 'Subversion of Copernican doctrine: the Earth, as primal Ark, does not move'.[14] Here, as will be the case for Merleau-Ponty, it is clearly a matter of re-introducing the human being with his 'flesh', his native 'soil', in a word, the earth itself as his primal habitat, the 'Ark' he shares with the animals, into the 'constitutive ego'. It is an astonishing text, since despite some hesitations and numerous obscurities, it attacks the Copernican revolution on its own ground, even claiming to recenter it. For the 'apodictic ego', which thus again becomes Ptolemaic, is at once the constitutive subject and the contingent subject of flesh and blood whose feet are on that Earth.[15]

This shows us that the stakes of the Copernican revolution – its acceptance or rejection – ultimately go beyond the simple technical domain of astronomical science.

My second testimony on this point comes from a certain N. Y. Marr. Today his name is forgotten, but in his own day it enjoyed a grim renown. He was a Russian linguist (1864–1934) who lived before the 1917 revolution, then radicalized his ideas under the revolution and at the beginning of Stalinism, in what was called 'the new theory of language'. He became a sort of Lyssenko of linguistics: 'Marrism' became synonymous with Marxist linguistics and anyone who did not show absolute allegiance to it found himself persecuted, forced to perform self-critiques and sometimes physically

14 [The German word *Arche* means Ark (as in Noah's Ark) but it may also allude to the Greek *arche* meaning the cause, origin or beginning. Husserl's text is to be found in English as 'Foundational Investigations of the Phenomenological Origin of the Spatiality of Nature', trans. Fred Kersten, reprinted in *Husserl: Shorter Works*, eds Peter McCormick and Frederick A. Elliston, Indiana: University of Notre Dame Press, 1981, p. 222. The editors report: 'The following descriptive comment was written on the envelope [of the manuscript]: "*Overthrow of the Copernican theory* in the usual interpretation of a worldview. The original ark, the earth, does not move"' (p. 231). Editor's note.]

15 '[W]e must not forget the pregivenness and constitution belonging to the apodictic Ego *or to me, to us*, as the source of all actual and possible sense of being . . .', *Husserl: Shorter Works*, ibid., p. 230 [Laplanche's italics].

eliminated. The Marrists were given total support by Stalin until 1950, at which point the tyrant himself, reflecting that this was all leading to extravagant conclusions (some even thought them deranged), liquidated Marrism (and possibly several 'Marrists' as well) by announcing the following revelation, truly as simplistic as what it was attacking: 'language is not a superstructure; language has no class character'.[16]

Marrism argued, then, that language is a class phenomenon and that its early stages can be specified according to the type of class-society: aristocratic societies/languages, followed by bourgeois societies/languages, and finally 'proletarian-speak', which is the most important for our thesis. For 'proletarian-speak' is 'science-speak', in that the classless society must correspond to the advent of a 'newspeak', a kind of esperanto – but far more ambitious than that (which itself, moreover, had its devotees both before and after the revolution). How is this connected with our problem? In so far as the Copernican revolution, which is scientific, 'science-think', has not yet entered into language, which has remained bourgeois, petit bourgeois or capitalist. Thus, the peasant who says that the sun rises in the east and sets in the west is actually a *kulak*, a bourgeois speaking the ideological language of pre-Copernican science. The man of the classless society, disencumbered of ideology, must by contrast invent a language in which to speak truthfully, according to science, that is, in which one might manage to express directly, through some kind of *decentering of language itself*, that it is not the sun which circles the earth but the earth which turns on its axis and also circles the sun, and so on.

With these two extreme positions, that of the late Husserl and that of the Marrists, equally foolish as they may be, we encounter perhaps a testimony both to the fundamental nature of the Copernican revolution and to the impossibility of sustaining its radicality consistently and to the end. We shall have to return to this at the close of our journey.

16 Cf. Stalin, 1950, 'On the question of Marxism in linguistics'. In the entire post-Marrist Stalinist era, Soviet commentary on Stalin's text was limited to repeating that language is not a superstructure. This, Stalin's only text on linguistics, had not only theoretical consequences: it posed the problem of national languages in the Soviet empire, and the taking-up of positions on the question of linguistic unification was even more important in practice than Lyssenkoism. Even Lacan quotes Stalin: at last, he comments not without irony, Stalin came along and decreed that language is not a superstructure! (*Écrits: A Selection*, trans. Alan Sheridan, London: Tavistock, 1977, pp. 125, 176).

The Unconscious: an Internal Other but not at the Center

It is well known that on several occasions Freud compared the discovery of psychoanalysis to the Copernican revolution, and saw in them two major affronts to human narcissism. I will not directly engage with these texts, which deserve a careful reading and possibly an uncompromising critique. Let us say at the outset that my vision of Freud's 'Copernican' revolution coincides only partly with what he says about it himself at the time. ·

Indeed, if Freud is his own Copernicus, he is also his own Ptolemy. The revolution in astronomy lasted nearly two millennia, with some intuitions of the truth almost from the start, but also with an initial going-astray. In psychoanalysis everything, essentially, is produced by a single man – *simultaneously: the discovery*, affirmed at a very early stage, and which is conjointly (and for me indissociably) that of the unconscious and that of seduction – *and the going-astray*, the wrong path taken each time there was a return to a theory of self-centering, or even self-begetting.

It is only in a schematic way that one might wish to date Freud's 'Ptolemaic' going-astray from the famous letter of the 1897 equinox or turning-point, where the abandonment of the seduction theory is solemnly announced. In Freud, one should speak, at almost every period, of an alternation between relapses into Ptolemaism and resurgences of the Copernican, other-centered vision. Resurgences and re-affirmations which are often deepenings: thus it is that seduction, although theoretically denied its foundational value, continues to pursue a secret pathway, an underground development, even under the reign of the dominant Ptolemaism – both in Freud's work and in some of his contemporary disciples.[17] Similarly, there are some major re-affirmations of other-centeredness, the most powerful of which is without doubt the adoption of Groddeck's id as an agency which lives us more than we live it. But it is also true that this re-affirmation is at least ambiguous, as the movement eventually ends up recentering the subject on the id – as that which is in him from the beginning and around which, so to speak, he grows.[18]

However, just as the Copernican line continues well after 1897, it is also true

17 Cf. *New Foundations for Psychoanalysis*, trans. David Macey, Oxford: Basil Blackwell, 1989, pp. 116–21; and Jacqueline Lanouzière, *Histoire secrète de la séduction sous la règne de Freud*, Paris: Presses Universitaires de France, 1991.

18 Cf. *Problématiques IV: L'inconscient et le ça*, Paris: Presses Universitaires de France, 1981, part 2: 'Problématique du ça'.

that Freudian Ptolemaism is already present at the moment when the seduction theory finds its strongest affirmation. This is particularly shown by the very construction of 'A Project for a Scientific Psychology' (1950a [1895]). The second section, 'The psychopathology of hysteria', broadly develops the idea of an exogenous origin of the unconscious, while the other two sections, III and above all I, are explicitly 'Ptolemaic' in inspiration: they aim to reconstruct the apparatus according to a sort of hierarchy, beginning with the ψ level conceived as unconscious and primary, onto which are grafted the problems of 'consciousness', of 'quality', or even simply of survival. The formula 'everything conscious was previously unconscious', which will infect the whole of metapsychology, is present here from the outset, alongside the thesis of a repressed unconscious, but without being articulated with it.[19]

In this double history of innovation and going-astray – a sort of braid in which at times one strand of the plait lies uppermost, at times the other – one should also take account of the enrichment due to numerous discoveries derived from analytic experience, and which must be placed either in the Copernican line or, more often, in the Ptolemaic system; thus the discovery of *narcissism*, of the *repetition compulsion*, the foregrounding of *aggressive* phenomena, etc.

All these discoveries, products of an enlargement of the field of experience – and one could list others – have to be integrated into a doctrine which, partly or totally, has effaced the initial revolution. Hence, exactly as in the Ptolemaic system, the trick is to integrate the new at the cost of supplementary complications, adventitious hypotheses designed to save appearances: the famous 'epicycles' of ancient astronomy.[20]

There are two facets to the Freudian revolution in the radical decentering it offers. The first is classical: the discovery of the unconscious, in so far as it is

---

19 *SE* I, pp. 283–387. See on this topic *Life and Death in Psychoanalysis*, Jean Laplanche, trans. Jeffrey Mehlman, Baltimore: The Johns Hopkins University Press, 1976, pp. 25–66.

20 The foremost example of one of these 'epicycles', these *ad hoc* pseudo-concepts, is the death drive. I have tried to show with increasing precision its value in restoring the balance of the Freudian system, its significance as a re-affirmation of something of the order of sexuality in its most savage dimension. What is completely remarkable is that in a system which has itself returned to the tame, the domesticated, to self-centering, to a biologization of the drive – the re-affirmation of what Freud calls himself the 'demonic' can only find a place in a totally distorted framework, in the form of an *instinct* itself biological.

precisely *not* our center, as it is an 'excentric' center; the other facet, the seduction theory, is hidden but indispensable to the first for it maintains the unconscious in its alien-ness.[21]

Das Andere, the other thing in us: this is the unconscious as it is discovered before 1897 and as it will re-emerge at numerous points in Freud's work, including the 1915 text 'The Unconscious' (1915e). It is what Leclaire and I tried to delineate in our article of 1966, under the banner of a 'realism of the unconscious'.[22]

I can only list some points, all of which are equally essential, in support of this alien-ness.

First, to take things in their proper order, the question of method. For one should never stop stressing that what distinguishes this hitherto inaccessible domain is a new method, a method of discovery and exploration. The domain of the unconscious is inseparable from the approach to it, something which already effects a break with all conceptions of a so-called 'pre-Freudian unconscious', which get stuck precisely on the question of method, either by simply positing the unconscious or by trying to divine it with some kind of soothsaying. The method is one of association and cross-referencing, a deconstruction, and only at the horizon of this dissolution (*Lösung*) or analysis can another reality be sketched: what is called an unconscious fantasy. There is no point-for-point correspondence, however, no analogy or similitude between the behavioural or conscious discursive sequence from which the associations start and the fragment of an unconscious sequence which can be outlined through cross-references. So much so that any method of a hermeneutic order

21 [*étrangèreté*: 'strangerness' translated as 'alien-ness'. Laplanche's description of the unconscious is a neologism connecting the other thing in us, *Das Andere*, back to *Der Andere*, the other person (*l'étranger*, the stranger/foreigner) who takes part in the seduction scene. The English 'strange' has a subjective dimension that is relative and reducible. Strangeness is in the eye of the beholder: the 'stranger' can become over time familiar, whereas 'alien' denotes an irreducible strangeness, the result of an *external* origin. While the foreigner may lose his effect of 'strangeness' over time, he never becomes a 'native' but remains a 'resident alien' however 'naturalised'. The hyphenated form 'alien-ness' allows the reader to hear the noun in Laplanche's neologism – *étrangèreté* – and distinguishes it from the usual abstraction 'alienness' – *étrangeté*. Editor's note.]
22 Cf. *Problématiques IV: L'inconscient et le ça*, op. cit., pp. 145–56; and 'The unconscious: A psychoanalytic study', Jean Laplanche and Serge Leclaire, trans. Patrick Coleman, *Yale French Studies*, no. 48, 1972.

— the direct transposition or translation of one discourse into another, be that second discourse Jungian, Kleinian, Lacanian or even Freudian[23] — is ruled out. Ultimately, the reciprocal implication of method and object consists in the fact that the former is not only adapted to the latter but oriented, magnetically attracted by it.

The second point, also leading to the notion of 'a realism of the unconscious' (which seems to me still as important as ever), is that the object searched for acts not only on the method but also in everyday life. This is what Freud calls the dynamic unconscious, and Leclaire and I stressed the fact that this activity implies that the unconscious cannot be a mere hermeneutic copy of the conscious.

In other words, just as due to the pathways of its discovery the unconscious is in no sense the analogue of conscious discourse, so in the formation of the symptom the latter is not a mere translation of the unconscious. Leclaire and I laid stress on the notion of compromise: it is with the same coefficient of reality that conscious tendencies, on the one hand, and those deriving from the unconscious, on the other, mingle and are mixed together in compromise-formations.

The third point at which the Freudian unconscious reveals its specificity is in its obedience to its own laws, which are named at a very early stage as the 'primary process' and the description of which dates from the Fliess correspondence, *Studies on Hysteria* (1895d) and 'A Project for a Scientific Psychology' (1950a [1895]). I will not dwell on these laws here.

Fourth: in the period before 1897 and for a long time afterwards, the unconscious will be considered as essentially the result of repression. In a text like that of 1915, there is still hardly room for a primordial unconscious which would not be generated by repression. Before 1897, one cannot even say that the repressed is the drive, for Freud practically does without the notion of drive until 1905. To state things in a lapidary formula, one could say that from a certain point in Freud's thought the unconscious will arise from the drive, then the drive from the somatic, but that before 1897 it is the drive which arises from the unconscious.[24]

23 A large part of current interpretive practice constitutes a fall back into hermeneutic illusions. See Jean Laplanche, 'Psychoanalysis as Anti-hermeneutics', *Radical Philosophy*, no. 79, Sept./Oct. 1996.

24 I am fond of quoting a passage from the Fliess correspondence (1895) (Draft N). It consists of two paragraphs whose headings are translated into French as *Pulsions* ('Drives') and 'Relation between drives and fantasies'. But in the German

The last characteristic is that this unconscious (memories, fragments of memories, fantasies – it matters little for the moment) consists of scenes or fragments of scenes, and above all that these scenes are essentially *sexual*. The significance of this is not merely contingent – why, after all, is sexuality accorded a primacy over, say, the alimentary or the need for security? Because the primacy of sexuality opens directly onto the question of the other, and in the case of the child, onto the adult other in his or her alien-ness.

But before we go on to the human other, I must stress two points concerning the other thing, the 'psychical other'[25] which is the unconscious: on the one hand, Freud's sharp vision of its alien-ness and, on the other, the fragility of that vision.

In the 'Preliminary Communication' of *Studies on Hysteria* the problem of the symptom's mode of causation is posed once it has been established that it is related to trauma. Two kinds of causality could be envisaged *a priori*: one historical, the other atemporal. From the first point of view, one could think that 'the trauma merely acts like an *agent provocateur* in releasing the symptom, which thereafter leads an independent existence' (*SE* II, pp. 6–7). Now, the experience of cathartic treatment, in that it concerns not history but actualized scenes and affects, requires an entirely different conception of causality: the cause is only effective because it is *present*; it is a foreign body[26] which is actually at work:

text one sees that Freud does not employ the term *Trieb* in this period; no doubt he is not yet sufficiently disengaged from his biological language. The word he uses is *Impulse*: 'impulsions', or if one prefers 'impulses': 'Relation between impulses and fantasies'. 'Memories appear to bi-furcate: one part of them is put aside and replaced by fantasies; another accessible part seems to lead directly to impulses. Is it possible that later on impulses can also derive from fantasies?', *The Complete Letters of Sigmund Freud to Wilhelm Fliess: 1887–1904*, trans. and ed. Jeffrey Moussaieff Masson, Cambridge, Mass.: The Belknap Press of Harvard University Press, 1985. Here the genesis is the exact opposite of what will be found, for example, in Susan Isaacs (cf. 'Nature and Function of Phantasy', in *New Definitions in Psychoanalysis*, eds M. Klein, P. Heimann and R. Money-Kyrle, London: Maresfield, 1955) where she declares that fantasies are merely the psychical expression of drives.

25 *Das andere Psychische*, *GW* XIII, p. 251. [Strachey translates this as 'the other part of the mind', *The Ego and the Id*, *SE* XIX, p. 213. Editor's note.]

26 [*corps étranger*: the adoption of Mehlman's translation, 'alien internal entity' (in *Life and Death in Psychoanalysis*) might have drawn the English reader's attention to this term's relation to *étrangèreté*, 'alien-ness' (see above, footnote 21); but the *Standard Edition* translation of Freud, in the passage quoted, has 'foreign body'. Translator's note.]

We must presume rather that the psychical trauma – or more precisely the memory of the trauma – acts like a foreign body which long after its entry must continue to be regarded as an *agens* that is still at work.[27]

Freud goes on to invite us to invert the proposition *cessante causa, cessat effectus* (thus: *permanente causa, permanet effectus*)[28] in order to

> conclude from these observations that the determining process continues to operate in some way or other for years – not indirectly, through a chain of intermediate causal links, but as a *directly* releasing cause . . . Hysterics suffer mainly from reminiscences.
>
> (*SE* II, pp. 6–7)

'Internal foreign body', 'reminiscence': the unconscious as an alien inside me, and even one put inside me by an alien. At his most prophetic, Freud does not hesitate over formulations which go back to the idea of possession, an idea which Charcot, to his credit, took seriously (even if he transposed it into scientific terms).[29] But on the other side of these Copernican advances – always hard to sustain beyond metaphor, *extravagant* in that they presuppose, as it were, the soul's *extravagation* – the dominant tendency is always to relativize the discovery and to re-assimilate and reintegrate the alien, so to speak.

At this point I will begin to comment on the particular text which is

27 '*Gegenwärtig wirkendes Agens*', *GW* I, p. 85; *SE* II, p. 6.
28 [With the cause ceasing, the effect ceases; with the cause persisting, the effect persists. Editor's note.]
I take this opportunity to re-affirm that psychoanalysis – and its object, the unconscious – is the place where a concept of causality based on the thing has taken refuge, as if to its homeland. This conception is no longer valid in the natural sciences, where the notion of law (classical or Stochastic) reigns supreme. On this *repatriation* of cause, thing and other metaphysical notions, see my 'Interpretation between Determinism and Hermeneutics' (in this volume, p. 144) and 'Psychoanalysis, Time and Translation', in eds John Fletcher and Martin Stanton, *Jean Laplanche: Seduction, Translation and the Drives*, London: Institute of Contemporary Arts, 1992.
29 'Preface and Footnotes to Charcot's *Tuesday Lectures*' (1892–4), *SE* I. It is quite remarkable that Freud, listing 'the ten most important books from a scientific point of view', limits his count to three names: Copernicus, Darwin and – between these two – 'old Doctor Johann Weier (1515–1588) on belief in witches'. Beside two authors to whom are attributed a major diminishment of human narcissism, there is a third who also deals with decentering – that witnessed by the possessed. (In 'Reply to a Questionnaire', *GW* NB, pp. 662–3.)

supposed to put the psychoanalytic discovery on the same footing as that of Copernicus, give it the same status as a blow to human egocentrism: 'A Difficulty in the Path of Psycho-Analysis' (1917a, *SE* XVII). For a careful reading of this text clearly shows, beyond an assertion on principle of the heteronomy of the human being, a continual pressure to return to self-centeredness.

'Man feels himself to be supreme within his own mind' – a first statement; but in reality psychoanalytic observation reveals that 'the ego is not master in its own house'. And here the word 'alien' or 'foreign' [Ger. *fremd*] recurs with insistence, at almost every line:

> In certain diseases . . . thoughts emerge suddenly without one knowing where they come from. . . . These alien guests even seem to be more powerful than those that are at the ego's command. . . . Or else impulses [*Impulse*] appear which seem like those of a stranger, so that the ego denies them; . . . the ego says to itself: 'This is an illness, a foreign invasion'.
>
> (*SE* XVII, pp. 141–2)

This 'alien-ness', however, falls victim to two attempts at reduction. The first comes from psychiatry, but is based on weak arguments, being content to 'shrug its shoulders and say: degeneracy, hereditary disposition, constitutional inferiority!' By contrast, the second plan for the re-assimilation of the alien – that of psychoanalysis – is a good deal more radical: 'Psychoanalysis sets out to explain these uncanny [*unheimlich*] disorders . . . until at length it can speak thus to the ego: "Nothing has entered into you from without; a part of the activity of your own mind has been withdrawn from your knowledge and from the command of your will"' (p. 142).

Thus the very movement of psychoanalysis would be to deny the alien-ness of the unconscious by offering to reduce it, both in theory and in the practice of treatment. This is the conclusion of the long *prosopopoeia* psychoanalysis addresses to the ego: 'Turn your eyes inward, look into your own depths, learn first to know yourself' (p. 143). In other words: you do not recognize that which in reality is clearly yourself. It is your own inner core that you fail to recognize; and the unconscious will reveal itself finally as 'something in the depths of man'.[30] The result is that the text even ends with a reference to

30 According to Groddeck's description of the id, a description I contest. Cf. *New Foundations for Psychoanalysis*, op. cit., p. 28.

Schopenhauer, which goes completely against what I have often stressed – namely, that to search for forerunners of the Freudian unconscious in the unconscious of the nineteenth century is to take a wrong path; but this assertion of dubious paternity takes place only to the extent that Freud himself denies the originality of his own discovery:

> It was not psycho-analysis, however, let us hasten to add, which first took this step. There are famous philosophers who may be cited as forerunners – above all the great thinker Schopenhauer, whose unconscious 'Will' is equivalent to the mental instincts [Triebe] of psycho-analysis.
>
> (pp. 143–4)

So that Freud reaches the point of conceding that 'the sole privilege' of psychoanalysis is to have given a clinical demonstration of Schopenhauer's theses and that the resistance to those theses is nothing but a by-product of the aversion produced by 'the great name of the philosopher'! Which goes to show that from the moment that the unconscious is reduced from its alien-ness to what one could call, along with theologians and those of a certain faith, an *intimior intimo meo* ['something more inward than my inwardness'] – we can only observe a return to centering: there is something in me which I've split off from, denied, but which I must re-assimilate. Certainly, the ego is not master of its own house, but it is, after all, at home there nonetheless.

One could endlessly demonstrate how the domestication of the unconscious never ceases to operate in Freudian thought, and this with regard to each of the foremost aspects of its alien-ness. So it is in the case of the primary process and in that of memory.

With the so-called 'primary' process Freud discovers a sort of lawfulness which escapes the rationality of our preconscious-conscious thinking. But to 'escape' could mean one of two things here: either that it has been withdrawn from that rationality, or that the primary process was never subjected to it in the first place, being more originary than it.

The very term 'primary' brings an entire theory with it. We unfailingly think of the primary as being there before the secondary, both in time – the secondary comes to exist after the primary – and also in priority, the structure of the secondary presupposing the primary as its foundation. Conversely, the idea of regression encompasses not only 'temporal'

67

regression, in other words a return to a time before the subject's existence – but 'topographical'[31] regression (regression to the system from which the excitation derives, the unconscious) as well as so-called 'formal' regression, the return to that lower level of organization which is the primary process, less structured than the 'secondary' process. But the notion of the 'primary', like that of 'regression', implies that these three aspects merge into one: that which is least organized and from which excitation arises is also the most archaic.

Freud sometimes paid homage to Hughlings Jackson, 'the great Jackson', who put forward the idea of a hierarchy of forms, and reciprocally, of a regression, a coming-apart or dissolution of the highest forms into the lower forms which preceded them. Freud takes up this conception of Jackson's not only, of course, in respect of aphasia, but also in the theory of dreams. What comes undone is what has been most recently acquired; what is uppermost dissolves, allowing what was there before it to appear; what is uncovered is therefore the most primitive. The Jacksonian notion of an organizational progression or regression thus forms part of that line of Freudian thought in which may be situated, along with chapter 7 of *The Interpretation of Dreams* (1900a) and the first part of 'A Project for a Scientific Psychology' (1895), a text exemplary in its going-astray: the 'Formulations on the Two Principles of Mental Functioning' of 1911.

The essential architectonics of the last two texts can be stated relatively simply. There is 'in the beginning' a purely associative mode of functioning in the organism, characterized by the fact that energy circulates in the system unhindered, and equally that it must be evacuated without hindrance, reaching the exit from the system as rapidly as possible – thus, a purely 'primary' mode of functioning dominated, Freud tells us, by the 'pleasure principle'. Then a secondary, regulated mode of functioning would appear, in which the energy is finally stabilized along certain pathways, allowing accumulation, reserve, inhibition and adaptive behaviour subject to the 'reality principle'. This reality principle, under the name *Not des Lebens* ('the needs of life'), far from being present at the beginning of the *Project*, is introduced at a certain point – so that it must be admitted that at the beginning we are given a description of an organism which would be as yet . . . *non-living*. It is only secondarily that the

---

31 [*régression topique*. This is translated, in accordance with Strachey's rendition of Freud's *Topik*, as 'topographical'. Translator's note.]

need for a reserve of energy (which would deal with excitations in accordance with the reality principle) is introduced. Constancy of level and homeostasis, although they characterize the vital function itself, would thus be introduced only *secondarily* into what should have been, supposedly from the beginning, an *organism*.

The term 'primary' is thus responsible for much of the damage, such as the genetic, hierarchical or constructivist model, wrought by the founder of psychoanalysis. The attempt to account, with so-called psychoanalytic concepts, for the whole of vital functioning – or even, simply the whole of psychical functioning – continually risks capsizing our boat. What must be affirmed is the following: if the primary is the unconscious, and the unconscious is the repressed, then this 'primary' has '*become* primary', so to speak. It is neither prior nor primitive, but a sort of 'reduced state'[32] caused by something else – so that the Jacksonian model of a construction through increasing complexity is misleading if applied to psychoanalysis.[33]

But even more pernicious than the notion of the primary – because it makes a greater appeal to personal experience – would be the apparently indisputable idea of repressed memory; would be, that is, if it were not brought into connection with that of 'reminiscence'. If the unconscious consists of memories which have been unable to lodge in the ego because they are irreconcilable with it, the fact remains that a memory, even if repressed, is historically *my* memory. If it is to become mine again, as it is nothing but a part of me from which, at some moment, I have been forced to separate, what could be more natural? Moreover, if the repressed is never

---

32 Cf. Jean Laplanche and Serge Leclaire, 'The unconscious: A psychoanalytic study', *Yale French Studies*, no. 48, 1972, pp. 152–5.

33 This model, which I call constructivist – from the simpler to the more complex, from the primary to the secondary – is fortunately opposed by the following fact (and this is where the situation turns around): the 'primary' level can in no sense be taken as a biological stage, describing something true in respect of a living organism. It is biologically unthinkable that the living being could pass through a first stage in which it was a mechanical system open to all the winds, seeking nothing but to empty itself completely of its enegy. On the contrary, the living being immediately 'defines' itself (delimits itself conceptually and in reality) by the existence of a specific level. Luckily, this first section of 'A Project for a Scientific Psychology' is fictional, so that it can be saved, if some of its hints are put to a different use. It is rightly interpreted as a model not of the living being but of the process occurring in a preliminary living being *from the moment when an unconscious comes to exist.*

anything but part of my stock of memories, the task of psychoanalysis, which is to do away with repression and suppress the unconscious, has rightly no limit: since it was already myself, there is no reason why it should not become, one day or another, me again!

Another way of putting the same thing would be to say: 'the unconscious is pathological'. In so far as what is at issue is a part of my ego from which I have separated through my own fault – through feeble-mindedness, weakness or defence – the pathological should properly give way to the normal, and the memory be fully re-assimilated. The only unconscious is a pathological one, or rather, the process which creates the unconscious is pathological. Hence, as reciprocal corollary, the delusion or mad hope of once more rendering all of the unconscious conscious. All will finally be revealed: once the memory because of which you fell ill has been re-assimilated, you will be ill no longer . . . and you will have an unconscious no more.

It is in 'the letter of the equinox' that one sees this very clearly emerging (a posteriori since Freud renounces it): an unbounded ambition to suppress or totally master the unconscious. Thus the disillusion, which is nothing but the reverse side of an illusion: 'If one thus sees that the unconscious never overcomes the resistance of the conscious, the expectation that in the treatment the opposite is bound to happen, to the point where the unconscious is completely tamed by the conscious, also diminishes'.[34]

In sum, the central question can be put as follows: how is it that the unconscious can consist of that which is repressed, and yet despite this be inexhaustible – be capable, that is, of endlessly slipping away from our grasp? Thus the about-turn of this letter (of 21/9/1897). First of all, in the negative: if the unconscious cannot be completely re-assimilated, this is because it is not made up of memories; unconscious fantasy is not simply the memory of lived scenes. To which I say, 'bravo!' We are not dealing with memory, so let us look elsewhere. From this point onwards, however, Freud finds himself compelled to put forth a positive double hypothesis on the nature of unconscious fantasy, to which all his work will never cease being indebted: under the banner of

34 *The Complete Letters of Sigmund Freud to Wilhelm Fliess: 1887–1904*, ed. Jeffrey Moussaieff Masson, op. cit., p. 265.

posteriority, the notion of retroactive fantasy;[35] and under that of anteriority, the idea of hereditary transmission.[36]

Would it not be possible, then, to maintain that the unconscious has a close link with the past, the past of the individual, *while at the same time abandoning the psychological problematic of memory* with its intentionality aimed at *my* past, but also its retrospective illusions and its ultimately undecidable nature? For Freud neglects here the innovative core of his own initial formulation: hysterics suffer, not from memories, forgotten or not, but from 'reminiscences'. The term could, of course, be reduced to memory – a memory cut off from its context – but it could equally be allowed to bear the value of *extravagance* which is not lacking in Platonic doctrine: something which returns as if from elsewhere, a pseudo-memory perhaps, coming from . . . the other.

The External Other: Cause and Guarantee of the Internal Other

We have reached the point which I consider is the essence of the Copernican revolution begun by Freud; the decentering, in reality, is double: the other thing (*das Andere*) that is the unconscious is only maintained in its radical alterity by the other person (*der Andere*): in brief, by seduction.[37] When the alterity of the other person is blurred, when it is reintegrated in the form of *my* fantasy of the other, of *my* 'fantasy of seduction', then the alterity of the unconscious is put at risk. Whence the question, formulated on another level: what is it that

35 'It seems once again arguable that only later experiences give the impetus to fantasies, which [then] hark back to childhood . . .'; ibid., p. 265.
36 '. . . and with this the factor of a hereditary disposition regains a sphere of influence from which I had made it my task to dislodge it – in the interests of illuminating neurosis', ibid., p. 265. This separation of *afterwardsness* [*l'après-coup*] into simple retrospective illusion, on the one hand, and an effect of hereditary disposition on the other is a constant of psychoanalytic thinking. Alongside Jung and Freud himself, an author such as Viderman does not escape it: having given the greatest possible space to invention relating to the past, he finally declares that this creation of the past is not so free as all that, oriented as it is by 'primal fantasies'.
37 At the same time, this does not mean that the unconscious is simply the other implanted in me. For in between the primary intervention of the other and the creation of the other thing in me, there occurs a process called repression – an extremely complex process comprising at least two stages in mutual interaction, and leading to a veritable dislocation/reconfiguration of (explicit and implicit-enigmatic) experiential elements. Metabolization and the 'translation' point of view are the essence of the theory of repression. Cf. *New Foundations for Psychoanalysis*, op. cit., pp. 130–3.

prevents the theory of seduction from 'maintaining' its affirmation of the primacy of external alien-ness? What, if not an imprecise grasp of this discovery's dimensions, and, let us not hesitate to add, of its philosophical dimension. How can the problem of 'the existence of the other person' not be completely overturned as soon as that other person is considered as primary in my own constitution – a primacy not only postulated by theory but implicated and experienced in the transference?[38]

The other person is the other of seduction, the adult who seduces the child. Now, from the moment when he formulates the seduction hypothesis and for a

---

38 Cf. 'Transference: its Provocation by the Analyst' in this volume, pp. 214–33. We hold back from exploring this question of the other from a philosophical point of view. Let us simply note that:

1) in philosophical thinking, the problem of the other person has on the whole been related to that of the existence of the external world; that is, ultimately, to the theory of knowledge. The various categories – solipsism, idealism, realism – include the existence of the human other within that of the objective world, as simply one of its specific cases. It is not until Husserl and Merleau-Ponty that the existence of others is made the object of an independent reflection. Here again, it must be said that this problematic remains derivative in relation to analyses deemed to be indispensable preliminaries: the constitution of a common objective and cultural world, the description of the irreducible experience of the body and the 'flesh' (Merleau-Ponty, the later Husserl). The existence of the other thus remains subordinate, in the history of reason, to that of 'the world' (the *Fifth Meditation* comes . . . fifth; 'The other and the human world' is a fairly short sub-chapter of the second part of the *Phenomenology of Perception* entitled 'The Perceived World').

2) In his explicitly philosophical statements, Freud does not depart from this, the inclusion of the problem of the human other within that of the external world. Concerning the latter he takes up alternate positions that are ultimately without contradiction: a naive empirical realism (Letter to Favez-Boutonier [11/4/30], *Bulletin Société Française de Philosophie*, janvier–mai, 1955 [Freud, 1930]; *GW Nachtragsband*, p. 671), and a more or less simplified Kantianism – 'do not neglect the subjective conditioning of our perception and do not take our perception to be identical with the unknowable percept' ('The Unconscious', 1915e, *SE* XIV, p. 161ff).

3) In the practice of his theory, Freud gives in more than once to the temptation to reconstruct from an endogenous source the relation of the living being to reality, out of the play of innate drives: something we describe as both a monadological project and an instance of biological idealism. In this sense his position could be called pre-phenomenological, not only in relation to Husserl but to what ethology and the notion of *Umwelt* owe to phenomenology.

4) Freud never develops the possibilities implicit in the seduction theory, such as we note them in the following pages: *the reversal of the problem of access to the other into that of the priority of the other.*

long time afterwards, Freud vacillates between two equally inadequate positions. On one side, what could be termed a subjectivist, 'internal' conception –
reducing the other to the subject's perception of the other (possibly to the trace
of that perception, or, when the notion of memory has been criticized, to the
imagination of this perception of the other). Nothing in this approach allows
the other any place other than in the depths of my subjectivity. And then
alongside this, from time to time, a philosophically more naive gesture,
consisting in . . . going to look for the other in the neighbouring room. Since
the other is always speaking to me from the neighbouring room, at a given
moment I go and see if he is really there. In the concrete situation of the
treatment, Freud allows himself to make suggestions, as if to locate the other
behind the patient's words: go and ask your servant or your mother; look in the
family archives to see whether such-and-such a person was alive when you were
a child, whether it is possible you could remember so-and-so.[39] Or even – and
again this persists until very late – Freud actually goes himself to look directly
in the neighbouring room for some real trace of the other; for after all, one can
never rely on investigations undertaken by the patient.[40]

Both of these positions – that of pure and simple subjectivism as well as the
'go and look over there' attitude – share the same presupposition: that the
other never manifests himself except in the subjective representation of brute
reality. Can one reproach Freud, though, for lacking something which would
have prevented the reduction of the other to the subjectivity of its recipient,
something which would have guaranteed its alien-ness?

What maintains the alien-ness of the other? Can one affirm here, with Lacan,
the priority of language? If, for my part, I speak rather of a 'message', this is for
at least two well-defined reasons: *first*, the message can just as easily be non-
verbal as verbal; for the baby it is principally non-verbal. *Second*, emphasizing
'language' effaces the alterity of the other in favour of trans-individual structures. To explain this *category of the message* I have often stressed the expression
Freud uses to describe the primal data offered to the infant: i.e. that part of its
experience which it has to master straight away, to order, to 'translate', so as to
assimilate it to its own system. The term used in a letter to Fliess (6 December

39 Cf., on this subject, the reconstruction of a memory in the 'Wolf Man' case-history
(1918b, *SE* XVII).
40 In a letter to Fliess (6/12/1896, Masson (ed.), op. cit., pp. 207–17), Freud confirms
the seduction of a young woman by her father thanks to an interview with the patient's
brother and to cross-referencing of memories and symptoms between brother and sister.

1896) is *Wahrnehmungszeichen*,[41] one which clearly indicates that these first elements to be translated are given to *perception*, but which leaves us with an ambiguity as to the meaning – and the translation – of these *Zeichen*: 'perceptual indices' or 'perceptual signs'? If one chooses the idea of 'indices', one is led to see them as purely objective elements of the situation, particularized for the infant to the extent that they allow it to discern something extra, to get a more complete view of the phenomenon.[42] One might say that Freud does not go beyond the relation we here denote with the term 'index' – something in a purely extrinsic relation to its signified, and which possibly is isolated from the perceptual whole by the perceiving subject. However, on the other hand, we could choose the translation 'perceptual signs', conferring on it a far more productive meaning: these elements are not mere side-effects of the situation or its concomitant details; rather, originating in the sender of the message, they *make a sign* in a double, linked sense – they acquire the force of signs and this is because, isolated by the sender, they are addressed to the subject.[43]

The absence of any notion of the message can be felt cruelly at numerous points in Freud;[44] for a moment I will dwell on one of these – what he calls 'the experience of satisfaction' (*Befriedigungserlebnis*). This is first described in Part One of 'A Project for a Scientific Psychology' – whose 'Ptolemaic' dimension will be confirmed by what I am about to say – and then in *The Interpretation of Dreams*.[45] Elsewhere, *The Language of Psychoanalysis* gives a clear outline of

41 Letter to Fliess (6/12/1896, ibid.). [Masson translates this as 'indications of perception'. Translator's note.]
42 Here I use the term index in Pierce's sense, to designate a relation of contiguity, possibly of mechanical causality, or even of a part to the whole, between the representation and the object. Smoke is an index of fire in the above three senses. Similarly one can use the term 'icon' to designate representation by analogy. As for the terms 'symbol' or 'sign', Pierce's definition is but one among hundreds.
43 Certainly an index can 'signal'; but there is all the difference between the smoke of a forest-fire kindled by lightning and that of a fire intended by Robinson Crusoe to signal his presence.
44 It is the absence of 'message' which splits the notion of afterwardsness into the inadequate and contradictory categories of deferred action and retroactive interpretation. I have discussed this in my seminar course of 1989–90, under the title '*La Nachträglichkeit dans l'après-coup*' (forthcoming). See 'Notes on Afterwardsness' in this volume, pp. 260–5.
45 'A Project for a Scientific Psychology', *GW Nachtragsband*, pp. 410–12, *SE* I; *The Interpretation of Dreams*, *GW* III, pp. 570–1, *SE* IV–V, pp. 565–6.

what is at stake here: the birth of the *Wunsch*, let's say the birth of the wish,[46] which is of the human order, out of need and its satisfaction, which are of the vital order. For need aims, precisely, at its own appeasement (*befriedigen* = to appease, to pacify); it is a question of a tension defined as such by an energetic system tending towards stability. This model of need, which is not necessarily obsolete in physiology, provides the concrete biological base on which sexual desire is constituted.

The first moment is indicated as the infant's *Hilflosigkeit*, in other words its incapacity to help itself, its 'helplessness'. Unable to provide on its own for its needs, the nursling organism is faced with an unbearable build-up of tension, comparable to the rising level of a reservoir,[47] to which it can respond in only two ways: either by letting the reservoir overflow (an action Freud considers 'non-specific', inadequate because it does not prevent the reservoir from remaining full); or, alternatively, in a 'specific' way, in a series of actions which allow the tension to be discharged for a certain period.

What characterizes helplessness is precisely the infant's inability to undertake for itself the action which could empty the reservoir in a lasting way. All it can do is cry, and its cries are themselves, moreover, nothing but the purely mechanical expression of a non-specific overflowing.[48] It is the cries which arouse 'foreign aid', the mother's activity, which first of all consists of the offering of nourishment.[49]

---

46 Or of desire. I will not explore this problem of translation here. Cf. entries on *souhait*, *désir*, *désirance*, *plaisir* in *Terminologie raisonnée* in André Bourguignon, Pierre Cotet, Jean Laplanche and François Robert, *Traduire Freud*, Paris: Presses Universitaires de France, 1989; translated in *Translating Freud*, New Haven: Yale University Press, 1992.

47 The model of excretion right up to the example of the 'lavatory flush' – the accumulation of anal or urinary products, sudden discharge leaving the system in peace for a time – is perceptible here.

48 The child's cries, according to Freud, are not a call for help. They are simple indices, in Pierce's sense. They only become messages, calls for help, through the subjective interpretation of the mother.

49 *Nahrungszufuhr* is transcribed by the editors, who nonetheless take the trouble to alert us that they have here corrected what must have been a slip of Freud's, who wrote *Nahrungseinfuhr*, meaning the 'insertion' or even the 'stuffing in' of food. The alien one, the mother, stuffs the breast into the child, or at least inserts it. If it is a question of a slip here, it directly follows the profound sense I give to the seduction theory: the intromission of something into the child.

What then follows is a specific sequence of satisfaction: a series of acts of feeding[50] leading to a prolonged relaxation. But just as important as this, according to Freud, are the mnemic traces, the inscribed images, of which there are three kinds: the memory of satisfaction and two sorts of sign — signs linked to the object (an image of the food) and internal images which correspond to a memory of the feeding sequence.[51]

At this point it is worth pausing over the description in *The Interpretation of Dreams*:

A hungry baby screams or kicks helplessly. But the situation remains unaltered, for the excitation arising from an internal source is not due to a force producing a *momentary* impact but to one which is in continuous operation. A change can only come about if . . . (through outside help) an *experience of satisfaction* can be achieved which puts an end to the internal stimulus [here is the turning-point: we move to the level of representation]. An essential component of this experience of satisfaction is a particular perception (that of nourishment, in our example) the mnemic trace of which remains associated thenceforward with the memory-trace of the excitation produced by the need. As a result of the link that has thus been established, next time the need arises a psychical impulse will at once emerge which will seek to re-cathect the mnemic image of the perception and to re-evoke the perception itself, that is to say, to re-establish the situation of the original satisfaction. An impulse of this kind is what we call a wish; the re-appearance of the perception is the fulfilment of the wish; and the shortest path to the fulfilment of the wish is a path leading directly from the excitation produced by the need to a complete cathexis of the perception. Nothing prevents us from assuming that there was a primitive state of the psychical apparatus in which this path was actually traversed, that is, in which wishing ended in hallucinating.[52]

---

50 These are not Freud's terms, but those of animal psychology and of psychophysiology.
51 What Freud calls *Bewegungsbild*, the kinaesthetic image of muscular movements involved in feeding. This aspect is neglected in *The Interpretation of Dreams*.
52 *GW* III, p. 571, *SE* V, pp. 565–6 [Laplanche's comments in square brackets]. One sees the point at which the *Wunsch* is linked to presentation: the wish is the reinvestment ['re-cathexis' in Strachey's English] of the presentation, to the extent that it could be said that in a certain way the satisfaction of the wish and the wish are one and the same thing: the wish, situated in fantasy, is already the (so-called 'hallucinatory') satisfaction of the wish. The 'wishing', the 'accomplishment' of the wish and the

I have quoted at length from this passage because the description it gives is both extraordinary and abortive. Extraordinary because it tries to bring about the birth of one thing (the wish) from another (need). Abortive because, of course, nothing can be born from the satisfaction of need but an hallucinatory reproduction of the satisfaction of need. The wish, whose 'genesis' we are given in this description, is the wish for food, nothing more. If we allow that the sexual is more than a simple transposition of the alimentary into representation or hallucination, it is clear that this Freudian alchemy, this attempt to make the base metal of the alimentary give birth to the gold of sexuality, has failed. Likewise, if Freud had described here a physiological experience of a sexual nature, it would in turn have been reproduced as a sexual wish.[53]

It is important to take account of what is missing in the 'experience of satisfaction', for this is a model unceasingly invoked by psychoanalysts who pay no heed to its inability to produce anything at all.

First, concerning 'foreign aid',[54] let us stress that it is found only at the initial stage of the process. The introduction of food simply triggers off the whole activity. Thereafter, the entire mode of functioning is solipsistic. There is no longer any trace of the alien in what is to take place, either in the object or in the aim of the drive. The object whose perception is reproduced is food; likewise, it is the sequence of alimentary consumption – ingestion, digestion – which recurs in the remembered scenario of the wish.[55]

'hallucinating' are conceived as simply different degrees of investment; something which moreover runs into the gravest objections, raised but not resolved in 1915 in 'A Metapsychological Supplement to the Theory of Dreams' (1917d [1915], SE XIV).

53 As if he sensed his failure to make the sexual rabbit emerge from the alimentary hat, Freud seems to suggest, in the *Project* (op. cit., note 45), a sort of relation between the two, no longer of emergence but of analogy: from alimentary satisfaction, the genesis of a wish for food, from sexual satisfaction, a sexual wish. This is the sense of several passages where he attempts to place feeding and sexuality *in parallel* (cf. 'the great needs': hunger, respiration, sexuality). In the context of the experience of satisfaction, he offers as two possible situations: 'the offer (*Zufuhr*) of food, the proximity of the sexual object'. A pity – or luckily – that Freud's 'slip' here effaces the parallelism: the 'insertion (*Einfuhr*) of food' replaces feeding itself in a sexual context, that of the adult who 'stuffs' something in. Cf. above, note 49.

54 [Strachey's equivalent is 'outside help'. Translator's note.]

55 For more detail, see my critique of leaning-on [*étayage*] in *Problématiques III: La sublimation*, Paris: Presses Universitaires de France, 1980, pp. 56–69; and in *Le fourvoiement biologisant de la sexualité chez Freud*, Paris: Synthélabo, 1993.

There are two aspects here, which are in the end identical. On the one hand, the exclusion of the adult from the sequence which follows; and on the other, the sampling by the nursling of purely objective perceptual indices, which are simply the representation without discrepancy of certain elements of the situation. So that, in the end, what is missing from all this is a sign, something that 'signals'. A sign offered to the infant by the adult, delimited by the adult in the situation before the infant itself finishes the process of sampling. It is thus, and only thus, that one can conceive the intervention of sexuality in the experience of satisfaction. Here, obviously, I am going well beyond Freud. It is the adult who brings the breast, and not the milk, into the foreground – and does so due to her own desire, conscious and above all unconscious. For the breast is not only an organ for feeding children but a sexual organ, something which is *utterly overlooked by Freud and has been since Freud*. Not a single text, not even a single remark of Freud's takes account of the fact that the female breast is excitable, not only in feeding, but simply in the woman's sexual life.

I have once again been discussing the archaic experience of breast-feeding; but what is called the 'primal scene' lends itself to analogous criticism. Whenever primal scenes are observed or discussed, two worlds without communication divide, so to speak: on one side, parental *behaviour*, the experience and content of which are by definition beyond the subject's grasp; and on the other, the side of the child, a traumatic *spectacle*, more often glimpsed or guessed than seen, suggested by a mere allusion (animal coitus) which the child must then fill out, interpret, symbolize. My point is that between these two worlds something is missing: the supposition (which should have occurred to a psychoanalyst!) that showing sexual intercourse is never simply an objective fact, and that even the letting-see on the part of the parents is always in a sense a making-see, an exhibition. But Freud is never to suspect this idea – that the primal scene only has its impact because it bears a message, a giving-to-see or a giving-to-hear on the part of the parents. There is not only the reality of the other 'in itself', forever unattainable (the parents and their enjoyment) together with the other 'for me', existing only in my imagination; there is also – primordially – the other who addresses me, the other who 'wants' something of me, if only by not concealing intercourse. What is it this father wants of me in showing me, letting me see this primal scene, even if only by taking me to a field to witness animal coitus?

What is missing in Freud – preventing him from maintaining the alterity of the other person (the seducer) which in turn requires the alterity of the other thing (the unconscious) – could be given different names, but in the end they are not greatly distinct: address, message, sign, something which signals, even signifier – a category which it has been the great merit of Lacan to have brought to the fore, even if he was to give it a very different value from that which it bears in the 'Saussurian algorithm'.[56]

We have felt that it was permissible to mock slightly the late Husserl, who puts the transcendental and constitutive subject in astronautical danger, as it were, by wondering how in its spaceship (its 'flying-arches') the subject could carry the 'Earth-ground', its 'arche-dwelling', stuck to the soles of its shoes (Husserl, op. cit., *passim*). The same interstellar journeys – well on the way to being made a reality from the time of this text, 1934 – raised a different, more exciting amd more genuinely philosophical problem: how to send across interstellar space a message which would signify my intention to communicate – and this beyond any sharing of codes with the possible recipient. Thus, on 3 March 1972, the rocket Pioneer 10 carried with it a 'message in a bottle', a message which 'aimed to communicate certain data on the spatio-temporal origins of the builders of the spaceship, and their nature'. Yet whatever the fabric of this message and the inventiveness shown by its authors,[57] all the difference resides – if we place ourselves on the side of the receiver – between, on the one hand, finding a rocket and detecting in its construction the *indices* of the presence of intelligent beings and, on the other, receiving *signifiers*[58] which, without presupposing any shared code or interpretive rule, testify to the intention to communicate and, perhaps, to conscious and even unconscious reasons for such an intention.

To address someone with no shared interpretive system, in a mainly extra-verbal manner:[59] such is the function of adult messages, of those signifiers which I claim are simultaneously and indissociably enigmatic and sexual, in so

---

56 Since linguists are most often in open civil war as to the meaning of their own technical terms, it ill befits them to reproach a lay thinker – who happens to be an analyst – with a deviant but rational use of one of their terms.

While the sign 'represents something for someone', and thus has a purely denotative function, 'the signifier represents the subject for another signifier' (*Écrits: A Selection*, trans. Alan Sheridan, London: Tavistock, 1977, p. 316). I do not wholly take on board this definition. However, that the signifier represents the other and that it 'makes a sign', that it 'signifies to' the subject – this is my understanding of a 'message'.

57 Cf. Carl Sagan, *Cosmic Connexion*, Paris: Seuil, 1975.

58 Whether indexical or iconic, it matters little.

59 Or, which amounts to the same thing, with verbal signifiers outside of their linguistic 'usage'.

far as they are not transparent to themselves, but compromised by the adult's relation to their own unconscious, by unconscious sexual fantasies set in motion by his relation to the child.[60]

Internal alien-ness maintained, held in place by external alien-ness; external alien-ness, in turn, held in place by the enigmatic relation of the other to his own internal alien – such would be my conclusion concerning the decentering revolution I have proposed here in continuation of the Freudian discovery. It remains for us to show in what respect it is *unfinished* and what is the nature – contingent or ineluctable – of that unfinishedness.

How can we doubt that Freud was capable of going – and could have gone – further than he did, in so far as that is precisely the ambition of our undertaking? With regard to the reasons for his blockage and then his going-astray, I have put forward on several occasions partial explanations – explanations which, moreover, are correlated: the centering on pathology, whence the rejection of a normal unconscious; the inadequate elaboration of the translation theory; and, above all, the absence of the category of the message as a third reality ranking alongside material and psychological reality. Here, I shall lay stress on another factor, which directly concerns the opposition between centering and decentering, by going back to Freud's assumptions regarding the three 'humiliating blows' inflicted on man by science.

I have, indeed, provisionally neglected to mention that Freud places between the Copernican and the psychoanalytic humiliations the wound inflicted on our pride by the evolutionary discoveries ascribed to Charles Darwin, his collaborators and precursors.[61] Man, believing himself to be of divine origin, an alien in the animal kingdom, learns from science that 'he himself is of animal descent'. Now, this place accorded to evolutionism and a so-called biological humiliation, alongside the decenterings introduced by Copernicus and Freud, seems to me both ambiguous and dangerous. Ambiguous – for is to reconnect man to his biological, animal lineage truly to decenter and humiliate him? Once the first few cries of outrage provoked by the notion that man 'descends from the ape' have died down, are we not thereby assured a much firmer basis? The family tree, which more than one has striven in vain to reconstruct, now goes

---

60 I am convinced that there is a kind of perception specific to the category of the message, and to that of the enigmatic message, so that a phenomenological 'eidetics' – à la Merleau-Ponty – of both would be possible.

61 'A Difficulty in the Path of Psycho-Analysis' (1917a), *SE* XVII. The opposition between Lamarck and Darwin is not relevant to the 'humiliation' in question.

back beyond Abraham, Isaac and Jacob, beyond Adam, to take in the history of all life to the point where the term 'phylogenesis', once restricted to the origin of a single species, ends up encompassing the entire evolution of life, of which the human species is the last link in the chain. Solidly in place, firmly centered on the animal pyramid, man does not fail to consider himself its culmination, the blossom of the family tree: a doctrine like Teilhard de Chardin's has clearly wiped away the so-called humiliation of evolutionism.

Wrongly placed by Freud alongside the revolutions of decentering, the doctrine of evolution in fact recenters man among living things; what is more, it is drawn on dangerously by Freud to jeopardize the essence of the psychoanalytic discovery. The invocation of phylogenesis, of the hereditary nature of drives and even of scenarios and fantasies, comes to the fore every time psychoanalytic decentering recedes from view. This is clearly what under-lies the very text which Freud believes to affirm the 'psychological humiliation' of man. 'Enter into yourself' and you will see that 'nothing alien has entered you': these repressed, alien sexual drives are ultimately nothing but the expression of somatic forces, on which the evolution of the species – and beyond that, of life itself – has left its indelible imprint.

The Constant Threat of Narcissistic Closure

To show that one can go further than Freud, that one can sustain more effectively than him the 'Copernican' aspect of his discovery, is the most important dimension of what we have named the 'new foundations' for psychoanalysis. This would be an inadequate claim if it simply referred Freud back to his mistakes, his blindness or even the inadequacy of the conceptual tools at his disposal. The correction of a going-astray, as I understand it, goes beyond a mere refutation of error, or even the explication of its contingent causes. A more radical view of causality must be ventured to reveal how, in Freud the theoretician, the going-astray is accompanied by a sort of connivance with the object; in other words, a covering-up of truth inherent in the very object to which thought conforms. The closing-in-on-itself of the Freudian psychical system, its *monadological* character, which results in the idea of an 'apparatus of the soul', would be radically linked to the closing-in-on-itself of the human being in the very process of its constitution. I have put forward – in a formulation which jokingly echoes Haeckel's law, according to which ontogenesis reproduces phylogenesis – a sort of 'Laplanche's law' which would claim: 'theoretico-genesis' reproduces ontogenesis. Without wishing thus to propose a universal law, subject to a

81

falsificaton test of a Popperian variety, I can only note that in the evolution of Freudian theory one finds more than once a parallel with the development of the human individual. I have previously been able to show this concerning the successive theories of the drive, or, again, that of pansexualism.

Keeping in mind this parallel between individual ontogenesis and the theory which accounts for it, one must ask the question: can the psychoanalytic Copernican revolution be finished? The Copernican revolution of Copernicus in astronomy miscarried, as we have glimpsed, in what Marr attempted: we cannot reform our language, and with it our perception and our inner sense, to the extent of giving everyday expression in a 'Copernican' language to the movement of the sun, moon and stars. The narcissistic wound inflicted by science is defeated by our narcissistic centeredness as living bodies. For the human psyche, things are a little different. Narcissism remains the key to the problem,[62] but it is caught up in the very evolution of the object of knowledge: one cannot say that the object of astronomy, the universe, *is* either Copernican or Ptolemaic – or again, first Ptolemaic and *then* Copernican. On the other hand, one is entitled to claim that the Ptolemaism of the human psyche, its narcissistic recentering, follows upon a 'Copernican' stage as its presupposition, in which the nursling child is caught up in the orbit of the other and has a passive relation to its messages. Furthermore, the moment of narcissistic closure – the constitution of the ego as an agency – corresponds in the sequence of primary repression to the constitution of the internal other, the unconscious. On the side of theory, Freud's endless Ptolemaic relapses – his way of continually taking the point of view of the subject in interpersonal matters and of the ego in intrapersonal ones – is nothing but a parallel to the ineluctable narcissistic closure of the apparatus of the soul.

If the human being closes in on itself at a very early stage, and if theory too is ceaselessly impelled, as if by some internal force of attraction, to close in on itself – what is the point in maintaining the opening which is introduced by the general theory of seduction? Is it meaningless to envisage 'seduction theory-speak', just as it was with Marr, in the case of 'Copernican-speak'?

Such an admission of defeat, of the inevitable closure of theory onto the

---

62 This was clearly seen by Freud, who prefaced his discussion of the three humiliations with a long exploration of narcissism. However, the conception of narcissism as a state *acquired* in development, which appeared in 'On Narcissism: an Introduction' (1914c), has definitively disappeared in this text, giving way to narcissism as a primal biological state.

subject, would only be definitive if psychoanalysis were nothing but a theory confronted with an object. But, as Freud always maintained, psychoanalysis is first of all a method, one from which the psychoanalytic situation is of course inseparable. To which we add that this situation *repeats* the originary situation of the human being; as such it is at once both Ptolemaic and Copernican. Copernican, in that it finds its immediate centre of gravity in the other: both in the observation of the fundamental rule, which aims to make visible the gravitational pull exerted by the sun and stars of the unconscious, the obscure way it drags the apparent coherence of our discourse into its orbit, as well as in the transference.

Psychoanalytic treatment itself, however, does not escape an endless recentering: the ego is tirelessly at work in it, striving to re-order the 'recuperated' elements of the unconscious.

Wo Es war, soll Ich werden.

The maxim is at root Ptolemaic, even if one allows that the *Ich* in question is not simply the narcissistic ego, in the narrow sense given it in the second topography. But the theory of seduction imposes the reverse or complementary maxim: *Wo Es war, wird (soll? muss?) immer noch Anderes sein*. There where there was id, there will be always and already the other. The permanence of the unconscious, the primacy of the address of the other − one of the functions of analysis is to uphold these truths, and it is the duty of the analyst to guarantee them the respect which is their due.

Translated by Luke Thurston

2

A Short Treatise on the Unconscious

Preamble

1. The unconscious in question here is the one Freud discovered, in analytic treatment and outside it, the one which is still – so we postulate, at least – the object of the psychoanalytic experience.

What I attempted to contribute in 1959,[1] and to elaborate in what came after, is a quite specific conception of the unconscious, with regard to its *mode of existence* and its *genesis*. Like every theory, this one is at a distance from the facts but aims to account for their interconnections: primarily for what we call the clinical in psychoanalysis, meaning by that what is revealed and unfolds in the psychoanalytic situation. To put things differently: my project consists in bringing that which is foundational in the *practice* of psychoanalysis into relation with the foundational process of the human being, in so far as this is characterised by the creation of an unconscious.

2. Historians can have endless debates as to the originality of the Freudian discovery and as to the novelty of the psychoanalytic unconscious. Freud himself oscillated between the idea that he had discovered a *terra incognita* and his occasional acceptance of links with an older tradition of thought: as

1 See in particular *Problématiques IV: L'inconscient et le ça*, Paris: Presses Universitaires de France, 1981, in which the report of Laplanche and Leclaire to the Bonneval conference (1959), 'The Unconscious: a psychoanalytic study', is also reproduced (translated into English by Patrick Coleman in *Yale French Studies*, no. 48, 1972). See also, *New Foundations for Psychoanalysis*, trans. David Macey, Oxford: Basil Blackwell, 1989.

when he makes the surprising declaration of allegiance to the 'unconscious will' of Schopenhauer.[2]

It is not my intention to enter into a discussion of the history of ideas, where others are much more competent than me. I simply wish to stress that it is overwhelmingly in relation to psychoanalytic *method* – namely, the perfectly original and meticulous description of the paths providing access to the unconscious – that the originality of this new domain is ceaselessly affirmed.[3] On the other hand, it is in the way the unconscious is conceived – how it is situated *topographically* and *genetically* – that the ambiguity emerges in Freud. Alongside texts (such as those of 1915) which give priority to the process of repression, and thus to the creation of the unconscious in the course of each individual existence, there is a constant temptation to situate the unconscious in some genetic lineage, in which it occupies the first, primordial position. Thus, the psychological lineage: 'Everything which is conscious was first unconscious'; the lineage of individual biology: the id is 'the great reservoir of the instincts' and constitutes the non-repressed part of the unconscious, which would open directly onto the body; and finally, the lineage of the species and of phylogenesis: whether by way of the so-called primal fantasies, which are supposed to constitute the kernel of the unconscious, or under the heading of metabiological and metacosmological speculation, which takes the unconscious drives back to an immemorial atavism.[4]

In Freudian thought, then, the concept of a mechanism of repression stands in opposition to a dynamic of emergence from a 'primal' moment, quite 'naturally' assimilated to the unconscious and lending itself to all sorts of romantic reminiscences (romantic in the widest sense of the term). But there is worse: the point of view of repression tends more and more to be subordinated to that of emergence: thus, the notion of *primal repression*, creator of the

2 I have discussed this sort of 'Canossa' in 'The Unfinished Copernican Revolution' in this volume, p. 67. ['Canossa': a moment of submission to a rival authority; from the name of an Italian town where the German Emperor Henry IV did public penance before Pope Gregory VII in 1077. Editor's note.]
3 Let us recall once again that the first point in the definition of psychoanalysis, to which *both* the clinical *and* the theoretical are subordinate, is that it is 'a procedure for the investigation of mental processes which are almost inaccessible in any other way' (*SE* XVIII, p. 235).
4 Cf. on this theme, *Le fourvoiement biologisant de la sexualité chez Freud*, Paris: Synthélabo, 1993.

unconscious as a place, only appears sporadically after 1915; from then on, repression will be essentially secondary, that is, bearing on drives-impulses already present and welling up from the primordial, non-repressed unconscious.

3. The postulating of such an 'id' – biological, primal, necessarily pre-formed – ran directly counter to the originality implied in the notion of the drive, as a sexual process not adapted, in human beings, to a pre-determined goal. It flew in the face of Freud's more complex elaboration of the mechanism of repression and its successive stages, notably in the Schreber case (1911c), and in 'The Unconscious' (1915e).

4. Last but not least, relegating the repressed unconscious to a secondary status compromised the specificity of the psychoanalytic field as a field of sexuality. From the moment when the unconscious is assimilated to a primordial id,[5] itself connected not only to the body but to a biologism, even a vitalism, the forces at work there become vital forces, independent, at their origin, of both sexuality and the fantasy inseparable from it. The terms 'life instinct'/'death instinct' designate perfectly these forces, predetermined in their finality, which can be defined in terms which claim to be independent of both orgasm and the fantasmatic: on the one hand, the constitution of increasingly all-inclusive totalities; on the other, the return to the inorganic.[6]

To sum up, what is at stake in the correct conception of the unconscious extends far beyond the purely theoretical sphere. It concerns in particular: 1) the foundation and the understanding of analytic practice; 2) the originality of the Freudian discovery and the break it introduces in the history of ideas and even that of mankind; 3) the notion of the drive; 4) the specificity of the sexual-fantasmatic field, which has to be re-affirmed as much in practice as in theory.

With these stakes in mind, I will limit myself here to five essential points,

5 I have shown, in *L'inconscient et le ça* (op. cit.), certain positive aspects of the notion and still more of the term 'id', if it is properly separated from its Groddeckian origin, which lingers on in Freud himself. I oppose to the idea that there is from the beginning, 'in the depths of man: it', the idea of the process of repression creating in me a genuine id, *more 'it' than nature [plus ça que nature]*, as it were. See *New Foundations*, op. cit., p. 28.
6 I would stress that they only *aim* to be independent, for there are evident fantasies linked to the notions of life and death instincts, from the myth of Aristophanes to images of Nirvana or of a cosmic mineral state, frozen and with energy levels near zero.

some of which are new emphases on ideas already presented, while others (III and V) comprise newer developments:

I   A realism of the unconscious
II The process of repression
III The consequences of repression for the (well-known) characteristics of the unconscious
IV The unconscious in life and in analytic treatment
V   The unconscious and metaphysics.

I A Realism of the Unconscious

It was under the rather provocative banner of 'a realism of the unconscious' that Laplanche and Leclaire put forward their report to the Bonneval conference in 1959. I see no need for any fundamental changes on this point,[7] and will simply retrace rapidly the most salient elements.

1. The reduction of the unconscious to a hidden *meaning* strikes me as being a constant temptation, dragging Freud's discovery backwards towards a centuries-old hermeneutics. Now, it is simultaneously in both the elucidation of symptoms (in the broad sense, taking in also slips, parapraxes, dreams, etc.) and in the method which arrives at this, that the *originality* of the 'formations of the unconscious' is attested, by comparison with the polysemy inherent in all systems of communication. The Freudian notion of compromise-formation implies a sort of mixed production deriving from (at least two) causal series, one of which, the unconscious chain, acts by way of the operations of displacement and condensation. A bungled action, to take that handy example, is not a simple everyday act, beneath which interpretation might discover hidden meanings; doubtless, the simple act of 'putting on the soup' could be, more or less legitimately, placed in different contexts which would relate it to a biological meaning (self-preservation), a sexual meaning (preparation of the totemic meal), a sociological one (rich classes and urban populations no longer

---

7 In 1977–8 (*Problématiques IV: L'inconscient et le ça*, op. cit.), I elaborated a long reflection, retrospectively, on that text, which still seems today, largely usable; with the one exception of the pointless discussion around 'the unconscious is the condition of language' / 'language is the condition of the unconscious', which, even with the best intentions, remained prisoner to a certain Lacanian problematic.

eat soup), etc. But the symptom, the irruption of the unconscious, only appears if I knock over the pot, or if I overdo the salt when one of my guests suffers from hypertension.

What is called, in terms allegedly derived from psychoanalysis and consecrated by habitual use, the analysis of content can be brought to bear equally on any text, with the aim of giving one or more 'readings': the unconscious of a text is by definition limitless; all discourse is, in Umberto Eco's phrase, an 'open work'. Freud's approach is quite different, however, when it comes, for instance, to 'the subtleties of a faulty action':[8] on a birthday card, a word 'totally foreign to the context' appears and is then scratched out: testimony to the irruption of an *other* causal chain.[9] That which comes from the unconscious intervenes as a reality (itself conflictual) in the midst of the conscious 'text', which therefore appears much less coherent: sometimes lacunary; sometimes, on the contrary, with moments of unjustifiable intensity and insistence. In a word, the notions of defence, conflict, compromise, condensation, etc. lose all their impact when psychoanalysis is reduced to a new version of hermeneutics: a hermeneutics in which the 'sexual meaning' is superimposed on the infinity of other possible meanings.

2. A realism of the unconscious seeks to solve certain impasses in Freudian theory. I will recall two of these.

First of all is the unresolved opposition between the functional hypothesis (the *same* representational content, a memory, belongs, according to the way it is invested, either to the unconscious system or to that of the preconscious/ conscious) and the topographical hypothesis (unconscious and conscious inscriptions are *distinct* and can co-exist; one does not abolish the other).[10] I discussed this point, which is far from academic, at length in 1959,[11] and above all in 1977.[12] What is clear, first of all, is that the 'reification' hypothesis – of two

8 1935b, *SE* XXII, pp. 233–8. [Laplanche quotes the title of Freud's essay 'The Subtleties of a Faulty Action'. Translator's note.]
9 But equally not a chain of *meaning*, or 'signifying chain'. See 'Psychoanalysis as an Anti-hermeneutics', *Radical Philosophy*, no. 79, Sept.–Oct. 1996.
10 [Laplanche is referring here to Freud's metapsychological paper 'The Unconscious' (1915e, *SE* XIV) where these proposed hypotheses are elaborated. Editor's note.]
11 In *Problématiques IV: L'inconscient et le ça*, op. cit., pp. 276–81. [For the 1959 discussion, see 'The unconscious: A psychoanalytic study', op. cit., note 1 above.]
12 Ibid., pp. 73–104.

separate and independent traces of the same event – for all its strangeness, is what is entailed by 'impressions given by analytic work', specifically the fact that making something conscious, however far it is pursued, does not do away with the unconscious inscription. The functional hypothesis, on the other hand, seems the most convenient when it comes to accounting not for the return of the repressed but for the opposite path, that is, repression. If it is the mnemic trace, the *representation of an event,* which is repressed, in other words which passes from the conscious to the unconscious state, there is no need to suppose that it has a double inscription.

Not without daring, Freud therefore lets two hypotheses, which are hard to reconcile, co-exist: repression is conceived on the model of the laying-down of a memory; by contrast, once repression has occurred, this very peculiar unconscious inscription shows itself to be very different in kind from a simple memory. But such a contradiction could also lead to the questioning of the claim – very broadly accepted – that repression is merely a particular case of committing to memory, the unconscious memory simply being more profound, more deeply buried, than ordinary, preconscious memories. What is the relation of repression to memory such as it is generally studied in psychology? The path I deliberately took consists in considering the unconscious element or trace *not as a stored memory or representation, but as a sort of waste-product of certain processes of memorisation.*

A second impasse in Freudian theory, also inherent in the attempt to include repression within a theory of memory and of making-conscious, is linked to the notorious opposition of terms *Wortvorstellung/Sachvorstellung,* translated by Strachey as 'word-presentation'/'thing-presentation'. These two compound terms clearly indicate that the content of the 'presentation' is, in the one case, the word, in the other, the more or less direct 'mnemic image' of the thing. Moreover – and despite all the nuances it would be appropriate to introduce here – the thing-presentation, characteristic of the unconscious, is for Freud essentially constituted of *visual* elements, while the word-presentation is of an acoustic nature made of words able to be *uttered.*[13]

Now, it is here that the theory of the unconscious – *wrongly to my mind* – lines up with a psychological theory which makes the possibility of a train of thought becoming conscious dependent upon whether or not it is possible to

13 This goes on up to *The Ego and the Id*: the 'mnemic residues of things' are assimilated to 'optical mnemic residues', while the 'verbal residues are essentially derived from acoustic perceptions' (1923b, *SE* XIX, pp. 20–1).

associate with it, here and there, acoustic verbal traces, able to be brought back to life, pronounced again at least in outline, and thus inwardly perceived. This theory, present from 'A Project for a Scientific Psychology' (1950a [1895]) onwards, deserves the greatest interest in the context of an account of normal processes; it is certainly what is taken up in the celebrated formula: 'The conscious presentation comprises the presentation of the thing plus the pre-sentation of the word belonging to it, while the unconscious presentation is the presentation of the thing alone' ('The Unconscious', op. cit., p. 201). But it is precisely this link – this 'plus' which ought to join up word-presentation and thing-presentation – which is problematic in analytic work.

There is no choice, then, but to raise the question of the type of reality which should be attributed to unconscious elements, and to refuse to see in them simple 'mnemic images of things', the more or less distorted copies of events or things. It was to make this understood that I put forward, for the Freudian *Sachvorstellung*, the term 'thing-like presentation' [Fr. *représentation-chose*], not as a more correct translation, but as a provocative mistranslation.[14] What I wish to make understood by this is that the unconscious element is not a representation to be *referred* to an external thing whose trace it would be, but that the passage to the unconscious is correlative with a loss of referentiality. The thing- or word-presentation (or, in more modern and more accurate language: the signifier), in becoming unconscious, loses its status as presentation (as signifier) in order to become a thing which no longer presents (signifies) anything other than itself.

3. A realism of the unconscious would set itself the objective of giving a precise meaning to the notion of psychical reality, which is constantly put

14 Cf. for instance *Problématiques IV*, op. cit., p. 96ff. *Problématiques V: Le baquet – Transcendance du transfert*, Paris: Presses Universitaires de France, 1987, pp. 112–13.

My friend Daniel Widlöcher will forgive my amusement at seeing him attribute to Freud the notion of 'thing-like presentation', which, properly speaking, is foreign to him. (Cf. 'Temps pour entendre, temps pour interpréter, temps pour comprendre', in *Bulletin de la Fédération Européenne de Psychanalyse*, 1993, n. 40, pp. 24–5). And, when he states that these unconscious representations 'do not relate to anything but them-selves', without realising it, he is following Laplanche (1959) and not Freud.

As for the suggestion that these thing-like presentations should be called 'action-like presentations' (*représentations-actions*), it corresponds to the idea that internal foreign bodies remain constantly active, that they are 'causes' in the 'metaphysical' sense of the term (see below, part V; also 'Interpretation between Determinism and Hermeneutics' in this volume, p. 144).

forward by Freud but of which he never truly gave an autonomous definition, or only on rare occasions, while most of the time he reduces it to psychological reality, that is to say in the last analysis to our subjective lived experience.[15]

In distinguishing not two orders of reality, as Freud most often did (external, material reality and internal, psychological reality), but three – that is, by adding the reality of the message or the signifier – I am thus adopting a position not unrelated to the outlines of a triple division in Freud, nor, of course, to the Lacanian tri-partition of Real, Imaginary and Symbolic.[16]

To make this clarification more brief, I will say that I in no way adhere to the first two categories in the sense in which Lacan defined them, contenting myself with the solid Freudian opposition:

> Freud: external reality – psychological reality
> and not Lacan: Real – Imaginary

As for the third category, I consider that the Freudian term 'psychical reality' is the index of a reality hitherto neglected, but which cannot in any way be assimilated to the Lacanian Symbolic, whose narrowly linguistic, supra-individual, structural (in a word *metaphysical* character, see section V below), I entirely reject.[17]

The category of the message, or of the signifier in so far as it 'signifies to',[18] is

15 On all this, cf. especially *Problématiques V*, op. cit., pp. 89–101. See also 'Seduction, Persecution, Revelation' in this volume, p. 169.

16 Cf., for example, *Problématiques V*, op. cit., pp. 89–91.

17 As a tribute to Lacan, and even having registered all my disagreements with 'Lacanianism', at least two aspects must be emphatically noted:
– the *man*, the *master*, was an extraordinary stimulator of thinking and research, in the midst of a post-Freudian world which was droning on and on;
– the *thinker* won acceptance for this certainty, which was unheard of in Freudianism: that the unconscious and the drive do not well up from the obscure depths of 'life', but their genesis and their nature are indissociable from the human world and interhuman communication.
Reread, from these two perspectives, the dazzling 'The Function and Field of Speech and Language in Psychoanalysis', in *Écrits: A Selection*, trans. Alan Sheridan, London: Tavistock, 1977.

18 Cf., for example, *New Foundations for Psychoanalysis*, op. cit., pp. 44–5. [Here Laplanche alludes to Lacan's distinction between a *signifier of* something, a meaning or signified, and a *signifier to* someone, an addressee. Laplanche's 'message' or 'enigmatic signifier' may have lost its signified and no longer function in the first sense, but it continues to interpellate an adressee. Editor's note.]

'addressed to', is absolutely different from that of the Symbolic: the message can be verbal or non-verbal, more or less structured, even have a minimal reference to a structure. The Lacanian model of language, directly adopted from Saussure and the structuralist school, is only, in the end, applicable to a perfect, well-made, univocal language, where the fixed differences between signifiers ('values') determine, or even render superfluous, the relation of a signifier to a determinate signified.[19] I therefore understand the category of the message or the 'signifier to' with the full extension Freud gives to language, comprising the language of gestures and all other kinds of expression of psychical activity.

However, this category is insufficient to account for what we call 'unconscious psychical reality': one must add to it the strange transformation, operated by repression, and leading to the formation of a thing-like presentation, or, to put it differently, a designified-signifier.[20]

4. Lastly, a realism of the unconscious is closely tied to what I have called its 'clinical-theoretical deduction',[21] a way of showing its necessity, starting from the primal, asymmetrical adult-child situation. I will return to this further on, but what I wish to underline from the outset is that this model of repression aims to account not only for the genesis of the repressed (the existence of the repressed), but for the production of a certain type of reality, called unconscious (the nature of the repressed).

19 This applies in mathematics. Cf., for example, *Problématiques IV*, op. cit., pp. 129–34.
20 To the extent that one introduces the notion of thing-like presentation, the opposition presentation *of* the thing/presentation *of* the word loses its pertinence for the psychoanalytic unconscious:

1) The presentation of the word (verbal representation) becomes in the unconscious, like the (visual) representation of the thing, a thing-like presentation.

2) The presentation *of* the thing is of no interest in psychoanalysis, it is 'treated' by repression only to the extent that it transmits a message, or 'signifies to'.

However, this opposition is still valuable for a psychology of memory, where it is a question of the remembering of a preconscious memory.
21 *New Foundations for Psychoanalysis*, op. cit., p. 151.

II Repression: The 'Translation' Model

Having repeatedly elaborated and sought to perfect[22] this model,[23] I will indicate only a few essential points, insisting on some new emphases.

1. The translation model of repression can be conceived only within the framework of the seduction theory. The thing-like presentations which form the kernel of the unconscious are to be conceived as that which eludes the child's first attempts to construct for itself an interhuman world, and so translate into a more or less coherent view the messages coming from adults. The partial but necessary failure of these attempts derives from the fact that these messages are enigmatic for the one who sends them, in other words they are *compromised* by the sender's unconscious. The only emphasis I would add here is to recall that the adult-child relation is eminently suited to re-awaken the conflicts and desires coming from the unconscious:[24] not all messages are equally enigmatic, but those sent out under certain conditions of re-activation are especially apt to be so.

2. The model of signifying substitutions or *metabola*, as it was advanced at Bonneval and after, seems to me still valid. Derived from one of Lacan's schemas, it was fiercely criticised, no doubt because it was at once too Lacanian and not Lacanian enough. It has the interest, certainly limited but a real one, of providing a suggestive model for thought. I have returned to it many times, in *Problématiques IV* just as much as in my *New Foundations* (pp. 130–3).

The process at issue here, it may be remembered, was, in the presence of the message (a signifier S_1) offered to the subject, one of trying to translate

---

22 The most recent references: *New Foundations*, op. cit., chapter 3. And 'Interpretation between Determinism and Hermeneutics' in this volume, pp. 138–65.

23 Which is known to be first put forward in the letter from Freud to Fliess, 6 December 1896. See *The Complete Letters of Sigmund Freud to Wilhelm Fliess: 1887–1904*, trans. and ed. Jeffrey Moussaieff Masson, Cambridge, Mass.: The Belknap Press of Harvard University Press, 1985, p. 207.

24 Cf. among others, my allusion to the article by M. Malev ('The Jewish orthodox circumcision ceremony'), in *Problématiques II: Castration-symbolisations*, Paris: Presses Universitaires de France, 1980, p. 239ff. Circumcision itself could be considered a symptomatic act, a 'compromised message' from the unconscious of adults. Cf. also, in relation to the 'threat posed by castration' and its seductive force: 'Seduction, Persecution, Revelation' in this volume, pp. 172–3.

it, by substituting a new signifier (S_2) for the initial signifier S_1. The relation of S_2 to S_1 is usually complex, made up of resemblances, contiguities, even oppositions.

The initial formula was written thus:

$$\underline{S_1} \quad X \quad \underline{S_2} \;=\; \frac{\dfrac{S_2}{s}}{\dfrac{S_1}{S_1}}$$
$$\;s\qquad\quad S_1$$

The process of translation being compared to the action of a multiplier S_2/S_1 upon a multiplicand S_1/s.

The formula, as it is reproduced here, would apply to the first translations of adult messages that the infant gives itself. These translations are (according to the formula of Freud himself) accompanied by failures of translation, which are precisely the first repressions or primal repressions.

The principal virtue of this schema is to offer for thought the paradox of a residue of translation which no longer signifies anything other than itself: S_1/S_1.

But, in simple equations such as this, mathematics insists on the conservation of quantity and is unable to account for the disruptive effect of a psychical *metabolism*. It must therefore be accepted that the two halves of the schema do not correspond to an equation (=) but to a transformation (→). On the left-hand side, there is the message to be translated (M_1), not a signifier (one never translates a single signifier). On the right-hand side is found, on the one hand the partial translation of the message (M_2), on the other the repressed signifier (or signifiers) S_1/S_1.

A formulation which gets closer to primal repression would thus be something like:

$$\underline{M_1} \quad X \quad \underline{M_2} \;\rightarrow\; \frac{\dfrac{M_2}{s}}{\dfrac{S_1}{S_1}}$$
$$\;s\qquad\quad M_1$$

This shows that the repressed signifier(s) S_1 is a remnant of the message M_1 and not the whole of it. The message is partly translated and partly repressed.

3. The crucial point for an understanding of the translation schema is to grasp

the idea that repression cannot be considered a particular case of committing something to memory.

Among the countless texts Freud devoted to memory, to the mnemic trace, to remembering, there are few devoted to the problem of memorial fixation. The most remarkable of these is a passage in the Leonardo study, clearly in response to the problem of the childhood 'vulture' memory.[25] So as to make himself clear, Freud compares the way that the human individual stores up his memories to the way in which, at the collective level, history is written. There are, he says, two quite distinct ways of writing history (or historiography, Geschichtsschreibung): one, in the fashion of the chroniclers, consisting of 'a continuous, day to day record of present experience'; while the other, casting 'a glance back to the past, gathered traditions and legends, interpreted the traces of antiquity that survived in customs and usages, and in this way created a history of the past'. This second type of historiography evidently distorts things, due to the interests of the present time and the aversion provoked by many an event from past times. We should note that in this second case, two moments of inscription are explicitly called for, as the reconstruction a posteriori is not based on nothing: there must have been a first inscription of the traces of the past, but this is independent of the historian. Conversely, I would add, the historian-chronicler is not a simple recorder of facts: in an era when audio-visual recording had not yet supplanted the chronicle, he had at least to transcribe the facts of experience, but in the most exact and neutral style possible: the passage from experience to writing is certainly not innocent, but the difference from history 'rewritten' much later is immense. Freud's favourite example concerning such a rewriting, is that of Livy refashioning, at the dawn of our era, the history of the origins of Rome: the huts of the founders of Rome were transformed into sumptuous palaces, chieftains into kings of illustrious heritage, etc.

According to Freud, in a way parallel to the two historiographies, there would be two types of memorisation in the individual. The first, 'in every way comparable' to the history of the chronicler, is '[a] man's conscious memory of the events of his maturity'. The second is that of the memories of childhood, which 'correspond, as far as their origin and reliability are concerned, to the history of a nation's earliest days, which was compiled later and for tendentious reasons' (pp. 83–4).

25 *Leonardo Da Vinci and a Memory of his Childhood* (1910c), *SE* XI, p. 82.

I note the following points:

The memory of the (normal) adult is supposed not to comprise any essential distortion. What this is, of course, is an ideal model which the psychology of everyday life would correct.

The memory of childhood experience is supposed to take place *a posteriori*, but, very obviously, it posits an initial moment in childhood, the leaving of traces. We therefore have a very exact resurfacing of the model of after-wardsness or the two-phase trauma.[26] What is subject to the work of distortion and rearrangement in memory are not the childhood events (intrinsically inaccessible), but the first traces of them.

Lastly, let us stress that this is a model of *conscious memory*. The result of the secondary elaboration which is Freud's interest here is the conscious memory: very precisely, the 'screen memory'. But to evoke this term (*Deckerinnerung*) is to indicate that it both covers over and prevents the resurgence of something: precisely, the repressed.

There has been so much interest in Leonardo da Vinci's childhood memory, about which real event it corresponded to, that it has quite simply not been seen for what it is: not a repressed unconscious element, but a screen memory, to which the model of memorisation as distorting and repressing applies fairly exactly. As the Leonardo text (especially pp. 120–3) is one of the foremost moments where the effects of seduction reappear in Freud, I think it is in no way arbitrary to apply to it the model of the repressive metabola, while of course simplifying its elements.

M_1 – the element inscribed at the first moment – let us designate it, with considerable simplification, as 'vehement caresses' (of the mother) (pp. 115–16).

M_2 – screen memory – let us call it the 'fable of the bird', thus avoiding the subsidiary argument about the kite/vulture.[27]

---

26 Laplanche's suggested translation for the French *l'après-coup*, Freud's *Nachträglich-keit* which Strachey translates as 'deferred action'. See 'Notes on Afterwardsness' in this volume, pp. 260–5.

27 Cf. Maïdani-Gérard, J.-P.: *Léonard da Vinci: mythologie ou théologie?*, Paris: Presses Universitaires de France, 1993. What Freud discussed, with his 'Egyptian' hypothesis about the goddess Mout, and what J.-P. Maïdani-Gérard discusses again with the Christian hypothesis and the theme of the Immaculate Conception, is the ideological context, the 'translation language' in which the substitutive message M_2 appears.

The repressive metabola, characteristic of the time of afterwardsness, would appear in a schema thus:

$$\frac{\text{vehement caresses}}{s} \quad X \quad \frac{\text{fable of the bird}}{\text{vehement caresses}} \quad \rightarrow \quad \frac{\dfrac{\text{fable of the bird}}{s}}{\dfrac{\underline{S_1}}{S_1}}$$

A long commentary would be required:

1. The mother's vehement caresses (cf. pp. 115–16) are messages addressed to the subject, to Leonardo. Their first inscription does *not* necessitate a translation, it is a pure and simple implantation. Again, in other words, these are elements of perception, but which 'make a sign';[28] they do not need to be transcribed as signifiers, as they are already 'signifiers to'.

2. These vehement caresses are *enigmatic* messages. Their signified is partly sexual, perverse, unknown to the mother herself.[29]

3. My schema would be erroneous if it gave the impression that what is located at the unconscious level is nothing but the initial enigmatic signifier. In reality, it must again be stressed that the enigmatic messages of adults undergo a reorganisation, a dislocation. Some aspects of them are translated, while some anamorphotic elements are excluded from the translation and become unconscious. This is why, moreover – despite the success it has enjoyed – the term 'enigmatic signifier' is unsuited to designate the complex and compromised message of the adult. On the other hand, at the unconscious level, the formulation 'designified signifier' seems to me more correct. In my schema I

---

28 These are *Wahrnehmungszeichen* ['Perceptual indices/signs']. See, for example, *New Foundations for Psychoanalysis*, op. cit., p. 130ff., and 'The Unfinished Copernican Revolution' in this volume, p. 74.

29 'A mother's love for the infant she suckles and cares for is something much more profound than her later affection for the growing child. It is in the nature of a completely satisfying love-relation, which not only fulfils every mental wish but also every physical need; and if it represents one of the forms of attainable human happiness, that is in no little measure due to the possibility it offers of satisfying, without reproach, wishful impulses which have long been repressed and which must be called perverse', ibid., p. 117.

leave its algebraic formulation as S_1/S_1, being no more able than Freud to pursue the 'analysis' of Leonardo any further.

Far be it from us to assimilate the analysis of Leonardo to an analytic treatment: it lacks the essential elements – transference and working-through under the power of the originary enigmatic situation – which cannot be supplied *in absentia*. However, the paths explored by Freud in his research are not without interest: first of all, he uses a method close to that of free association, by using the freely juxtaposed material of Leonardo's notebooks. Moreover, despite appearances, he does not seek to discover the meaning(s) of the fable of the bird. On the contrary, he dismantles the fable by relating it to the ideological, cultural and linguistic elements which intersect there, and give it the appearance of consistency. Eventually, he discovers correlations, associative connections, between the elements of the fable and those of the originary situation (itself partly conjectured on the basis of certain historical facts about Leonardo's family); this allows him to draw close to a designified-signifier, something that turns around the smile, the penetrative kiss . . . a veritable source-object of the drive and of a part of Leonardo's artistic creativity.

III The Characteristics of the Unconscious and their Explanation on the Basis of Repression

In more than one place, Freud listed the characteristics of the (systematic) unconscious or those of the id, which he rightly considers to be identical. By what means does he arrive at this conclusion?

The idea, that, inside the psychical apparatus or outside it, only something directly accessible to consciousness is knowable, is one of the most dubious. Out of simple reverence for the term 'un-conscious', and because of the essential closure which corresponds to it in the person in question, we have lost the kind of audacity shown by Freud when, in 'A Child is being Beaten', he claims to know, to articulate, a fantasy which in the majority of cases is absolutely incapable of becoming conscious ('I am being beaten by my father'). Even were it to turn out that Freud was wrong as regards the object of his inference, at the very least he fully assumes the implications of his move: it is possible to speak of the unconscious, some of its contents can be outlined, even reconstructed (Freud, 1919e, *SE* XVII; see also 'Interpretation' in this volume, pp. 154–9).

Beyond what can be directly observed (which of course in no way implies that such knowledge is correct!), certain facts and entities can be inferred on the basis of other phenomena that are more directly observable than they. This is the case for many physical entities. Thus, before it was observed, the atom was for a long time deduced.[30] Likewise, astrophysics has 'black holes', which *by definition* are not visible (since they absorb all light-rays) and can only be established indirectly from their gravitational effects. It is to such an *indirect* method that Freud resorts when the id is in question: '[W]hat little we know of it we have learnt from our study of the dream-work and of the construction of neurotic symptoms'.[31] Finally, properties and even entities can be deduced from a model, itself produced in contact with observed facts. We recall from Popper that a contradiction between one of the consequences deduced from the model and a fact of experience will result in the falsification[32] of the model, entailing either its abandonment, its profound modification or its integration, as a particular case, into a more general model.[33] This model may itself be of different sorts: static – that is, describing a relatively motionless state;[34] or genetic – that is, predicting the properties of an object from its genesis. In this sense, the translation model of repression is of a genetic nature, as it describes how the unconscious comes into being: it should therefore be possible to deduce from it not only the existence[35] of the unconscious, but also certain of its properties – its consistency, so to speak.[36]

30 The fact that the atom was not observed but deduced allowed, for a very long time, a certain idealism of the 'constructed' scientific object to be given free rein. The atom, it was said, is nothing but a bundle of equations.

31 *New Introductory Lectures* (1933a), *SE* XXII, p. 73.

32 I retain the word 'falsification', which does not include the whole of refutation. Falsification is the breakdown of a theory in relation to one of its major *consequences*.

33 The famous example is Einstein and Newtonian physics. Another example of falsification is the abandonment of the theory of seduction by Freud, because certain of its consequences contradict experience.

34 Thus Einsteinian physics described the gravitational bending of light rays before it was observed.

35 Cf. 'The wall and the arcade', in *Jean Laplanche: Seduction, Translation and the Drives*, eds John Fletcher and Martin Stanton, London: Institute of Contemporary Arts, 1992, pp. 197–216.

36 A few more remarks on the fact that the characteristics of the id are above all negative. Freud links this to the fact that the id 'can only be described in opposition to the ego' (*New Introductory Lectures*, 1933a, *SE* XXII, p. 73). But such a 'negative' characterisation is equally relevant to its genesis, to the extent that this suppresses certain aspects of the 'conscious' psychical network (this was indicated in the Bonneval Report, in the section entitled 'The Fiction of Language in a Reduced State', *Yale French Studies*, op. cit., p. 152). Let us further note that for one of these major characteristics, a sort of negation of a negation is at work: 'the absence of negation in the unconscious'.

1. Unconsciousness and Timelessness

For various reasons I link these two problems, which for me illuminate each other. In separating them, Freud inevitably gave priority to the problem of the emergence into consciousness [Bewusstwerden],[37] and mortgaged himself to a consciousness-centred theory, whereas in my view his conception of the 'systematic' unconscious locates it in a different realm from that of the conscious illumination we may bring – or not, as the case may be – to particular preconscious memories or affects. In this sense, I have hardly anything to retract from – only something to add to – my brief elaboration in 1959 of 'The unconscious and the problem of consciousness'.[38]

In two recent articles on time,[39] I have proposed the distinction between four levels of time, two of which correspond to our object: the psyche of the human being.

Level II is perceptual time, that of immediate consciousness; it is also . . . the time of the living being. Level III is the time of memory and the project, the temporalisation of the human being. I situated Freud's contributions at these two levels, unfortunately badly distinguished by him. Level II, that of immediate temporality, is described by him in elaborations which appear to be psycho-physiological, where 'time' is related to perception and its rhythmic quality. As for level III, Freud – without having truly thematised it – brought in a decisive advance: that of afterwardsness. I also showed that the confusion between these two levels, and above all the inclusion of the (extra-psychoanalytic) problematic II in problematic III, was one of the forms taken by the forced reintegration of psychoanalysis into a general psychology. However, it can be seen that the distinction is sometimes clearly present in Freud: in the passage from the Leonardo study discussed earlier, memory of the 'chronicler' type corresponds to level II temporality, and memory of the 're-writing and distorting' type corresponds to level III.

Lastly, from the point of view of proof, negative characteristics (no man is a quadruped) can lend themselves to falsification just as much as positive ones (all men have a thumb opposable to the other fingers).

37 Bewusstwerden or 'devenir-conscient' [becoming-conscious].
38 In Yale French Studies, op. cit., p. 126.
39 'Psychoanalysis, Time and Translation', in Fletcher and Stanton (eds), op. cit., pp. 161–77; and 'Time and the Other' in this volume, esp. pp. 237–41.

To deal with things from the point of view of the unconscious, the level of perceptual temporality and of immediate consciousness primarily involves the preconscious-conscious relation – that is, access to my personal archives. By contrast, it is at the level of *temporalisation*, conceived as narrativisation, as the translation of enigmas coming from the other, as continual 'self-theorisation', that repression is located: in as much as it involves precisely the failure of temporalisation and the deposit of untranslated residues.

It follows that the word 'conscious', which can be heard in our psychoanalytic term 'un-conscious', is not the immediate, vital consciousness [*consciencialité*], connected to perception. The use of the word 'consciousness' by Hegel, in expressions such as 'unhappy consciousness', 'pious consciousness' or even that of Freud himself in 'consciousness of guilt' (*Schuldbewusstsein*), brings us closer to what is in question. With the word 'con-sciousness', one should let etymology play its part (*cum-scire*) – it is a 'knowledge'[40] of oneself in every human being, of one's surroundings and one's fate which is relatively organised, coherent (*co-haerens*). This 'knowledge of self', constituted in afterwardsness, thus returning to the past from the present in order to aim towards a future, this movement of translation has as its origin the 'fixed mover' of the enigmatic address of the (external) other. It necessarily leaves something of that address outside itself, something untranslatable which becomes the unconscious, the internal other. This internal other, in turn, functions as an agent, a source-object, which constantly seeks to penetrate con-scious existence (which is *entirely different* from coming into the light of consciousness-perception).

According to this perspective, the adjective 'atemporal' (*zeitlos*) does not refer to an accidental quality of the 'other thing' in us, but to its very being, determined by its genesis: the exclusion of the work of temporalisation, proper to the preconscious-consciousness system.[41]

---

40 Not, of course, scientific knowledge; it is mostly fantasmatic, ideological: see the 'sexual theories of children'.

41 'The processes of the system *Ucs.* are *timeless*; i.e. they are not ordered temporally, are not altered by the passage of time; they have no reference to time at all. Reference to time is bound up, once again, with the work of the system *Cs*' (in the 1915 edition, 'the system *Pcs*'. ['The Unconscious', 1915e, *SE* XIV, p. 187]).

It could not be better put. However, Freud's hesitation between the 'Consciousness system' and the 'Preconsciousness system' shows his uncertainty about the distinction between what I call 'consciousness II' (immediate consciousness) and 'temporalising con-sciousness III', which corresponds in Freud to the system *Pcs*.

If the term 'atemporal' can thus be considered as more pertinent than that of 'unconscious', the exclusion of this atemporal with regard to consciousness [*la consciencialité*][42] is much less direct and essential than one might have thought. There is no *a priori* reason why the contents of the atemporal, the thing-like presentations, should not reach consciousness without passing through temporalisation (the system Pcs) and without ceasing to belong fully to their system: ecmnesic resurgences with or without hypnosis, hallucinations. . . .[43] Conversely, the simple addition of a word-presentation to a thing-presentation – which Freud ultimately makes the essence of access to consciousness – is quite inadequate when it comes to reintegrating the thing-like presentation into the space of temporalisation.[44] That requires, at the very least, the work of analytic treatment.

2. The Absence of Coordination and Negation

I see nothing to add on this point to the fundamental description of the systematic Ucs. or the id, which Freud repeats several times; for instance in the *New Introductory Lectures*:

> It is filled with energy reaching it from the instincts, but it has no organization, produces no collective will, but only a striving to bring about the satisfaction of the instinctual needs subject to the observance of the pleasure principle. The logical laws of thought do not apply in the id, and this is true above all of the law of contradiction. Contrary impulses exist side by side, without cancelling each other out or diminishing each other: at the most they may converge to form compromises under the dominating

---

42 To make things easier, I use this term [*la conscientialité*], *Bewusstheit* in German, to refer to consciousness II, linked to immediate temporality. This is the perception-consciousness system in Freud.

43 Cf. *Problématiques IV*, op. cit., pp. 53–5 and 98–101. The most striking text of Freud's is the end of 'Constructions in Analysis' (1937d), *SE* XXIII.

44 Let us recall again that the nature of the thing-like presentation depends neither on the (visual/auditory . . .) sensorium, nor on the (verbal/non-verbal) content of the representation from which it emerges. A word-presentation, in being repressed, becomes equally a thing-like presentation. Nothing prevents such a thing-like presentation made of verbal material from directly reaching consciousness by being respoken 'in outline': phrases in dreams, verbal hallucinations.

economic pressure towards the discharge of energy. There is nothing in the id that could be compared with negation. . . . [45]

Lack of coordination and the absence of contradiction[46] clearly go together, the principle of the excluded third being essential to the coordination of thoughts. The same is true of the notion of 'value', of capital importance in linguistics and semiotics, which allows a signifier to be marked as different from its neighbouring signifiers. It is precisely these links, differences, coordinations, which are abolished by repression. Freud had already noted, correctly, that this operated in a 'highly individual' manner ('Repression' [1915d], SE XIV, p. 150). But, despite his affirmation that 'repression and the unconscious are correlative to a (very) great extent' (pp. 147–8), he always shrinks away from the hypothesis of using the very process of repression to explain the characteristics of the unconscious. Later when the notion of the id appears, the description of a system without organisation and 'collective will', which had been necessitated in large part by analytic experience, is still maintained, although it seems hardly to accord with an endogenous origin of the id, especially if the latter is now conceived as 'taking up into itself instinctual needs'.[47] Nothing, indeed, in the observation of living *organisms* allows any such *disorganisation* of needs to be asserted – which would moreover be incompatible with life. And if it had to be admitted, according to a conception increasingly prevalent in Freud, that '. . . in the id, which is capable of being inherited, are harboured residues of the existences of countless egos',[48] and in particular those *organisers* which are the com-plexes (*organised groups* of representations) and primal fantasies (typical fantasmatic *structures*), the contradiction with the former description of the unconscious system would become still further apparent.[49]

45 New Introductory Lectures (1933a), SE XXII, pp. 73–4. [Strachey's 'instinct', 'instinctual' correspond to Laplanche's more accurate translation of *Trieb* as *pulsion*, 'drive'. Translator's note.]
46 For an isolated formulation which goes against this, and which I consider a slip, cf. *Problématiques IV*, op. cit., p. 103, note 1.
47 *New Introductory Lectures* (1933a), *SE* XXII, p. 73.
48 *The Ego and the Id* (1923b), *SE* XIX, p. 38.
49 It is in *Moses and Monotheism* (1939a) that this becomes the most obvious: with the powerful return of notions of instinct, of phylogenesis, even the idea that 'the course of events in the id, and their mutual interaction, are governed by quite other laws than those prevailing in the ego' (*SE* XXIII, p. 96). For this is something quite different from saying, as previously, that they 'exist side by side without being influenced by one another' (*SE* XIV, p. 186).

That the id (the unconscious system) is the result of repression, and repression may be understood through a translation theory – these are *my* hypotheses; they have the advantage, at least, of accounting for the characteristics of the system, as Freud drew them from analytic experience. To put things succinctly, translation treats the message as a coherent whole, while the untranslated signifiers do not cohere together and do not form another chain. Repression, the negative side of the translation of the enigmatic message, has an effect of dislocation.

I offer here an *illustration* of this specific point (translation dislocates what it rejects), without claiming in any way to give an example of repression, in the psychoanalytic sense; not only because it is a case of an interlingual translation, but for many other reasons too.

The following French sentence is to be translated: *l'étalon court dans la ferme* [the stallion runs in the farm]. The two words *étalon* and *ferme* each conceal homonyms.

$étalon_1$ = English 'stallion'
$étalon_2$ = English 'standard'
$ferme_1$ = English 'farm'
$ferme_2$ = English 'truss' or 'truss girder' (carpentry equipment).

The English translation, according to the meaning and the context, clearly chooses $étalon_1$ and $ferme_1$, giving 'the stallion runs in the farm'. Thus the following signifiers are left to one side:

$étalon_2$ = standard
and
$ferme_2$ = truss.

But these abandoned signifiers have no relation between them, neither syntagmatic nor paradigmatic. They do not form a second 'signifying chain' as Lacan would claim; to paraphrase Freud, they persist side by side without influencing or contradicting each other.[50]

50 The choice, for this example, of homonymic and not polysemic terms, takes on a further signification. Let us recall that the *polysemy* of a word consists in the fact that there are several meanings, with a common relation of derivation (metaphoric or metonymic). *Homonymy* refers to two words of the same pronunciation, even the same spelling, which have no common derivation, having different histories and contexts, and often even dissimilar etymologies. The interest of homonyms is as an illustration

It is explicitly from the *absence of negation* in the unconscious that Freud derives the absence of an unconscious representation of *death*.[51] Without wishing to go into the depths of this extremely complex question here,[52] it is important to remark that Freud ought to have extended this inference to the idea of castration, to which we can also give, in good Freudian doctrine, 'only a negative content'.

But, in a still more general manner, the notion of 'unconscious complex', whether it be the 'Oedipus' or 'castration' complex, is specifically worth re-examining, in so far as a complex corresponds to a structure with complementarities, coordinations, reciprocities and exclusions. If the Oedipus is a major form of kinship structure and one that founds exchanges of people, goods and ideas, it is unclear how this 'binding' of the contemporary soul could be located in the realm of the 'unbound'. This is no reason to reject the presence in the unconscious of elementary but uncoordinated impulses directed at the parents. The same is not true of castration, an idea sustained entirely by the negation at the heart of the opposition phallic/castrated,[53] and which can be conceived only as a force of organisation, imposing its binary logic at 'higher' levels; with, as its most tangible benefit, the binding of the anxiety caused by

---

of *compromise*, in the symptom, the dream, parapraxis, etc., being a *mechanical signifying convergence* of two causal series, and not a 'second meaning' hidden beneath the first.

Thus, in Freud's little article 'The Subtleties of a Faulty Action' (cf. p. 88 above) the word *bis* is a perfect homonym in this sense, as it at once belongs to Latin (*bis* = twice) and to German (*bis* = until), so that one cannot be said that here there is a superimposition of *meaning* such as would lend itself to a hermeneutics.

51 'What we call our "unconscious" . . . knows nothing that is negative, and no negation; – in it, contradictories coincide. *For that reason* it does not know its own death, for to that we can only give a negative content', 'Thoughts for the Times on War and Death' (1915b), *SE* XIV, p. 296 (my emphasis).

52 Are there, in general, ideas in the unconscious?

What is the relation of this Freudian thesis to those concerning the representation of death in the child and primitive peoples, once the idea that the unconscious is what is most 'primitive' in us is rejected?

If death appears to me through the death of the other, what sort of metabolism and repression processes this message?

53 Cf. *The Language of Psychoanalysis*, op. cit., articles on 'castration complex' and 'foreclosure'; *Problématiques II: Castration-Symbolisations*, passim; *New Foundations for Psychoanalysis*, op. cit., pp. 36–7.

the attack of the drives into the fear of a danger which can be isolated and mastered.

3. The Unconscious and the Primary Process

A new consideration must, however, lead us to qualify slightly these last affirmations: following Freud, we often state that the unconscious is ruled by the primary process, characterised by mobility of investments and the mechanisms of displacement and condensation. Yet such a mobility, implying incessant exchanges between unconscious signifiers, seems to accord ill with the conception of thing-like presentation as fixed, separated from one another by the process of repression.

Let us first note that it is in relation to the dream, and more generally to the formation of symptoms, that the primary process is discovered. More precisely, it is postulated as characterising the unconscious work culminating in the dream, the joke, the symptom, etc. This work, moreover, most often bears upon 'residues' which are not unconscious, but preconscious.

On the other hand, in support of the rigidity of the unconscious, clinical experience shows some striking manifestations, to which some of Freud's formulations bear witness. Foremost among these is the 'repetition compulsion', which in *Beyond the Pleasure Principle* (1920g) is described as the model of the return of the same, almost the identical. In *Inhibitions, Symptoms and Anxiety* (1926d), this compulsion is referred to as 'the resistance of the unconscious' and defined as 'the attraction exerted by the unconscious prototypes upon the repressed instinctual process' (*SE* XX, pp. 159–60).

The solution is, in fact, close to hand – if one bears in mind the distinction between primal repression and secondary repression. The latter is characterised precisely by the existence of an attraction deriving from the primal repressed. There would therefore be a case for distinguishing *schematically* between two levels in the systematic unconscious: that of the primal repressed, made up of unconscious prototypes, characterised by their fixity and the effect of attraction they exercise, not on each other but on the representations which come within their reach; and that of the secondary repressed, to which the primary process applies. Not to mention, obviously, the momentary attraction of preconscious residues, subject in turn to displacement, condensation and overdetermination in the course of symptom-formation.

If one considers that, despite its strangeness for logical thought, the primary process constitutes nevertheless a sort of binding, and if one recalls that the sexual death drive is a principle of unbinding, whereas the sexual life drive (or Eros) functions according to the principle of binding, it follows that the deepest level, the primal repressed, is the privileged site of the first ('a pure culture of otherness'),[54] while in the secondary repressed, site of the primary process, the two kinds of drive begin to engage in contest with each other and to form compounds.[55]

It is clear that this stratified arrangement of unconscious contents and processes provides us with a slight modification of what was said at the end of the previous section: that it is only from the 'primal' unconscious that the presence of complexes should be excluded. For, even if they are found at the level of the secondary unconscious, they nonetheless take on quite special forms there, not yet governed by *contradiction*: the castrating wound may be present as a perforation,[56] as a 'buttonhole' or even as a cut, but not as a subtraction. A body can be cut into a thousand pieces, it can be cut incompletely: but to *subtract* the 'phallus' part is actually a negation, culminating in 'castration'. As such, the castrating subtraction does not belong to the unconscious.[57]

4. The Unconscious and Affect

I would not return (summarily) to this question, were it not that it lends itself to an accusation based on certain assumptions: that to deny the presence of affects in the unconscious is to promote an intellectualist psychoanalysis, allowing no place for the affective relation, the expression of feelings, etc. The targets of this accusation include Freud's 1915 text, Lacanian theory and, quite clearly also, the position of the author of these lines, from 1959 until today. Very briefly, therefore:

54 [Laplanche is here alluding to Freud's formulation that in melancholia what holds sway in the superego is 'a pure culture of the death instinct' (Cf. *The Ego and the Id*, (1923b), *SE* XIX, p. 53). Editor's note.]

55 A conflict which is pursued at higher levels between the ego, the superego and the id: 'The struggle which once raged in the deepest strata of the mind . . . is now continued in a higher region, like the Battle of the Huns in Kaulbach's painting', *The Ego and the Id*, ibid., p. 39.

56 Cf. my discussion of the prehistoric paintings described by Leroi-Gourhan, *Problématiques II*, pp. 268–9.

57 'In analysis we never discover a "no" in the unconscious', 'Negation' (1925h), *SE* XIX, p. 239.

1. My theory of repression – which derives from that of Freud in 1915, reinterpreted through the notion of translation – implies that 'in the unconscious' there are thing-like presentations. Thus there is no affect . . . but nor are there any 'representations of'.

Conceiving the contents of the unconscious as psychical 'things', 'internal foreign bodies', entails a mental effort. The only question is to know whether the effort is worth it!

2. The messages which are the object of the first translations are not essentially verbal, nor are they 'intellectual'! They include in large part signifiers of affect, which can be either translated or repressed: a smile (in Leonardo), an angry gesture, a grimace of disgust, etc. These signifiers, if they are repressed, will be designified, in the same way as are more 'intellectual' signifiers. The 'exclusion' of affect here is nothing but a general consequence of the exclusion of the signified.

3. The site of affect is primarily the body, and secondarily the ego. Affect is the experience of the way the body and the ego are *affected*. In other words the unconscious or id affects the ego, and this in diverse ways, from anxiety to the most elaborate of affects, including shame, guilt, etc. To exclude affect from the unconscious, to give it a *different* topographical location, in no way means excluding it from analysis!

4. The demand to find repressed affects in the unconscious seems to me to go back to the old theory of double personality, or rather multiple personalities, which Freud relies on at one point, at the outcome of the first para-hypnotic treatments (Anna O.). According to that theory – which puts rather too much trust in appearances – there is supposed to be an unconscious personality (or several), alternating with the conscious personality but just as complete as it – with its affects, its representations, a quite specific moral awareness, sometimes a different language, etc.

But if Freud relies at one point, in a dialectical manner, on the argument for a '*double conscience*' ('The Unconscious', op. cit., p. 164), he very quickly shows its limits. The unconscious is thus in no sense an other 'myself' in me, possibly more authentic than me, a Mr Hyde alternating with a Dr Jekyll, the one with his hatred, the other with his love. . . . It is an other thing (*das Andere*) in me, the repressed residue of the other person (*der Andere*). It *affects me* as the other person affected me long ago.

108

IV The Unconscious in Life and in Analytic Treatment

1. The Ptolemaic Unconscious

I have tried to show, in 'The Unfinished Copernican Revolution',[58] the move-ment by which, on the basis of an initial Copernicanism (of the little human's orbiting round the sexual adult), man closed in on himself, in a Ptolemaic system. This closing-in is correlative to the continual movement of translation; but there are two sides to the latter: translation properly speaking, which leads to the predominant ideology of the ego; and repression, which rejects, casts into the interior, the unconscious thing-like presentations. These are well and truly included in the ego, contained by it through a constant counter-investment; to that extent, they certainly participate in a Ptolemaic system. But at the same time they constitute an irreducible kernel, almost a quintessence of otherness: and thus the promise of a reopening.

The everyday manifestations of the unconscious, the 'formations of the unconscious', do not escape this closure: they appear within the narcissistic space of the ego, and also, due to the almost machine-like mechanism of the primary process, they cannot be considered as messages. The dream is most often dreamt without being recounted, without any communicative intention: the model of the tub, as I have termed it,[59] clearly schematises its initial 'unrelatedness',[60] its 'narcissism'. This could be shown equally for the symp-tom, which is not immediately relational, allocutory – or only in the way its secondary benefits are employed. There are bungled actions, slips of the pen, which have no witness and no 'address', even a virtual one.

---

58 'The Unfinished Copernican Revolution' in this volume, pp. 52–83.

59 *Problématiques V: Le baquet: transcendance du transfert*, Paris: Presses Universitaires de France, 1987. The course in question was given in 1979.

It is remarkable to see the idea taken up, shamelessly, even if it is indirectly attributed to Freud, without even a mention of my initiative in choosing the term and elaborating the model for psychoanalysis. Cf. René Roussillon: *Du baquet de Mesmer au 'baquet' de S. Freud*, Paris: Presses Universitaires de France, 1992.

What quotation do the inverted commas around *'baquet'* point to in this title? One looks for it in vain in the text.

60 Here I take up the movement of *Problématiques V*, op. cit., pp. 57–9, which goes from closure to opening.

2. Openings in Life

There is, however, a *compulsion to recount* certain dreams. Can this be considered as something purely internal, the maintenance of an allocutory opening at the heart of the most 'closed', 'private' phenomenon? Without passing a categorical judgement, I would incline to give the determining role to 'provocation' by the other.[61] I do not think that the dream becomes an address *by the mere fact* of being told: it is the fact that the dream to come is 'to be told' which turns it into an address. This 'turning' [*version*] towards the other seems to me to be of a quite different nature from the 'transferences' which are common currency in all dreams, and which are only modalities of displacement and condensation, the image of one person taking the place of another, or being superimposed on it. Such transferences are modalities of 'filled-in' transference.[62]

> . . . [A]n unconscious idea is as such quite incapable of entering the preconscious and . . . it can only exercise any effect there by establishing a connection with an idea which already belongs to the preconscious, by transferring its intensity on to it and by getting itself 'covered' by it. Here we have the fact of 'transference', which provides an explanation of so many striking phenomena in the mental life of neurotics.[63]

The dream-interpreter, the soothsayer, the prophetess are indispensable characters in all cultures. They are sought out because they are 'supposed to

---

61 Cf. 'Transference: its Provocation by the analyst' in this volume, pp. 214–33.

62 [Laplanche makes a distinction between transference *en plein* ('filled in') and transference *en creux* ('hollowed out'). 'Filled in' transference is a positive reproduction of childhood imagoes and relationships which must evolve towards 'hollowed out' transference, which reproduces the originary enigmatic relation to the other. See *New Foundations for Psychoanalysis*, op. cit., p. 160 ff, and 'Transference: its Provocation by the Analyst' in this volume, p. 229. Editor's note.]

63 *The Interpretation of Dreams* (1900a), *SE* IV–V, pp. 562–3. The *Argument* of the current number of *Nouvelle Revue Psychanalytique*, 'L'inconscient mis à l'épreuve' (no. 48, 1993, p. 7), recalls that the 'Bonneval journées curiously neglected' transference. So, equally curiously, do Freud's 1915 article and most of his elaborations of the unconscious or the id: 'Bonneval' was in good company! Perhaps it was necessary to begin to connect up the otherness of the unconscious and the otherness of the other in childhood, in order to attempt to address the relation of the unconscious to the other in transference, which would not be the pure reduplication of the same 'cliché' which is the 'filled in' transference (cf. Freud, 'The Dynamics of Transference' [1912b] *SE* XII, p. 99).

know' more about these strange phenomena, thus reactivating in an undeniable way the relation to the adult who 'knows more of . . .'. More generally still, I have postulated as one of the major dimensions of the cultural domain this provocation by the enigma of the other. The cultural message, the artistic 'creation', is situated beyond a purely pragmatic aim (to produce such and such an effect on an addressee, by using some particular means). It is, in its depths, provoked by the 'nameless public', 'scattered into the future', who will receive (or not) this message in a bottle.[64]

The 'cultural' thus seems to me to be one of the precursors of the analytic situation, specifically because of the 'hollowed-out' transference it installs.

3. The Opening of the Analytic Treatment

The 'tub of the analytic treatment', as I have tried to show, is quite different from the 'tub' of the dream: quite simply because it includes the other, the other person, in its enclosure.[65] It is therefore not a paradox that one is able to affirm that it constitutes an unprecedented site of *opening*, one which is, properly speaking, quite unheard of in human existence. Let us again recall that if the id has its origin in the first communications, what is proper to it is that *it does not talk*. What brings the id to language, and more broadly to expression, can only be the result of the complex process which is the analytic treatment. Many different factors are involved: the preservation of the enclosure of the 'tub'; the interior attitude of the analyst, comprising listening, refusal and respect for the enigma of his own unconscious; the method of free association[66] and freedom to speak[67]; and finally interpretation and construction, whose complementarity I have tried to show –

---

64 [For an elaboration of the relation between cultural production and the modalities of the transference together with the Mallarméan allusion see 'Transference: its Provocation by the Analyst' in this volume, pp. 221ff. Editor's note.]

65 Laplanche discusses various homeostatic models of enclosure in Freud through the model of the 'tub' (*le baquet*). See especially *Problématiques V. Le baquet: transcendance du transfert*, Part I. Editor's note.]

66 *Problématiques V, passim.*

67 Where else can one say, where has one been able to say, at any moment in the history of man, what is said in analysis ?

interpretation (in the narrow sense) being *mainly* on the side of the analyst, and construction on that of the analysand.[68]

I can only reformulate things: it is in the hollow of the enigma offered by the analyst that the analysand comes to situate and re-elaborate the hollow of his own originary enigmas. This takes place through the dismantling of his own constructions (notably, the Oedipal ones), the tracking of signifiers towards the repressed, and lastly the production of new constructions/translations, which necessarily originate with the analysand, and with which he tries to 'allow passage to' something of the repressed. 'Which necessarily originate with the analysand', for this must be forcefully stated: if the human being is endlessly translating – both translating the messages of the other and self-translating – he is his own hermeneut. But the obverse of hermeneutics, or translation, is repression, and it cannot be free of this. The analyst, every time he claims to translate or to help translate, *assists repression*. It is not for him to be the hermeneut, whether or not by means of the psychoanalytic ideologies which are at everybody's fingertips. For instance, what is known as a 'psychoanalytic reading', whose banality we are sick and tired of, is a direct means of repression.[69] *The hermeneut*, well before psychoanalysis and probably after it, *is the human being*. The heart of analysis is not part of this universal tendency, but runs counter to it: in this sense, and while recognising the place of the hermeneut, psychoanalysis is very precisely an anti-hermeneutics.[70]

What portion of the id can be reintegrated into speech? What part – 'unconscious prototypes' – remains anchored and perhaps immutable? Lastly and above all, what portion of the 'hollowed-out' transference can be transferred, at the end or by an interruption of analysis, thus escaping a Ptolemaic reclosure which is only too natural? These questions lack a general response, allowing one all the more to envisage a typology of processes and ends of analysis.

---

68 'Interpretation between Determinism and Hermeneutics' in this volume, pp. 161ff.
69 The 'death drive' reading or the 'depressive position' reading, the Oedipal or castration readings, reading according to the Law . . . readings, readings. . . . The theory of seduction is not a reading 'language', but an attempt to understand analytic practice.
70 See 'Psychoanalysis as Anti-hermeneutics' (1994), *Radical Philosophy*, no. 79, Sept./Oct. 1996.

V The Unconscious and Metaphysics

The most active currents in contemporary psychoanalysis seem caught between two temptations, which, for convenience's sake, I will refer to as the phenomenological and the metaphysical.

1. The *phenomenological current*: this I discussed as early as 1959, in a study of Politzer's enterprise. One of the most notable representatives of this tendency (even if his success has not measured up to the quality of his efforts) is Roy Schafer in the United States. To put it briefly, the point in every case is to restore to the human being his quality of 'first person' subject, the author of his acts and his signifying intentions. All descriptions in terms of metapsychology, of apparatus, of system, etc. are in this view alienating descriptions, in which psychoanalytic theory becomes complicit with a too natural slide towards 'abstraction' and 'realism'. These last terms are Politzer's, but Schafer's critique, much further elaborated by a thinker who is familiar with ego psychology and is an experienced practitioner, develops along exactly the same lines: 'it is not the agency [the ego] but the person who perceives, judges and thinks'; the unconscious is the subject's 'self-trickery', which finds an accomplice in the psychoanalytic theory of a 'mind-place', etc.

I term these initiatives 'phenomenological' in the broadest sense; even if they are inspired by other philosophies as well, they posit that one should be able to find the intentionality of a subject at the heart of all psychical acts, and that this should give an integral account of them.[71] Seemingly, such a phenomenology takes on a task less insurmountable than the one which would give an account, by a more or less transcendental constitution, of the world of apperception of all *cogitata* [objects of thought].

Let us note, firstly, that in Politzer, and even more so in Schafer, this attempt to disalienate the subject or the person passes above all through theory or through 'language'. To put forward 'a new language for psychoanalysis'[72]

71 An excellent critical account of the thought of Roy Schafer is given by Agnes Oppenheimer, 'Le meilleur des mondes possibles. A propos du projet de R. Schafer', in *Psychanalyse à l'Université*, 1984, vol. 9, no. 35, pp. 467–90. Cf. also *Problématiques V*, op. cit., pp. 226–9.
72 Roy Schafer, *A New Language for Psychoanalysis*, New Haven: Yale University Press, 1976.

(first of all in books, but also in treatment) is said to be the essential step for the subject to take to recover the mastery of, and responsibility for, his psychical acts. Now, even supposing that one can rely on such a system of programmed 'self-theorisation',[73] it could only be viable if it took account of the fact that 'third person' language is nevertheless so successful. In different terms, resistance and defence, before belonging to theory, belong to the human being himself, and the thought of disalienation ought to encompass the thought of alienation.[74]

Second, the whole Freudian experience is constituted as the discovery of an other thing in us, acting not according to meaning, but according to modalities which are causal. The critique of this 'realism of the unconscious' continues to fall apart when faced with this same experience, especially with what takes the form of the repetition compulsion, and when it attempts to rival 'mechanical' descriptions of the dream-work which remain unsurpassed to this day.

Finally – and this is my personal contribution – in refusing to recognise in us the existence of a foreign body hard as iron, 'disalienating' thought denies itself the path leading from the other thing in us to the other person who is its origin. Thus it fails to discover that internal alienation is the residue of a fundamental decentering whose center for the child is the other adult, and whose force of gravitation is designated by the enigmatic message. Thus, by promoting a new 'language'[75] one fails to give its rightful value to the category of the message, of the 'signifier to', and, finally, of the other.[76]

2. In speaking of a *metaphysical current*, I will refer to Freud and to Auguste Comte – firstly to get rid of the claim that one must be a metaphysician, and if not, one is not a philosopher. As if there did not exist a critical philosophy, a positive philosophy, a Freudian philosophy, and several others.

Auguste Comte – forgotten, barely read nowadays – sets out a 'law of the three estates', through which the evolution of the human mind (in a collective, but also an individual, sense) passes: the *theological estate*, in which phenomena are held to be 'produced by the direct and continual activity of supernatural agents'; the *metaphysical estate*, in which supernatural agents are replaced by

---

73 [*auto-théorisation*] In the term which I use.

74 Cf. *Problématiques V,* op. cit., pp. 226–8, where I use the polemical formulations: 'Metapsychology is dead . . . but it doesn't know it' (Politzer); 'The subject is not alienated . . . but he doesn't know it' (Schafer).

75 In the sense – very 'Poincaré', very 'Condillac' – of a 'well made language'.

76 A phenomenological psychology lacks the other thing. A phenomenology of perception lacks the other person. Cf. 'The Unfinished Copernican Revolution' in this volume, p. 72, footnote 38.

abstract forces, veritable entities (personified abstractions) held to be capable of producing by themselves all observable phenomena, the explanation for which now consists in assigning each its corresponding entity; and lastly the *positive estate*, with its notion of law as a constant relation between phenomena.

Freud, for his part, subscribes to a sequence which, despite its somewhat different terms, is not very far from this: the animist, religious and scientific views of the world.[77] 'Animism' in Freud is very close to Comte's 'theology', their common point being the intervention of *anthropomorphic* agents. As for metaphysical concepts, when Freud speaks of them he does so less precisely than Auguste Comte, in order to include religious notions, such as original sin, God, etc.[78] Let us therefore keep the Comtean definition of metaphysics as the creation of abstract entities to which real powers are attributed, a definition which does not fail to find yet another echo in Freud, when he assimilates a *certain* kind of philosophical thought to schizophrenic thinking, in which 'what concerns words predominates over what concerns things' ('The Unconscious', op. cit., p. 200).

Creating abstract entities and attributing to them their own efficacy: the procedure is beginning to become a current one, especially in a sort of neo-metapsychology or neo-metaphysics in France. The move from adjective to substantive particularly lends itself to this. I have already pointed to the Lacanian sequence:

symbolism → symbolic → the Symbolic

But examples abound:

mother → maternal → the Maternal
origin → originary → the Originary[79]

Quite recently, we were told that it was essential to 'bring ourselves up to date on the henceforth central notion of the Negative'.[80] The capital letter comes to seal the derivation from the greatest metaphysician of all time, Hegel:

---

77 *Totem and Taboo* (1912–13), *SE* XIII, p. 77.

78 This is the famous passage on 'the transformation of metaphysics into metapsychology', *The Psychopathology of Everyday Life* (1901b), *SE* VI, p. 321. I have given some indications about the 'repatriation' of the metaphysical notions of self, of cause, of archaeology, in 'The Wall and the Arcade', in Fletcher and Stanton, eds, p. 210; and 'Interpretation between Determinism and Hermeneutics' in this volume, p. 144.

79 I have used this word, although I have made clear that I do not accord it any transcendent or causal value, but see it as a category to be outlined in experience.

80 Programme of the 'XII Journées occitanes de psychanalyse', November 1993.

negation → the negative → the Negative

And yet, in the Freudian texts referred to, one finds the term *Negation* (or *Verneinung*) and the adjective *negative*, but not, to my knowledge, the metaphysical entity *das Negative*.[81] Now, all the difference is there: while a certain qualification of something (such as: negative) occurs at different moments, 'the Negative' will be solemnly declared to manifest itself in 'different figures', and the trick is done. Thus, as Auguste Comte recalls, 'phlogistics' would give rise to the 'different figures' of fire. . . .

You're lying in wait for me, I know; and, for once, our metaphysicians can join in with Politzer and Schafer, to ask: 'So what about "*the* unconscious"? Isn't it the very epitome of an entity formed from an adjective? Did Freud not give, with this, the example of a metaphysical concept *par excellence*? And it's no good, in some hypocrisy of translation, simply avoiding the capital letter! . . . '.

I will ask our metaphysicians of the Negative, incidentally, if they have already exhausted the joys of the metaphysics of the Unconscious, such is their need to plunge 'to the depths of the Unknown to find the New'.[82]

Above all, though, I will plead guilty. Not on my own account, nor Freud's, nor even that of 'the unconscious'; but on behalf of 'unconscious things' which are truly 'words (or rather signifiers) taken to be things'; taken to be things in the mechanism of 'refused' translation. It must be fully admitted that 'the unconscious' is not a metaphysical entity, but a collective notion encompassing 'entities' which *for their part* have taken on a 'metaphysical' or metapsychological value. These entities work according to the 'metaphysical' principal of *cause*, withdrawn as they are from the *laws* of meaning.

We shall end with Auguste Comte. Although he refuses, in his classification of the positive sciences, a separate place for psychology, between physiology and sociology, it is amusing to observe how 'theology' and 'metaphysics' powerfully re-emerge, precisely *in that place*, with psychoanalysis: in the *anthropomorphism* of the agencies and the *metaphysics* of the entities in the psyche. But this re-emergence takes place *in the human being* and not in the classification of sciences: from that place, anthropomorphism and metaphysics are not ready to be dislodged.

Translated by Luke Thurston

---

81 While elsewhere German, the metaphysical language *par excellence*, lends itself all too easily to the substantivisation of the adjective or the verb.
82 'Au fond de L'Inconnu pour trouver du *nouveau*', the final line of Baudelaire's 'Le Voyage', *Baudelaire: Selected Verse*, ed. with trans. Francis Scarfe, Harmondsworth: Penguin Books, 1961, p. 190.

3

The Drive and its Source-Object:
its Fate in the Transference[1]

The drive: what use is it? Lurking within this question as proposed at this conference,[2] to my mind, there lies a trap. As there is, of course, in any question if one answers it in its own terms. The question itself has to be *questioned*. The way this particular question is formulated – fortunately – leaves it ambiguous: is what is meant 'the drive' itself, or 'the concept of the drive'? I have little doubt that in the minds of the vast majority of us what is at issue here is the concept, the so-called scientific and theoretical concept. What, indeed, is it for? How should we use it? And what use is it to us? In posing the terms of the question in this way, all we are doing is to show our support for the pragmatist conception that is everywhere current in the world of the natural sciences and probably in psychoanalysis too. Assuredly, modern science (to make a slight detour) is not in thrall to short-term usefulness of the purely technical kind. Indeed, the question: 'what use is it?' rather than having anything to do with direct action, may simply mean: what use is it for our understanding? (I am thinking here, for instance, of the role of concepts in astrophysics.) But unfortunately, I would say, analysts seem in some respects to want to give lessons in pragmatism to physicists. Bound to a daily practice, they expect every concept to help them on a daily basis, if not in supplying

1 Laplanche's title purposely echoes that of Freud's 1915 paper, 'Triebe und Triebschicksale', which appears as 'Instincts and their Vicissitudes' in the *Standard Edition of the Complete Psychological Works of Sigmund Freud* (1915c), *SE* XIV, pp. 109–40 [translator's note].
2 Proceedings published as *La pulsion pour quoi faire?*, Paris: Association Psychanalytique de France, 1984.

117

constructions and making interpretations, at least in deciding what general direction to take. From the 'what for?' levelled at the concept of the drive, it is not unusual among analysts for the next move to be an open and more general 'what for?' directed at theory itself. Theory: what use is it? Theory is becoming one of the scapegoats of psychoanalysis, with the other scapegoat being so-called applied psychoanalysis, what I call extra-mural psychoanalysis (outside the clinical). Both from theory and from extra-mural psychoanalysis there is a double movement of repulsion which is but one and the same thing. For the reason for this double banishment may be found in a certain conception – which might even be called a technicist one – of theory as having to be *applied*.

To the initial question of 'what use is it? ' I want by way of answer to formulate a double question of my own: first, should the drive be of any use at all? and, second, what is the status and function of theory, its distance with regard to experience (i.e. our own experience, that of analytical practice)? And if I have posed as a preliminary these two questions which are in fact one and the same question, the reason for this is that the *very content* of what I aim to put forward should help us to answer them. Analytical theory ought to help us understand the status of theory itself. I shall return to this issue towards the end of this essay.

My second preliminary remark is as follows, and has to do with history. The problem we are addressing is of course the drive, for us as analysts, in 1984. But we surely cannot jettison every historical approach and problematic, and all reference to the work that has gone before us, notably the work of Freud. I have given my views on the topic too often to make more than a brief allusion necessary. I think there can be no question, here amongst us, of indulging in Freudology. But Freudianism, both that of Freud himself and of his successors, is an experience, and I think that it is unfortunate we have in French only the one word – *expérience* – to refer to what is acquired experience and to what is codified scientific experiment.[3] German like English has two words. What I mean by this is that when I speak of experience I use the word in the English-language sense of experience, irrespective of whether practical or theoretical experience is at issue. Theory too is an experience and precisely not in the experimentalist sense. There is a living experience of concepts, their borrowings, their derivations, their straying or wandering. There is a way in which the evolution of theoretical experience re-enacts the various metamorphoses in the

3 [As Laplanche indicates here, the French word 'expérience' means both *experience* (in the usual, empirical sense) and *experiment* in the scientific sense. Translator's note.]

evolution of the thing itself, in this case of the human being, including of course the errors that human beings fall into about themselves, as if these were reduplicated in the mistakes of theory, which to be sure need to be delimited and overcome.

I would like now to start from experience, and notably from the common fertile soil of practical experience, i.e. from so-called 'clinical' experience, which, to my mind, is the yardstick of any theory of the drive. I will endeavour to list the *requirements* that practical experience makes on theory under four headings.

1. The first *requirement* is psychic determinism. There is a general belief in psychical determinism that no analyst can deny. The psychical domain, just like any other, ought to be able to be ordered by reason. Chance must be excluded from it, and so on. This is a fairly general Freudian postulate; although it is a postulate for psychologists as well as for analysts. Freud here places himself openly on the side of science in the sense that man is seen as part of nature. But (there is always a but) if that were all, psychoanalysis would be nothing but a psychology; it would be a science like any other and have to follow the progress common to all the sciences, i.e. from muddled, subjective notions (such as the will, motivations, even causes, which is *the point*, of course), and would have to move on from the notion of cause, as has long been said of the natural sciences,[4] to drawing up *laws*, that is, constant or quantifiable relations between phenomena. It may be argued, rightly enough, that the notion of cause is derived from a certain subjective experience of the psychical act and that it is in the first instance projected by us onto the outside world, which we suppose to be acted upon by something in much the same way that we feel we act or are being acted upon ourselves. Gradually, in the objective sciences, cause gives way to the drawing up of regular sequences, the ideal for which are mathematical functions. So if one follows the movement of science, there ought at some stage to be a reverse movement, consisting in a reinteriorisation of a law-governed determinism, or even of a mathematical (some would say mathemic)[5]

4 First formulated by Auguste Comte.
5 [An allusion to Lacan's term 'matheme' which he coins by analogy with the morphemes and phonemes of linguistics and Levi-Strauss's 'mythemes' (the minimal units of language and myth respectively). They are attempts to formalise in an algebra-like way the relations between the fundamental components of Lacanian theory. See the entry on the matheme in *An Introductory Dictionary of Lacanian Psychoanalysis*, Dylan Evans, London: Routledge, 1996, p. 108. Editor's note.]

119

determinism on the inside; there ought therefore to be a reconquering of the psychical by natural science.

There is, however, something that gets in the way of this reverse movement. The obstacle isn't the recourse to meaning, nor is it the personalist grievance. It is the resistance and the deepening of the notion of cause that psychoanalysis provides. The investigation, analysis, and interpretation of symptoms, dreams, slips of the tongue, parapraxes, etc., all this may be thought of as a quest for meaning. Beyond meaning, however, what Freud teaches us is that what we are searching for is another *content* and consequently a real cause. And in the constant evolution of Freud's thinking on this subject, the idea of the *id*, the idea that we are acted upon by this set of obscure causes to which he gives that name, puts a virtually definitive seal on this recognition of our fundamental decenteredness.

2. My second point, still in connection with the *requirements* against which any notion of the drive should be measured, may be put as follows: the cause or causes that psychoanalysis searches for and uncovers are of the order of representation, they are memories, fantasies or imaginings, and imagos, with two sets of distinctive features. They are representations that are so to speak frozen, fixed beyond the meaning that may inhabit them, beyond the multiple meanings that may be assigned to them. These frozen and fixed representations have the generative power of schemas as well as the materiality of *quasi-things*. This is the way in which I approach the problem of translation posed by Freud's *Sachvorstellung*, which is of course a presentation of the thing in the intentional sense, but which becomes in the unconscious a veritable thing-like presentation. The movement from the presentation of the thing to the thing-like presentation means precisely this fixing beyond all meaning, or even, in linguistic terminology, beyond all referentiality.[6] The second characteristic of

6 [Strachey's translation in the Standard Edition of Freud's *Sachvorstellung* is thing-presentation by contrast with word-presentation (*Wortvorstellung*). According to Freud the unconscious as a system consists of thing-presentations which are perceptual traces, predominantly visual, of the object, denied access by repression to corresponding word-presentations, essentially auditory and belonging to the preconscious system where language is located (see the entry on 'Thing-Presentation/Word-Presentation' in *The Language of Psychoanalysis*, J. Laplanche and J.-B. Pontalis, trans. Donald Nicholson-Smith, London: The Hogarth Press, 1973, p. 447). Laplanche argues here and elsewhere that the effect of repression as a partial and failed translation is to

these presentations is that they are unconscious, or that they have their roots in the unconscious, and that a part of them at least is incapable of becoming conscious again, as we are all well aware, even in analysis. Analysis can but accept the fact that a part of the unconscious will never be recalled and brought back to consciousness, but can only be grasped within a network of constructions that attempts to approach it but which never reaches the thing itself, the thing-like presentation itself.

3. My third *requirement* involves the fact that these presentations have, to a large extent, to do with bodily processes, whether they are organised around the body itself, or one or other of its zones or functions. The essential point here is to recognise those libidinal 'organisations' – or complexes – that are the fantasmatic organisations well described by Freud. To go from centering on these modes of organisation to seeing in the erogenous zone itself (whether oral or anal, etc.) the source of the drive as such is but a short distance to travel, and Freud himself seems to do this without much second thought in the *Three Essays on the Theory of Sexuality* (1905d), and indeed it is perhaps relatively easy to do so in the case of the genital zone (to say that the penis or the female sex organs are the source of the drive seems straightforward enough), or with regard to the anal or even oral zone (but *where* in fact is the somatic source of oral excitation? There has ultimately never been a clear answer to this). Far more difficult to maintain, at any event, is this kind of metamorphosis of the source in respect of something like the scopophilic drive (is the drive to look an excitation of the eye, is there such a thing as an ocular orgasm? few of us would be prepared to say so) or with regard to the sadistic drive that supposedly comes from muscular excitation.

4. My fourth *requirement*, finally, is the need to account for the phenomena of displacement. The fact that one and the same affective reaction finds itself bound to an entirely different representation from the real circumstances of its genesis is a type of experience that Freud highlights from the outset, in his earliest writings, notably the *Studies on Hysteria* (1895d), and that is something

produce an unconscious residue that has a reified and alien materiality. The preconscious intentional presentation-of-the-thing (Ger.: *Sachvorstellung*, Fr.: *représentation de chose*) is transformed into an unconscious presentation-as-a-mental-thing (*représentation-chose*) or thing-like presentation, a designified signifier. See also 'A Short Treatise on the Unconscious' in this volume, p. 90, p. 92, n. 20. Editor's note.]

we cannot avoid, either in our experience or the way we think about it. Much the same is true of the suppression of affect, the so-called 'belle indifférence' of hysterics and its supposed reappearance or the semblance of its reappearance elsewhere, in somatisation or the hysterical attack; or of the detachment of affect from any representation, its dequalification, and, in place of a qualified, specified affect, the sudden occurrence of anxiety; or else of phenomena like transference, in all senses of the term, including transference in the dream, i.e. transference onto the residues of the day, or the transference of certain affects, certain wishes, or else transference in our everyday meaning of the word, transference within the psychoanalytic session itself. There are, in analysis, many different experiences such as these, which serve perhaps only to radicalise a spontaneous mode of perception; I mean by this that displacement is indisputably an analytic experience, but that it is already an everyday experience as well, and an experience in everyday language. What else are we doing when we say, for instance, (and we say it without Freud's assistance) that we have transferred our love from this or that person to another, or that we have a potential for aggressivity which is only waiting for the first available opportunity, regardless of what object first comes to hand? In short, phenomena of displacement, and even condensation, encourage us quite naturally to construct a theory of the radical separation between affect and representation, and to produce a schematisation that makes the one independent of the other, with the one (affect), on the physical model, being the motive force, the other (the associative path) being the railway track leading from one representation to another. To this one could add all Freud's other metaphors about connections (referring to the linkages in a chain as well as the points on a railway track) taking one from one representation to another. There is here a very strong, very persuasive if not indeed convincing experience, and one that leads straight to physicalist models, in terms of quantity and neurones, energy and structure, or, as the talk was in the seventeenth century, figure and movement. The model is one that dominates Freud's thinking throughout the whole of its development.

I shall indicate in more detail my position on the economic hypothesis in a moment. I want only to emphasise that no metapsychological thinking can neglect to take account of the displacement which is our daily experience. But it must also be acknowledged, inversely, that absolute displacement, the displacement in which affect retains nothing of its original representation, is only an asymptotic, theoretical case, that is never attained in reality, as with an absolute primary process. Obviously, psychopathology (in the broadest sense, up to and including *The Psychopathology of Everyday Life* [1901b]) provides the model for the most radical displacements (or as I am wont to put it: 'the most forgetful' displacements, forgetful, that is, of whence they have come). But a radical displacement, an absolute primary process, ought to be translatable into the sequence: 'I've forgotten – what? – I've forgotten – what? – I've forgotten', which is precisely the absolute limit set upon analytical investigation, so long indeed as it seeks to uncover what has been forgotten, but which presupposes of course that the primary process is not absolute.

A *causalist* determinism that renders us foreign to ourselves and alienates us in an id; a determination by unconscious representations; representations interweaving in complexes *bound to the body* or one or other of its parts or functions; the phenomenon of *displacement*, which can neither be neglected nor pushed to the limit of the absolute: these are four of the results of analytic experience. What I mean by this is not raw experience (there is no such thing, in the empiricist sense), but experience that is relatively independent of any theoretical system. This is where the theory of the drive, if drive there be, can be inserted. The fact is that Freud, with remarkable success, introduces here two types of model which are in fact quite different from one another: the first is the physicalist model which, as I said a moment ago, reduces every phenomenon to energy + figure, or energy + representation; and the second is a biological model, based on the constancy principle, i.e. the undeniable tendency of all organisms to maintain their distinctness from their environment both in terms of structure and of energy level. These two models in Freud are at times in competition with one another, but most often they work in conjunction with each other, and their respective places must constantly be re-evaluated. To sum up in a word my personal re-evaluation of these two models, I would say that the chief virtue of the physicalist model is in its physical falsity, which at best makes it well suited to account for that alien materiality – as hard as nails, or harder – which we term 'unconscious psychical reality' or the 'internal foreign body'. What one sees here is indeed the return – the reintrojection, one might say – of a false physical causalism to its site of origin: the unconscious psyche. As for the homeostatic, biologising model, it is most readily verified, throughout the elaboration of Freud's thinking, in relation to the ego.

My aim is in no sense to provide a summary of Freud's theory of the drive, which operates as a kind of synthesis or compromise between physicalism and biologism. I will content myself with enumerating: source, pressure, aim, and object, together with the much-vaunted contingency of the object which is the basis of so many problems. And I shall only recall, in Freud's view, the biological origin of the sexual drive, as well as the biological origin of the functions of self-preservation. The most synthesising formula is one with which you are all familiar: the concept of the drive, says Freud, is 'one of those lying on the frontier between the mental and the physical'; the drive itself is 'the psychical representative of an endosomatic, continuously flowing source of stimulation', 'a measure of the demand made upon the mind for work'.[7]

Let me set this massive recourse to the biological alongside the four requirements I outlined earlier. The requirement for a cause that alienates us and turns us into foreigners to our own acts: certainly, indeed, the reference to the biological turns us into foreigners to our own acts. The link with bodily zones (my third point above): that too seems to fit . . ., though one would have to say that the state of tension – tumescence followed by detumescence – is a fairly rudimentary model when it comes to accounting for the source of the drive (I referred earlier to the drive to look). And how do things stand with our third point, displacement? Well, Freud's theory, the biological theory of the drive does account for this, but at the cost of turning it into an absolute. The contingency of the object is total. The drive comes to be seen merely as pressure (ultimately, the only element that remains of this device with completely interchangeable parts called the drive is pressure, *Drang*), as pressure or energy which attaches itself to (or detaches itself from) anything whatever, as it might to a decoy. However, it is in respect of my second requirement, the relation to representations (memories and fantasies), that the biological theory is at its weakest and most arbitrary, because it denies these representations any activity of their own, treating them only as a kind of hook or site of investment for the benefit of undifferentiated and free-floating energy. To my mind, the recourse to some biological drive in order to account for the force of unconscious determinism is little more than an unverifiable and contestable hypothesis, and one that in any case belongs outside analysis.

Let us go further. The hypothesis of some innate drive apparatus necessarily entails the idea that fantasies are but a burgeoning outgrowth, the psychical translation of an endogenous, and ultimately maturational evolution. This is clearly visible in Freud, at the biologising highpoint of his thinking between 1897 and 1905, in the aftermath of the notorious letter of 21 September 1897. The same proves to be the case in someone like Melanie Klein, in whom fantasy and drive are tightly bound together, and are ultimately endogenous (as she has

7 Sigmund Freud, *Three Essays on the Theory of Sexuality* (1905d), *SE* VII, p. 168.

often been criticised for thinking) not only in their force but also their modalities of manifestation. What one finds here, in my view, is a biological idealism for which lived experience is only ever a point of attachment and anchorage. The objection is a decisive one, and it applies to any psychoanalytic theory that aims to contrast a biological or somato-psychical organism with an environment that is taken, in its very essence, to be non-psychical.

Is another theory of the drive possible or must all notion of the drive be abandoned? Is it possible to put forward another version of Freud's theory, and return to another Freud, to a third model, sketched out but left in his bottom drawer by Freud himself? Surprisingly enough, a clue may be found in the fact that the *Trieb* or drive was not really elaborated till 1905 (even if the term does appear once before in the *Project* [1895]).

Of course, the notion of an excitation with an internal origin was in evidence before then. Internal excitation, Freud reminds us, is that which one cannot elude by motility. The definition is incontrovertible, but from the outset the question remains an open one: that which one cannot elude by motility, is this the body? Or is it the investment of reminiscence by the body? Is it *the internal foreign body itself, i.e. the reminiscence itself*? There is another term used in the letters to Fliess, which may also be translated by the term 'drive', which is the word *Impulse*, which is found in a limited number of passages all belonging to the same specific period.[8] Without any doubt, these are not bodily forces or even investments of fantasy. These *Impulse*, or impulses, in the sense in which one might refer to them in the field of physics or electronics, are the very action of the repressed memories and fantasies, that which arises from them and flows from them as from their source. You will find all this in Draft N particularly. These texts, with this earlier usage preceding that of *Trieb* proper, are at the heart of what is called the seduction theory, which is to say that the

8 [Laplanche is referring here to the current French translation of the Freud/Fliess Correspondence, in which Freud's original German term 'Impulse' is indeed translated as 'pulsions' (drives). In the standard English translation of the volume by Eric Mosbacher and James Strachey, the word is rendered as 'impulses' (see *The Origins of Psycho-Analysis: Letters to Wilhelm Fliess, Drafts and Notes: 1887–1902*, London: Imago, 1954, p. 207). Masson's more recent edition also translates it as 'impulses', see Letter of May 31st, 1895 (Draft N), in *The Complete Letters of Sigmund Freud to Wilhelm Fliess: 1887–1904*, trans. and ed. Jeffrey Moussaieff Masson, Cambridge, Mass.: The Belknap Press of Harvard University Press, 1985, p. 250. Translator's note.]

Freudian model that I am attempting to set up, at the very origins of the drive, is that of *primal seduction and repression*.

The presentation that follows should be taken only as a general schema. It ought not to be understood as strictly chronological, though it is a schema of engendering and thus, in the broadest sense, a genetic one (if the term is taken in the very wide sense of engendering). Whereas the classical theory of the drive proposes one antecedent and only one, that of endogenous somatic stimuli, my view is that it is indispensable to think in terms of a double antecedence: on the one hand, the presupposition of an organism devoted to homeostasis and self-preservation and, on the other, that of an adult cultural world in which the child is totally immersed from the outset.

Let me fill in a few details. I draw a sharp distinction between sexuality and the functions of self-preservation which I see as biological and bio-psychological functions that aim to maintain the organism, its structure and its constants, all of which are assimilable to a homeostatic energy level: the model is one that, ultimately, physicists have used for all their regulatory, feedback systems. Self-preservation, in humans as in all life forms, is primary. However, I want to emphasise that it implies from the outset an opening to the world and, in terms of both perception and motor development, an opening of the organism onto its own environment. The idea of an organism initially closed upon itself, and only then opening itself to the object (or constructing it, even?) is one of the modalities of biological idealism or solipsism that so many theorists of psycho-analysis have imprudently adopted.

In return, in contrast to this priority of self-preservation, along with Freud and also, marginally in relation to him, in the wake of Bolk, the emphasis has rightly been placed on the partial deficiencies in humans, or on the lagging behind of their adaptive mechanisms. The dependency of young humans on adults, which is much more marked than in other species, fosters the delay that is at the origins of humanisation, i.e. the early sexualisation of human beings. However, modern research (like the work of Brazelton) shows how far the adaptive and perceptual opening of small babies to the object should not be underestimated. So much then for the first precondition, with all the necessary qualifications that have to be applied to the notion of self-preservation.

As for the second precondition, this concerns the adult world that confronts the nascent organism. Briefly, let us remember that this is a world of significa-tion and communication, swamping the child's capacity for apprehension and mastery. Messages are offered on all sides. By messages I do not necessarily nor chiefly mean verbal messages. Any gesture, any mimicry functions as a signifier.

These originary, traumatic signifiers I propose to call 'enigmatic signifiers'.[9] These signifiers are not enigmatic by virtue of the simple fact that the infant does not know the code, which he or she would need to learn. We are well aware of the fact that the infant begins inhabiting verbal language without being provided with a code in advance, in the same way that one learns a foreign language by simple everyday usage. That is not the point. What is crucial is the fact that the adult world is entirely infiltrated with unconscious and sexual significations to which *adults themselves* do not have the code. Furthermore, there is the fact that the infant does not possess the physiological or emotional responses corresponding to the sexualised messages it is being offered; in short, the child's means of constituting a substitutive or temporary code are fundamentally inadequate.

What then is seduction, both as a fact of experience and as theory? At the moment, the whole issue is being blown out of all proportion in relation to Freud's correspondence with Fliess, as regards what Freud might or might not have kept silent about or repressed, including the historical facts of seduction with which he was confronted (as much in his self-analysis as in his own early case-histories). Anecdote is one thing, seduction as a structural phenomenon is another. One might even say the one got in the way of the other. What I mean is this: the partial abandonment of the seduction theory in 1897 was perhaps due to Freud's own confusion between the contingency of so-called perverse sexual behaviour on the part of the adult and the generality of the situation of seduction. Freud throws his 'neurotica' overboard when he should perhaps have refined it, in the direction of a fundamental, primal seduction. Later, he was partly to correct his aim by stressing the generality of seduction linked to caring by the mother. However, this is not enough; beyond exciting behaviour, whether perverse or simply naive, one has to look at everyday practice.

Let me quickly return to the example of the breast, with all the extreme, exorbitant importance that it has for psychoanalysis. Now, alongside this efflorescence of the breast – good or bad, given or refused – alongside the omnipresence of the breast among analysts and particularly among child analysts, I would like to emphasise the absence of the erogenous breast, the

---

9 For a further discussion of the terms 'enigmatic signifier', 'enigmatic message' see 'A Short Treatise on the Unconscious' in this volume, p. 91ff.; New Foundations for Psychoanalysis (1987), trans. D. Macey, Oxford: Basil Blackwell, 1989, pp. 44–5, 130–3.

erotic breast from analytical thinking. The breast is a major erogenous zone in women, which cannot fail to function as such in relation to the infant. This breast that feeds but also excites me, that excites me as it excites itself, what does it want of me? What does it want to tell me that it doesn't already know itself? The example of the breast is perhaps only a fable, particularly for the modern child who increasingly has infrequent contact with it. It has the advantage of making clear on what basis the constitution of the first *source-objects*, these interiorised or rather introjected objects, occurs. From the beginning, there is a relation centered on self-preservation, the satisfaction of a major adaptive need (feeding). From the beginning, too, there is the centering on a zone of exchange between the inside and the outside of the body, which is the oral zone, and one can understand why it becomes a point of convergence and fixation of an erogenous sensitivity, without there being any need to attribute to it any particular physiological erectility. From the beginning, too, concomitant with the providing of food (i.e. milk), there is the instrumentality of the breast, which cannot be other than an enigmatic message, charged as it is with a pleasure both unknown to itself and impossible to circumscribe.

In passing, and without lingering on this point, let me take the opportunity of saying something about the theory of 'leaning-on', as put forward, placed on one side, and taken up once more by Freud, then by others such as myself. The theory of leaning-on holds that the sexual drive arises to the extent that it props itself up against (*in Anlehnung an*) the function of self-preservation. This leaning-on takes the form of the fact that both the sexual drive and the function of self-preservation originate at the same place, in relation to the same source, within the same activity, but then object and aim begin to diverge by a movement of gradual splitting, with the object, as you know, undergoing a metonymic type of derivation, i.e. by contiguity, substituting for instance the breast for the milk, and with the aim diverging in metaphorical fashion in relation to the goal of feeding, that is, modelling itself by analogy on incorporation. 'Leaning-on' has currently become a rather overworked term. It has been used to refer to the propping of mind on body, and there has even been talk of counter-propping, and so on. But even taken in the best (i.e. Freudian) sense, learning-on is only an extreme instance of a physiological conception of the sexual drive, one that must be inverted and turned back on itself. It is inconceivable that sexuality should emerge biologically from self-preservation, even were it to be by virtue of a displacement affecting both aim and object. This is the last word in Crusoesque enterprises, by which I mean the attempt to reconstruct the world of culture on the basis of the endogenous resources of the solitary baby Robinson. My formula then is this: the only truth of 'leaning-on' is primal seduction. It is because the adult's gestures of self-preservation are the bearers of sexual messages that are unconscious for the adult and unmasterable by the child that, in the so-called erogenous zones, they produce the movement of splitting and drifting that may lead to auto-erotic activity. But the obligatory vehicle of auto-eroticism, that which stimulates it and brings it into existence, is the intrusion and then repression of the enigmatic signifiers supplied by the adult.

We must return then to primal repression, for it is in one single movement that primal repression splits off from the psyche a primordial unconscious which thereby *becomes* an id, and constitutes the first *source-objects*, which are the sources of the drive. In accordance with the Freudian theory of afterwardsness [*Nach-träglichkeit*], I take primal repression to have at least two phases. The first, passive phase is, so to speak, the implanting, the first inscription of the enigmatic signifiers, without these as yet being repressed. They have a sort of dormant status, which is both internal-external or (as Freud also has it elsewhere) sexual-presexual. The second phase is bound to a reactualisation and reactivation of these signifiers, which are henceforth attacking-internal ones, which the infant must endeavour to bind. It is this endeavour to bind, to symbolise dangerous and traumatic signifiers, that culminates in what Freud calls the infant's theorisation (the infantile sexual theories), and in the partial failure of such symbolisation or theorisation, and by that token in the repression of an unmasterable, uncircum-scribable remainder. These are the presentations-of-the-thing (*représentations de chose*) having become presentations-as-mental-things or thing-like-presentations (*représentation-choses*), which take on an isolated status, outside of communication and signification, in what is called the id.

The drive is therefore neither a mythical entity, nor a biological force, nor a concept lying on the frontier between the mental and the physical. It is the impact on the individual and on the ego of the constant stimulation exerted from the inside by the repressed thing-presentations, which can be described as the source-objects of the drive. As for the relation of the drive to the body and the erogenous zones, far from being conceived by starting from the body, this is the action of the repressed *source-objects* on the body, taking place by way of the ego, which is initially a body-ego, and in which, naturally enough, the erogenous zones become the sites for the precipitation and organisation of fantasies.

A word about the *dualism of the drives*, in order to recall the idea that the dualism here is an articulation, a *dichotomy internal to the sexual drive*. Life-drives and death-drives may be distinguished according to the very nature of their *source-object*. In the death-drive, the object finds itself reduced to a single aspect, unilateral, fragmented, exciting, even destructive. In the life-drive, the object always has unified and totalised aspects, even when it is what is called a part-object, i.e. a part of the body. The result of this is that the *source-objects* of the death-drives and life-drives are ultimately the same; but they are diminished, pared-down so to speak, reduced to indices of excitation in the first case, while in the second the tendency to unify and synthesise may be found in the very presentation of the *source-object*.

I would like to say a few words more about the so-called 'economic' conception, in order to differentiate between the quantitative aspect and the process aspect. First of all, the idea that there is a relatively constant force to the drive remains a plausible postulate, even if it is entirely utopian to want to quantify the force involved. There is nothing different here from the 'demand [. . .] for work' made by 'repressed unconscious prototypes'.[10] If I had to formulate a quasi-metaphysical hypothesis as to the ultimate origin of this force, I would say it is the measure of the difference or disequilibrium between what is symbolisable and what is not in the enigmatic messages supplied to the child. If you will, it is the measure of the quantity of trauma.

Second, in any case, irrespective of any quantifying ambition, the constancy of the pressure of the drive is only approximate, valid for a specific lapse of time. Against the idea that there is an absolute constancy stands the hypothesis that sexual 'energy' is always being generated anew, along the same lines as preside over its original creation.

There is another aspect of the economic model, however, whose importance remains undiminished. This is the distinction between the two modes of functioning, the primary process (so-called free energy) and secondary process (so-called bound energy). It is possible to imagine that the circulation involved – the types of circulation, whether free or bound, whether more or less free and more or less bound – can be conceptualised according to a non-physicalist model, based on what may be called the circulation of meaning or information in communication circuits, with the paradox that one would then also have to refer to the circulation of non-meaning, i.e. the non-symbolised.

Finally, still within the realm of the economic problem, I want to return to the notion that the independent existence of affect and *representation* is postulated by Freud on the basis of indisputable clinical evidence. The idea deserves,

10 *Inhibitions, Symptoms and Anxiety* (1926d), *SE* XX, pp. 159–60.

on the one hand, to be translated into the kind of model of circulation mentioned a moment ago and, on the other, to be modulated according to each specific case. The more qualified an affect is, the less mobile it becomes; the more dequalified it is, the more the process at issue is closer to the primary process. But it is only asymptotically that one can postulate an absolutely unbound discharge (anxiety) or displacement of affect.

I said at the beginning my purpose here was to relate the drive to transference. To do that properly would involve much lengthy discussion, so I shall content myself with indicating the main crux of the argument. Transference, as I conceive it, is characteristic of the analytical situation and of some other specific intersubjective constellations which all have in common the fact that they reproduce and renew the situation of primal seduction. This is the way I interpret Lacan's formula, which is more suggestive than established with precision, of the 'subject supposed to know'. The subject supposed to know, initially, is the adult for the child, so much so that it is possible to say that the primary situation of the drive is a relation both of transcendence and of transference, already: of transcendence on this side of the relation since there is a void in signification or a lack of signified which constitutes the enigmatic character of the adult message; and of transcendence and transference on the other side, since the whole movement of symbolisation consists in adding new signifiers with the purpose of displacing, transposing, and thus binding the most traumatic signifiers. Transference – in the analytic sense of the word – can only be the continuation or resumption of this movement of symbolisation. In that sense, far from being the kind of playing with roles and disillusionment that it is sometimes taken to be, transference may be said to be the reopening of the primal transference, and its fate, in turn, may be said to be nothing other than its capacity to be transferred itself (and this formulation – the transference of the transference – is found in Wilhelm Reich, though probably without it having the same meaning).

I also promised to return to my two initial questions: should the drive be of any *use* at all? and what is the status of theory? Well, the very content of what I have been suggesting offers various avenues of response. First, in relation to the question: 'what use is the drive?', it is impossible to disregard the fact that this sort of question (what use?) is inseparable, in its goal, from an adaptive intent. This aims to adapt a concept to an external goal, however purely technical and value-free this may appear. Does the question 'what use?' have a rightful place in the field of the sexual? Ought one not, before all else, ask *how the drive uses us* and what we can manage to do with it?[11]

As for theory, its status cannot be separated from the function of knowledge and infantile theorisation in the genesis of the psyche (let me recall once more the formulation of 'infantile sexual theories'). This is not in any way to devalue theory, as is often done, by turning it into an avatar of fantasy, while at the same time proceeding to devalue fantasy by seeing it simply as something fictitious, with all the emphasis being put purely on its derealising aspects. If my account is accepted, it follows necessarily that analytical theory, at its most general level (notably the theory of the drive and the *source-object*), should show us how, in what conditions, with what results and what failures, and at what cost, the subject 'theorises' or metabolises the enigmas that are posed to it from the outset by interhuman communication. In a certain manner, analytic theory is in this respect a metatheory in relation to the fundamental theorisation that all human beings carry out: not primarily in order to appropriate Nature, but to bind anxiety in relation to the trauma that is the enigma.

This means that analytic theory can in no way be imposed on, nor even interfere with the process of individual symbolisation as it operates from the beginning and as analytic treatment claims to pursue it. Theory states that there is a strong case for helping the patient to 'theorise' in his or her own terms, with all the elements of his or her individual history that are still in place. The theory of the drive, of a drive having its source in the representation-objects of each individual, is an inducement to maintain analytic theory at a distance from clinical practice and its transferential process.

Translated by Leslie Hill

11 Laplanche's wordplay contrasts *faire de nous* with *faire avec elle*.

4

Implantation, Intromission

We recall an old argument in which Pasche and Renard[1] raised objections, of the most radical kind, to the thought of Melanie Klein. By situating the process of projection at the origin, they said, Klein took up definitively an idealist position. Everything came from the interior; objects, whether good or bad, only emerged, like rabbits or doves, from the magic box of tricks. Their objection is well-founded, but the reason for this was perhaps not clearly seen: a conception of the unconscious as primal, endogenous and ultimately biological, permits no other type of thought in psychoanalysis. We should not forget, too, that the reduction of the unconscious to a biologism of the drive, before it was taken to extremes by Klein (who goes as far as leaving out repression), was first of all Freud's doing.

There is no doubt some advantage, on the other hand, in giving priority to introjection in the play between projection and introjection. Introjection – and its most visible modality, repression – indicates that the subject first takes something inside itself, setting up an unconscious, before constituting through projection a sexual object-world, according to the lines of force emanating from the repressed. I have myself stressed the priority of this process (primal repression) above all others, in the constitution of the psychical subject. The source-object, while it is indeed the 'source', is at the same time primarily an object which has 'fallen down below', been repressed. Lacan, with his

---

1 F. Pasche and M. Renard, 'Réalité de l'objet et point de vue économique', in *Revue française de Psychanalyse,* XX, Octobre–Décembre 1956, no. 4, pp. 517–24.

idea of a primal symbolisation or *Bejahung* (affirmation),[2] was clearly heading in that direction.

Nonetheless, to introject or project, repress, symbolise or affirm are verbs and processes whose subject, both grammatical and real, is 'the subject', the individual himself.

Let us turn to the defence mechanisms and the attempts to account for what is most alien to the subject: psychosis and its surroundings. Freud attempts to outline this 'alienness',[3] in perversion but also in psychosis, with the concept of disavowal (*Verleugnung*); a bit of reality is disavowed, placed in a sort of intermediate zone, where the subject 'knows very well, but all the same . . .'[4] Lacan's effort, with 'foreclosure', is more radical. The 'paternal signifier' is not admitted by the subject into his 'symbolic' world. What is foreclosed from the symbolic, as we know, is supposed to return in the real. . . .

There too, however, disavowing or foreclosing entails an *act*, that of an *indestructible* subject.[5] In order to disavow or foreclose, for all the somewhat too easy declaration that 'he wishes to know nothing about it', our subject, Jacques, Anatole or Sigmund, must indeed know or at least apprehend something of what he is going to expel, however radical that expulsion is supposed to be. From projection to disavowal, from disavowal to foreclosure, psychoanalysis, an illusionist caught in his own trap, exhausts itself striving to believe that the rabbit pulled out of the hat, 'returns in the real'.

It is too commonly ignored that Aristarchus of Samos, in the third century B.C., discovered heliocentrism.[6] The ignorance of this continued up to the work of Copernicus, whose 'revolution' was only a rediscovery, a resurgence

2 Several references, notably, 'On a question preliminary to any possible treatment of psychosis' (1955–6), in *Écrits: A Selection*, trans. Alan Sheridan, London: Tavistock, 1977, pp. 200–1.
3 'étrangeté'. Elsewhere Laplanche's neologism 'étrangèreté' has been translated 'alien-ness'. See 'The Unfinished Copernican Revolution' in this volume, p. 62 n. 21.
4 Octave Mannoni, 'Je sais bien, mais quand même . . .', in *Clefs pour l'imaginaire de l'autre scène*, Paris: Seuil, 1969.
5 Laplanche is alluding to a formulation of Lacan in his critique of the notion of projection: 'this same indestructible *percipiens*' (*le même percipiens increvable*), in *Écrits: A Selection*, op. cit., p. 187.
6 We are also indebted to him for his unprecedented efforts to measure the distances between the earth and the moon, the earth and the sun, and the diameters of the moon and the sun. This priority of Aristarchus over Copernicus was certainly drawn to Freud's attention.

after a long period of scotomisation.[7] When Freud speaks of the three blows or major humiliations inflicted by science on human narcissism,[8] he adds to the cosmological humiliation due to Copernicus (the earth is no longer the center of the universe) and the biological humiliation brought by Darwin (man is no longer sovereign of the animal kingdom), the psychological humiliation due to Freud himself (the ego is no longer 'master in its own house').

Yet this was an imperfect, unfinished revolution which Freud himself put at risk. For if the individual is henceforth governed, in classical psychoanalytic theory, by the unknown drives of the unconscious, this 'id' – however strange it is supposed to be – is nonetheless not an alien. It is supposed to dwell *at the center* of the individual,[9] whom it governs in its own way, even if it has dethroned the ego. One sovereign in place of another, but well and truly installed in the keep of the castle.

To project, to introject, to identify, to disavow, to foreclose etc. – all the verbs used by analytic theory to describe psychical processes share the feature of having as subject the individual in question: *I* project, *I* disavow, *I* foreclose, etc.[10] What has been scotomised, as in the case of Aristarchus? Quite simply, the discovery that *the process originally comes from the other*. Processes in which the individual takes an *active* part are all secondary in relation to the originary moment, which is that of a passivity: that of seduction.

---

7 It is probable that Copernicus knew the works of Aristarchus.

8 'A Difficulty in the Path of Psycho-analysis' (1917a), *SE* XVII, p. 137.

9 This centered, concentric conception of the human being is testified to many times in Freud. Thus, among others, this stupefying formulation – that the unconscious sends out 'from the interior', towards the external world, 'through the medium of the system Pcpt.-Cs', some kind of retractible antennae, characteristic of perceptual functioning. This sort of unconscious no longer has anything to do with the repressed, nor therefore with the unconscious discovered by analysis. Cf. 'A Note upon the "Mystic Writing Pad"' (1925a, *SE* XIX, pp. 225–32).

10 Or indeed – Anatole projects, Anatole disavows, etc. My distinction is not between the first and the third person (a distinction dear to the personalists and to Politzer), but between oneself and the other.

Autocentrism, to coin this term, has made (almost immediately) a powerful return; it has imposed its hegemony over the whole of metapsychology, the clinical and the practical. There has been a return of the old philosophy of the subject (spiced up with a biological, or eventually a phenomenological, dressing),[11] after the timid 'Aristarchan' opening of 1895–7. At that point, Freud seemed about to dethrone 'Anatole' from his original active status. Sexuality came to him from the other, was implanted in him by the other. A fugitive moment. . . .

We propose to give a full place, in metapsychology, to processes irreducible to an autocentrism: those whose subject is quite simply the other. Not the metaphysical Other or some 'little other' (Lacan), but the other of originary seduction, first of all the adult other. Central among such processes is *implantation*. By this I wish to indicate that the signifiers brought by the adult are fixed, as onto a surface, in the psychophysiological 'skin' of a subject in which the unconscious agency is not yet differentiated. It is these signifiers, received passively, that are the object of the first active attempts at translation, residues of which are the primally repressed (the source-objects). Here, I refer back to *New Foundations for Psychoanalysis*.[12]

Implantation is a process which is common, everyday, normal or neurotic. Beside it, as its violent variant, a place must be given to *intromission*. While implantation allows the individual to take things up actively, at once translating and repressing, one must try to conceive of a process which blocks this, short-circuits the differentiation of the agencies in the process of their formation, and puts into the interior an element resistant to all metabolisation.

I have no doubt that a process related to intromission also has its role in the formation of the *superego*, a foreign body that cannot be metabolised.

However great the opposition between the classical 'autocentred' processes and those 'allogenic' ones introduced here, it will have been noticed that all take as their model well-known *bodily processes*, bringing into play the volume of

11 Just as empty as the efforts, mentioned above, to make an 'alien' or absolute 'alienness' emerge from the interior, would be the elaborations of the late Husserl, and his poignant search for a 'synthesis' or a 'passive constitution' of the object.
12 Trans. David Macey, Oxford: Basil Blackwell, 1989, schema on p. 135. What is described in the *Fort-da* game could be used as an example here: the signifier implanted there is the absence of the father or the mother; it is taken up actively by the child, in the translation of the *Fort-da* game.

the body, its skin-envelope and its orifices. Intromission relates principally to anality and orality. Implantation refers, rather, to the surface of the body as a whole, its perceptive periphery.

Translated by Luke Thurston

5

Interpretation between Determinism and Hermeneutics: a Restatement of the Problem

The debate about interpretation in psychoanalysis is not of recent origin and it is by no means over. Ricoeur's great book, *Freud and Philosophy* (1965), represents an important stage in this controversy. The significance of this work, whose impact can still be felt today, should not be underestimated; it is one of the few to have truly overcome the language barriers to the spread of French psychoanalytic ideas, and also one of the few to be constantly quoted as a major philosophical disquisition on psychoanalysis.

It is no detraction from this monumental, profound work to say that it offers, not a prospect that extends beyond Freud, but an attempt to reconcile Freudianism with substantially earlier conceptions. More precisley, it marks a resurgence of the centuries- if not millennia-old classical tradition of hermeneutics at the very center of the Freudian problematic of interpretation. A resurgence it may be, but it is not the first incursion of hermeneutics into psychoanalysis – that first incursion dates explicitly from Jung and Silberer and can, in its simplest terms, be accommodated under the banner of 'anagogic' interpretation, a form which is not content to describe what is or has been but denotes 'a state or process which is to be lived'. More than one passage in Ricoeur could be adduced in support of such a line of descent, which does not, in my sense, imply any disapprobation. While I am not claiming that Ricoeur's influence has been decisive in every respect, it may be convenient to regard the current debate as being conducted so to speak in a 'post-Ricoeur' situation.

In France, particular importance attaches to the discussion that has arisen concerning the writings and theses of Viderman, a discussion that ended on a sustained note with the colloquium organized by the Paris Psychoanalytical

Society, published in 1974 under the title 'Constructions and reconstructions in psychoanalysis'.

The debate in other countries has been no less keen, even if it has been relatively disconnected from French psychoanalysis. A good example is the book by Spence (1982), the foreword to which by Robert S. Wallerstein (President of the IPA) is indicative of the capacity to call received ideas into question; further examples among many others are the textbook by Thomä & Kächele (1988), which explicity places itself in the hermeneutic line, and, from another point of view, the entire work of Roy Schafer.

All these questionings of the conventional theory of analytic interpretation exhibit a subtly differentiated range of viewpoints. In particular, the challenge from the English-language authors is characterized by a radical critique of metapsychological thought as a whole, and is based on a theory of propositions and narrativity derived from the 'philosophy of logical analysis', which remains quite alien to French thought.

Ultimately, however, although the various protagonists' starting points and philosophico-epistemological foundations differ, we are left with two positions, nicely summed up by the antithetical terms of *reconstruction* and *construction*.

The first is a 'realistic' standpoint, which claims that neurosis is a 'disease of memory' and that only the recovery of the subject's *real* history (whether by a lifting of infantile amnesia or by a reconstruction) can allow the ego to detach itself from blind mechanisms and achieve some degree of freedom.[1]

The second position is a 'creative hermeneutic' one, taking cognizance of the fact that every object is *constructed* by my aim and that the historical object cannot escape this relativism. The psychoanalytic approach to an individual's past cannot constitute an exception to this rule: there are no crude facts: 'there is no experience but that which is inquired into'. It is in this precise sense that Viderman speaks of the interpretation's invention and creativity. Ultimately,

---

1 Thus Viderman summarizes 'the historicist conception and its justifying postulate, that of determinism' as follows: 'In Freud, neurosis was a disease of memory; and the recovery of the subject's history, the re-establishment of a historical pattern broken by the effect of defences, followed by reintegration into a consciousness which had lost essentially traumatic memories or guilty wishes, were required to prove by the effect of interpretational construction that access to the totality of the significant history is not only possible but also within the reach of psychoanalytic technique, and that once this task has been accomplished, we have completed the *restitutio ad integrum* that is the fundamental aim of analytic treatment' (Viderman, 1974, p. 350).

the approach of the psychoanalyst should not differ greatly from that of any scholar: he confronts the data, dreams, memories and associations with the aid of preconceptions without which he would simply see nothing at all. Never mind what Leonardo saw or said: 'What matters is that the analyst, without regard to reality, adjusts and assembles these materials to construct a coherent whole which does not reproduce a fantasy pre-existent in the subject's unconscious but causes it to exist by telling it' (Viderman, 1970, p. 164).[2] Analytic interpretation should then finally remember that it is *sovereign*, because any past is determined from my present, or even from my future, my pro-ject.

To intervene in a debate is, if possible, to cause another voice to be heard – not a conciliatory voice, nor yet a voice that embraces one of the positions against the other, but the voice of a third party.

However, as a measure of the temerity of my argument, I should like to point out that both of these voices are equally entitled to claim kinship in one way or another with Freud. They are, for example, the two alternating attitudes that lie behind the successive versions, the second thoughts, of the case-history of the 'Wolf Man'. One is the search for factual, detailed, chronological truth about the primal scene, while the other, at a stroke wholeheartedly embracing Jung's objections and abandoning almost all of the reality so painstakingly reconstructed, admits that all this may be nothing but retroactive fantasy, with only a few clues, if that, as foundation; but it must be added that for Freud such a fantasy in turn finds its full justification only in the

---

2 Such deliberately provocative formulations were bound to call down on Viderman the qualification of analyst-as-demiurge, if not the charge of so being. However, his reply or defence, the second stage of his argument, may well surprise: the analyst's interpretation, while it must be 'inventive', 'plural' and often even 'arbitrary', is nonetheless definitely guided by the hypothesis of a primordial biological id and innate primal schemata or fantasies: 'It is upon the deep, fundamental form of the primal fantasy that the modulations of the events which singularize the subject's history and which historicize him act'. Thus, in Ricoeur's rather than Viderman's terms, the *telos* of the interpretation is not arbitrary but in effect coincides with what consitutes each individual's *arche*: his primordial, hereditary and – why not? – phylogenetic id. Whatever he may say, Viderman is therefore contrasting one Freud with another, a Freud-as-historian with a Freud who could be described as a Kantian, in that he postulates *a priori* categories, the common heritage of all men which regulates their apprehension, their 'construction', of the real. And indeed, if the primal fantasies are so to speak the entities that control the whole of the subject's imagination, why should they not also, as it were homothetically, guide the 'poietic' activity of the analyst?

existence of phylogenetic schemata, tantamount to categories which *a priori* inform every individual experience.[3]

How then are we to proceed, confronted as we are with two positions which at first sight appear equally Freudian? If we claim that the debate is spurious, we are so to speak trying to show that Freud himself became trapped in it, even if we have to go back with him to the point where he begins to go astray. To do this, however, we must at least specify what the trap is.

In simple terms, *the major illusion here is the comparison with the historians, historiography.* Rather than a comparison, it is an attempt to apply to psychoanalysis an epistemological model that belongs to an entirely different field.

And it is indeed the historian's history, historiography, that is constantly appealed to as a witness in this debate – whether it is rejected in its classical form as doomed to reflect a purely factual truth (Spence's 'historical truth'), or whether we follow Viderman in embracing a modern historiography which has succeeded in going beyond a naive realism and draw all the consquences of the fact that the historical object, like any other, is constructed.

I am therefore unavoidably compelled to embark on a brief, non-specialized digression exploring the collective history of mankind. Before – radically, as we shall see – questioning the relevance of this paradigm to our discipline, I must say a few words about it.

What is forcing history to redefine itself is first and foremost the new awareness on the part of historians of the relativism of their science. It is not the absolute of the historians of the past, whether providentialists or positivists, but the product of a situation, of a history. This singularity of a science which has only one term for both its object and itself, which swings between history as lived and history as constructed, undergone and manufactured, compels historians, now that they are conscious of this original

---

3 When Pontalis and myself rescued 'primal fantasies' from the total oblivion into which they had fallen in the analytical community, we certainly had no idea of the grandiose fate that was in store for them, in particular in the French analytical community. Such is the destiny of the exegete or the critic: because we rediscovered this concept and demonstrated its importance in the Freudian system, we virtually of necessity became its champions. Twenty-five years later, people are dumbfounded and incredulous when I affirm my steadfast opposition to the fable of fantasies transmitted phylogenetically from the father of the primal horde.

relationship, to inquire again into the epistemological foundations of their discipline.

(Le Goff & Nora, 1974, vol. I, p. X)

This ambiguity can be illustrated by apportioning it – but is this always so easy? – between history that happens, the history that is narrated, and history as a discipline, or historiography. Historical positivism – which is perhaps somewhat too hastily caricatured and stigmatized – may be said to aim, in its naive realism, at a seamless reproduction of 'the history that happens' in historiography. Leopold von Ranke's oft-quoted, notorious statement that the historian should merely show 'what really happened' has become virtually a scapegoat of the epistemology of history. Let us only recall two major stages in this criticism, at least in France: Aron on the one hand and the Ecole des Annales on the other.[4]

Aron's *Introduction to the Philosophy of History* (1938) presents a radical critique of positivism. Whereas the philosopher's proclaimed intention is to stake out the limits and to find an acceptable position between a naive realism of the object and an absolute relativism, the main onslaught is against positivism, with the result that relativism in fact appears to prevail totally. Years later, Aron himself reacted against this, describing his old position, as it were in a new swing of the pendulum, as speculative and vigorously opposing the easy approaches of 'perspectivism': 'In Parisian circles the formula "there are no facts" is totally in favour. Of course, I know that in a sense this formula is true: there are no facts that are not constructed . . . but ultimately, I am at times tempted to act the philistine'.[5]

While the 'dissolution of the object' proclaimed for a moment by Aron may have opened the way to the most subjectivistic interpretations and, at the limit, to the negation of all historical knowledge, the French school known as *la nouvelle histoire*, or the École des Annales, adopts a very different approach: its protagonists, as practitioners of the 'historian's profession', take as their

---

4 On this point as on many others, see Ricoeur's valuable study (Ricoeur, 1983–5) – in particular, volume I.

5 Aron, 1968, p. 124 (quoted by Sylvie Mesure on p. viii of the 1986 edition of Aron, 1938). Where historical relativism is accorded a definite place, nothing can stop it. Thus, in a way, certain formulae from the 'Introduction' could be wielded to justify the negation of the 'fact' of the gas chambers by an author such as Faurisson, or Maître Verges's relativization of the massacres of the Khmers Rouges. This is a use of relativism which Raymond Aron would, of course, have scorned.

starting point this practice and the 'new techniques' offered by modern investigative methods, to define 'new objects', correlative with 'new approaches'. These new approaches do indeed go hand in hand with a critique of conventionally accepted objects; this critique is levelled at the two traditional 'atoms' of conventional history: on the one hand, the historical individual and, in particular, the great man (to whom Freud devotes a chapter in his book on Moses), and, on the other, the 'event'. However, their place is taken by new objects, which are no less credible or scientific for being constructed: 'long-term' history, sometimes extending to a history of climates, a history of social facts, up to and including a history of festivals, a history of mentalities, and even a history of death or a history of institutions, rather than of political facts; conversely, on the particular level, there are monographs on objects from which the individual is deliberately ousted from the central position: for instance, the famous 'Montaillou, a village in the *Occitan* region' usurps the 'history of the reign of Louis XIV' or the 'history of battles', of which the notorious 'Battle of Marignan in 1515' has become the paradigmatic object of derision.

However, beyond the espousal of positions that is essential to any innovation, what we are witnessing is an enrichment and not an arbitrary selection. Even this history of prominent figures emerges renewed rather than abolished by the intersecting approaches which here overlap. The event itself is rehabilitated when it is seen that, before it becomes an arbitrary creation of the chroniclers, it is constituted as such, at the very moment when it is lived. Not only elaborations improvised 'hot' but also successive re-elaborations form part of the historical object, and from this point of view we may agree with Pierre Nora (Ricoeur, 1983, vol. 1, pp. 210–28) that we are seeing 'a return of the event', albeit in completely renovated form, which attempts to take account simultaneously of the three aspects of the word 'history' which make up its entire specificity: history that happens, history that is narrated and the history of the historian. Such a synthesis may be possible or impossible – for example, one that aims to give an overall view of the history of the Vichy regime and of the history of the memory of the Vichy regime (cf. Rousso, 1987).

Can psychoanalysis take a historiography of this kind, which has undergone a profound renewal, as its inspiration? Or, conversely, might it be a fallacious model for our discipline – fallacious where it reduces Freud's search to a quest for a historical truth which would be that of the conventional historians (according to von Ranke's notorious formula: the event 'as it really happened')? However, the model would *also* be fallacious in attempting to set up against this positivism a pure construction of the historical object which would be valid for the psychoanalytic construction too.

As an indication of my meaning, I shall pause for a moment, as if at two *signs or clues*, at two paradoxical points where (so to speak) psychoanalysis and historiography run counter to each other.

The first point is *determinism*. Here I should like only to note that historians (whether 'old-fashioned' or 'modern') never make deterministic demands as rigorous as those in the psychoanalytic debate in the matter of the so called predictability of the present from the past. If determinism does exist for modern historiography, as well as, probably, for the vast majority of historians of the past, it can only amount to correlations valid for precise sequences, for short 'items' capable of being repeated; or, alternatively, in a completely different dimension, to long-term correlations, the actual events being made dependent on other factors such as, for example, geography, economics or even climate change.

Now it is really odd to see psychoanalysts fighting, pro or contra, over a conception of historical determinism which has never been that of the histor-ians, and which invokes as its authority, in particular, Pascal's excursion on . . . the length of Cleopatra's nose. But this singularity of the deterministic demand among the psychoanalysts is not a quirk, but is one of the most important documents in our case. We are entitled to wonder whether it has not been grafted, transposed, on to the diachronic sequence from the observation that is the daily stuff of psychoanalysis, that the length of Cleopatra's nose . . . may really be the strict determining *cause* of a symptom.

Its cause is by no means its law. It does not establish constant relations between phenomena but simply, almost magically or mechanically, exerts its effect. In this sense, it has been well and truly ousted from all sciences, including history, in favour of the establishment of correlations capable of being formulated as a function. Yet I should like to suggest that with psychoanalysis, the cause, however old-fashioned and archaic, has in effect rediscovered its true home in the deep sense in which metapsychology is the *repatriation* of metaphysics.

Perhaps *archaeology* has suffered the same fate as the concept of the cause: after some ill-treatment in certain quarters, we may wonder whether it does not assume a deeper sense again in psychoanalysis.

While modern history may in a way be regarded as a broadening, a perfecting or even a fulfilment of the historiography of all times, and while someone like Leroi Ladurie is not ashamed of his kinship with Thucydides or even Michelet, modern archaeology certainly tolls the death knell for its classical predecessor.

Archaeology has at least three ancestors, but, it might be said, it strongly repudiates this line of descent. The first ancestor is the lover of art and curiosities, the 'antiquary' in search of beautiful or curious objects: in this sense, Hadrian was already an 'antiquary', an enlightened collector. The second origin of archaeology is the traveller. Archaeology discovered its objects and sites in the great 'journeys' of the seventeenth, eighteenth and nineteenth centuries and in their painstaking and irreplaceable descriptions of monuments. And what is the third ancestor of the archaeologist? Well, it is something less commendable: the robber of graves and monuments.[6]

In any case, what our three characters, the traveller, the robber and the art lover, have in common is without any doubt love of *the object for itself*, an object which is at one and the same time beautiful, strange and lucrative. It is the search for the emotion connected with the object unearthed from the past, be it intact or partially reconstituted.

The whole of modern archaeology contrasts totally with this archaeology in search of the object or the city, an activity nowadays denounced as 'approximate' (Leroi Gourhan), or, even more often, roundly condemned as having irrevocably ruined important excavation sites.

Modern archaeology, for its part, is also aware that excavation constitutes irreparable destruction, but, in a sense, considers that it does not matter, once the essential has been extracted from the site: 'An archaeological stratum is like a book of which each page is destroyed as we read it, and which it must be possible to reconstitute later' (Duval, 1961, p. 226). Excavation is thus necessary destruction; it is irremediable, but, at the same time, it must endeavour to preserve each stratum by a variety of different means (photographs, samples, analyses, card indexes, diagrams, etc.). But if methodical destruction is now coextensive with the work of the archaeologist, this is because he now seeks something other than material objects or even ruins: the search for connections, relations, has become more important than that for

---

6 However, it would be wrong to be over-fastidious by accepting only the first two, the traveller and the art lover, because all three are interdependent. The art lover has always obtained his supplies from the grave robber, and sometimes the traveller is all three in one: traveller, art lover and pillager. For instance, Lord Elgin completely stripped the Parthenon of its famous sculptures and took them away to the British Museum. Was this action harmful? We may still ask ourselves this question today when we see the destruction wrought in Athens by modern pollution. Might he not be said to have rescued the representations of the Panathenaea?

objects. We can say no more than that modern archaeology has become a mere service activity, a technique in thrall to the prehistorians or historians and subordinated to their aims: the most complete documentation, the tidiest possible indexing of human phenomena.[7]

Archaeology's sole value henceforth is through the mosaics of *historical* correlations which it helps to make more explicit. Its objects are now mere bundles of relations and techniques. The moment when they are reassembled, reconstituted and displayed is just a concession to popularization or, if it is preferred, to education.

Let us go into any archaeological exhibition. Ah! What we see is no longer the incredible Capernaum of the old Cairo Museum, still less the artistic jumble of the 'curiosity cabinet' of old, specifically designed to stimulate desire and to arouse wonder. Now, before we encounter the slightest object, we are assailed by huge panels bursting with maps, charts and diagrams, telling us all about population migrations, changes in customs and living conditions and the evolution of techniques. The vase or statue is meaningful only when 'didacticized', placed in relation, set in the context of the invention of the potter's wheel and the clay or tin trade. Held captive by the wish to learn, I am absorbed in the reading of one of these panels, from which I am only torn away when my wife impatiently exclaims: 'Just look at this extraordinary horse!'

Exhibition organizers are well aware of this temptation, and ultimately they always yield to it, while inwardly regretting their demagogy. For this entire route, so well signposted by historical reason, is in fact completely 'magnetized' by one thing: the wonderful object of the exhibition. This unique object, isolated (and in this sense genuinely *archaeological*), displayed in a casket of light and, preferably, in a separate sanctuary draped in black velvet, this object usually made of an indestructible material, this gold object that constitutes the main draw of the posters (the gold of the Scythians, the gold of the Celts or the gold of the Incas), this timeless object – having journeyed through centuries and millennia to address itself direct to us – this mask of Agamemnon, what

7 The two recent excavation sites in the two courtyards of the Louvre illustrate this antithesis, both of methods and between those implementing them: in the Cour Carrée, traditional archaeology for a moment regained its splendour, in unearthing the magnificent palace of Philippe Auguste and the helmet of Charles VI. By contrast, in the Cour Napoléon III, a *chantier du President* par excellence, the daily life, craft techniques and socio-economic relations of olden times were documented by painstaking work with the scraper and brush, chemical analysis and photography.

does it want from me? *Che vuoi?* to quote Lacan quoting Cazotte. This comeback, this return (a *Wiederkehr* which is perhaps also a *Heimkehr*) of archaeology will be one of the guiding threads in my examination of Freud.

Putting Freud to work, or, in other words, 'interpreting Freud with Freud' (Laplanche, 1968a), does not mean trying to find a lesson in him – still less an orthodoxy. Nor is it a matter of choosing one Freud against another, or of 'fishing' here and there for a formulation which suits me. Putting Freud to work means demonstrating in him what I call an *exigency*, the exigency of a discovery which impels him without always showing him the way, and which may therefore lead him into dead ends or goings-astray. It means following in his footsteps, accompanying him but also criticizing him, seeking other ways – but impelled by an exigency similar to his.

To put it in more colloquial terms, what is it that makes Freud tick? My answer, my proposition, is this: *it is not history*. Or, to be less provocative, it is something that has nothing to do with the history of the historiographers.

On this route, I shall spare myself two detours, at least for the purposes of this paper. The first, which might be dubbed 'Freudological', would have examined in detail Freud's positions on the history of societies – on historiography.[8] The second detour would have been a point-by-point comparison, showing the resemblances and differences between, and the possible transpositions of, the historiography of societies, with that of human individuals. However interesting it might be, such a comparison – which would be somewhat academic – would miss the essential point: what Freud is aiming at is not, transposed to the individual level, a life history or biography; nowhere in Freud is such a life history to be found, in any sense of the term – either a history of events or a history of the Ernest Jones type ('life and work'), or even a history tinged with psychoanalysis. He admittedly often applies the word history (*Geschichte*) to the individual, but the word *Lebensgeschichte* (life history or biography) is usually relegated to a subordinate position after the history of the disease or of the patient (*Krankheitsgeschichte* – *Krankengeschichte*). His 'historical' bravura piece, which still calls forth commentaries from the psychoanalytic community, is entitled: 'From the history of an infantile neurosis'. The word 'history' is

8 Among many others, the repeated reference to Livy's distortion of the Rome of the kings would show that Freud was no stranger to a relativistic questioning of historical objectivity – a questioning which antedates Raymond Aron's thesis by many years.

certainly there, but accompanied oddly by the words *infantile* and *neurosis* and, even more strangely, preceded by '*aus*': 'from' or 'out of'.

When I reread the definition imposed by Viderman as a demand on the orthodox Freudian thesis which he opposes – 'restoration of the continuity of a broken historical pattern . . . reintegration of lost memories . . . access to the totality of the significant history, etc.' – I tell myself (and Viderman would, of course, agree) that this is not what Freud succeeds in achieving; contrary to Viderman, however, I claim that it was also not Freud's profound aim, even in the apparently 'historiographical' work on 'the Wolf Man'. What he is aiming at is a kind of history of the unconscious, or rather of its genesis; a history with discontinuities, in which the moments of burial and resurgence are the most important of all; a history, it might be said, of repression, in which the subterranean currents are described in as much detail as, if not in more detail than, the manifest character traits. Is this an account of events? It would be paradoxical to deny that moments in time, situated and dated, constitute essential reference points in the investigation. But what are these 'events', which mark the transition from one age to another? Let us quote a passage on one of the most important:

> The date of this transformation can be stated with certainty; it was immediately before his fourth birthday. . . . But the event which makes this division possible was not an external trauma, but a dream. . . .
>
> (Freud, 1918b, p. 28)

What a strange history of events, in which one of the turning-points is a purely internal event!

But, I will be told, you are denying the obvious! What could be more obvious throughout this paper of Freud's than the almost forensic search, exploiting the slightest clue, for a primal scene which (in von Ranke's terms) 'actually happened' (*eigentlich geschehen*). However, since this statement is generally associated with the most decisive arguments of the commentators to show that the scene could neither have happened nor have been observed, and that it could not have been consigned to memory in this way, how can we fail to see this combination – imposition of a maximum positivist demand on Freud/proof of its minimum satisfaction – as a way of stifling Freud once and for all in the straitjacket of his realistic postulate?

The reference to a so-called Freudian orthodoxy seems to me here, as often, to be a trap: either it is adhered to blindly or else, more subtly, it is invoked in order to incarcerate Freud in it and condemn him. Our position should be one beyond, or rather short of, orthodoxy – specifically, in an interpretation of a large number of clues, incoherences, breaks, minor details, etc., which contradict the overall picture but, in accordance with our analytic method, trace out as many convergent tracks. To return again to von Ranke's term, which at the end of the day suits me well – *eigentlich*: 'actually' or 'in actual fact' – what Freud is seeking 'in actual fact' is not what 'actually happened', in the sense of the crude event or, as Raymond Aron put it, of the elusive 'John Lackland went that way'.

Among a thousand other clues in 'the Wolf Man' case is the fact (already mentioned) that he suddenly considers that the reality of the primal scene as an event can be 99 per cent swept away without *any* change in its traumatic effect; a mere mating of dogs is enough. Another clue is the statement that the relevant intercourse was 'three times repeated' . . .: what would be an actual memory of an event three times repeated if not the memory of a sequence of three events: 'John Lackland went that way on 9 April, and then on 10 May, and then on 15 August'? Here, however, in the primal scene 'reconstructed' by Freud, the 'three times' *is included in the content* as a detail among others. Surely this is what happens, for instance, in the logic of the dream, in which the 'three times', like any other comment on the account ('that is not clear' – 'that happens again and again', etc.), is to be taken as a part of the content and not as a characteristic extrinsic to the dream.

We are plainly shifting from the factual event to something other than that. However, I do not wish to move on too directly to the 'fantasy' because I am very well aware that, not finding its reason within itself, the fantasy would in turn be liable to lead us on to the archetypal – i.e. to an atavistic experience. Let us therefore say, more modestly, that we are moving from the *event* to the *scene*.

Event or scene: how are we to distinguish between them? Perhaps by the ways in which they are recorded, which we are too quick to combine under the single heading of a memory or the faculty of memory: conscious-preconscious on the one hand and unconscious on the other.

Here again, regarding memory, Freud is not unequivocal. His theory of memory, where it approaches a psychology of fixation, reshaping and evocation, is highly credible, as in the following quotation from 'Screen memories': 'It may indeed be questioned whether we have any memories at all *from* our childhood: memories *relating* to our childhood may be all that we possess' (Freud, 1899, p. 322).

So much for conscious memory. In contrast with this genuine but fairly trivial relativism, we may recall the grandiose image from *Civilization and its Discontents* (1930a). In mental life, Freud tells us, 'nothing which has once been

149

formed can perish'. His well-known metaphor is that of an archaeological site, Ancient Rome, but it is chosen precisely to demonstrate the difference from real archaeology. In the Eternal City (the epithet is used not without irony), every new construction has obviously necessitated a prior destruction. The archaeological strata do not coexist in the intact state but only abraded, reduced to the condition of mere foundations. It is impossible to construct a monument without having in practice destroyed all the superstructures of what preceded it. However, the opposite is the case in that hyperarchaeological site that is a human being:

> Now let us, by a flight of imagination, suppose that Rome is not a human habitation but a psychical entity with a similarly long and copious past – an entity, that is to say, in which nothing that has once come into existence will have passed away and all the earlier phases of development continue to exist alongside the latest one. This would mean that in Rome the palaces of the Caesars and the Septizonium of Septimius Severus would still be rising to their old height on the Palatine. . . . But more than this. In the place occupied by the Palazzo Caffarelli would once more stand – without the Palazzo having to be removed – the Temple of Jupiter Capitolinus; and this not only in its latest shape, as the Romans of the Empire saw it, but also in its earliest one, when it still showed Etruscan forms. . . . On the Piazza of the Pantheon we should find not only the Pantheon of today, as it was bequeathed to us by Hadrian, but, on the same site, the original edifice erected by Agrippa; indeed, the same piece of ground would be supporting the church of Santa Maria sopra Minerva and the ancient temple over which it was built.
>
> (Freud, 1930a, p. 70)

Two conceptions of 'memory', one historical and the other archaeological – one conscious-preconscious and the other unconscious: that is quickly said. But let us take a closer look.

This image of Rome, in which time is developed like a fourth dimension of space, could be made plausible as follows: an observer is looking at Rome from a distance of 2,700 light-years from Earth. What he sees is the Rome of Romulus, whose image reaches him at that instant. At the same time, carried by a continuous train of light waves, he receives the successive images of the same city, the combination of which really does constitute the kind of four-dimensional hologram described by Freud. The observer need only move along this hologram ('change the direction of his glance or his position', as Freud says), to concentrate on a particular image, monument or epoch.

150

Why do I find this rationalization only half-satisfying? It is because, in our train of waves travelling between Earth and Sirius, we shall never find this or that monument, taken in isolation and finished once and for all, but instead *all* stages, in each second, of its construction and destruction. Freud's image of unconscious memory therefore becomes strangely unrealistic compared with our physical model: it is neither a reshaping of living, conscious-preconscious memory nor a complete hologram of everything experienced (which would be an absolute jumble), but a succession and superimposition of fixed images, independent of each other; as Freud says of the unconscious, '[c]ontrary impulses exist side by side, without cancelling each other out or diminishing each other' (1933a, p. 73).

The imperceptible stages, the moments of transition, are abolished here, in favour of a succession of fixed archetypes, each forming a whole. To paraphrase what we said about the Wolf Man's 'three times', the 'three years' it took to build Nero's Domus Aurea are not represented by the memory of three years of works constituting a time sequence, but become a characteristic inherent in the Domus Aurea itself, in its representational content: 'The Domus Aurea, which was built in three years'.

It is therefore an odd coexistence, made up of fixity and manipulation, of veracity and artifice, that characterizes the singular archaeological field in which the 'psychical object' is considered to be preserved. We have no wish to deny that Freud sees in this a paradigm of memory, and the text of 'Constructions in analysis' does indeed begin under the combined banner of memory and archaeology. However, the addition of the word 'unconscious' — 'unconscious memory' — here changes everything, because what is then meant is not a trivial memorization, and not the trivial reshapings of memories by subsequent experiences, social contexts, ageing, etc. What is involved here is a psychical phenomenon which is at one and the same time a cataclysm (like the engulfment of Pompeii) and a permanent preservation (like the burial of Tutankhamen's objects in his tomb).

Hence the image of archaeology, which dogs every psychoanalyst just as it dogged Freud from the letters to Fliess until his very last day, has by no means yet given up all its truth. If, like Suzanne Bernfeld (1951), we associate this 'dogging' with nostalgia for the golden age in Freiberg, with the wish for the intact object represented by the eternally young and beautiful mother, and with an atheistic sublimation of the infantile belief in immortality, we are surely magnifying one aspect out of all proportion, while invoking causes that exist in

151

all human beings while most are heedless of the archaeological object, which, in fact, they blithely destroy in working their fields or building their motorways.

This Freudian archaeology ought to be described as *hyperarchaeological* or *hyperrealistic* – being even more fascinated by the *object* than was the archaeology of former days. It is an object which is not merely a thing but which contains within itself the phases of its construction, the affects to which it gave rise, and presumably even more, as we are beginning to suspect. It is an archaeology which is not subordinated to history, as modern science would have it, but which subordinates history solely to the revivifying of the object. So it is with Schliemann, Freud's hero and model: his entire knowledge of history – the poetic history of the Iliad or the history of the ancient historians – is used to one single end: the patient identification on the ground of the co-ordinates of the precise point to dig in order to unearth Troy.

This was an exciting model for Freud, and constitutes a major clue among others. Perhaps it is another sign, another line of association, to note his preference, in the matter of this unconscious preservation, for the term 'trace': traces in the memory (*Gedächtnisspuren*) or mnemic traces (*Erinnerungsspuren*), as if the important thing were not memorization itself but the trace – which is so to speak secondary – left by the memory, and in fact the result of repression.

The term 'reminiscence' is equally evocative, even if no further notice was ultimately taken of it. It is, of course, a term that goes back to Plato, and may still signify a kind of memory – but a memory cut off from its origins and from its access routes, isolated and fixed, reduced to a trace. It is a trace which is not on that account necessarily more *false*, but which contains a 'kernel of truth' that is more essential than the trivial conscious memory.

We can now gauge the gulf between the formula that 'the hysteric suffers from reminiscences' and Viderman's statement that neurosis (in Freud) is a 'disease of memory'. The unconscious, if the reader is prepared to follow us, is *not* memory; repression is not a particular modality of memorizing. Repression – cataclysm and burial in the unconscious – is as different from memorization as the engulfment of Pompeii is from Joinville's Chronicle of the Seventh Crusade of Louis IX, perhaps even more different. This is why we hazard the term 'hyperarchaeology', even if we must then discover in this the deep roots of our fascination for archaeology.

Hyperarchaeology = *hyperreality*. This is the locus of another demand – and another aporia – of Freud's search, the one called 'psychical reality'.

Let us state the problem from the outset: the existence, the postulate, of a third domain, which is not material, factual, perceptual reality, but which is also not subjectivity, that which is 'merely a presentation' (*das bloss Vorgestellte*, [Freud, 1925h, p. 237]).

> Whether we are to attribute *reality* to unconscious wishes, I cannot say. It must be denied, of course, to any transitional or intermediate thoughts. If we look at unconscious wishes reduced to their most fundamental and truest shape, we shall have to conclude, no doubt, that *psychical* reality is a particular form of existence not to be confused with *material* reality.
>
> (Freud, 1900a, p. 620)[9]

Freud was never to fulfil what he describes here, that intentional aim (to put it in phenomenological terms), or else he was to find only substitutes (*Ersatz*). The first *Ersatz* is to reduce psychical reality to psychological reality, and this is the entire trend of the *Introductory Lectures on Psycho-Analysis* (1916–17, chapter XXIII): under the cloak of the fundamental rule and of the 'absence of any indication of reality in the unconscious',[10] all transitional thoughts (associations) and intermediate thoughts (fantasies) should strictly speaking be placed on the same level as, for instance, memories. After all, they are all part of the 'real', being as real as the material world, and it is their combination which, from a purely subjectivist point of view, is now called 'psychical reality'; but Freud has shifted from one sense of this term to the other: from a particular psychical entity that would be reality, a *thing* in the unconscious, to the finding, trivial as it is, that any thought, even if it is fiction, is a psychical *phenomenon* among others, worthy of consideration and study as such.

There are other returns (distorted like a 'return of the repressed'), of that entity whose existence Freud suspected and which he constantly tried to grasp, that psychical entity that is as hard as iron, and perhaps stronger than the perceptual fact itself; one of these returns is called 'primal fantasy' and the other, still in Freud, the primordial 'id' anchored in the biological; in Lacan, however, we may detect in the guise of structuralism a derivative of the same exigency, something that would like to occupy the same position: 'the symbolic'. I do not have the space for a critique of these here.

Let us return to *reminiscences* and their principal form, *scenes*.

---

9 Note in passing the terms 'transitional or intermediate thoughts'. It is everything that is *relation* – in particular, that is history – that is devalued, derealized, in comparison with the supreme 'psychical reality' that is archaeological reality.
10 Letter to Fliess (21 Sept. 1897), Freud, 1985, p. 264.

Throughout the discussion about the famous scenes – their reality, their improbability and the possibility of remembering them – it seems to me that we have confined ourselves to two antithetical elements which oppose each other as would the crude physical fact and the theorization of the physicist (in what would actually be a highly debatable epistemology). So it is, since Viderman helps us to clarify matters, with the Grusha scene in 'the Wolf Man' case:

> It is a historical scene, in the sense that it is a matter of a real, dated event –
> it is not history – any more than 'Caesar crossed the Rubicon'. . . . These
> are objective facts, comparable for historians with the trajectory of a body
> in the physical world. . . . In order for this scene to be animated, to come
> alive and to speak to us, it is first necessary for Freud himself to speak.
> (Viderman, 1970, p. 343)

Two points are ignored here (not only by Viderman but also by his contra-dictors, and presumably by Freud himself): (1) that Freud's interpretation is preceded by a proto-interpretation by the subject himself, so that the psycho-analytic interpretation always only comes second; (2) even more importantly, what is to be interpreted is not crude factual material, or even historical fact, in the sense of the banal 'John Lackland went that way'. However, my objection is not that, as has been demonstrated to excess, 'human facts are not things' and, in the most general sense, that they 'have a meaning', but that *infantile scenes – the ones with which psychoanalysis is concerned – are first and foremost messages.*

Here I shall rest my case on a Freud paper which seems to me exemplary from more than one viewpoint. It is exemplary in showing a process of repression at work; and it is exemplary in demonstrating that the memory is very different from the unconscious fantasy that has arisen from it, and, incidentally, from the conscious fantasy derived from the former. The paper is 'A child is being beaten' (Freud, 1919e). I commented some years ago on this paper, when I made use in particular of the concept of 'leaning-on' (Laplanche, 1970, chapter V).[11] I return to it today with a conceptual arsenal more directly derived from the generalized seduction theory: message, transla-tion and partial failure of translation.

11 [The French term *étayage* translates Freud's *Anlehnung* for which Laplanche suggests 'leaning-on' in English rather than Strachey's 'anaclisis'. In Laplanche's *Life and Death* (1970) Jeffrey Mehlman has translated it as 'propping'. See my commentary fn. 29, 'Introduction' to this volume, p. 25. Editor's note.]

I should therefore like to recall the three formulations proposed by Freud as a chronological sequence, derived, he tells us, from several analyses (four female patients):

1. My father is beating a child (a little brother-or-sister).[12]
2. I am being beaten by my father.
3. A child is being beaten.

Regarding the third stage, I have nothing to add to Freud's description and perfect explanation: we have to do with a perverse conscious fantasy accompanying masturbation and culminating in orgasm. This fantasy is a derivative of the unconscious fantasy (No. 2), and it is derived from it by a number of routes: neutralization, compromise between the sadistic form of the fantasy and the masochistic type of its satisfaction, displacement of guilt, masculinity complex, etc.

Let us concentrate on Stages 1 and 2. Freud sometimes describes them as two stages of one and the same fantasy, but, if we look at them closely, how can the same type of reality be attributed to each?

Stage 2 really is what we call an unconscious fantasy. It has the fixed and stereotyped character of such a fantasy; and being inaccessible to any reshaping, it is all the more fixed and stereotyped because it can never become conscious. It is constructed only by the analysis:

> This second phase is the most important and the most momentous of all.
> But we may say of it in a certain sense that it has never had a real existence.
> It is never remembered, it has never succeeded in becoming conscious. It is
> a construction of analysis, but is no less a necessity on that account.
>
> (Freud, 1919e, p. 185)

On the other hand, Freud hesitates openly about the first phase and inclines towards deeming it real:

> One may hesitate to say whether the characteristics of a 'phantasy' can yet
> be ascribed to this first step towards the later beating-phantasy. It is perhaps
> rather a question of recollections of events which have been witnessed, or

---

12 *Geschwisterchen*: the German does not specify the sex of the sibling; *Kind* [child] is also neuter in German.

of desires which have arisen on various occasions. But these doubts are of no importance.

(p. 185)

This last quotation betrays a very different position from that adopted in the case of 'the Wolf Man'. The real scene is variable, its details are of little importance, and it is perhaps this very variability that bears witness to its having been lived. Different circumstances, we shall say, have been able to convey one and the same message, and it has been possible for this to be repeated in different ways. . . . 'These doubts are of no importance', Freud concludes.

A significant qualification is that the second scene, which is unconscious, is described as the 'original phantasy' (*ursprüngliche Phantasie*) (Freud, 1919e, p. 199); on the one hand, this shows that the fantasy proper only begins with it, but, on the other, such a formulation as it were competes with and even invalidates the conception of 'primal fantasies' of phylogenetic origin, formulated two or three years earlier. An unconscious fantasy may thus be *'original' without ceasing to be the product of an individual process* and without any need to refer to the archetypal and the unconscious of the species.

Another important point is that the unconscious fantasy is not a copy of the conscious scene, a faithful memory that has simply succumbed to infantile amnesia. *Repression is something quite different from a memorization.*

It is time to attempt a different description of the process whose stages are so well marked out by Freud.

In the first stage, the real events that have taken place between the family protagonists are something quite different from mere material sequences. It seems to me obvious that, in one way or another, they are *presented* to the child. If a little brother-or-sister is beaten in the presence of the child, it is not like beating an egg white in a kitchen. Nor is it neutral and innocent (in Grusha's unconscious) to scrub the floor in front of the child with her buttocks projecting.

The fact that the father is addressing himself to the spectator of the scene is illustrated in Freud in his addition to the initial formulation: 'My father is beating the child [brother-or-sister]/whom I hate'.

This 'whom I hate' is not a factual, perceptual component of the scene. It is a *contextual* component. It does not belong to one or other of the protagonists, but is their secret or common possession. If I hate the little brother-or-sister

156

and, knowing this, my father beats him or her in front of me, this confirms that he is addressing a message to me.

I now come to a second addition, which Freud wishes to make to what he calls the first stage: 'My father is beating the child [brother-or-sister]/whom I hate/he loves only me'.

This addition belongs even less than the first to the perceived. We are perfectly safe in proposing that it constitutes an interpretation or, more precisely, a *translation*, made in the past by the child and reconstructed in the analysis. I shall now develop the sequence, following Freud very closely: 'My father is beating [in front of me] the child [little brother-or-sister] whom I hate'. 'It means [*das heisst*]: "My father does not love this other child, he loves only me"' (Freud, 1919e, p. 187).

In passing, lest anyone consider the process of translation to be something purely 'intellectual', note the major role of the affect, which here appears both in the source context and in the target translation.

It now remains for me to justify thoroughly this translation theory of repression; its original formulation is to be found in Freud's letter to Fliess (6 Dec. 1896):

Thus an anachronism persists: in a particular province, *fueros*[13] are still in force; we are in the presence of 'survivals'. A failure of translation – this is what is known clinically as 'repression'.

Why *translation* and not interpretation? It is because the latter word, while roughly correct, is insufficient. It is too general, and also lends itself too readily to the facile explanations of hermeneutics. Admittedly I interpret a discourse (and a translator is also called an 'interpreter'), but I also interpret the storming of the Bastille as a sign of a weakening of the nobility and a precursor of the guillotine.

What is *translated*, specifically, is not a natural, or even an historical sign, but a message, a signifier or a sequence of signifiers. In order for there to be translation, someone must have meant something.

It will be seen that I am again resorting to the category of the *message* or enigmatic *signifier*. The term 'message' insists on the fact that the signifier

13 Masson the editor comments: 'A *fuero* was an ancient Spanish law still in effect in some particular city or province, guaranteeing that region's immemorial privileges' (Freud, 1985, p. 208).

represents someone (Lacan says 'the subject') to another; it is what may also be called the 'address' aspect of the signifier.[14]

Whether signifier or message, I qualify it as 'enigmatic'. However, I immediately reject the idea that every signifier is enigmatic, if that is understood to mean – a trivial enough statement – that it is polysemous.[15] If I had to give up the term 'enigmatic' to my objectors, I should then coin the expression 'compromised signifier', in the dual sense that it is *a* compromise, like the symptom, as well as being *compromised by the unconscious* of its originator. After all – and one is slightly ashamed to say so – psychoanalysis with and since Freud has omitted to note that repression and the unconscious exist in the other before being present in the child: in the Wolf Man's parents, in Grusha and in the beating father.

The father who 'is beating the child' *says* more than he consciously means. He means to say, for example: 'Disobedient children must be punished to teach them how to behave'. More directly, addressing himself to the child: 'so you see you are better behaved than he is . . . you are not the one that deserves such a spanking . . .'

Yet this father barely knows that he means something like: 'Spare the rod and spoil the child' [in French: *Qui aime bien, chatie bien*, who loves well, punishes well]. This expression is ambiguous, because, consciously, loving and punishing are the two poles of any good upbringing, but, unconsciously, they tend to merge.

Finally, the father has no idea at all that he is saying a whole lot of other things, such as: 'Loving means beating, sexually assaulting, and having intercourse, as, for example, I do with your mother . . . and furthermore, not only genitally but also anally – for how else could one assault a little "brother-or-sister", etc., etc.'.

Confronted with this enigmatic message, a message compromised by any number of unconscious resurgences, the child translates it as best he can, with

14 The concept of an 'address' is essential for understanding works of culture, as well as for restoration of the junction between these works and the 'transference'. See below, pp. 221ff.

15 There is no doubt that Freud, and Jones after him, use the word 'symbol' in the psychoanalytic sense to denote not any indirect and polysemous representation, but only ones in which what is symbolized is unconscious. In this way the symbol is directly linked to the old formulation dating from 1895: it is the symptom as a production of the unconscious, which is a 'mnemic symbol'.

the language at his disposal.[16] This translation coincides precisely with the words that are spoken/lived/felt: 'My father does not love this other child, he loves only me'.

What is lost in this translation is the obscure aspect of the message, to the effect that, from the sexual point of view, loving involves beating and violent attack. It is this *fuero*, this 'survival' (*Überlebsel*) which forms precisely the unconscious fantasy, a fixed and immutable fantasy, not historicized but designified, senseless and inaccessible directly – a truly original fantasy, which can only be identified by the perverse derivatives with which we are all familiar.[17]

In order to discuss psychoanalytic interpretation and its status between determinism and hermeneutics, I could not avoid this long introduction to the third category, which I suggest locating in the position postulated by Freud when he speaks of 'psychical reality'. Alongside perceptual reality and psychological reality – of which conscious-preconscious fantasy constitutes a major sector – we should place a third reality, that of the message, i.e. of the signifier in so far as it is addressed by someone to someone. If we say that this category is practically absent from Freud's thought, we are also saying that the other, the human other, is also absent from it, as a source of messages. The other – in particular, the parental other – is barely present at all, and then only as an abstract protagonist of a scene or a support for projections; this is the case with Freud, but also, and to an even greater extent, with Klein.

Interpretation therefore finds itself trapped in the unresolvable dualism of pure factuality on the one hand and a creative imagination on the other: in the one case, it patiently reconstitutes 'facts' which it hopes will prove to be the source of a determinism, explaining the present by the past.[18] It is an

16 I am, of course, here using the word 'language' exactly as Freud does, to denote any kind of expression of psychical life, and not just verbal language (cf. Freud, 1913j).
17 'My father is beating me.' Is this unconscious fantasy a buried individual memory, or is it not? Is it or is it not an archaic schema, handed down by heredity, a kind of fifth 'primal fantasy' to be added to the other four? If one's answer to these two questions is no, as ours is, why should we not once and for all cast doubt on the idea that the representational contents of the id are, on the one hand, hereditary schemata of memory and, on the other, repressed memories?
18 That is the usual sense of 'afterwardsness' in Freud (*Nachträglichkeit*): an action deferred from the past to the present. (see Laplanche, 1991b, pp. 338–9, for an explanation of the use of 'afterwardsness' and 'Notes on Afterwardsness' in this volume, pp. 260–5.

explanation that will always fall into the famous parody of psychoanalysis, brilliantly anticipated by Molière: 'And that is why your daughter is dumb'.

In the second case, the interpretation notes that human facts always have 'a sense', but it adds too quickly that this sense is imposed on an inert datum by the individual – an infantile subject, and then the subject of the treatment, conceived as a kind of collective interpreting entity. However, the creativist hypothesis, the conferring of sense whose action is retroactive,[19] cannot remain suspended in mid-air: when Freud himself ventures to do this with Little Hans, so to speak injecting the Oedipus complex into the situation, he immediately draws down on himself the question: 'Does the Professor talk to God . . . as he can tell all that beforehand?' (Freud, 1909b, pp. 42–3). Similarly, Jungian or Ricoeurian hermeneutics – 'incorporation of a discourse in another discourse' – barely attempts to conceal its normative aims and theological reference points.

Between determinism and hermeneutics, what is the contribution of the concept of the enigmatic message and the correlative concept of translation? With the *message*, there is the idea that an existing, pre-existing sense is offered to the subject, of which, however, he is not the master and of which he can become the master only by submitting to it. With the concept of *enigma*, a break in determinism appears: to the extent that the originator of the enigmatic message is unaware of most of what he means, and to the extent that the child possesses only inadequate and imperfect ways to configure or theorize about what is communicated to him, there can be no linear causality between the parental unconscious and discourse on the one hand and what the child does with these on the other. All the Lacanian formulae on the unconscious as 'discourse of the Other', or the child as 'symptom of the parents', disregard the break, the profound reshaping, which occurs between the two, and which may be likened to a metabolism that breaks down food into its constituent parts and reassembles them into a completely different entity.

Metabolism – *metabole* – why, for that matter, speak of translation? Mainly because (as I have tried to show elsewhere [Laplanche, 1988]) every authentic translation presupposes a detranslation, i.e. postulates that what is presented to it is already in some way a translation. The translator is the human individual.

___

19 This is the sense which the hermeneuts attribute to Freud's afterwardsness: a retroaction of the present on the past, reversing the arrow of time (cf. Thomä & Kächele, 1988, pp. 111–15).

He has been translating since early infancy, but it would be a misunderstanding of the word to regard it as a merely ideational process. The infantile sexual theories, which are one of the prototypes of this 'translation', imply the adoption of a comprehensive position – at one and the same time affective, imaginative, intellectual and active – relative to the adult message.

The individual will certainly not subsequently stop translating, as long as he lives. Usually, however, unlike the child, the adult merely translates his old translations, so to speak, turning out 'rehashes' of them. The comparison with translation, in the technical sense of the term, however imperfect it may be, can help us: the individual thinks he is translating Freud, but he is actually translating Strachey.

Yet we do not insist on a monopoly for this term and are quite ready to allow some equivalents to be added to it: construction (or self-construction), ideologization, or self-theorization (theory here being used in the sense of 'infantile sexual theories').

How, in relation to a process as old as Man himself, are we to place psychoanalysis, its unprecedented discovery and the dynamic it introduces – in other words, how are we to allow a more all-embracing self-construction, less subject to the dictates of the 'untranslated'? The answer is not by means of a lifting of amnesia but by a deconstruction of old constructions, concomitant with a (partial) lifting of repressions.

'What sort of material does he (the patient) put at our disposal . . .?' asks Freud in 'Constructions in Analysis' (Freud, 1937d, p. 258). We may answer this question by organizing this material in a slightly different way from Freud:

1 Memories or fragments of memories, admittedly distorted and ideologized to a greater or lesser extent, but which it would be futile and hypocritical to place on the same level as fantasies, as this would be to deny that they are intentionally and irreducibly directed towards an actual past. It is within these memories that the major scenes are to be found, scattered and often fragmented or repeated – the scenes that are in effect shot through with the enigmatic parental messages.

2 Constructions or ideologies or theories representing the way the individual synthesizes *his* existence *for himself*: approximately but also compulsively.

3 Derivatives of the original repressed, which is in itself inaccessible: what we call 'unconscious formations'.

161

It is only for the sake of convenience that we distinguish these three types of material, because obviously they are constantly mingled, in a wide variety of compromises.

What is the contribution of Freud's discovery? Is it tautologous – or simply a reaffirmation of something that has been substantially forgotten – to say that it is primarily . . . *analysis*: primarily, as Freud insists, a method? It could be defined as follows: 'a method of free associations polarized by the transference'. Since I cannot here develop a conception of the transference (as transference of the enigmatic original-address situation), I must simply emphasize that psychoanalysis, along the chains of free association, analyses – that is to say, it breaks down material and reduces it to discrete components.

This in my view is the significance of the terminological changes introduced in 'Constructions in Analysis': it is a reaffirmation of the fact that the analyst's interpretation correlates exactly with the free associations, whose course it merely punctuates by emphasizing their overlaps or nodal points. So there is nothing to add to Freud's redefinition: '"Interpretation" applies to something that one does to some single element of the material, such as an association or a parapraxis' (1937d, p. 261). The German *deuten, Deutung*, is here much more eloquent, and much less 'hermeneutic' than our word 'interpretation': *deuten auf* means to indicate with a finger or with the eyes – 'to point' as the Lacanians would say.[20] We must never cease to emphasize the unprecedented, revolutionary and, at the same time, scientific character of the Freudian method. Even if this method appears to be something acquired once and for all, it must be continuously reconquered against the ever-recurring facile temptations, even in our circles, of an interpretation which 'is its own sole authority'.[21] The 'revolution' brought about by the Freudian method is constantly on the wane: a 'permanent revolution' is essential.

Let us proceed further in our assignment of positions to the different activities in analysis, following Freud very closely as we do so. What then is

20 I know that *deuten* is connected by etymology with an ancient root (from which *deutsch* is also derived) meaning to make popular or public. However, there is nothing to suggest any communication between etymology and present-day connotations.
21 In my 1968 paper (Laplanche, 1968a) I dwelt at length, in connection with the works of Ricoeur, on the opposition between the Freudian method and all forms of hermeneutics. Guardian and guarantor of the method, guardian and guarantor of the transference (in my sense of the term): the 'function' or 'task' of the analyst could be redefined from these two points of view.

to be said of *construction*? Can we take the paper so entitled as justification for claiming that the analysis, and the analyst, 'construct' a new fate? Two points seem to us obvious in Freud's thought as a whole: (1) what he means by the term 'construction' is always a *re*construction of the past[22] and (2) the construction of a new fate for the subject, from the analysis, cannot be a task of the analyst. The one who translates his primal messages, who constructs his fate, in analysis just as in childhood, is the analysand and only the analysand. When Freud is accused of not undertaking a 'psychosynthesis' and not helping the subject to construct himself, we must hear him thundering that synthesis, or the compulsion to synthesise, is so dominant (at least in the normal or neurotic subject) that 'whenever we succeed in analysing a symptom into its elements, in freeing an instinctual impulse from one nexus, it does not remain in isolation, but immediately enters into a new one' (Freud, 1919a, p. 161).

It would be too easy to show how this opposition of principle to any demiurgic manipulation is sometimes contradicted by the founder of psychoanalysis in his own practice. Here, however, we hold fast to the distinction between *reconstruction* in the analysis (a joint task of the analysand and the analyst) and *construction*, or a 'new version' of self which may result from the analysis, but is an operation of the analysand alone.

What is it that can be *reconstructed* in the analysis? In terms of our idea that the *original* repressed is not a forgotten memory, the reconstruction will not be essentially that of historical events of the past considered to have succumbed to amnesia. To be sure, we do not deny that fragments of memory, as well as less temporal elements, are drawn as such into the unconscious by secondary repression. The forgetting of the name 'Signorelli' remains a paradigm of this process (Freud, 1901b, chapter 1). However, the phrase emphasized by Freud, 'I have always known that', when placed in dialectical relation with that other phrase, 'I would never have thought of that', surely means that the reconstruction relates to something other than a history of pure events. It is a kind of reordering of elements supplied by the method, many of which are already within reach. In a nutshell (the demonstration would be by way of the example of reconstruction given by Freud in his 1937 paper), let us say that what is reconstructed is a certain process including the

---

22 'his work of construction, or, if it is preferred, of reconstruction' (Freud, 1937d, p. 259).

message, the attempt to translate the message, and what was lost in this translation: it is essentially the reconstruction of a defence or a repression.[23] The aim here is not to restore a more intact past (*whatever would one do with that?*) but to allow in turn a deconstruction of the old, insufficient, partial and erroneous construction, and hence to open the way to the new translation which the patient, in his compulsion to synthesize (or, as the German Romantics might have put it, in his 'drive to translate'), will not fail to produce.

In conclusion, the work of the analysand in the analysis is both determined and free.

It is *determined* first by the force which moves it: this driving force (*Triebkraft*) which impels the subject to translate has its origin in the forcible entry of the other and in the need to bind this forcible entry: the other (*der Andere*) of the enigmatic message in infancy, and then that internal 'other thing' (*das Andere*) that is the unconscious, and finally, the representative of the other that is the analyst.

However, it is *free* in that the other's messages, being enigmatic, will never yield up all their sense in a 'revelation' sufficient unto itself.

It is also *determined* by the work of association, which compels it again and again to pass through 'nodal points' which are not inventions of the analyst but derivatives of 'psychical reality', and to go back over the compulsory routes of old translations and repressions.

Yet it is *free* – and this point is basic – in that the repressed no longer acts completely blindly and mechanically but can be reintegrated in a wider and more significant context.

It is *free* in that this new translation is in the most favourable case a new

23 It is in the reconstruction that some reference to theory can – albeit in great moderation – be introduced. This will be the theory of repression (and, more generally, of defence) on the one hand, but also, on the other, a knowledge of the ideologies which served as the individual's translational framework. Foremost among these ideological systems is the Oedipus complex itself. A compilation of the 'levels of theory' and their involvement in the treatment remains to be made. For instance, we might ask whether an injection of Kleinianism is of the same order as a use of the Oedipal reference, in so far as the latter (but not the former) merely retraces the paths of a structure of family relations offered culturally to the individual since childhood as a privileged system of self-theorization (for material that could be used to help answer this question, see Société Psychanalytique de Paris, 1989).

formulation, richer and more all-embracing, precisely because it is preceded by a detranslation.

But it is *determined* in that the binding schemata are (or, if it is preferred, the subject's 'target language' is) not invented out of the blue: they are supplied to the analysand by an entire social and cultural environment, so that, like any discovery, every fate, however singular, is never more than half as new as it appears at first sight.

Summary

I have opposed the two principal conceptions of interpretation: the *determinist* conception predominant in Freud, in which the present is determined by the subject's actual past; and the *creative hermeneutic* conception which traces its origins back not only to Heidegger and Ricoeur but also to Jung; in the latter view, interpretation cannot but be retroactive, assigning significance to a meaningless past.

The author shows that Freud, in exactly the same way as the hermeneuts in the opposing camp, remains the prisoner of the antithesis of *factual reality* and a purely subjective interpretation close to *fantasy*. He lacks a third category, that of the *message* whose meaning is immanent, in particular taking the form of the mostly non-verbal sexual messages conveyed by the adult to the small child.

The development of the human individual is to be understood as an attempt to master, to translate, these enigmatic, traumatizing messages.

Analysis is first and foremost a method of deconstruction (ana-lysis), with the aim of clearing the way for a new construction, which is the task of the analysand.

Translated by Philip Slotkin and revised for this volume
by Jean Laplanche

6

Seduction, Persecution, Revelation

To Jean-Pierre Maïdani-Gérard

I'm putting my cards on the table. They fall into three suits:

1) I say 'seduction' and the answer I get is: 'To be sure! Seduction fantasy'.
2) The psychotic says 'persecution' and the answer he gets is: 'To be sure! Delusion of persecution'.
3) The religious man says 'revelation' and the answer he gets is: 'To be sure! Revelation myth'.

'To be sure' features in all three answers. To be *sure*: that *reassures* us when faced with the idea that the neurotic, the psychotic and the religious person might 'be right in some way'. The phrase is Freud's, although he actually uses it to refer to the *content* of the symptom. It must be admitted that, as regards the content of fantasies, delusions or beliefs, there is if anything a glut of interpretations. Here, however, I propose to go much further, and discover how much 'rightness' lies in the very *form* of the statement concerned. Seduce, persecute and reveal are after all active verbs, and it is this activity of the other that I wish to investigate.

The person who answers 'to be sure' is Freud, and it is simultaneously anybody and everybody if it is true that it is an intrinsic human tendency to deny and reassimilate otherness, and that the trend of Freud's theory is to reproduce this closure and this process of recentering.[1]

---

1 This term is part of Laplanche's location of contradictory tendencies in Freud's thought towards both a decentering of the human subject in relation to the other and a recurrent recentering of the human subject back on itself. He designates these tendencies Copernican and Ptolemaic respectively by analogy with cosmological speculation. See 'The Unfinished Copernican Revolution' in this volume, pp. 52–83.

Given that the most radical discovery of otherness is the discovery by psychoanalysis of the other thing in me and of the link between the other thing and the other person, it is surely paradoxical that this discovery should lead, through various transformations, to an ever clearer recentering.

However, Freud's tendency towards reclosure is not a linear, one-way movement. Different routes lead, for example, from seduction to the seduction fantasy, from fantasy to the biological, or again, on another level, from the drive (*Trieb*) to the instinct (*Instinkt*). An attentive reading of a late text, such as *Moses*, reveals a much more pronounced and extensive return to the term 'instinct' than had previously been suspected.[2]

Before proceeding to discuss my three topics, the three moments of decentering and recentering, I wish to acknowledge a debt to Guy Rosolato; my own paper echoes, in particular, the ideas expressed in his discussion (1992) of primal fantasies and the myths that correspond to them.

An echo implies not only resonance and harmonics but also divergences; for all the depth of the former, only he himself is really qualified to judge whether the differences are minor or significant.

Seduction

My first topic is the *seduction/seduction fantasy* controversy, in which I accord seduction priority over the fantasy. I do not mind if I am therefore seen as a softy or – as the case may be – a terrible crank. We all surely know what unitary visions lead to. Does psychoanalysis not teach us pluralism, plurality or even juxtaposition – the very juxtaposition that reigns in the unconscious, where everything remains side by side and synthesis is not demanded? But 'side by side' with seduction, you will object – with stubbornness equal to that with which I defend my thesis – are there not 'also' the other scenarios, which are no less important and no less primal? The primal scene – what could be more primal? Castration – what could be more fundamental? And the return to the womb – what could be more primordial?

Why then should seduction be privileged, among the three or four major

2 For example: 'We find that in a number of important relations our children react, not in a manner corresponding to their own experience, but *instinctively*, like the animals, in a manner that is only explicable as phylogenetic acquisition' (Freud, 1939a, pp. 132–3; my italics).

scenarios? And why should I be so pigheaded as not to accept the little word that would reconcile us all: 'fantasy'? After all, does psychoanalysis not center itself on fantasy? Surely the practice of psychoanalysis postulates fantasy as the only field in which it functions from beginning to end?[3]

The two objections raised against my thesis – forgetting that seduction is a fantasy, and wrongly giving it priority over other, no less primal factors – ultimately turn out to be just one. If seduction is merely a fantasy, it has no right of precedence over other productions of *my* imagination. The primal scene, castration – all these imaginings are of equal value, as scenarios created by myself under the pressure of the drive or of the wish.

Conversely, however, upholding the *reality of seduction* is to affirm its priority, its primacy over other so-called primal scenarios.

Is *seduction* more real than observation of the primal scene? What experimental, statistical confirmation could I adduce in support of such an absurdity? Similarly, I could rightly be challenged to prove that children are masturbated by an adult more often than they are threatened with castration by that adult.

---

3 I am here setting myself up as the devil's advocate, but this devil actually wins most of the votes. In the *early days* of psychoanalytic treatment, the fundamental rule would entail a reduction to the subjective level – which would in turn imply that all contents are placed on the same level. 'There are no indications of reality in the unconscious', Freud reminds us when explaining the abandonment of his seduction theory in 1897. However, Freud extends this lack of indications of reality to the treatment itself, and does so without any precautions – presumably because the treatment is in effect intended to approach as close as possible to the unconscious. Saying everything and doing nothing except for saying, must imply the introduction of an element of unreality into the 'saying', thereby favouring imagination. From then on, however, every kind of confusion is possible: for example, claiming that the psychological reality of the treatment *is* the psychic reality of the unconscious; claiming that the words spoken in the treatment are capable of abolishing the referential dimension of any words; and so on. I discussed the modalities of this reduction of the analytic situation to the level of illusion in Laplanche, (1987a), pp. 88–134.

As to the *purpose* of the treatment, there seems to be a consensus, too – like a lowest common denominator – that it is the full assumption of the position of the person who says 'I'. While the grammatical quibbles about *wo Es war, soll Ich werden* are admittedly interesting, whether Freud's *Ich* is an ego or an I, and/or an I, ultimately what 'must happen' is always a process of recentering (cf. 'The Unfinished Copernican Revolution' in this volume, pp. 81ff). The same applies to Lacan: more than one formula brings us back to this ideal of a 'full word', i.e. ultimately, one that is centered on itself. However, as we shall see, Lacan's contribution goes further.

The whole question turns here on the term 'reality', on the kind of reality at issue, and whether or not psychoanalysis has contributed anything new in this field, whether it has affirmed the existence of a *third domain of reality*.[4]

As for 'psychical reality', I have more than once had occasion to emphasise that Freud uses this term as an *index* of a separate domain in the mind, but also that he fails to maintain a firm definition of it, as distinct from the reality of the psychological field in general. *Psychological* reality is the fact that it is always I who think 'seduction', and that seduction cannot be anything other than my way of apprehending it. Compared with the psychological level, the *material* reality is seemingly easy to distinguish, comprising as it does observable sexual gestures. However, when we come to think about it, that 'observability' quickly becomes disputable. 'Observable' is justifiable in terms of a genital conception of sexuality: touching a child's penis can surely be regarded as a real seduction. But what about touching the lips or the anus? Is this to be deemed seduction because these are preformed erotogenic zones? Yet in spite of appearances, this is still a pre-Freudian conception, if we accept Freud's view that the entire body is initially a potential erotogenic zone. On the basis of this fundamental postulate, how should we see the gesture of touching the child's big toe? Is this a seduction or not? Under what conditions is it a seduction? What is the type of reality in question? What are the 'indications' of this reality?

The answer that suggests itself is the presence of a sexual fantasy *in the adult*. Here again, however, a distinction must be made: either we postulate an immaterial communication from unconscious to unconscious, from fantasy to fantasy, which would quite unjustifiably presuppose the pre-existence of a fantasy and an unconscious in the baby; or we begin to contemplate the idea that there is a *third domain of reality*, which is *neither* the pure materiality of the gesture (assuming that this could in any case be grasped) *nor* the pure psychology of the protagonist(s).

So we have the reality of the message and the irreducibility of the fact of communication. What psychoanalysis adds is a fact of its experience, namely that this message is frequently compromised, that it both fails and succeeds at one and the same time.[5] It is opaque to its recipient and its transmitter alike.

---

4 As it happens, my first stammering address to the analytic community many years ago, to the old Société française de psychanalyse, was on the subject of reality in neurosis and psychosis (Laplanche, 1961).

5 Oddly enough, the account given of the development of Freud's ideas in the *Introductory Lectures on Psycho-Analysis* (1916–17) begins not with dreams but with parapraxes, which are phenomena of the life of communication.

Put simply, seduction is neither more nor less real than a parapraxis, the reality of which is not reducible to its materiality. A slip of the tongue is no more *nor* less real materially than a correctly pronounced word. But a slip also does not boil down to each of the interlocutors' conceptions of it, which are often incomplete and reductive. It conveys a detectable, observable message, which is partly interpretable by psychoanalysis. It is in terms of this third domain of reality and not of material reality that I persist in saying 'seduction' rather than 'seduction fantasy'.

The priority I assign to it is based on the fact that the other scenarios invoked as primal have seduction as their nucleus, to the extent that they too convey messages from the other, always at first in the direction from adult to child.

I shall leave aside the return to the mother's womb and its correlate, rebirth. Freud lucidly demonstrates that it is by no means as fundamental as Jung claims. It is rooted in the primal scene, and is based on the wishes stemming from it, in particular, that of being sexually satisfied by the father (Freud, 1918b, p. 100).

What interests me here is *the seduction content — i.e. the unconscious message content — of the primal scene and of castration*. Freud makes an enormous effort to manufacture the primal scene from just two ingredients — perceptual reality on the one hand and the child's fantasy on the other — the relative proportions of which are infinitely varied. It is the old story of the Wolf Man on which I won't dwell here. However, the reality that is other than material but also other than purely subjective is never questioned: the adult *proffering* the scene to be seen, to be heard, suggesting by a particular behaviour, a gesture, or even a conjugal kiss. Surely, allowing something to be seen is often equivalent to offering it to be seen? However, there are more explicit ways of allowing something to be seen than mere negligence. When the Wolf Man's father takes the child to watch animals copulating, are we really to imagine that nothing but an innocent stroll is intended?[6]

The primal scene conveys messages. It is traumatising only because it proffers, indeed imposes its enigmas, which compromise the spectacle addressed to the child. I certainly have no wish to make an inventory of these messages, for there are, in my sense, no objective enigmas: the only enigmas that exist are ones that are proffered, and that reduplicate in one way or

6 What could be less innocent than a stroll? I remember that, during the occupation, the few French words the German soldiers knew were: *'Promenade, mademoiselle?'* — a sexual invitation, coded as such.

another the relationship that the sender of the message has with his own unconscious. The messages of the primal scene are frequently ones of violence, savagery, castration and anality. A message of exclusion is virtually inherent in the situation itself: I am showing you – or letting you see – something which, by definition, you cannot understand, and in which you cannot take part. Klein's 'combined parent' denotes precisely this knot, which is enigmatic and even incorporates a double bind.

Waxing somewhat rhetorical on fantasies of origins, Pontalis and I once wrote: 'the primal scene pictures the origin of the individual' (Laplanche & Pontalis, 1964, p. 19). With hindsight, I confess that I now totally distrust this statement and I should like to make my position clear. Let us first of all dispose of the idea of any 'objective' enigma. For what right do we have to imagine that the sight of parental intercourse may raise the question of fertilisation in the mind of the little researcher that a child is? And hence, that of childbirth? And finally, the problem of his own origin? As I just said, there is no enigma – as distinct from the purely scientific *problem* – other than that whose components are to be found, not in the objectivity of the data, but within the person who *proffers* the enigma. So we must put ourselves in the position of the adult protagonists of the primal scene in order to discover whether this enigma has to do with the origins, i.e. with human procreation. We should therefore have to accept that human intercourse is teleological and somehow informed by the wish for procreation. This is an idea that Freud opposed throughout his life, from the *Three Essays* of 1905 onwards, suggesting instead that sexual desire initially arises in both men and women separately from the wish for a child, the two eventually coming to be connected only by complex, contingent links that are highly variable from one individual to another.

Before invoking the big philosophical questions – where do we come from? where are we going? and so on – in connection with the primal fantasies (as we ourselves have done), we should remember that the wish for a child, whether or not conscious, is by no means general and preponderant, and that it is far from being an irreducible element of sexual desire. But it must also be recalled that, in another context, Freud *does* consider the child's questioning about origins and procreation. However, he places it in a very different context from the primal scene – in the arrival of a younger sibling. I would add that this too is not a purely objective fact, for 'You will be getting a little brother' is also an enigmatic message from the other.

It is interesting to note here that Freud deals with the enigmas of birth and

171

death in almost the same terms. It is wrong to maintain, he says, that the child's researches about birth result from 'some inborn need for established causes' (Freud, 1908c, p. 212). Similarly, he writes that 'the philosophers are thinking too philosophically' by seeing death purely as an intellectual enigma: primaeval man – and, we may also say, the child – does not believe in his own death. Nor does he 'rack his brains about the enigma of life and death . . . beside the body of his slain enemy' (Freud, 1915b, p. 293). Here again, *the enigma is presented to him by the message* addressed by the other at the moment of dying: the death of someone he loved.

This, of course, is the ultimate limit of the category of the message: the message conveyed to us by the other in taking his leave of us once and for all. I mention this merely to point out that mourning, too, cannot be reconceived in terms only of the two categories of material reality and fantasy, i.e. without taking account of the message, here (irremediably) interrupted for ever ('Time and the Other' in this volume, pp. 248–54).

Castration

This is a complex question that, especially since Lacan, has been cloaked in a pathos that has inflated the concept until it has come to mean death, finitude and simply the human condition in general. Already with Freud, however, it is not a simple matter even to reduce it, as he constantly insists, to its precise, genital, anatomical context. It is after all made up of different 'ingredients', themselves situated on different 'levels', which I have previously tried to distinguish (Laplanche, 1980b). On the level of 'theory' (the 'theory of Hans and Sigmund') it presents itself as an answer, an ordering, and, as such, as a bulwark against anxiety. At a deeper level, though, it belongs to the category of enigma: always set, and proffered, by the other. As for the ingredients of this enigma, let me dwell for a moment on the threat of castration. A kind of index of the problem I am raising is to be found in Freud's use of two different words for 'threat', *Drohung* and *Androhung*. In our French translation, the *Oeuvres Complètes* (*OCF*, Paris: PUF, 1988–), we carefully distinguish between them. We have translated *Drohung* by menace [threat] and *Androhung* by *menace prononcée* [pronounced or spoken threat], i.e. a threat addressed by someone to someone.

A pure threat is objective: a storm threatens, unless, of course, we posit a Jupiter brandishing bolts of lightning; but then, precisely, it becomes an *Androhung*. However, the *spoken* threat is not reducible to its mere content: you'll have it cut off. It cannot be taken to lack an unconscious substratum. If a father, or a mother, utters the words 'you'll have it cut off', this cannot be deemed purely and simply a matter of the Law, as has been maintained since Lacan. It seems to me that the main effect of the reduction to this legislative and univocal aspect is to mask the underlying unconscious wishes. Might the castration threat not be the vector of, or a cloak for, other wishes on the part of the person who utters it – for instance, to mention only the most common, the unconscious wish to penetrate?

To conclude these very brief comments on the primal scene and castration, what is lacking in both Freud and Lacan is a consideration of the enigmatic dimension, otherness, on the part of the child's adult protagonists: the others of the primal scene, the other of the castration threat appear as if they themselves had no relationship with their own unconscious. This is in accordance with the Lacanian formula – which is also valid for Freud and with which I take issue – that 'there is no Other of the Other'.

Persecution

Are human beings once and for all closed in on themselves? Are they irremediably Ptolemaic, centered on themselves? So one might believe without psychoanalysis, and sometimes even within psychoanalysis itself, when we observe its ridiculous efforts to reconstruct the outside, objectivity, on the basis of the inside. Some psychoanalytic constructions of object-relatedness lack nothing to rival the most complex, and precisely the most delusional systems of the great idealists, Berkeley, Fichte, or even Hegel. The last mentioned represents perhaps the most radical attempt to conjure the other out of the hat of the same. The basic idea is alienation (*Entfremdung*) or externalisation (*Entäusserung*). But, however peremptory this 'external' entity, this 'alien', the situation is ultimately not as serious as all that. In the last analysis, I create the alien in order to recognise myself – in order eventually to reappropriate him for myself.

Unlike these self-centered delusions, psychoanalysis in spite of everything carries within itself the germ of a break with Ptolemaism. The germ of this break is present in Freud's seduction theory, and in the transference. Yet psychoanalysis is in turn perfectly prepared to reverse the direction of the movement, as if seduction and transference were themselves but externalisations and alienations, the essential point being to rediscover and recognise oneself in them.

There are still other traces, other testimonies to this priority of the other.

These include the superego, which I mention only in passing, and psychosis, or more precisely, persecution.

Before turning to Schreber, I shall overcome my misgivings and tell a so-called 'funny story', one that makes us laugh precisely because it is unfathomable. It is the one about the madman who thinks he is a seed and is afraid of being eaten by chickens. He is sent to a psychiatric hospital and treated not only by psychiatrists but also by psychoanalysts. In what we call the 'critique' of delusion, the psychoanalyst worthy of the name goes much further than the conventional psychiatrist: he not only confronts the delusion with the reality but also explains very clearly how the proposition 'I, a man, want to devour him, a chicken' leads – by negation of the wish and in accordance with the model demonstrated by Freud (Freud, 1911c, p. 63ff.) – to the proposition 'he, a chicken, wants to devour me, a seed'. The whole thing, then, has been properly explained, 'criticised' and the day comes for the patient to be discharged from hospital. It is an old-style asylum, out of town in a rural setting, and in the yard there is a hen-house. As soon as the man leaves the psychiatrist's office and passes the hen-house, he breaks into a run. The psychiatrist immediately catches him up, saying: 'What on earth is happening, you were cured, surely you know that it is all wrong and just a projection of your own wishes'. The patient replies: 'I know perfectly well I am not a seed, I know he can't eat me up, I even know he doesn't want to eat me up, that he can't want to eat me up. But does he know that?'

The character of this question is irreducible. It is not a statement, not a delusional belief: the belief, for its part, has been reduced, explained, internalised. But a *question* about the other is something that cannot be explained. It is the residue of all explanation. It falls within the domain of faith (or trust) and of mistrust.

Persecution obviously leads us to the case of Schreber, with which I shall assume familiarity, and which, Freud notes, as if in passing, could make an important contribution to the psychology of religion. However, if you look up the chapter on religion in Jones's biography of Freud and also the Freudian texts explicitly devoted to this subject, you will not find a single word about the Schreber case; this is astonishing given that we have here what still remains the most complete psychoanalytic account of an individual relationship between man and God. The case-history tells of Schreber's amorous persecution by Flechsig (which we may decode as father-based transference) and then by God. It includes the extraordinary religious construction embracing God, His multiplicity (the upper God, the lower God, the anterior God, the posterior God, etc., the proved souls, nerves, and so on) and His relationship to man, which is made up of revelation and fundamental incomprehension. From my point of view – that of seduction – this is quite extraordinary: God understands nothing of men and, we could without doubt add, He understands nothing of Himself either, including in the end the destruction of the world, its redemption and its reconstruction.

However, an attentive reading of the text shows that this destruction and reconstruction apply not to the world in general but to the human and interhuman world, and specifically the sexual world. The reality involved in this destruction and reconstruction is only secondarily material reality, what I call (somewhat restrictively) the reality of self-preservation. The Schreber case-history explicitly coincides with the period in Freud's career when self-preservation and sexuality are still kept happily distinct from each other. Moreover, the discussion with Jung to be found both in this text and in the paper on narcissism is steeped in this distinction, which conflicts very specifically with Jung's monism of the drive. This is a vital point: the concept of 'loss of reality' was not yet unified at this time, as it was later in the texts dating from 1923 and 1924, when self-preservation disappeared as an independent dimension, having been completely incorporated in the second dualism of instinctual drives. It is striking that, as a result, the 1923 and 1924 texts on neurosis and psychosis (Freud, 1924b and e) actually fail to make any distinction between sexual reality and reality . . . pure and simple.

Freud's Schreber discussion falls into two main parts, one on the content and the other explicitly devoted to the paranoid mechanism.

Having decided to concentrate my critique on the second part, I must emphasise that the first part of the Schreber essay is an amazing demonstration of the interest represented by this delusion on account of its conformity with psychoanalytic theory.[7] The brilliant, demonstrative use of the analytic method takes 'extra-clinical psychoanalysis' to its very limits. Even more surprisingly, however, the psychoanalytic contents of this first part is almost entirely forgotten when Freud turns to the study of the 'mechanism': I mean, very specifically, its sexual content and its potential implications for the theory of seduction.[8]

7 Freud constantly emphasised this conformity, both at the end of his Schreber case-history (1911c, p. 78) and in his correspondence with Jung.
8 This contrast between the two parts of the Schreber case-history is clearly brought out by Bertrand Vichyn in his innovative thesis on paranoia.

Admittedly, this content will be re-encountered, but in the watered-down and sublimated form of the father 'complex', as we shall see in a moment. For it is not long before Freud points out that the basic theoretical problem to be explained is the mechanism of paranoia and, in particular, the *persecutory form* of the delusion. The Freudian doctrine of neuroses and psychoses is precise: however interesting the content (genital and pregenital sexuality, homosexuality, castration, etc.), that content is presumed to be the same in all disorders; it is universal:

> But in all of this there is nothing characteristic of the form of disease known as paranoia, nothing that might not be found . . . in other kinds of neuroses. The distinctive character of paranoia . . . must be sought for . . . in the particular form assumed by the symptoms; and we shall expect to find that this is determined, not by the nature of the complexes themselves, but by the mechanism by which the symptoms are formed or by which repression is brought about.
>
> (Freud, 1911c, p. 59)

However, let us pay close attention to what follows: there is a major change of tack, a contradiction of the above point of doctrine on the basis of clinical experience, and yet it is a change of tack that does not go far enough. A major change of tack: whereas we should henceforth be speaking only in terms of mechanism (defence and return of the repressed), we must accept that the 'content' is after all exceedingly important: experience drives us 'to attribute to homosexual wishful phantasies an intimate (perhaps an invariable) relation to this particular *form* of disease' (p. 59, my italics).

Again – and here we are on the most classical ground possible – a distinction must be made, within the mechanism itself, between repression on the one hand and the return of the repressed on the other. Freud, however, insists, as a point of doctrine, that the two are not symmetrical: the return does not necessarily take place by the same route as the original repression. What then determines the choice of neurosis is this final stage, i.e. the return itself, which is a specific mechanism (cf. Laplanche & Pontalis, 1967, 'Return of the repressed').

The development of Freud's argument in the second part utlimately covers these three points in succession: the (homosexual) complex, the return (projection) and repression. The paradox, though, is that he attacks something that according to doctrine should be an essential point: the independence of the

176

return mechanism, which is solely and specifically responsible for the 'choice of neurosis', i.e. the independence of the mechanism of projection, since that is what is in question.

Freud tells us that projection must be the essence of paranoia, but then proceeds to dispose of it in a single page (Freud, 1911c, p. 66). He merely gives a general psychological definition of it, and immediately points out that it is a universal mechanism, so that paranoid projection is reduced to the model of 'normal' projection: instead of seeking inside myself 'the causes of certain sensations', presumed to be initially 'inside', I look for them in the external world. The model is avowedly psychological, with a kind of reminiscence of the classical 'neurological' definition of projection as a point-by-point correspondence between a given area of the brain and a given peripheral receptor of sensations. This model of 'normal projection' is therefore constructivist, and to some extent follows the sensualist pattern, which remains dominant in all psychoanalytic attempts to arrive at a so-called genesis of reality: Winnicott's 'first not me possession' takes us back willy-nilly to Condillac and his famous 'smell of a rose'. Finally, as presented on the relevant page of the Schreber case-history, this model in fact scorns the distinction between the two domains of reality – self-preservation and sexuality – which I was just praising Freud for having kept distinct at this stage in his thought.

Lastly, the attitude displayed by Freud to projection in this text is very curious indeed. On the one hand, the exhaustive investigation of projection is put off to some future date (it was actually never written); while, on the other hand, the *essence* of paranoia – stated to lie in the projective 'return' to the external world – is in fact displaced on to what is allegedly not specific, i.e. on to the two other elements: the contents and the process of repression. However, to complicate matters still further, this projection – postponed to the Greek *calends* and in effect ejected from the passage that was supposed to examine it – returns in different guises to haunt the other two studies, of repression and of the 'complex' respectively.

As to the description of *repression*, I shall not go into detail except to point out that, here again, total ambiguity reigns. Freud gives a canonical description, abstract in its generality, of *neurotic* repression with its three phases, and tries unsuccessfully at the same time to accommodate the paranoid process within it. I have no intention of embarking on a comparison of the psychotic process with neurotic repression, which would raise considerable problems. After all, it seems to me that the main preliminary question is whether we should not *first*

177

re-evaluate the theory of repression in the light of a theory that I call translational, connected with the idea of seduction and of a message.[9]

For all their ambiguity, Freud's description and discussion are extremely
rich. However, I must cut across country to reach the major passage, which
other authors have also found worth commenting on, about projection:

> What forces itself so noisily upon our attention is the process of recovery,
> which undoes the work of repression and brings back the libido again on to
> the people it had abandoned. In paranoia this process is carried out by the
> method of projection. It was incorrect to say that the perception which was
> suppressed internally is projected outwards; the truth is rather, as we now
> see, that what was abolished internally returns from without. The thorough
> examination of the process of projection which we have postponed to
> another occasion will clear up our remaining doubts on this subject.
>
> (Freud, 1911c, p. 71)

Summarising the basis of the argument, we find the following statements in
succession: it is a projection, it is wrong to say that it is a projection ('it was

---

9 A number of questions are raised by the manner of Freud's introduction of a general
description of repression in his discussion of the Schreber case. In order not to dodge the
issue by a mere terminological distinction, it should first be noted that Freud does not use
the term here simply as a synonym for 'defence'. What Freud actually gives is a canonical
description of repression, quite similar to the one that was to be presented in his 1915
paper. To get to the point of this text, a number of essential questions must be considered:

i) How meaningful is it to apply a model of *repression in the unconscious* to all forms of
psychopathology?

ii) Can the schema of repression be used, so to speak, in reverse in the case of
psychosis? This is to some extent the schema employed in the papers dating from 1923
and 1924 (mentioned later).

Decathexis of the object in psychosis would thus ultimately correspond to decathexis
of the representation in neurosis. However, the analogy by symmetry does not hold
good for long: for example, the 'return' of the repressed takes place in the same
direction in both cases.

iii) Another possible conception of the psychotic defence in the context of repression would be as a fundamental failure of repression; this approach is not alien to us,
but in our opinion calls for an in-depth re-examination, involving the introduction of
the 'translative' dimension.

iv) Finally, to complicate matters, it must be remembered that every concrete
psychosis *also* includes an element of classical neurotic repression, and of the classical
'return'.

incorrect to say that the perception which was suppressed internally is projected outwards') and the investigation of the projection will explain everything. It is a projection, it is not a projection, and 'just wait and see until I finally get around to discussing projection'.

Those familiar with Lacan and, in particular, his paper on psychosis, will see this passage as an anticipation of foreclosure. In these terms, 'what was abolished internally returns from without' is to be understood as 'what has been foreclosed from the symbolic reappears in the real'. Once again, I must insist that we first ask ourselves which of the (three) categories of the real, discussed earlier in this paper, is concerned here.

This text on the psychoses is great, not to say inspired. Its attitude to Freud is Machiavellian, as Lacan criticises Freud's classical successors (Lacan's own adversaries) by assigning to them the responsibility for certain ideas which are explicitly Freud's, while at the same time attributing his own ideas to Freud. In the critique of projection on which he embarks, Lacan attributes the following simplistic formulation to his adversaries: 'The property store is within, and the properties are taken out as and when the need arises' (Lacan, 1966 [1955–6], p. 542). This formula has in fact been directly lifted from Freud himself: 'the world of phantasy . . . is the store-house from which the materials or the pattern for building the new reality are derived' (Freud, 1924e, p. 187).

Lacan always declined to stick the knife into Freud. The knife concerned is not that of the conventional image of murder but the one of splitting and dialectic: making use of the contradiction in Freud, who appeals to the good old theory of projection . . . only to reject it two lines later.

My own critique of Lacan's text runs along the following lines: its beginning is astonishing, showing as it does that the conception of delusion or hallucination cannot be a matter merely of a return to the primacy of the perceiver over the perceived, that old, indestructible *percipiens*, whose synthesis, unity and even uniqueness Lacan calls into question. This opening grippingly brings out what I call the dimension of the message, and what delusion highlights as irreducible otherness.

I shall not deliver a lecture on Lacanian theory. I do not know if it is still fashionable to read Lacan these days. At any rate, I commend this practice to all who are not strictly orthodox in their reading. This is by no means an easy text. The central part, which presents the theory, becomes harder and harder to grasp, with its mathematical or geometrical schemata. I personally feel that the otherness of the other is thereby, if anything, weakened. The persecutor has become more and more abstract, 'structured like a language', as one might say –

and, in particular, less and less sexual. The same applies to the introduction of the concept of foreclosure: 'foreclosure of the father's name' is a curious euphemism compared with what in Schreber 'reappears in the real' (as he puts it), i.e. full-blown, sodomitic, anal-sadistic persecution.

This brings us back to Freud and the first aspect that he develops: the content of the delusion, the drive, the homosexual wish, condensed in the formula 'I (a man) love him (a man)'. Could it be said that Freud, in his grammatical deduction of delusion, is already Lacanian? This may well be so, by the way he develops, like logical propositions, all the forms of negation of this formula, as so many types of delusion: persecution, jealousy, erotomania, etc. Such a structuro-logico-linguistic matrix, which is truly structuralist before its time, yields nothing to the permutation formulae which, for example, would allow Lacan to define the famous 'four types of discourse'. However, we have good reason to take a closer look at Freud's deduction, without excessively prolonged transports of delight over the beauty of the demonstration.

1) First of all, we may note, as it were, a token of surprise on Freud's part at the fact that, whereas doctrine dictates that the form of the illness should depend solely on the mechanism, i.e. on the metapsychology of the return – experience compels us to realise that persecution is always connected with a precise libidinal content. This for Freud remains a fact of experience that contradicts the theory, but it does not on that account induce him to delve more deeply into the relationship between what he calls 'projection' and what he calls 'homosexuality'. On the contrary, he keeps them separate in the famous negations of 'I love him'. Projection remains a mechanism extrinsic to the libidinal tendency, like an unexplained additional 'compulsion' (*Zwang*). What demonstrates that the projection remains extrinsic, without being truly determined by the content, is the arbitrary manner of its use by Freud at different times and in effect *ad libitum*. For example, two different schemata are given for the mechanism of persecution. In the first (Freud, 1911c, p. 63), the progression is described as follows:

1) I love him.
2) I hate him.
3) He hates me.

There are two quite distinct reversals, the first of which transforms love into hate, while the second corresponds to a subsequent projection, as the ego cannot tolerate the hate within.

Later in the same text, however (pp. 65–6), the projection is described first:

1) I love him.
2) He loves me.
3) He hates me.

Here, the transformation into hate would be a secondary, subsidiary distortion, to prevent the projection from being recognised.

2) Again, the homosexuality postulated is a very odd one. Contemporaneously with the Schreber case-history, Freud was developing a complex psychogenesis of homosexuality in his *Leonardo* (1910c), involving narcissistic identification with the mother. He was later to suggest another psychogenesis, also entailing psychic conflict. Here the situation is quite different: we have a kind of direct, preconflictual homosexuality, not mediated by the unconscious: a direct love for the father, a primary, and one might almost say, prehistoric love.

3) This homosexuality is strange not only by virtue of its genesis (or rather, absence of genesis) but also on account of its formulation, which tends to desexualise it, i.e. to formulate it in terms of love and also of hate. This desexualisation contrasts glaringly with what Schreber openly describes, which Freud followed in the first part of his text, only to take hardly any account of it later: on the one hand, an inseparable blend of sexual advances and persecution from God, and, on the other hand, the mainly anal-sadistic character of His behaviour. Does the reduction of this positive sexual harassment to love and hate really constitute progress in its analysis?

4) The final point is to my mind vital: the material to which Freud applies his transformations are neither fantasies nor scenarios. A comparison with, for example, the descriptions given in 'Instincts and their Vicissitudes' (1915c) shows that, in that work, the inversions and reversals upon the subject's own self related to libidinal actions: seeing, looking, beating, etc. Here, in the Schreber case-history, the reversals apply to abstract formulations of more or less desexualised feelings, of so-called drive movements, but *without* the wishful fantasies that theory would demand as their representational supports, the 'ideational representatives'.

In his now classical paper 'Paranoïa et scène primitive', Rosolato (1969) concentrated on theories that put masochism at the center of the paranoid delusion. The relevant authors include Bak, who sees paranoia as a 'delusional masochism' and describes a 'regression from sublimated homosexuality to masochism' as its first stage. In my view, this position rightly reverses the entire sequence of the Schreber text: the homosexuality is sublimated and not primary; what lies at the root is masochism, as I have maintained constantly since *Life and*

Death in Psychoanalysis and my paper on the primary position of masochism in the field of the sexual drive (Laplanche, 1968b). Pathological masochism, that of Schreber, would be a particular, and of course aberrant, case of this primary position of masochism.

Another noteworthy point is that Freud himself (as Rosolato incidentally points out) came very close to this theory in 1919, some years after his Schreber study, in 'A Child is being Beaten'. On the second (masochistic and unconscious) phase of Freud's famous sequence, that of 'being beaten by the father', Rosolato writes: 'I should not be surprised if someone were to succeed one day in showing that this same fantasy lies at the root of the querulent delusion of the paranoiac' (1973, p. 235).

I consider this comment to be of vital importance because it completely overturns the entire sequence previously described by Freud.

1) The formula 'I am being beaten by my father' (which, incidentally, is presented as strictly equivalent to 'my father is beating me', an equivalence consistent with the structure of the unconscious fantasy) is on the level of the concrete sexual scenario and no longer of the disincarnate affective logic of 'I love him'.

2) In 'A Child is being Beaten', Freud describes this second unconscious phase as following a conscious first phase in which *the father beats a little brother or sister.*

3) In 'Interpretation between Determinism and Hermeneutics' (in this volume, pp. 154–9), I dwelt at length on the character of the first phase as an enigmatic message: my father is beating a little younger sibling *in front of me, he is showing it to me.* I tried to demonstrate how repression, operating between the first and the second phase, can be conceived of by the translational model, a partial translation of the message with the means at the subject's disposal; the partial failure of the translation leaves an untranslated, but distorted 'anamorphotic' residue, namely, unconscious fantasy.

With what we sense about psychosis, this model could be invoked only to demonstrate its own radical failure – the failure that Freud sometimes calls repudiation and sometimes disavowal, and that Lacan terms foreclosure. Progressing one step after another, we must perhaps suppose that, in psychosis, there is ultimately little or no difference between the first and second phases. What precedes 'my father is beating me' would be . . . 'my father is beating me', accompanied, of course, by the sexual and possibly metaphorical dimension of that act. This is consistent with what is known about Schreber's father, and also with the absence of a little brother or sister who could have been beaten in the presence of his or her elder sibling.

Must we therefore presume that in psychosis, the message remains unchanged, pending, suspended? In what state? And where?

The models throng in upon us, all of them exposing us to the risk of including them 'in', i.e. in spite of everything, 'in a subject'. Of course we are unsatisfied with the concepts of repression and the unconscious; but must we on that account reinvent other modes of inclusion? The crypt presupposes the ego, and the splitting of the ego presupposes the ego, on either side of the split. What of foreclosure? It is still me (*moi*) – or I (*je*) – that forecloses.

In my translational two-stage model of repression, I myself once suggested an image whereby, in an initial stage, the other's message, which is sexual-presexual and enigmatic, is, as it were, actually implanted in the body – that is to say, it is not taken into account by an ego or an I. For it is important to emphasise that primal repression is a correlate of the constitution of the ego, of the entity that says 'I'. We must therefore ultimately think of a process that is not in the first person, and perhaps not even in any person. However, any model, even one of foreclosure or of seclusion, is necessarily exposed to the risk of being captured by identity-based thought, which is, in the last analysis, a Ptolemaic model. That reassures us, to be sure.

Revelation

We are supposed to be talking about religion at this symposium. I am certainly not an expert in this field – not even on Roman Catholicism, the religion of my family and my youth – let alone on other religions, their history and particularity. Here again, a work such as Rosolato's on the sacrifice (1991) offers in-depth knowledge: it is an admirable mine of information as well as a wealth of ideas and comparisons.

I wish to consider religion here from the point of view of *revelation*. The 'revealed religions' include not only the three religions 'of the Book', but many others too, for example, it seems, that of the Etruscans.

I must say that the choice of the theme of revelation is consistent with my vision of psychoanalysis and of the priority I give to message from the other. I could have gathered references on the theology or philosophy of revelation, but I have in fact consulted only isolated documents on these subjects. Instead, I have had a look at a very interesting work by Fichte, dating from 1792–3, entitled *Versuch einer Kritik aller Offenbarung* [*Attempt at a Critique of All Revelation*].

The history of this text is entertaining. While the ageing Kant was enjoying his years of glory, Fichte, an illustrious unknown, brought out his book in the form, and with the title, of a 'Critique'. Its wily publisher saw fit to omit the author's name, and everyone immediately supposed that it must be Kant's fourth Critique. So the philosophical public showered praise upon it. But then, out of honesty and also because he wanted to claim his own, Fichte disclosed his authorship: the critics immediately changed tack and declared his opus to be worthless!

It seems to me that this text opens the way to a theory of communication, and hence to the possibility of a process of decentering whereas Kant remains within what I call the Ptolemaic field. Its central section, entitled 'Formal discussion of the concept of revelation', is essentially an exposition of the concept of *Bekanntmachung*. We who were in France at the time of the German occupation know the word *Bekanntmachung* as the heading of those notices posted on walls, which – perhaps under the influence of surrealism – we made fun of by deforming into '*bécane machin*' ['thingummy contraption']. A *Bekanntmachung* informed the population that bread coupons would be given out at such and such a time, but also that such and such a person was going to be shot; it was a *notice* or an *announcement*. This last term allows us to distinguish – as Fichte in fact does – the announcer, the 'announcee' (the recipient of the announcement) and the announced. So Fichte, proceeding along Kantian lines, develops two points: the *necessity* of the *Bekanntmachung* and its *possibility*. As to the 'necessity', he shows that, except for truths demonstrated *a priori*, the entire field of what we know is 'historical', and is therefore transmitted, communicated, announced, made known (*bekanntgemacht*) to us through the mediation of another. This is even the case for most of the truths that can be demonstrated in other ways, in so far as we do not constantly repeat their demonstration but instead merely trust in another's reasoning. We live almost exclusively in the field of historical truth, i.e. of announcement by the other.

As to the 'possibility' of *Bekanntmachung*, this raises a typically Kantian problem: whereas the sensible world is entirely determined, doomed to unmitigated determination by so-called efficient causes, the 'communication' of a truth must be of a different order; it must be teleological. Fichte's solution is strictly Kantian: the existence of a free subject (which is presupposed by a subject-to-subject communication) is a postulate of the moral law.[10]

The important point in this discussion is the promotion of the category of the communication from the other and the subordination of revelation – as a

10 Fichte is here referring to Kant's third antinomy of pure reason, which directly sets the determinism of the sensible world against the need to posit a free subject – who is obviously the moral subject.

The question is whether this antinomy could not be formulated more exactly by

particular case that ultimately has little specificity – to this category. I make this point provisionally, while noting that Fichte's *Bekanntmachung* is obviously not a matter of an enigmatic message compromised by the unconscious.

Let us examine for a moment the title of this symposium, 'Beginnings', or rather its subtitle, 'Neurotic formations, religious formations'. Whether formations or models, a plurality of models of religion can be found in Freud, a diversity and perhaps a unity that is not easy to maintain. First of all, as Rosolato points out (1991), we must distinguish the model for rites, which is

setting determinism (the world of physical laws) against the inescapability of a communication of truth that postulates that this communication is not governed by a physical causality: if my interlocutor is an 'automaton', an 'animal-as-machine', I should be interested only in the laws that move him, and not in the alleged content of what he says. The Kantian antinomy remains extrinsic: it opposes a thesis and an antithesis on two different levels (the phenomenal and the noumenal; science and morality), which can co-exist without any real conflict. The real antinomy is much keener and more conflictual, because it undermines any statement, or rather any *communication*, of the thesis of complete determinism: it is that, by the very act of writing the words 'neuronal man', I am contradicting myself by addressing myself to a reader and trying to convince him on the level of reason and not that of neurones.

The antinomy therefore needs to be reformulated as follows: (1) man is a being of nature and all his acts should be explicable in accordance with the laws of nature (cf. Kant, 1781 [1934], pp. 270–5); (2) communication from one man to another, and in particular communication of the previous statement, presupposes that I do not regard this communication as determined by the laws of nature.

The two terms of this antinomy are inescapable, and attempts have often been made to overcome it by seeking in physical science a utopian point of dehiscence where freedom might be introduced: this is what I call the 'pineal gland' type of solution. Descartes, as we know, thought that the 'soul', located at a particular point in the brain, could act on the body by influencing the *direction* of the movements of the 'animal spirits'. Such a change of direction would not call for the intervention of an additional force. This conception is based on an erroneous statement of the principle of the conservation of energy in the form of a so-called 'conservation of the quantity of motion'. The modern 'solution' – of the 'pineal gland' type – is to attempt to introduce 'freedom' or 'meaning' through the door opened slightly by Heisenberg's relations and by quantum theory.

The third antinomy in the form I have given it above is tenable (speculatively) only if it is recognised that science is not and never will be a completed totality, and that determinism – just as much as its opposite, the communication of truth – is a regulating principle of theoretical practice. I say 'speculatively' because, in everyday life at any rate, it is tolerated perfectly well, as an inconsistency without consequences, even by those who espouse an absolutist determinism, as soon as they communicate.

the model of obsessional neurosis, and the model(s) for belief. However, where belief is concerned, the Freudian model is more complex and more fragmented than it seems. First of all, there is the schema presented directly in *The Future of an Illusion* (1927c), i.e. that of illusion itself, which Freud defines as a belief based on a wish and not susceptible to proof. Delusion is explicitly included in this context, as a part of illusion, the part that is demonstrably inconsistent with reality. The inadequacy of this theory of delusion is plain: an illusion could become a delusion according to the state of our knowledge at a given moment. Anyone who believes in spontaneous generation before Pasteur's discovery is labouring under an illusion, but once Pasteur has demonstrated the error, it becomes a delusion. In individuals with different levels of knowledge, but also if one civilisation is compared with another, the problem becomes almost insoluble: at what point does it become a delusion to believe in spontaneous generation? Can we define delusion merely by weighing it against a 'rational critique'?

Let me now return to the model of illusion as applied to religion. The underlying wish, in the first instance, has to do with the helplessness of the human being (the adult, at the beginning of Freud's analysis), his inability to help himself when confronted with the forces of nature, the cruelty of fate, death, and, finally, the sufferings and privations imposed by life in society. As has been noted, this conception had nothing specifically psychoanalytic about it; it may even be a legacy of the philosophy of the Enlightenment, possibly by way of Feuerbach. As it happens, Freud himself raises this objection in *The Future of an Illusion* and answers it clearly there. This comforting function for the adult is but the manifest aspect of religious belief. What is latent is the Oedipus complex and, more precisely, the father complex (to present Freud's argument in a nutshell). In theory, however, the religion of the modern adult could be derived from the father complex in two ways. The first is the individual trajectory, involving a return to the helplessness and ambivalence of the child-individual towards the father. In fact, Freud is never satisfied with this approach alone. For instance, in 'the Wolf Man' case-history, he is not content merely to go back from the Wolf Man's beliefs to his personal relationship with his father. The religious edifice of the adult is irreducible to the fantasies and wishes of a particular child confronted with a particular father. It is never a matter of an individual creation, but always a cultural creation. In every case a link is required between the individual Oedipus complex and that of mankind. Where religion is concerned, what predominates is the childhood of humanity, its prehistory, with *Totem and Taboo* (1912–13) on the one hand and *Moses and Monotheism* (1939a) on the other. However, there is a clear change of

186

emphasis between the qualification of religion as infantilism in the texts dating from the 1920s and the evaluation of the 'advance in intellectuality' in *Moses*.

Let us consider this question of the childhood of the individual and that of mankind. Can the Oedipus complex of the former be made to correspond to that of the latter? Freud finds the right word for the purpose in his *Moses*; a whole section of the work has this word as its title, and it is one of the points he considers at length: it is *analogy*. How is the analogy between an individual and a people to be conceived? Fortunately, the problem is not raised on the general level, but only in connection with a precise question, memory, or even more precisely, transmission.

At different times in his career, Freud attempted again and again to explain both individual and group transmission by this analogy.

Civilization and its Discontents (1930a) presents a grandiose fresco of the archaeology of ancient Rome, which unfolds in space-time before our eyes as a model of the preservation of the unconscious in individual 'memory'.

An often misunderstood passage in *Leonardo* (Freud, 1910c, p. 83) compares two ways of writing history (*Geschichtschreibung*) and two types of individual memorisation: the day-to-day 'chronicle' of events on the one hand, and ordered, retroactive reconstitution on the other. It is no longer a question here of repression or of the unconscious.

In *Moses*, unlike the previous two texts, Freud invokes the individual process to cast light on collective memory. Several types of transmission of the history of peoples are mentioned, to be clearly distinguished precisely where religion is concerned.

First, there is *transmission by communication*, tradition. Freud deals with this mode of transmission at length, in particular comparing religious tradition to the epic. The essential point is that linear tradition, transmission pure and simple through the manifest and through language, is insufficient for religion.

The second model is *repression and the return of the repressed*; this constitutes the core of Freud's *Moses*. The Mosaic doctrine must have been obliterated by the murder of Moses, only to arise again with the force of a symptom:

> A tradition that was based only on communication could not lead to the compulsive character that attaches to religious phenomena . . . it would never attain the privilege of being liberated from the constraint of logical thought. It must have undergone the fate of being repressed, the condition of lingering in the unconscious, before it is able . . . to bring the masses under its spell. . . .
>
> (Freud, 1939a, p. 101)

I shall consider in a moment this model of collective and historical repression, involving latency and return, but should like first to mention the third model, which is juxtaposed with the other two. This is the model of atavism, of the *hereditary transmission* of memory traces. Freud dwells briefly on this, presenting as evidence, as you know, the discoveries – or so-called discoveries – of psychoanalysis, such as the symbolism of language leading to the hypothesis of a primal language, and also the idea of primal fantasies. This is the famous phylogenetic model of *Totem and Taboo* and of the 'Overview of the transference neuroses'; I shall not discuss this as such, since I have often done so in the past.

What is its effect here? Purportedly to support Freud's argument, but in fact to confuse the issue. It is adduced to support his argument because he wants to prove the existence of a kind of internal transmission, not mediated by tradition, by culture, or by the spoken word. However, this model of phylogenetic transmission confuses the issue, because it is a model of inscription by repetition, by summation, and not a model based on repression.[11] Again, it is an inscription model necessarily mediated by the biological aspect of each individual. Yet the development of the Mosaic religion in fact involved something quite different: the repression of a single event, or possibly a two-stage event (and not the additional multiplicity of repetition), and, what is more, its inscription in the Jewish people-individual, considered not as a genetic succession of individuals but as analogous in its totality to what Freud elsewhere (e.g. 1915b, p. 278) calls 'collective individuals' (*Grossindividuen*).[12]

What then would be the analogy of Freud's view of the Moses episode to religion? What is it whose genesis is involved? Religion? Certainly not: the Moses book does not go back over explanations previously advanced. Is it the genesis of monotheism? Yes and no, but ultimately no, because monotheism, that of Akhenaton, has an earlier origin. Freud himself seems disconcerted at the realisation that he has perhaps gained nothing by replacing Jewish monotheism with Egyptian monotheism (as emphasised by Moscovici in his foreword, [1986, p. 53]), particularly as there is a perfectly natural sociological

---

11 Freud is explicit on this point: 'under what conditions does a memory of this kind enter the archaic heritage? . . . if the event was important enough, or repeated often enough, or both' (Freud, 1939a, p. 101).

12 There is in fact an even more important underlying confusion here, in that Freud equates repression with a memorisation, with a certain type of memory. Here I must mention my own view that the differences are fundamental: memory bears, virtually, on every perception or experience, whereas repression bears exclusively on a message, on something meaningful.

explanation in the case of Egypt: the constitution of a big, centralised empire, leading as it were naturally to a unitary religion. The problem is therefore: what happens between the Egyptian belief and that contributed by Moses? As if by a miracle, belief becomes revelation and election. But revelation and election are not enough; the compulsive force of monotheism is not sufficiently accounted for by the mere fact of Moses having chosen his people and revealed monotheism to them: for this, repression is necessary.

The society-as-individual: here the 'analogy' meets with a major difficulty which, for me, is quite simple: in order for a message to be repressed, a repressing ego must be constituted. A repression is effected in the first person. The constitution of the ego is a correlate of repression. But then the idea of collective neurosis immediately – when used in the *proper* sense, and not as a sum of individual neuroses[13] – comes up against the impossibility of conceiving of a repressing ego in the group, and of a locus and status of the repressed. On the other hand, the concept of collective *psychosis* remains tempting, and it is not without justification that the status of collective paranoia has been claimed for religion, in particular by Rosolato in the case of the three monotheistic religions, and also by Enriquez and by Lyotard more specifically for Judaism.

If the paranoid process has no subject, no repressing ego, or (in more subtle terms) if paranoia corresponds to a sector where there is no repressing ego, we may be inclined to take things literally where the 'collective individual' is concerned too. It is suggestive to say, for example, as it seems to me Lyotard does, that the sacred writing may be the locus of the untranslatable – and initially unpronounceable ('foreclosed') – message (Lyotard, 1984, pp. 69–110).

Religion and Paranoia. Freud does not by any means proceed along this path. The importance of this link is not explicitly brought out, even in the Schreber case-history. On the subject of religion, Freud does mention *Wahn* (delusion) in *Moses and Monotheism* (1939a, p. 130), but a curiously revealing translation problem arises here. The French translator of the Gallimard edition, Cornelius Heim, takes the trouble to explain that *Wahn* in Freud's text must be translated at one point by 'illusion' and, three lines lower down, by 'delusion'. In my opinion, he is, of course, wrong in terms of translation theory, because, by changing the French word used to translate *Wahn*, he is making the ambiguity of the text itself inaccessible. Remarkably, however, he does so not without a semblance of justification, by interpreting a particular trend in Freud's thought,

---

13 'Collective hysteria' can be regarded as a sum of individual hysterias. There is a convergence of individual unconsciousnesses, and in particular a locus of convergence of the repressing agencies: the leader in whom the *egos* are identified.

for it is Freud himself who constantly reduces delusion to a mere variety of illusion.

I shall not enter into a discussion of a delusional model of religion. On the other hand, I shall say a few words about the model of seduction in religion, including the delusional model as a particular case. It seems to me that the concept of seduction is evident, and indeed almost omnipresent, in the Bible. Some research on the word itself is indicated, by way of the Greek of the Septuagint or the Greek of the New Testament (πλανάω = to lead astray), to seduce); the verb 'to seduce' will certainly be found, in particular for seduction by Christ and also for seduction by God, especially in *Jeremiah*. However, a widening is involved in the transition from the word 'seduction' to the *fact* of seduction. The fact of seduction features already in *Genesis*, in the form of knowledge that is offered and prohibited, and moreover offered by someone duplicitous, if we are prepared to include the tempter *within* God Himself. Perhaps 'temptation' is inseparable from 'revelation' and 'seduction'.

What then is to be said about those ingredients and prerequisites of seduction that are the message and the enigmatic? It seems to me that these are precisely the elements that are lacking in Freud's theory, in both his theory of religion and, of course, his general theory. What Moses transmits, according to Freud, is Akhenaton's monotheistic belief; it is a dogma (*Lehrsatz*), an object of belief (*Glauben*) that is repressed with the murder of the founder. This repression merely gives the force of compulsion to Akhenaton's monotheistic belief, but not to a *message* from him, the question of which never arises.

The enigmatic element is even more characteristic. Considering it from the point of view of the unconscious of the speaker, none of the protagonists in this story has an unconscious: not Moses, not Akhenaton, and, in particular, not the primal father. The father of the horde communicates nothing; he has no unconscious. Nor – to bring the matter closer to home – do the fathers of the Wolf Man, of the Rat Man, of Hans or of Dora. At the origin of the Oedipus complex, there is no Oedipus complex. In *Moses*, it is the series of repressions that creates a stand-in for the priority of the other. Repression, as if *ex machina*, creates the compelling force, the *Zwang*, of religious belief. The enigma is, so to speak, displaced or transferred by the series of repressions without ever being located in the simultaneity of an enigmatic message, in the compulsion of a 'to-be-translated'. I see the 'translation drive' as the root of the temporalisation of the human being, and I consider its driving force to lie not in the translator but in the internal, non-temporal, simultaneous disequilibrium of the enigmatic message, which supplies the force of a 'to be translated' (cf., for example, Laplanche, 1988).

190

This is a long way from Freud. Is it so far from a certain conception of 'revelation'? That God is a god who speaks and compels the hearer to listen is obvious throughout the Book, which is but a variant of the paradigm 'Hear, O Israel!' That God is enigmatic, that He compels one to translate, seems obvious in the entire Judaeo-Christian tradition of exegesis. Whether this enigma presupposes that the message is opaque to Himself is plainly a different question. Does God have an unconscious? I shall leave the discussion of this point (or indeed the anathema) to the theologians, and shall merely quote Rosolato here: 'The enigmatic element of the (primal, analogical) signifiers is transposed and collected in the religious mysteries' (1992). In this sense, perhaps, the Mystery of the Trinity, together with the bloody conflicts occasioned by it, can be regarded as a failed attempt at appropriation, at translation, of a primal enigmatic element.

As far as enigmatic messages and seduction stories are concerned, Job provides us with a fine example. There is more than one evident parallel with Schreber, with the primal destruction of the world and its final reconstruction, with the duplicity of the seducer (which is of the same order as the 'perfidy' of which Schreber speaks), if we are prepared to include here, within a sulphurous unity, Satan himself. Another parallel is the anal aspect of the persecution, identifiable in the dung, and even in the stinking excrement that Job himself has become. A final parallel, the most important of all, is the repeated attempt at translation, justification, delimitation and mastery, which are the main points at issue between Job and his questioners.

This translation is the work of an ego, and its completed aspect is dogma, even in the domesticated form of enigma represented by the mystery – in other words, the modalities of belief.

Belief: Glaube, Glauben. The German word is difficult to translate; in Freud, for example, it is sometimes rendered by 'belief' and sometimes by 'faith' (article of faith, faith as a theological virtue, etc.). One word in German corresponds to two words in French, English and many other languages. If a language has only one word for the two concepts, is that indicative of its wealth or its infirmity? With regard to *Lust,* whose situation is somewhat similar (the word can be translated as either 'pleasure' or 'desire'), Freud vacillates between a polysemy of the German language that allows a fertile confusion, and a kind of inability to make essential conceptual distinctions (cf. 'Terminologie raisonnée', Laplanche, 1989a). In the case of *Glauben,* I have no hesitation in saying that this is a fundamental infirmity of the German language. The difference between faith and belief goes virtually unnoticed by German speakers and it takes a long time to explain it to them. When it is noticed, it is not readily understood. For example, one philosophical dictionary, having pointed out that German does indeed not have a word corresponding to the English 'faith' (*foi* in French), equates it with the religious aspect of belief, or with the latter's affective aspect. In general, the distinction is not even perceived; Freud himself certainly overlooks it.

A telling passage in this respect is to be found in his paper 'A religious experience' (1928a). Freud's interlocutor is an Englishman who describes in a letter how he lost his faith and regained it after seeing someone on the dissecting table who obviously reminded him of his mother. Freud first gives a masterly analysis of all this, and then quotes another fragment of the letter, in which the correspondent hopes that God will give Freud 'the faith to believe' (in English in the original). This expression could be rendered into French without difficulty, by *la foi de croire*, but Freud misunderstands it, as is evident from his spontaneous but utterly 'flattened' translation *das rechte Glauben* – literally, 'the right belief'.

Benveniste says that 'it is what can be said that delimits and organizes what can be thought' (1966, p. 70). Is this still so with languages belonging to one and the same civilisation, such as German, on the one hand, and English and French, on the other? How, for example, is this famous passage from the second preface to Kant's *Critique of Pure Reason* to be translated: 'I must, therefore, abolish knowledge, so as to make room for belief [*das Glauben*]'? As stated earlier, Kant is an apostle of Ptolemaism and not a Copernican, in spite of his reference to Copernicus. One of the chapters in the *Critique of Pure Reason* is entitled *Meinen, Glauben, Wissen* ['Of opinion, belief, knowledge'], and thus defines various possible positions of the cognising subject towards the object. In this trilogy, *Glauben* is obviously not to be translated by 'faith'; belief alone is meant.

Faith. In its entry for 'foi', the French *Dictionnaire Robert* gives first what it calls an 'objective' sense, that is, a sense based on the position of the speaker, or the announcer according to Fichte's distinction mentioned earlier: he who is faithful to his word, in expressions such as *jurer sa foi* [to swear on one's honour] or *violer sa foi* [to break one's word]. It then gives a 'subjective' meaning: trust in the word of the other; this is therefore based on the position of the addressee of the statement, the 'announcee'. In religious parlance, we speak of the faithful, but we also say that God is faithful, in the sense of keeping faith. It is the compulsion of the message that demands that it be translated.

However, as a counter-offensive to this priority of the message of the other, along comes a positive invasion by belief, a kind of reconquest of faith by belief, through the Kantians, through Freud, and, of course, through psychoanalysis. Entire works have been published on belief, without any examination of faith. I am thinking of the special issue of the *Nouvelle Revue de Psychanalyse* on belief (1978, no. 18), in which no one explored the route mapped out by Pontalis in his introduction entitled 'Se fier à, sans croire en' ['Having faith in, without believing in']. 'Do not believe in psychoanalysis! Have faith in it', he adds. This statement is perhaps untranslatable into German and into Freudian. It is to my mind perfectly consistent with the idea that transference, like faith, comes from the other.[14]

Conclusion

I began by adopting a critical position towards the concepts of fantasy, persecution as projective delusion, and myth, central as these are to psychoanalysis.

Of course, I had no intention of denying their existence or importance, but wished to try to show that they are correlative with a process of closure towards the other's address, which is an enigmatic and seductive address. I must also say that it is a sexual address. The distinction between the vital and the human (cultural and sexual) orders is of fundamental importance. When I refer to a primal decentering, a basic Copernicanism, I am speaking not in general but in specifically sexual terms.

The confusion between the sexual element and self-preservation, accepted by Freud after 1920, probably contributed to the impasse reached in the discussion of Romain Rolland's 'oceanic feeling'. The 'ocean', if we are willing to retain this word, is well and truly that of the sexual. Only in this field, that of the message and of psychic reality, is the movement centripetal and not centrifugal. 'Psychical reality' is not created by me; it is invasive. In this domain of the sexual, there is too much reality at the beginning; and it is to this 'too much reality' that the model of the 'project for a scientific psychology' can be applied (Laplanche, 1970, p. 96ff.): the ego processes part of this inflow of

---

[14] 'Opinion, knowledge and belief' (Kant) are modalities of the subjective attitude to the true. They are convertible into each other: what is believed can be known, by way of verification. That is how Freud deals with the objection that virtually all of our lives are based merely on belief in dogmas (*Lehrsätze*) transmitted by others: one can always go and see, and repeat the demonstration for oneself (cf. *The Future of an Illusion* (1927), beginning of chapter V).

Freud was acquainted only with the man of belief (and knowledge), but, in this anecdote about Saint Thomas recounted by Claude Imbert, the man of belief is contrasted with the man of faith: 'A disciple asks Thomas: "Master, if I told you that there was a winged ox in the yard, would you believe me?" "I would tell you to go and have another look." "But if I came back and told you again that there was a

reality in order to integrate it into its system and to lower its own level of investment. However, there always remains an element of irreducible otherness: perhaps what Rolland calls the 'oceanic feeling', which would be, precisely, the perception of the enigmatic as such.

Reductionism. Psychoanalysis obviously has reductionist intentions where religion is concerned. However, this attitude is not specific, on the part either of the 'reducer' or of the 'reduced'. After all, the reduction is not directed only at religion and, furthermore, the psychoanalytic attempt links up with a historical movement which hugely surpasses it. The reductionism towards religion is often merely a transformation of a more general reductionism, a correlate of the centrifugal illusion. I create the object, reality, from my fantasy. The transitional stage of the 'first not me' is necessary if I am to attain the capacity for object relations and objectivity. I create persecution from my internal demons. Revelation is but the correlate of the myth, a creation of the collective imagination. In all this we always rediscover the 'indestructible percipiens', always projection as a universal, normal and pathological, or even neurological, mechanism.

What I contrast with this reductionism, in every field, is the inalterability of what I once called 'transcendence'. In the past I referred to the 'transcendence of the transference': the term is more or less apt, as there is no question of verticality, or of surpassing, let alone of self-surpassing. If I were to see the situation in terms of the expression 'I transcend myself towards', I should not retain the term 'transcendence'.

However, the point at issue is the existence of a vector and the direction of this vector. Consider the following example from the field of engineering. To feed cables or small pipes through a large diameter duct, a 'guide' or 'pull line' can be used. When the duct is laid, a rope is left inside it, to which the cable can subsequently be attached in order to pull it through. Instead of pushing the

winged ox in the yard, what would be your answer?" "In that case," said Thomas, "I would rather believe that God had worked a miracle than that a son of Dominic had wanted to deceive me"' (Imbert, 1978, p. 43).

Note that the faith concerned here is not faith in God but in a modest disciple, who cannot 'want to deceive'. Saint Thomas certainly does not review the series of causes as Imbert claims ('your words are the token of what you have seen, and what you have seen is the token of the thing'): his faith is based on the 'fidelity' of the 'son of Dominic'. The Cartesian thesis of the 'evil demon' would here constitute a major aspect of the argument. Again, let us not forget the other Saint Thomas, the one who 'believes only what he sees', who receives the answer: happy is he who has not seen and who 'gives his allegiance' (*adhère*, to use Chouraqui's term).

194

cable in a centrifugal movement (by 'projection'), we in fact pull it towards the outside, the original starting point of the guide. The movement of the cable remains centrifugal, but a prior relationship had been established; there was a pre-existing opposing vector, allowing the cable to be pulled.[15]

I have tried to trace this vector from the other in three parallel fields: infantile seduction, persecution, and revelation, as follows:

other → ego (1) infantile seduction
other → ego (2) persecution
other → ego (3) revelation

This priority of the other in no way precludes the possibility of centrifugal movements and then reciprocal ones (interactions). But these are actually guided (exactly as in the example of the engineer's 'guide') by the primal vector, which is centripetal. The priority of the other does not rule out any attempt to establish a hierarchy, a genesis, a correlation, or even a reduction between the three parallel vectors. Vector 2, the persecutory vector, is certainly a transformation, but also a token, of Vector 1. As for Vector 3 (revelation), I merely wished to draw attention to its kinship with the other two, without any *a priori* intention either of denigrating it by putting it in a subordinate position or, conversely, of giving it any priority.

After all, does 'religion' lose or gain from a comparison with the major co-ordinates of the human condition? I had such a comparison in mind in pointing out, post Fichte, that revelation is merely a mode of *Bekanntmachung*; and I also wished to point out that faith, which is irreducible to belief, being a movement originating in the other, is not merely a religious feeling in the narrow sense of the term.

Summary

To seduce, to persecute, to reveal are active verbs. To speak of the *fantasy* of seduction, of the *delusion* of persecution, the *myth* of revelation appears like a

---

[15] Just when suggesting the image of the guide, I happened upon this passage from Freud:

'We begin to see that we describe the behaviour of both jealous and persecutory paranoiacs very inadequately by saying that they project outwards on to others what they do not wish to recognise in themselves. Certainly they do this; but they do not project it into the blue, so to speak, where there is nothing of the sort already. They *let themselves be guided* by their knowledge of the unconscious . . .' (1922b, p. 226, my italics).

reversal of passivity into activity through which an autocentered or re-centered subject claims to be at the origin of what, primarily, he has submitted to. One must wonder whether, in referring to their primal passivity, the neurotic, the paranoiac, the religious person are not 'in some way right after all' (Freud): not only with reference to the *content* of fantasies, delusions and beliefs, but also with regard to the centripetal, rather than centrifugal, vector of the intervention of the other.

Concerning *seduction* I have emphasised that it is not primarily a fantasy but a *real* situation to be found at the heart of both the other so-called primal scenarios, i.e. castration and the primal scene. But, in order that such an assertion be not mistaken for a factual realism, it is essential to put forward a third category of reality that is continually reduced to those of material and psychological reality, i.e. the reality of the message and, more specifically in the framework of analytic theory, the enigmatic message.

The priority of the other person in paranoia is considered with reference to the Schreber case. The sexual other and his intrusion are the main issue in Freud's analysis in the first part of the study. But, in the second part, desexualisation (in the name of love), and a recentering on the subject are both triumphant, obvious as they are in the so-called primal sentence from which Freud wishes to derive everything: *I (a man) love him (another man)*.

Finally, the religious field gives us the opportunity to refer to the Fichtean notion of *Bekanntmachung*, the 'announcement' by the other person, at the root of *a criticism of any revelation* and, on the other hand, to the notion of faith (originating from the other person), to be precisely distinguished from that of belief which, being the only one known to Freud, is too easily debased into *illusion*.

It is my aim to stress the existence of the very same vector coming from the other person, irreducible to a projection coming from the subject, within the three parallel fields of primal seduction, paranoia and religion, whatever the articulations, priorities or even reductions between them that one might be tempted to suggest in other respects.

Translated by Philip Slotkin and revised for this volume
by Jean Laplanche

Freud seems to have clearly anticipated the need for a centripetal 'guide' to underlie centrifugal projection. It is precisely at this point that he introduces the idea of communication from unconscious to unconscious. Further discussion of this concept is needed, on the basis of the generalised seduction theory.

7

Masochism and the General Theory of Seduction

The title proposed for this lecture should be given its exact scope: in no way am I aiming to put forward a complete theory of masochism *within the frame of* the general theory of seduction. The *and* which joins up the two terms, 'Masochism *and* the general theory of seduction', indicates that what is in question here are two elements – for me, essential elements – in the theory of sexuality, and that their conjunction, their intimate connection, is at the very centre of that theory. It is for others, if they consider the elements I put forward valuable, to develop and set out a psychopathological theory of masochism, in its multiple aspects.

My paper aims to develop the following arguments:

I   Freud's thinking goes astray on masochism, in a way which parallels the going-astray of the theory of sexuality.
II A critical analysis of the text which marks the extreme point of this going-astray, 'The Economic Problem of Masochism' (1924c, *SE* XIX).
III My own trajectory in relation to this Freudian development.
IV A digression (in the form of a simple reminder) on the essential notions of pain and passivity.
V   The close tie between the general theory of seduction and the theory of masochism.

I Freud's Going-Astray

What I call the *going-astray* of Freudian thought does not amount to a simple error, which it would be sufficient to refute. It concerns the moment when thought, confronted by an obstacle, chooses the wrong path. Demonstrating the existence of such a going-astray requires several complex elements:

indicating the causes of the going-astray;

showing the possibilities of another path;

showing how the avatars of the thought one is criticising (Freud's thought – at its different stages) pay homage, so to speak, to the truth which has been abandoned, with attempts – often acrobatic – to retrieve, rediscover, or reintegrate that which has been lost.

As is known, in my opinion the major Freudian going-astray is that of 1897: the abandonment of the seduction theory. Elsewhere,[1] I have indicated what were its causes, what prevented Freud from overcoming the obstacle in the right way; and likewise, which path, to my mind, could have been taken at the same crossroads.

Today, I would like to point out two stages, two successive Freudian compensations for the initial disaster. To give this disaster a definition, let us say that it is the abandonment of a theory of human sexuality as exogenous, intersubjective, and intrusive. From then on, as Freud writes in the famous letter to Fliess of 21 September 1897, the endogenous factor, 'the factor of a hereditary disposition regains a sphere of influence . . .'.[2]

The return to an endogenous account of the sexual drive will be from then on definitive in Freud. Fortunately, this still leaves room for numerous powerful returns of the specificity of this drive by contrast with all instinctual functioning. Powerful returns. Sometimes, too, redistributions, and, among the latter, I will point out two of the most important:

the theory of leaning-on,[3]

the introduction of the death drive.

1 *New Foundations for Psychoanalysis*, trans. David Macey, Oxford: Basil Blackwell, 1989, pp. 114–15. [For Laplanche's discussion of the idea of a 'going-astray' (*fourvoiement*) see *Le fourvoiement biologisant de la sexualité chez Freud*, Paris: Synthélabo, pp. 5–28. Editor's note.]

2 *The Complete Letters of Sigmund Freud to Wilhelm Fliess: 1887–1904*, trans. and ed. Jeffrey Moussaieff Masson, Cambridge, Mass.: The Belknap Press of Harvard University Press, 1985, p. 265.

3 [Laplanche uses the term *étayage* to render Freud's *Anlehnung*, which Strachey translates as 'anaclisis'; in English he suggests a literal translation: the active 'leaning-on' in preference to Mehlman's passive construction of being 'propped'. Translator's note.]

The theory of leaning-on. Its extraordinary theoretical ambition can be summed up as follows: how, starting from a dualism which sets up, apparently in parallel, two types of drives which are equally biological (self-preservation, sexuality), can something of the specificity of the sexual – precisely its non-vital, marginal character (*Nebenprodukt*) – be regained?

From this point onwards, leaning-on will be defined by the hypothesis that the sexual is capable of arising at the edges of all somatic activity, all kinds of shock (this is the notion of 'co-excitation', which will keep all its force in masochism). But even if, in such a process, a small space is left for sexual excitation generated by a shock coming from the exterior, the theory as a whole remains profoundly biologistic, and above all, endogenous. It is only ever a theory of the *emergence* of the sexual from another mode of functioning, which is thus substituted for the theory of its implantation.

A second upheaval takes place, this time covering over, burying the sexual beneath a theorisation impossible to disentangle: the *second theory of drives*, that of life drives and death drives.

The profound function of the death drive, as I have tried to show,[4] is to be a final avatar, a last re-affirmation of sexuality in its diabolic character, in its radical tendency to unbind. This theory is nevertheless to become truly alienating – its function from then on, in the whole of psychoanalytic thought, being that of a lure or trap, both in the false equation Eros = sexuality and in the infinite interpretations to which the 'death drive' lends itself. The mere joining-up of these two simple words has the effect of unleashing speculation, favouring the revival of a romanticism and an irrationalism which, in a second moment, has, appropriately enough, been tacked onto a 'clinical practice', itself equally lacking in rigour.[5]

4 *Life and Death in Psychoanalysis*, trans. Jeffrey Mehlman, Baltimore: The Johns Hopkins University Press, 1976, chapter 6.
5 More than any other, the great dualist theory of 'death/life drives' lends itself to a re-introduction of hermeneutic interpretation (especially Kleinian), which I have shown is opposed to the Freudian method of access to the unconscious. Cf. 'Interpréter [avec] Freud' in *La révolution copernicienne inachevée*, (Paris: Aubier, 1992); 'Psychoanalysis as Anti-Hermeneutics', *Radical Philosophy*, no. 79, Sept./Oct. 1996; and 'Interpretation between Determinism and Hermeneutics' in this volume, pp. 138–65.

II 'The Economic Problem of Masochism' Revisited

My second part is a rereading of 'The Economic Problem of Masochism' (1924c, SE XIX, pp. 155–70). A sharp, critical rereading, working over an eminently contestable and contradictory text in order to make it yield its elements of truth.

This, Freud's most comprehensive text on masochism, dates from 1924, an important date, when the theory of the death drive – initially put forward 'tentatively', as a purely 'speculative' hypothesis – took on the appearance of dogma, or rather, of metaphysics (the metaphysical age being characterised, for Auguste Comte as for Freud, by the recourse to purely abstract entities).

Freud, it is true, did not go the whole distance with metaphysics, always refusing to speak of *Thanatos* or *destrudo*.[6] To push reification to its full extreme, we had to wait for Melanie Klein.

Why take on a text which I consider to be a hazardous construction, made up of imbalances and contortions, whose intricacy is almost baroque? Doubtless because it is an exciting text, as exciting as a neurosis, especially when one starts to see things a little more clearly. One finds there the strata of successive theorisations, revealing contradictions, irritating but fertile once the shell is cracked, and also the creativity which is always at work. And in fact, even in an edifice to be deconstructed, how many splendidly carved pieces there are, worth using again!

I hope not to lead you too far afield in this reading which seeks to be at once incisive, aggressive and respectful.

The opening words – 'may justly be described as enigmatic'[7] – give me pause for thought, for the *enigma* is neither a simple problem to be resolved, nor an unfathomable mystery. In Freud, for instance, feminine sexuality, the primal scene, and so on, are enigmatic (*rätselhaft*). When Freud speaks of the enigmatic dimension of a question, my usual response is to make this dimension

6 [Laplanche refers to Freud's refusal to assign an independent source of *energy* to the death drive, to posit a 'destrudo' which would match the 'libido' of Eros. The term 'Thanatos' is not used by Freud in any of his published texts, see entry in Laplanche and Pontalis, *The Language of Psychoanalysis* (1967), trans. Donald Nicholson-Smith, London: The Hogarth Press, 1973. Editor's note.

7 [Strachey's translation (1961, SE XIX, p. 155) has 'mysterious' (op. cit., p. 155) where Laplanche has '*énigmatique*' in accordance with Freud. It has been altered in keeping with the discussion of *énigme*. Translator's note.]

double: an enigmatic question is one in which the enigma has a function in the very content of the question, and not merely in its form.

Masochism – to go back to the most banal level – is something obscure, even contradictory. Freud seeks to bring two kinds of clarifications to this: clinical and theoretical.

First, the *clinical*; or rather – for this is not really a clinical text – nosography and psychopathology.

The great distinction Freud introduces is well known: there are three types of masochism – erotogenic, feminine, and moral. It is striking to see how this categorisation remains, despite everything, usable and used, even though it deserves discussion, or should even be contested, regarding both the contents and the descriptions of *each category* as well as the *sequence* to be established between them.

Erotogenic masochism – 'a mode of sexual excitation', says Freud. We would comment: masochistic behaviour is enacted, orgasm is obtained by real means, through bodily suffering.

Feminine masochism – 'the expression of essential femininity', according to Freud. What emerges from his description is above all that orgasm is obtained due to fantasy.

Moral masochism – 'a behavioural norm in life', and Freud adds, curiously, the highly-stressed word *behaviour*. Orgasm has disappeared. It is a question of apparently non-sexual behaviour.

The scenes where these three kinds of masochism are played out are thus, successively:

the body
fantasy
interpersonal/intrapersonal relations.

First, I will quickly go into the content of each category to show the difficulties or points where they connect up. Then I will examine the problem of their sequence, which is directly linked to metapsychological explanation.

1. *Erotogenic masochism.* This is the most meagre description of the three. It is practically non-existent, even compared with that of the *Three Essays* (1905d). Freud had doubtless always thought the descriptions of sexologists adequate on this point; and doubtless these patients – like most perverts – hardly ever

consulted the psychoanalyst. But all the same, some essential points are missing here:

– the continuity between normality and perversion is not mentioned (no more than it is in the *Three Essays*). The *preliminary pleasure* of masochism, notably, is absent, although it is a widespread phenomenon which causes no astonishment and contradicts, openly and in a very simple way, any purely genital account of sexual pleasure in terms of discharge;

– even the description of *extreme masochism* is absent, or engaged in ways which can be contested: thus, the declaration that 'all other masochistic sufferings shall emanate from the beloved person and shall be endured at his command' ('The Economic Problem of Masochism', op. cit., p. 165); thus, the affirmation of the non-serious, playful (*spielerisch*) character of a form of behaviour which will never put life in danger, nor threaten the integrity of the genital organs.

A case which has become famous, the one described by M. de M'Uzan, 'A case of perverse masochism',[8] counters these two affirmations. The masochist one sees there chooses his partners outside of any amorous consideration. He pushes his practices to the limits of what can be conceived: to the extent of very serious lesion to the genital organs (absolute castration only being avoided due to 'hemostasis') and fatal consequences.

As well as the inadequacies of the Freudian description, a major problem is raised by the categorisation itself, which is not taken up here by Freud, although it had been clearly addressed previously, prior to Freud: the existence of *two versions* of erotogenic masochism:

– one in which the accent is placed on passivity, submission and voluntary servitude. The prototype is Masoch. Here, the tyrant is indeed the beloved person, and precise contractual limits are set for sexual manoeuvres;

– the version where only physical suffering counts. The only limit being (in the de M'Uzan case), 'the sadist chickening out'.

Had Freud read Masoch? In any case, he only mentions in passing, in the *Three Essays*, the difference between masochism à la Masoch and 'algolagnia'. A difference which, from the metapsychological peaks of 'The Economic Problem of Masochism', he treats as negligible. If the description of erotogenic masochism

8 M. de M'Uzan, «Un cas de masochisme pervers», *De l'art à la mort*, Paris: Gallimard, 1977, pp. 125–50.

is absent – Freud's only aim seeming to be to rush towards a metapsychology of the death drive – the *two other* descriptions are a little richer.

2.   *So-called feminine masochism* can be defined, following Freud's text itself, as the location of suffering on a psychical scene, that of fantasy. By the same token, Freud's reflections should have returned, automatically, as it were, to the major text 'A Child is being Beaten' (1919e, *SE* XVII), whose subtitle is 'A Contribution to the Study of the Origin of Sexual Perversions'. Yet, remarkably, this inter-relation is not even sketched. And if the two texts are compared, curious contradictions emerge.

This kind of masochism is called 'feminine' *a potiori*, in so far as the fantasies which support it 'place the person in a characteristically feminine position'. Freud gives a list of these fantasmatic contents: 'being castrated, being copulated with, giving birth'.

It is remarkable that 'being beaten', the central fantasy in the 1919 article (and the most manifestly masochistic of all) . . . has disappeared. 'Being beaten' is, no doubt, replaced by 'being castrated'. One sees here the beginning of the curve of Freud's re-interpretation of the treatment of fantasies of beating, resulting from his theory of the primacy of the phallus.[9]

No less remarkable is the surreptitious introduction in this series of the fantasy of 'giving birth', of which one would like to see the proof, at both a clinical and a metapsychological level, that it takes on a masochistic character and function.

The Freudian elaboration of feminine masochism begins with the words 'in men': such an opening to this topic is provoking and paradoxical, but the justification Freud immediately gives is very flat, a disappointment to the curiosity which has been momentarily aroused in us: '. . . in men (to whom, owing to the material at my command, I shall restrict my remarks)'. The justification would be, then, purely factual, even statistical. The argument of 'available material' is belied, however, if one recalls that in 'A Child is being Beaten' Freud looked at four cases of women and two of men, and that the whole analysis relies on the first group.

Another particularity of the paragraph on feminine masochism is the repeated affirmation of a sort of *superimposition* of purely fantasmatic scenarios

9 Cf. Jacques André, «*La sexualité féminine: retour aux sources*», in *Psychanalyse à l'Université*, vol. 16, no. 62, 1991, especially pp. 32–4.

onto the arrangements acted out in erotogenic masochism. Such a coincidence is anything but proven, as was visible above in the severe cases of algolagnia, and it seems to aim to render the latter less 'serious': 'the performances are after all, only a carrying-out of the fantasies in play' ('The Economic Problem of Masochism', op. cit., p. 162).

Finally, to come back to the term *feminine*, let us take up a strange affirmation, suggestive but perfectly erratic: 'This superimposed stratification of the infantile and the feminine will find a simple explanation *later on*' [emphasis added].

One would like to know where this 'later on', which is so promising, is to be found. Especially if one decides to bring this statement into confrontation with the *canonical* thesis, solidly anchored in the Freudian theory of castration, of the masculine character of precocious sexuality in both sexes. The allusion to an originary infantile state, in which femininity, passivity and masochism are superimposed, can only be out of place in relation to the dominant dogma.

3. *Moral masochism*. Here, in a certain way, things work quite well. Freud is quite comfortable between the Oedipus complex and his new topography. The opposition of a 'masochism of the ego' and a 'sadism of the superego' is *relatively* convincing.

Relatively, for if it is possible to give a phenomenological – or clinical – sense to the *masochistic pleasure* of the ego, on the other hand, the 'sadism of the superego' risks appearing more dangerous, more difficult to conceive. For if there is a solid point in the Freudian theory of sadism and sado-masochism, it is clearly that the sadist himself finds masochistic enjoyment in the pain he provokes in others through an identification with the suffering object.[10]

How, then, is a 'sadistic superego' to be represented? If the superego is an agency which is itself identificatory, how could it find its enjoyment in the identification with the suffering object – that is . . . with the ego? Here, the anthropomorphism of agencies, which elsewhere is justified, finds its absurd limit.[11]

It remains true that in this description of moral masochism an essential element is certainly highlighted, i.e. the resexualisation of morality, via the

10 Cf. 'Instincts and their Vicissitudes' (1915c), *SE* XIV, p. 129 ff.
11 'Freud . . . always considered *the pleasure of causing suffering* as more *enigmatic* and requiring a more complex explanation than *the pleasure of suffering*: which is to say that the "superego pleasure" just invoked can by no means serve as an irreducible and unquestionable axiom', *Life and Death in Psychoanalysis*, op. cit., p. 104.

Oedipus complex and the masochist fantasy which supports it: 'being beaten, being copulated with, by the father'.

There is no masochism without sexuality, no masochism unless one can – and must – find traces of sexual excitation, if not of orgasm. Freud is always imperturbably steered, in his description of moral masochism, by the compass of sexuality.

Passing to the final *level of explanation*, that is metapsychology, is also to confront the problem of the *explanatory sequence of the three types of masochism*. The classic sequence, for Freud, is that the 'moral' type sits on the 'feminine', which in turn sits on the 'erotogenic'.[12] It is a quasi-genetic, even normative sequence, which de M'Uzan takes up when he considers that the pervert is an individual whose evolution towards moral masochism has been aborted.

However appealing it may appear, such a sequence is profoundly erroneous: it situates at the foundation a purely biological phenomenon, upon which a second level, that of fantasy, would spread out, ending up eventually with a desexualised level, 'morality'. What is more, the primacy accorded to erotogenic masochism (and thus, ostensibly, to the body) offers ideal terrain for Freud's metaphysical demon, allowing him to plunge back into the meta-biological fantasmagoria of two great drives and their epic conflict.

It is, however, remarkable that Freud does not, for all that, give up his earliest explanation, based on the notion of 'co-excitation', which is explicitly recalled in particularly clear terms which deserve to be quoted:

In my *Three Essays on the Theory of Sexuality*, in the section on the sources of infantile sexuality, I put forward the proposition that 'in the case of a great number of internal processes sexual excitation arises as a concomitant effect, as soon as the intensity of those processes passes beyond certain quantitative limits'. Indeed, 'it may well be that nothing of considerable importance can occur in the organism without contributing some compo-nent to the excitation of the sexual [drive]'. In accordance with this, the excitation of pain and unpleasure would be bound to have the same result, too. The occurrence of such a libidinal sympathetic excitation when there is tension due to pain and unpleasure would be an infantile physiological mechanism which ceases to operate later on. It would attain a varying degree of development in different sexual constitutions; but in any case it

12 Cf. *Three Essays on the Theory of Sexuality* (1905d), *SE* VII, pp. 71–2.

would provide the physiological foundation on which the psychical structure of the erotogenic masochism would afterwards be erected.

('The Economic Problem of Masochism', op. cit., pp. 160–1)

This theory is considered 'inadequate' by Freud, but it is nonetheless
reinserted in the great struggle, which goes on essentially *inside* all human
beings (even all living beings), between the life drive and the death drive.

Let us be clear: this priority Freud gives to what happens 'inside' – priority
of the moment when the subject makes himself suffer, priority of the internal
attack – can take on a precise meaning, which I have attempted to outline with
the term 'auto-time'; this designates a series of founding moments in which
unconscious fantasy and the excitation linked to it (the 'drive') are constituted
in a single process (that of *repression*). The excitation, too, is necessarily
experienced in a masochistic way as the painful assault of an *internal foreign
body*, in relation to which the ego is passive and permanently in danger of being
invaded.

But what Freud begins to do with this *auto-time*, an essential moment
locatable in the *constitution* of the psycho-sexual individual, is to hypostasise
it as an absolute, primal *ontological state*; and, moreover, he takes it backwards,
so to speak, to *living beings* in general. From then on, every living individual
will be seen as closed in on itself at the outset, a solipsistic monad which would
be the arena of the infernal struggle of the two great drives – of life and death –
and which would open to the exterior only because it was necessary to expel
death (originary self-destruction) . . . to be able to live. We know the ingenious
schema Freud then proposes: the internal residue of this self-destructiveness is
bound in place by Eros (here unduly assimilated to 'sexuality'), to give birth to
'originary erotogenic masochism'.

It is remarkable that into this perfectly abstract (and as such unverifiable)
biological metaphysics, whose opposing entities are supposed to have existed
from the dawn of time, Freud wishes to reinsert the theory of 'co-excitation', a
theory of the origin of sexuality born of the humblest concrete observations
concerning the provocation of sexual excitation by emotions, intellectual work,
or . . . train journeys.[13] This leads to a triple aporia:

1. *What is produced* by co-excitation is sexuality. But how could this be formed

13 Reread the entire chapter (to which Freud himself returns) on 'The Sources of
Infantile Sexuality' in the *Three Essays*.

206

anew by co-excitation if, elsewhere, it is the great originary, timeless drive called Eros? The aporia thus reflects on the notion of the life drive, whose 'erotic' character becomes extremely doubtful.

2. *What produces* co-excitation would be the 'death drive'. But if this obeys the 'Nirvana principle', if it aims at the abolition of all tension to finish in the peace of the interstellar void, how could this absolute relaxation provoke the shock which is needed to give rise to co-excitation?

3. Finally, starting from a sort of vital, objective sado-masochism, which is never anything but the struggle of two great biological forces, how can one trace the origins of the masochist *fantasy*? Could biological drives put on borrowed psychical clothes, rather as in Susan Isaacs' conception of the nature of fantasy?[14]

Here, on the question of fantasy, one should mark the point where things come to a halt. Fantasy would only be introduced in a secondary way, as a sort of epiphenomenon, the psychical adornment of a purely biological process. Putting fantasy back at the origin is to reset the whole process and its derivation the right way round. It is impossible to start with a pure erotogenic masochism if one is to understand anything at all about masochism. Its true derivation can only set out from the genuine, non-speculative domain of psychoanalysis: that of fantasy, in its originary link to excitation and orgasm.

Freud, of course, still holds the trump cards, i.e. 'feminine' masochism and the principal fantasy: that of beating. But once again, everything must be recentered on what constitutes the site of origin.

III From Emergence to Implantation

Before getting to this, I would first like to give an account of my *personal trajectory*. This will not be a narcissistic account, but a clarification.

Because I take Freud as my support, 'put him to work', as I say, it is necessary from time to time to sketch my own trajectory. This is a trajectory which draws on the essential – that is, on the essence of human sexuality, of the 'sexual drive'. At first sight the trajectory could be considered *regressive* in comparison with Freud's own. This does not mean that I have been ceaselessly

14 Cf. Susan Isaacs, 'Nature and Function of Phantasy', *International Journal of Psychoanalysis*, 1948, XXIX, pp. 73–97.

in search of illusory origins, of a proto-Freud, as for others there has been a proto-Marx. My regression is different, and the unearthing of a proto-Freud is only of middling interest to me. I am not a specialist in the pre-1900 Freud; other people are much more competent there than I am. What interests me is not to return to textual sources, but to refind *the* source or well-spring, to seek to release its waters from the twists and turns and subterranean leaks, where they have drained away.

In *The Language of Psychoanalysis* (1967), in the article *'Position originaire du masochisme dans le champ de la pulsion sexuelle'* (1968),[15] in *Life and Death in Psychoanalysis* (1970), my journey back along the Freudian trajectory focused on two major points:

- the aporias and the structural signification of the death drive; to be more explicit, its remedial function in a structure whose details were extremely faulty;
- the rehabilitation of leaning-on (and its correlative, co-excitation). The *unearthing*, one should say, by Laplanche and Pontalis of a concept which had been completely forgotten, and *by Freud himself*.

Every archaeological discovery arouses the passion of the discoverer, so understandably I spent a long time on leaning-on – which is not regrettable because it can be a productive and, above all, propaedeutic notion, introducing the essential distinction between, and also articulation of, the domains of sexuality and self-preservation. The concept is nevertheless susceptible to ambiguous uses. In its general formulation – where it corresponds to the notion of co-excitation – it is absolutely central: 'it may well be that nothing of considerable importance can occur in the organism without contributing some component to the excitation of the sexual drive' ('The Economic Problem of Masochism', op. cit., p. 160). Clearly, the entire distinction turns on this 'nothing of considerable importance'. The accent could be placed on the individual's self-preservative function, onto which would be grafted pleasure of a sexual nature, as a marginal product. Alternatively one could consider that the shock 'of considerable importance', giving birth to sexual excitation, is the intervention of the other.

In the first case, one is led to give an essentially endogenous account of

15 Reprinted in Jean Laplanche, *La révolution copernicienne inachevée*, Paris: Aubier, 1992.

leaning-on, to describe it without the other appearing, except as *natural object* of self-preservation, then of sexuality.

In the second interpretation, the self-preservative function[16] serves to call in the *intervention of the other*, which, moreover, though it is generally attracted by the physiological sites of exchange (especially the mouth, anus and urogenital membranes), is far from limiting itself to these, and can cause 'shocks' in any part of the organism, in particular on any part of the bodily surface, to set up all kinds of currents of exchange. It was in this sense that, some years after *Life and Death in Psychoanalysis*, I took up again the question of the genesis of sexuality, proposing to clarify things more radically: 'The theory of seduction provides the truth of the notion of leaning-on'.[17]

However, the *'Position originaire'* article, a little earlier than *Life and Death in Psychoanalysis*, had still partially yielded to the inclination to the endogenous, in so far as it thought it indispensable to set out from an activity whose origin was the subject – the aggressive subject, transformed by the 'drive for mastery' – in order to define a moment of turning-around which would be the sexual position of masochism. To put it briefly, the 1968 article continued on the track of a leaning-on conceived as a process of endogenous emergence.

Nevertheless, I still maintain and subscribe to the central thesis of the 'originary position of masochism in the field of the sexual drive'. For the necessarily traumatic intervention of the other must entail – most often in a minor way but sometimes in a major one – the effraction or breaking in characteristic of *pain*. That the 'drive' is to the ego what pain is to the body, that the source-object of the drive is 'stuck' in the envelope of the ego like a splinter in the skin – this is the model which one should constantly keep in mind.

IV Pain and Passivity

This would be the point to recall two Freudian aporias, which it is indispensable to shed preliminary light on. As I have set forth this illumination elsewhere, I will simply mention it here.

16 Itself interactive, opening immediately onto its environment.
17 *Problématiques III: La sublimation*, Paris: Presses Universitaires de France, 1980, p. 69 [translation mine].

1. Concerning *pain*: in the text of 1924, Freud sets up an incessant confusion between *unpleasure* and *pain*, neglecting the specific theory of pain (as the breach of a limit) which runs through all his work.[18] Thus, the too clever paradox of masochism, 'pleasure = unpleasure' tends to become easier to conceive if one substitutes for it the expression the 'pleasure of pain'. But the term 'pleasure', in turn, is not certain, since it is unable to signify, in an unequivocal way, discharge. Freud recalls this countless times, especially concerning 'preliminary pleasure', and precisely in the text of 1924: 'it cannot be doubted that there are pleasurable tensions and unpleasurable relaxations of tension. The state of sexual excitation is the most striking example of a pleasurable increase of stimulus of this sort . . .' ('The Economic Problem of Masochism', op. cit., p. 156).

From this point on, this new shift – from the pleasure of pure discharge to pleasurable excitation – leads to a complete metamorphosis of the formula of masochism, which becomes 'excitation due to pain'. Too bad for dialectics that it has thus lost its romanticism, the mystery of the immediate conjunction of two contradictory terms (pleasure/unpleasure).[19]

At the risk of 'Germanising' the problem I would only stress, following Freud, that the term *Lust*[20] can very often mean 'as much the sensation of sexual tension as that of satisfaction', which makes it very 'instructive' concerning the role of 'preparatory sexual excitations' (*Three Essays*, op. cit., p. 210).

The conjunction of pain, excitation and preliminary pleasure thus largely functions to dispel 'the economic problem of masochism'.[21] If this conjunction is completed by the idea of the *fixation of preliminary sexual aims*, either as the necessary precondition of orgasm or, in extreme cases, as its replacement, it offers a general key to the different forms of the 'masochist perversion' which is merely an exacerbation and a fixation of a major dimension of human sexuality, *ab origine*.

Again, one must not exclude from these considerations representation and

18 Cf., for instance, *Problématiques I: L'angoisse*, Paris: Presses Universitaires de France, 1980, pp. 190–4.
19 Cf. *Life and Death in Psychoanalysis*, op. cit., pp. 104–6, where this is clearly developed.
20 Translated in the *Oeuvres Complètes de Sigmund Freud* as *plaisir-désir*, 'pleasure-desire', 'the pleasure-desire of looking'.
21 There is no *mystery of* masochism, but there is an *enigma at the heart of* masochism.

unconscious representation. This is where my second remark, on passivity, comes in.

2.   Concerning the problem of *passivity*, and of its correct definition, without which no clinical outline is possible, Freud, as I have insisted, went definitively astray. For, if he recognises the masculinity/femininity pair as difficult to grasp, he never seems bothered about accepting banal prejudices concerning activity/ passivity. 'A drive with a passive aim' – he never clearly tells us what he means by that. I have attempted, for my part, to fill in this lacuna by furnishing a precise criterion: that of there being 'more' of representation on the active side (the adult with his conscious *and* unconscious representations) than on the passive (the infant, in the beginning).[22] Now, it is this introduction of the dimension of fantasy, rightaway, into a process which cannot be described as purely 'economic', that links up with the description in terms of 'pain'. For it is the breaking in of an 'excess of message', emanating from the other, which functions like pain, originating first from the outside, then coming from that internal other which is repressed fantasy.

V Masochism and Primal Seduction

Having got to my last point, I can only state again the exemplary character (the example being the 'thing itself', according to Freud and Hegel) of the sequence Freud describes in 'A Child is being Beaten' (1919e).[23]

The blindness (Freud's and partly my own in 1968) consisted in not having noticed that this is a sequence of seduction. It is indeed the second moment – masochist, unconscious, repressed – which *inaugurates sexuality*, the sexual drive in the subject. However, the first moment is not that of the subject's mastery of those around him, as I thought for a while and Freud thought for a long time, tracing sado-masochism back to the 'drive for mastery'. 'My father beats a little brother or sister' is a message *addressed to the child in question*, a message at once non-sexual and sexual, which from then on is implanted in the child as something 'to be translated': the movement which sets sado-masochism in motion is not centrifugal, but centripetal.

22 Cf. *New Foundations for Psychoanalysis*, op. cit., pp. 109–11 and 121–3.
23 Analysed at length in its metapsychological sequence, in 'Interpretation between Determinism and Hermeneutics' in this volume, pp. 154ff.

The theory of seduction affirms the priority of the other in the constitution of the human being and of its sexuality. Not the Lacanian Other, but the concrete other: the adult facing the child. A perverse adult? Yes, one must say; but intrinsically perverse because his messages are 'compromised' by his own unconscious.

This situation could be called, objectively and originally, sado-masochistic. But the mistake would be to center it on the physical action, the father hitting the little 'brother or sister'; the breaking-in is directed towards the child receiving the message: the other introduces his message, steeped in fantasy, which the child must in a second moment attempt to master, *at once* symbolise and repress.

What I have tried to make available in a *generalisation* of the theory of seduction can be summarised in several points, which I am not able to develop here:

- the fact that the process is neither pathological nor exceptional: no more so than is the unconscious;
- the idea that the phenomenon in question is a message, and a message to be translated;
- to that extent, the idea that there is no ultimate scene, whether of seduction or not. Successive scenes, however diverse, are the vehicles of the parental message. The first of these, if there is a 'first', has no privilege.

Since time is lacking, I can only refer you again to Jacques André's foundational article,[24] which develops, concerning femininity and its priority, an underlying theory in Freud which is suppressed by the dominant phallic thesis.

Confronting the essential passivity of the infantile situation is the major task of symbolisation. What symbolisation, conceived as impossible translation, is fated to let drop becomes unconscious fantasy. This alone is the source of the human sexual drive. In relation to this we are in an essentially passive position, a position of 'originary masochism'.

By way of conclusion, in order to focus my views I will take as pretext the formulation 'Masochism between life and death':[25] as sexuality, masochism

24 Jacques André, « *La sexualité féminine: retour aux sources* », in *Psychanalyse à l'Université*, op. cit, reprinted in *Aux origines féminines de la sexualité*, Paris: Presses Universitaires de France, 1995.
25 The title of the conference Laplanche was addressing: Journées occitanes de Psychanalyse, *Le masochisme: entre vie et mort*, Nice, 1991.

212

cannot be located *between life and death*. Life and death are two concepts linked to the vital order, that of self-preservation. They are biological concepts, or more precisely, metabiological if it is true that biology does without them quite well.

Human sexuality – like masochism, like culture – has nothing to do with the self-preservation of the human individual. The relations between the two domains can only be secondary, no doubt eventually of some importance, but in the end fragile, inessential.

'Life and death in psychoanalysis': I appreciate, of course, the implicit reference to my book made by those who organised these study-days, but I was careful in the title of the book to add 'in psychoanalysis', in order to suggest that in moving from the vital order to psychoanalysis these terms had undergone a transmutation.

It is a total metabolisation of the biologistic concepts in Freud which allows him to take them as the banners – life drives and death drives – of forces whose only field of activity is the human psyche, or more precisely, its sexual psyche. However, the words have become so weighty that the terms are still flourished, even if they are given most diverse and contradictory meanings. The 'death drive' offers, nowadays, a screen of immunity to whoever wishes to develop in psychoanalysis any 'romantic', 'pessimist' and eventually Heideggerian conceptions. It is a moment to abandon slogan-terms and think on our own.

Translated by Luke Thurston

8

Transference:
its Provocation by the Analyst

Analyst: You are taking me for someone else, I'm not the person you
think.

Analysand: But the other in the originary relation was, precisely, not the
person I thought. So I'm perfectly right to take you for someone else.

The transference, or more particularly the accounts which are given of it,
has always been a source of dissatisfaction to me. The formulations I have set
forth correspond to a broader view, that of the theory of seduction. Terms like
'transcendence of the transference', 'hollowed-out transference',[1] 'transference of the transference' or even 'originary transference' are formulations open
to discussion and 'work'. It is often difficult to work over one's own formulas.

If I have adopted, as an introduction to this presentation, the opposition
between 'ordinary' and 'extraordinary' transference, this is not to add two
supplementary categories, two new concepts; it is more a possible guiding
thread, which I have grasped as such, in a series of lectures on 'ordinary and
ideal psychoanalysis'. The binary ordinary/extraordinary can have at least two
meanings: it is one and the same transference – ours, that of psychoanalysis –

---

1 [Laplanche makes a distinction between 'filled-in' transference – *'en plein'* – and
'hollowed-out' transference – *'en creux'*. The former is a positive reproduction of
childhood imagoes and behaviours, while the latter is a reproduction of the originary
relation to the enigma of the adult other to which the former is in some sense a
response and a translation, which must be worked through so as to allow the latter
relation to emerge. See *New Foundations for Psychoanalysis* (1987), trans. David Macey,
Oxford: Basil Blackwell, 1989, pp. 160–2. Editor's note.]

which can be described as both ordinary and extraordinary, familiar when it appears, disconcerting when one tries to think about it: at the same time *heimlich* and *unheimlich*.[2] Also perhaps, from another perspective, there exists somewhere an ordinary transference, and elsewhere an extraordinary variety of the same species – something which is less surprising because the word 'transference' itself implies the transportation of the same thing to somewhere else.

I will return later to this second formulation, which concerns the opposition between transference within psychoanalytic treatment and transference outside it. For the moment, I will pause over this notion that a single transference constitutes our ordinary quotidian experience, even if, for Freud, it was extraordinary, the moment of a divine – or rather diabolic – surprise: a moment which seems, moreover, to have become a thing of the past. For Breuer, in his misadventure, it was something diabolic; but it was, too, for Freud, this transference he considered a 'cross', an 'unwanted devotion' which blocked remembering. Let us recall *Beyond the Pleasure Principle* (1920g): transference is one of the major reasons – *the* major reason – for positing a 'repetition compulsion' which would escape the pleasure principle. Let us also recall 'Observations on Transference-love' (1915a, *SE* XII), an article often discussed, at least since Octave Mannoni. The article appears thoroughly *dramatic*, in the true sense of the word, since it concerns a theatrical performance where suddenly, on stage, a fire breaks out: the fire of real love. Will I provoke objections if I say that this article is most often used as a pretext for this bit of rhetoric, a way of scaring ourselves a little, of recalling how, in practising what is termed the 'cure by love', we are handling explosives? It is also a means of showing that Freud was – just as we still are ourselves (which reassures us) – trapped when it comes to distinguishing normal from pathological, love from transference-love. As far as clinical practice goes, however, we seem to manage not so badly with transference-love, at any rate when it is contained within non-psychotic limits (but in the case of psychosis, should we not also speak of transference-hate?).

In analysis, our day-to-day experience – the existence or even the declaration of transference-love – often appears immediately, which confirms, if

2 [The German terms for canny and uncanny. For Freud's discussion of the ambiguities and shifting relations between them, see 'The Uncanny' (1919h), *SE* XVII, p. 219. Editor's note.]

confirmation were necessary, its 'lightning' quality. It is rare for us to draw back, or encourage someone in supervision to draw back, and not to engage with this development in the treatment. A certain vigilance is current, a certain attention to structural dimensions, for instance the 'mirroring' aspects of the relationship. In passing – is it not remarkable that Freud does not, in that article, make any reference to the principal text in which he introduces precisely the problem of love, amorous passion, *Verliebtheit* – that is to say, the text on narcissism? One has to check the dates and to rub one's eyes, so to speak, on realising that the text on transference-love is from 1915, and that it nevertheless contains not a word about the developments concerning love in 'On Narcissism: An Introduction' which dates from 1914.

I will continue with the 'ordinary' transference. Guy Rosolato, in a quite remarkable article, 'La pratique: son cadre, ses interdits',[3] gives us in summary a description of what usually takes place, as opposed to what is said. What takes place, that is, in France, in what he terms a 'basic practice' reckoned to be orthodox, average, marked (but in a considered fashion) by Lacan's influence, but not the practice of true-believers. The description is done with humour, but like all forms of humour, it bears traces of sympathy, even in its criticism. Actually, Rosolato's description only refers to transference in passing, not that it is absent for it impregnates the whole, but the author mentions it explicitly only a few times. Is this not also the result of our clinical exchanges, centered in an important way on cases in supervision? The location of the transference, together with a discreet allusion to the counter-transference, is considered vital; but one never insists either to oneself or to the other on what, for decades, was called the technical management – the *Handlung* or *handling*[4] – of the transference, and still less (a point to which I will return) on its dissolution.

Let us regard this 'basic practice' Rosolato talks of with the same benevolence as he does, a benevolence which is not unquestioning. Let us say that on the whole we have moved from the analysis *of* transference to analysis situated *in* transference. This implies a 'basic' transference, which would be in the end the very *milieu* of analysis, in the sense of its surrounding environment. One ends up getting used to a *milieu*, no longer noticing it. The very idea that the transference has to establish itself, evolve, disappear, becomes blurred. Transference, it has been correctly remarked, is present straight away, from the first

3 *Psychanalyse à l'Université*, 1987, vol. 12, no. 47, pp. 469–85.
4 [The terms are in German and English in the original. Translator's note.]

interview; it is often noticed even before the beginning of the treatment, for instance in a dream, and is frequently observed in the period which elapses between the first interview and the beginning of analysis. One notices a *milieu* less when one is plunged in it; more so when it is rather briskly altered or when one leaves it. Thus the interest there has been in what is called 'lateral transference'. Is this a term of Freud's? It is not clear. Lateral transference, acting out, an infidelity to the analytic relation – what is to be done with it? It may be drawn back into that relation, interpreted, in sum, as a *transference of transference*: 'What you could not, did not wish to tell me, you have signified, enacted, outside'.

Characteristic of this perspective is an interpretation, or rather a persistent misinterpretation, of the Freudian term *Übertragungswiderstand*. This misinterpretation has been pointed out by Lagache, Pontalis and myself; the term, that is, always means the resistance *of* the transference, in other words, the resistance which the transference opposes to the treatment: transference as one of the major resistances. For it is a mistake to think that Freud ever speaks of resistance *to* transference: such a notion absolutely fails to occur to him. Now, this mistranslation should give us pause for thought. It indicates a crucial development since Freud, for transference has become the outright equivalent of the treatment, so that resistance to one is identical to resistance to the other. Is this to say that we do not speak about transference in the treatment, that we fail to analyse the transference? It is certain that we exercise the 'caution' underlined in the first place by Rosolato. If we interpret a transferential movement, it is not to attack it as a defence, nor to resolve it; it is in the end to make it evolve, to help in its evolution.

Like the terms 'resistance of transference' and 'resistance to transference', the term 'dynamic' would provide interesting material for our reflection. Freud's article 'The Dynamics of Transference' (1912b) is a big disappointment if one hopes to find anything in it about 'dynamics' in the modern sense of the term: a dynamic movement internal to transference. What Freud describes is the determination of the transference by forces, thus the unconscious dynamics which produce it; but as for dynamics as movement, as evolution, as the changing relation of forces, as 'dynamism' – there's no question of this in the article. Rosolato connects the 'basic practice' he describes[5] to what he

---

5 The five axes on which Rosolato situates all psychoanalytic practice are: logodynamic, transgressive, ideal-inducing, technical and negative, ibid., p. 483.

terms the 'logodynamic' axis. Adopting what he says fairly freely, I will propose something along these lines: speech in the transference reveals the unconscious, but is also the bearer of new meaning. In this second sense of the word 'dynamic', precisely that of logodynamics, there is very little that is dynamic in Freud.

Interpreting the transference: enabling it to develop. The notion of *Lösung*, resolution or dissolution of the transference, which is so important for Freud and whose presence was so strong for a long time in analysis, seems to have taken a secondary place in our concerns. Not without justification, perhaps: isn't the dissolution of the transference sawing through the branch one is sitting on? Analysis remains analysis up until the last second, which means that until the last second there will be transference. Not without justification, then. But also not without error, if the almost instantaneous dissolution of the transference as an 'illusion' has to give way, in our time, to a sort of gradual disappearance of the limits of analysis, a process of attenuation too frequently embodied in certain ways of ending analysis: one moves on to two sessions, then one session; why not to a half-session or a quarter-session? One moves from lying-down to sitting; why not, in caricature, have a couch equipped with a crankshaft which would progressively bring the patient into a sitting position?

Briefly, this problem of ending replays, precisely, the whole problem of analysis. The move from the extraordinary situation of analysis to the ordinary one of life can be conceived in at least three ways: as a radical shift of level (from illusion to reality), as an imperceptible transition, or – and this will be my proposal – as *transference*.

Whatever its nature, there is no question of demolishing this basic practice to which I have just added a little on the topic of transference, nor of aggressively reforming it. It is tried and tested, but in a certain way it lacks *real* examination, lacks self-reflection. It always refers, to be sure, to Freud, but this reference can become reverence. Yet its differences, even its divergences, from Freud are major. What remains of Freud is no doubt an essential element, but one which is not necessarily well theorised – rather an intuition or a lived experience: the specificity, the unprecedented character of what takes place in analysis. The certainty that sexuality is at work, and not only psychological transference in general, is connected to this extraordinary quality.

The last great reference to Freud, the last coherent explication of the Freudian position, is clearly the great 'Rapport' of Daniel Lagache.[6] This report may seem at a certain distance from contemporary practice, but nevertheless it is not out of date in so far as the problematic it sets out has not been given any theoretical renewal. This problematic, as you know, is that of 'psychological unity', and I would immediately stress my differences with Lagache, for I think it is precisely a psychological duality, or a duality of the psyche, which should be spoken of if one is to understand anything at all about transference. By duality, I mean simply the opposition between self-preservation and sexuality. To talk of the unity of psychology is to return the unfamiliar to the familiar, the extraordinary to the ordinary, to return the psychoanalytic transference to the psychological transference of habitual behaviour, which is the unavoidable common destiny of all humans, even of all living beings.

I will not follow this work of Lagache's in detail; I did this a few years ago in my book on transference.[7] It constitutes an historical step, one of whose most important moments is assured by the transition from Freud to an author who was a contemporary of Lagache, and who is perhaps now rather forgotten, Ida Macalpine. In Freud, the specificity of analytic transference is due to the specificity of the neurotic. It is neurosis – unresolved, unconscious conflict – which produces transference. Neither the analyst nor the situation do so in the slightest. This 'clearing' of the analyst is strongly denounced by Lagache, precisely following Ida Macalpine. For this last author, by contrast, it is the analytic situation, analysis *as situation*, which creates transference.[8] This is certainly an important step, to be hailed as such; but a step whose failure, I should immediately state, is due to its inadequate exploration of what is properly the analytic situation. Ida Macalpine defines the situation as unreal, infantilising, regressive. In analysis, she says, the subject regresses because he adapts to a situation which is itself regressive. The formula cannot be contested

6 D. Lagache, 'Le problème du transfert'. Communication à la XIV Conférence des Psychanalystes de Langue française, 1951, in D. Lagache, *Oeuvres III. Le transfert et autres travaux psychanalytiques*, Paris: Presses Universitaires de France, 1980, pp. 1–114. See Lagache's two essays on transference in *Selected Writings*, trans. Elizabeth Holder, London: Karnac Books, 1993.

7 *Problématiques V: Le baquet: transcendance du transfert*, Paris: Presses Universitaires de France, 1987; especially pp. 13–29.

8 Ida Macalpine, 'The Development of the Transference', *Psychoanalytic Quarterly*, vol. XIX, 1950.

in behavioural or object-relations terms. Nor is this incontestable formula contested by its advocate, Ida Macalpine: transference, she says, is an infantile reaction, but one which, given the situation, is perfectly justified. One can help it to evolve further; its 'resolution' is doubtful – or to tell the truth, it is out of the question.

For his part, even if Lagache is on board with Ida Macalpine at first, at a certain point he disembarks. I am doubtless schematising his thought, but it is very clear that he cannot follow Macalpine the whole way. Once on board with the 'relation' and the 'situation' defined as regressive, how is one to get off? In the name of what? In the name of what should really be called an act of violence: the return – in order to pass judgement on a transference considered, all the same, to be *true* to a situation which is itself derealising – of another norm, in the form of an adaptation to a present and actual situation: a reasonable relation to the 'real analyst'. The term 'interpretation as confrontation', created by Daniel Lagache, is perfectly explicit. It is this which, in a certain sense, I aimed at in the little dialogue which I used as my epigraph: 'I'm not the person you think, you are taking me for someone else'.

In the end, is this idea of 'confrontation' all that out of date? It could be said that in a sense it has left everyday use, and *thus* it is not part of concrete practice. Nevertheless, it is by no means certain that it does not remain present at the heart of current practice and, even more so, in every psychoanalyst's conviction. At the most intimate level of practice, it remains as the guarantee of a division between the pathological and the normal, the imaginary (or fantasy) and the real, the atemporal and the present, and so on. Probably (or at least we hope so), the contemporary analyst is not so fatuous as to present himself as 'the measure of all things'. The idea of reality-testing or the examination of reality is no longer an explicit axis of practice. Apprenticeship to reality remains more implicit.

Let us be irrational together – says Daniel Lagache – and then, at a second moment: let us now be rational! The formula is democratic, if it states that on both sides there is both irrationality and rationality. Yet despite everything, what is infantile, atemporal, transferential – in short, irrational – remains, according to this conception I would criticise, what has to be more or less reduced, that which should diminish. The infantile is, despite everything, considered as a 'minus'.

At this point my short opening dialogue ought to foreshadow the nub of what I am proposing: beyond all the splits which can be traced at the heart of the transference – between past and present, unreal and real, unadapted and adapted – there is the primordial split, which means quite simply that *the other is other*, but with this paradox or amphibology: he is other than me because he is other than himself. External alterity refers back to internal alterity.

Before following that path, however, of the relation between analysis and the originary situation, I will take a detour. My reason for returning to the theme of transference was a recent conference on 'Psychoanalysis outside the clinic [*hors cure*]', and a round-table discussion entitled 'Transference and counter-transference in psychoanalysis outside the clinic'.[9] Four things I was not satisfied with, four questions, which were connected, led me to formulate, first to myself, then to the round table, a sort of response.

1. Whatever the formulation chosen – psychoanalysis *hors cure*, 'extramural' [*hors les murs*], transposed or exported psychoanalysis – we never get away from the schema of *application*. Witness the very title of the discussion. It is always a question of finding a clinical paradigm (here, the paradigm of transference and counter-transference) and seeing how it can be transported beyond this setting, in other words into a *second* location.

2. Nevertheless . . . hasn't psychoanalysis found one of its most productive aspects in its relation to culture? Can it not be maintained that it is *originally* at home in its reflections on Sophocles, on Shakespeare, on jokes? In *culture*, therefore.

3. Whatever the unprecedented character of Freud's inaugural gesture in founding analytic treatment, is it possible to think the psychoanalytic relation has no antecedents in human history, or correspondences beyond the clinical? If one thinks that is not possible, if one admits that the foundation of psychoanalysis took place as a rupture on the basis of a continuity, one is then led to posit and search for predecessors of, or correspondences to, transference, beyond the clinical. But in such a search, the reverse claim is no less mistaken if it is given an inappropriate generalisation: that repetition in psychoanalysis is nothing but a particular case of the repetition proper to all human beings, or rather to all living beings. If, in the broadest sense, everything is 'transference',

---

9 Conference of 24–5 November 1990; the *table ronde*, in which Roger Dorey, André Green, Guy Rosolato and Gérard Bonnet (chair) participated, has been published in *Psychanalyse à l'Université*, 1991, vol. 16, no. 64, pp. 3–28.

everywhere and always — as Lagache reminds us[10] — and if it is vain to think that we can transport ourselves somewhere else, without taking our habits with us, then analytic transference, dissolved into a 'psychological' transference, totally loses its specificity. Now, for us it is not so much a question of such a psychologisation, such a generalisation of transference, as of the need to find a kinship between what is most specific to the clinical situation and what is produced, not everywhere, but in some privileged places existing outside it.

4. Finally, the last unsatisfactory point. We cannot accept the schematic reduction of transference to a transition between only two points in time; between these two points, alongside them, there must certainly be intermediary stages; and beyond them, succeeding points.

I then said to myself, in the course of this discussion (perhaps too rapidly): perhaps we are looking for something which has already been found. Or perhaps we are looking the wrong way round: we wish to transpose the model of clinical transference onto what lies beyond it (psychoanalysis 'outside the clinical'), but maybe transference is already, 'in itself', outside the clinic.

If one accepts that the fundamental dimension of transference is the relation to the enigma of the other, perhaps the principal site of transference, 'ordinary' transference, before, beyond or after analysis, would be the multiple relation to the cultural, to creation or, more precisely, to the cultural message. A relation which is multiple, and should be conceived with discrimination, but always starting from the relation to the enigma. There are at least three types of such a relation to be described: from the position of the producer, from that of the recipient,[11] and from that of the recipient-analyst.

Putting Victor Hugo, Jules Verne or Leonardo 'on the couch': the approximate, journalistic character of such a formula is clear. Of course, the author is always absent, definitively or not; but is he perhaps *essentially* absent, whether or not he is dead? The author, allegedly psychoanalysed by Freud or by one of

10 'If one takes transference in the largest sense, it becomes difficult to set its limits. All conduct is in fact a blend of the assimilation of the present situation to old habits, and the adjustment of old habits to the present situation. In man, the notion of absolutely new conduct, which would not in any way involve the transference of old habits, is unthinkable; what can be new is the organisation of old habits on whose repertoire the individual has drawn.' D. Lagache, *Oeuvres III. Le transfert . . .*, op. cit., p. 80 [translator's translation].
11 On the choice of this word [*réceptionnaire*], see below, p. 224.

us, cannot respond to the interpretation with new associations. Where is the 'logodynamics'? On his side or on that of the reader? André Green has drawn from this a conclusion which takes things forward: 'In applied psychoanalysis', he says, 'the analyst is the analysand of the text'. The formulation has the merit of putting back into question a too-easy equation (the analysis of Dora = the analysis of Leonardo). But perhaps this is to rush too far ahead. Before asking, concerning the cultural domain, what is the position of the recipient-analyst and where analysis is situated, one should first investigate the position of the recipient (the reader) *in general* and ask where – not analysis – but transference is situated; for transference is not the whole of analysis.

Der Dichter und das Phantasieren, 'the poet and the activity of fantasy':[12] it is a rich text, but it is limited, and it leaves us on our guard. It shows the origin of the *content* of the imaginative work marvellously, then it skims over, in the last two pages, the so-called question of *means* or of effects. Doubtless some recollection of seduction is tracing itself out, but only in a faint outline. But Freud, as always, keeps to the major, and wholly inadequate, opposition between content and form, or fantasy and technique. Nowhere is the question asked: what, quite simply, drives the *Dichter* – *sit venia verbo* – to 'dicht'?[13] Why create *in order to* communicate, and communicate through creating? And above all, why communicate *in this way* – that is, by addressing no-one, aiming beyond any determinate person ?

Modern studies of language have clearly shown that communication is a pragmatics: to communicate is to manipulate, to produce an effect on someone. There is no question of denying that cultural production has its own effects as well, realistic, self-preservative effects – glory and profit. Let us go further. Cultural production can be partially submitted to a directly sexual pragmatics. A jazz saxophonist said, in a recent interview: 'Don't forget to tell those who don't know which instrument to choose, one thing: girls can't resist a saxophone'. Here, it is a question of what I call 'restrained' seduction. No doubt the sax enables conquests; so do the novel and painting. But what a laborious path, what an extraordinary going-beyond it takes to get there. Going beyond oneself, but above all going *towards* another who is no longer determinate,

12 'Creative Writers and Day-dreaming' (1908e), *SE* IX.
13 [In other words: 'what . . . drives the Poet – pardon my saying so – to "poetize"?'. Translator's note.]

and who will only incidentally be the object of an individual sexual conquest. Going-beyond, transcendence towards an other = X.

Through this dimension, cultural production is situated from the first *beyond all pragmatics*, beyond any adequation of means to a determinate effect. The problem of the addressee, of the anonymous addressees, is an essential part of any description of the poetic situation. The addressee is essentially enigmatic, even if he sometimes takes on individual traits. So it is with Van Gogh's Theo, who is as much an analyst without knowing it as is Fliess for Freud, for behind him looms the nameless crowd, addressees of the message in a bottle.

Am I in the process, here, of describing an elitist phenomenon, the privilege of certain people, and not a constant human dimension? I do not think so, for what can be termed 'the cultural' exists from the moment the human becomes human: cave-paintings, idols and probably music and poetry. What can be isolated here as characteristic of the cultural is an address to an other who is out of reach, to others 'scattered in the future', as the poet says. An address which is a repercussion, which prolongs and echoes the enigmatic messages by which the *Dichter* himself, so to speak, was bombarded: 'A quiet piece, fallen down here, of an obscure disaster'.[14]

What name should we give to the one who welcomes in, gathers up, the cultural work? 'Consumer' is too prosaic, taking us back to self-preservation. 'Addressee' implies a relation of direct address to an individual in order to have effects on him. 'Reader' only applies to writing. '*Amateur*', perhaps? 'Recipient' is the term which I would choose. It is of the essence of the cultural product that it reaches him with no pedigree, and that it is received by him without having been explicitly addressed to him. The recipient's relation to the enigma is thus different from the author's, a partial inversion of it. But here too, this relation is essential, a renewal of the traumatic, stimulating aspect of the childhood enigma.

What I have just proposed, sketched out concerning the cultural is too hasty; one would have to add to it the situation of the recipient-analyst (or simply 'art critic'), who is, in turn, caught between two stools: the enigma which is addressed to him, but also the enigma of the one he addresses, his public

14 A renewed study of the phenomenon of 'inspiration' could take as its guiding thread the idea that here we have a transference of the relation of primal seduction. [The quotations here are from Mallarmé's poem, 'Le tombeau d'Edgar Poe': 'Calme bloc ici-bas chu d'un désastre obscur', *Mallarmé*, ed. with trans. by Anthony Hartley, Harmondsworth: Penguin Books, 1965, p. 90. Editor's note.]

(for it is too easy to forget that one always does non-clinical psychoanalysis in order to write about it, to communicate it in turn).

It is the offer which creates the demand: a constant proposition in the cultural domain. The dominance of human needs, undeniable but truly minimal in the domain of biological life, is completely covered over by culture. The biological individual, the living human, is saturated from head to foot by the invasion of the cultural, which is by definition intrusive, stimulating and sexual. How has analysis been able to lose sight of this truth, which was ready to emerge alongside the theory of seduction?

This forgetting, and the long going-astray which was its result, can be verified both in the psychoanalytic theory of the human being and in its conception of transference and the treatment. In both cases one cannot escape from a monadological, auto-centered conception. Everything is constructed from the center, all mechanisms are conceived with, as subject, the person in question – Pierre, let's say, or Sigmund. It is Pierre who does the transference, Pierre who projects. And even if the movement is centripetal, it is still Pierre who introjects.

With Freud, transference has a subject fully equipped with his conflicts; with Klein, someone burdened with instincts and objects, who brings them along to analysis. With Ferenczi, perhaps the notion of reciprocity is introduced, but only ever to relate two monads, about which *from that moment* that author is right to wonder why one should be termed the analyst, the other the analysand. Reciprocity, mutuality, the response of the shepherd/counter-transference to the shepherdess/transference, and the other way around – all of this stems from the fact that the arrow of analytic asymmetry has not been noticed. With Lacan, one sometimes seems to have emerged from monadology. But the Hegelian formulations on desire as desire of the other easily become circular (the desire of desire of desire . . .); an endless circle which favours the assimilation of the unconscious to a language, and the claim that it is transindividual. No doubt things are opening up in Lacan, but it is an opening onto all the winds of language. As for the categories of need, desire and demand, henceforth easily accepted, integrated, rendered banal in today's clinic, they lend themselves only too well to monadological recentering. The desire or the demand *of* the analysand: departure-points for *his* transference.

Is it possible for us to succeed in this intellectual conversion, this unimaginable 'version'? to abandon the centrifugal arrow, free ourselves from the idea that everything is already in Pierre's pouch, in that 'indestructible percipiens' Lacan speaks of – an expression which is from one of his inspired moments, his article on psychosis? There he is right to denounce the primacy accorded to projection, which is assumed by the conception of hallucination. Everything would be in the internal 'convenience store', and would be reduced to the simplistic question of 'moving the inside to the outside'.[15]

Is it possible for us to conceive that the arrow, the originary vector, goes in a reverse direction? Reversing the arrow is not to fall back into the symmetry of transference and counter-transference, not to ask which desire of the analyst's would correspond to the analysand's desire. The 'desire of the analyst' – no doubt there is one, even several, and very diverse; but my question is a different one. Are we able to conceive that it is the offer of analysis, the offer of the analyst, which creates . . . what? Not analysis, but its essential dimension, transference. Not, perhaps, the whole of the transference, but its basis, the driving force at its heart, in other words, the re-opening of a relation, the originary relation, in which the other is primary for the subject. A re-opening, because the entire process of the constitution of the subject takes place through a closure, which is, precisely, repression, the formation of topographical agencies, the internalisation of the other and its enclosure in the form of the unconscious.

What does analysis offer? What is the analytic situation? It can be formulated, reformulated, again: I have attempted to do so at length, with the image of the tub.[16] Here, I will propose three dimensions, three functions of the analyst and of

15 Jacques Lacan, *Écrits*, trans. Alan Sheridan, London: Tavistock, 1977, pp. 187–9. Lacan's failure to succeed fully in the radical de-centering required, as well as the fact that he does not truly formulate it in his seminar on transference, is due, we think, to two reasons: 1. An abstract and purely linguistic conception of the signifier, the 'Other' being reduced to the 'treasury of signifiers' in a completely impersonal way. 2. The total misrecognition of the seduction theory, which alone enables the so-called 'supremacy of the signifier' to be put back into its originary frame: the real primacy of the concrete adult over the child.

16 *Problématiques V: Le baquet: transcendance du transfert*, op. cit., esp. pp. 30–46. [Laplanche locates the model of the the tub – le baquet – as one of a series of homeostatic models of enclosure in Freud's work whether of the living organism or vesicle, the psychic apparatus, the ego or the dream. The analytic situation is also modelled in similar terms as an enclosed space, artificially constructed, from which is bracketed out through the fundamental rule and associated conventions the everyday realm of needs and interests; a space in which fantasy, the sexual drives and their derivatives can be brought into play through speech. The difference from these other models of enclosure is that it includes the analyst and his offer of analysis and so incites the re-establishment of the situation of primal seduction and its relation to the originary enigma of the other. Editor's note.]

what he inaugurates: the analyst as the guarantor of constancy; the analyst as the director of the method and the companion of the primary process; the analyst as the one who guards the enigma and provokes the transference.

The first two functions are correlative: the guarantor of constancy and the director of the method. Without these, there is no analysis; more precisely still, without the second, there is no analysis. This is what Freud says: analysis is a method to gain access to phenomena which would otherwise be more or less inaccessible. The method is precisely decomposition, which is steered according to the current, or the currents, of the primary process. It ana-lyses, that is, it dissolves. It is governed by the 'zero principle', setting in motion what Freud, in his way, designated as the 'death drive'; which has nothing to do with biological death, but which, potentially, leads to the dissolution of all formations – psychical, egoic, ideological, symptomatic. But as a counter-balance to this force of unbinding, this liberation of psychical energies, psycho-analysis offers itself as a guarantor of constancy; of containment, as it has been called; of support. It offers the constancy of a presence, of a solicitude, the flexible but attentive constancy of a frame. The principles of *constancy* and of *zero* are, for me, the true principles of psychical functioning.[17] The images of the cyclotron, the tub and the dream link up here: in the dream, the ego takes up a wholly peripheral place, that of the desire to sleep, leaving the field open to the primary process. On this very point, the same takes place in the analytic situation: it is only because there is containment that analysis is possible. It is because the principle of constancy, of homeostasis, of *Bindung* is maintained at the periphery, that analytic unbinding is possible.

The dream as model: André Green has taken note of this in order to set out a critique – that the analytic session is conceived by Freud in terms of a solipsistic model, that of chapter VII of *The Interpretation of Dreams* (1900a). But I'm not sure that a model which would be 'intersubjective' could fully remedy this. Here, I must return to the idea of the 'offer', and to the third function of the analyst: as the one who guards the enigma and provokes[18] the transference. What is *offered* is a place for speech, for free speech, but not,

17 Cf. 'Les principes du fonctionnement psychique' in *La révolution copernicienne inachevée*, Paris: Aubier, 1992.
18 The term *Reiz*, so difficult to translate in its double usage, is our guide here. The *Reiz*, in neurophysiology and in Freudian metapsychology, is a stimulus: that which attacks from the exterior, and provokes change. But it is also the *Reiz* of a person: attractiveness, seductiveness, *sex-appeal*, temptation (a temptress . . .). In Germanic,

properly speaking, the place of an exchange. There is an essential dissymmetry in the relation. Lacan was already talking of 'subjective disparity'. But one must go further, towards something which is difficult to think, as difficult to think as the priority of the other in the constitution of the sexual subject. I have also attempted to take up again the formulation of 'the subject supposed to know', noting how little elucidation Lacan had given it. Let us try it, then!

What is put forward with the offer of analysis in so far as it is social, everyday, banal is certainly a response to the patient's questions: What do I have? What should I do? I would add Kant's third question: What am I permitted to hope? What is proposed is a certain path towards truth, supposed to lead towards the good, towards well-being. But analysis is not a guru, nor a preacher, nor an oracle – despite the impression given by certain practices. It does bring experience and knowledge – that of the method – but also a radical refusal to know the good of its patient, to know the truth about his good.

Benevolent neutrality – two terms which are one, and which take us deeply into paradox. Bene-volence: 'to want the good' of the other without ever claiming to know what it is, without manipulating the patient, even for his supposed good. With the word neutrality, things are even less in focus, and this goes back to Freud. The image of neutrality is inevitably that of the blank screen or, rather, the mirror. Offering projection as much room as possible, allowing solipsism its full space, finally to overthrow it in a confrontation: you clearly see that *it's you that*. . . . In short: *you have projected, and I give you back your projection, I counter-project*. This is neutrality's artificial, almost experimental conception of the mirror: it should be possible to deduct the conditions of the experience or experiment, and for everyone to get back his marbles.

One must arrive at a positive, creative conception of neutrality, productive of the enigmatic dimension. It is here that we should complete our short dialogue, with this response from the analyst:

Analyst: Yes, you can take me for an other, because I am not what I think I am; because I respect and maintain the other in me.

It is maintaining the dimension of interior alterity which allows alterity to be

---

wraitjan means, to be exact, 'to cause to break up' (*reissen machen*), 'to cause someone to come out of himself'; (cf. also *herausfordern*, to challenge, provoke, unhinge). The French word *provocation* would take in both meanings, in line with the theory of seduction.

set up in the transference. Interior relation, relation to the enigma, 'the relation to the unknown': 'If the relation is free enough . . . it becomes for the psychoanalyst the support of his alertness regarding his own psychical reality, his theory and his analysands. For the latter it guarantees access to the diversity of their desires.' I have quoted Guy Rosolato.[19] I will not indicate here my slight differences vis-à-vis this notion of the relation to the unknown;[20] but I find there something corresponding to what, for me, is the maintenance of the analyst's interpellation by the enigma; the maintenance which not only guarantees access to the diversity of desires, but truly *creates, provokes transference.*

'Filled-in transference', 'hollowed-out transference'. It is something simple, in the end, which I have tried to express in this way. We offer the analysand a 'hollow', our own interior benevolent neutrality, a benevolent neutrality concerning our own enigma. The analysand can place there something 'filled-in' or 'hollowed-out'. If it's something filled-in, he empties his pouch into it; if hollowed-out, *another hollow*, the enigma of his own originary situation, is placed there. So we are sent back to the originary infantile situation. The sexual enigma is presented to the child by adults in an *address*, and this address is enigmatic in so far as the other (the one who sends it) does not entirely know what he is saying: he is other to himself. It is in this sense that I have spoken of the *transcendence of the transference* and the transcendence of the originary situation. This originary situation could be called, paradoxically, '*originary transference*'. It is not, of course, the transfer of another thing, but it can nonetheless be given this name, by a sort of movement to the limit — because it already contains the driving force of transference, that is, the doubling, the diplopia which is proper to it. The adult's sexual, provocative, traumatising enigma is, for the child, what has to be ceaselessly mastered, translated, brought back into constancy. All development takes place, therefore, in the direction of a double closure to the message of the other. The closure on the side of what can be translated, theorised, in other words, more or less given ideological form; and also closure through the sealing-off,

---

19 Laplanche quotes the title of Guy Rosolato's book, *La Relation d'Inconnu* — 'relation of/to the unknown'. *La Relation d'Inconnu* (1978), Paris: Gallimard, p. 15 [translator's translation].

20 In particular: that the unconscious is not necessarily, in my opinion, on the maternal side.

the repression of the anamorphic residue of messages, that is, of what resists symbolisation.[21]

Analysis offers – and perhaps in this it is allied to the site of culture – a re-opening of the dimension of alterity. In this opening, of course, something must also take up its place: that which, precisely, had been sealed off.

Taking up a place to open things out, but also to analyse things. For what is new in analysis, in relation to culture, is not transference, it is . . . analysis – that is, *Lösung*. Again, I come back to this definition of Freud's: analysis is before anything else a method of access to unconscious processes. *Lösung*: analysis, solution and resolution, dissolution; a term which unfortunately cannot be translated into French, with all its compounds (*Auflösung, Erlösung, Ablösung* . . .). There is no dissolution of the transference as such; there is the resolution or dissolution of 'filled-in' transference into 'hollowed-out' transference.

From this point on, in that outcome which I consider to be the most analytic, what becomes of the 'hollowed-out' transference? This leads me to conclude with my notion of the 'transference of transference'.[22] If transference, like our interpellation by the enigma, exists before and outside analysis, if it is a fundamental dimension of the human being, any outcome worthy of analysis cannot entail an end to that opening.[23]

21 In the face of the alterity of the other, the methods of defence are immutably the same: attempt at assimilation, denial of difference, segregation, destruction. These are quite clearly found again in attitudes to cultural and ethnic differences. But what is lacking in all the analyses of 'racism' is any consideration of the internal split inherent in the other himself: it is this *internal alterity* which is at the root of the anxiety provoked by external alterity; it is this that one seeks to reduce at any price.
22 I have noted, very much in passing, that these words were first used by Reich, who wished them to indicate that the analytic process was the assumption of, the arrival at genitality and the orgasm, and once the analysand had reached this point, he was to transfer himself beyond this recovered genitality. There is, in fact, between this conception of Reich's (transference of one 'fullness' to another) and my way of proposing the terms 'transference of transference', a total antinomy. Hollowed-out transference is not the result of a development or a process. It cannot be measured in terms of normality and abnormality. Its irreducible dimension of alterity is the basis of transference.
23 Lagache, it is well known, wished to relate transferential repetition to the 'Zeigarnik effect': unfinished tasks tend to be better remembered and more often taken up again than finished tasks (cf. *Oeuvres III*, op. cit., pp. 93, 135, 166). The only meaning we can give to this relation is that the transference cannot aim at closure, since it is the return to, the re-elaboration of our relation to originary enigmas – a relation, in essence, unfinished.

In other places – during analysis, outside analysis – other possibilities of 'transference' are available to the analysand, other poles for the elaboration of an individual destiny. This complex situation, where discrimination is necessary, cannot be envisaged without considering a principal factor, which until now has been ignored: the cyclical character of the dynamics of transference. This fact of experience – that the subject's elaboration passes periodically through points, memories, fantasies whose sequences are organised in analogous ways – finds an exact correspondence in the 'translation' theory we are developing: there is no new translation which does not first pass through the old translations, in order to detranslate them in the interests of a new translation. The process could be purely repetitive, with the same furrows or ruts being indefinitely retraversed. Hollowed-out transference – the point of attraction which constitutes the enigma, and which is re-activated by the analyst – although it is the very origin of the movement of gravitation, is no guarantee that an orbit should not remain stationary, either temporarily or indefinitely. Further cycles, on the other hand, carry the certitude of some gap, some change of level. The same themes are, to be sure, gone through again, 'retranslated', but the 'target language' is enriched; in exceptional cases, it is changed.

I introduce here, concerning the transference, a model familiar to me, the spiral.[24] The circle and the spiral both define gravitational movements. With the former, the movement takes place around a point; with the latter, along an axis. But the spiral can only move forward by passing through, on the horizontal axis, the same enigmatic signifiers (ES):

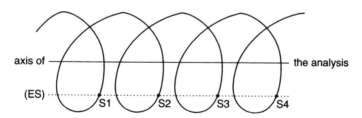

Figure 1

In astronautics, the precise lapse of time when the launching of a spaceship is possible is called a 'window'. It would be a question either of going into orbit

24 In rigorously mathematical terms, it is in fact a 'helix'.

from the earth, or the departure, from a satellite already in orbit, of a vessel aiming to leave the earth's gravitational system.

Likewise for departures from analysis: there are favourable windows, which it can be judged opportune to take advantage of – failing which, gravitation re-asserts its pull for another turn of the spiral.

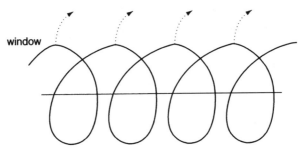

Figure 2

The parameters at stake, nevertheless, are no less complex – and above all, more conjectural and aleatory – than those of interstellar navigation. Will one more turn be a turn for nothing, pure repetition, or is a certain potential for elaboration still present in the analysis? Likewise, that which 'makes a sign' outside can take on diverse meanings: saturation; the arrival at a given point; valencies released by the hollowed-out transference and leading to a new and eventually definitive closure; lateral transference, which perhaps appears under the sign of something new but at the price of breaking, out of time, the current spiral; the transference of transference, in which is set out, outside the treatment, a true site for the confrontation of the enigma.[25]

To distinguish these different modalities can be considered one of the analyst's major tasks, when it comes to proposing the termination of analysis, or acquiescing in one. Again, it must be admitted that often the ways out are

25 We have no hesitation in considering, among the circumstances favourable to the end of the analysis, not only the internal dynamics (turns and windows) but also the external situation. To be still more precise: not only the subject's capability to face up to new difficulties and conflicts (cf 'Analysis Terminable and Interminable', 1937c, SE XXIII), but also the new poles of gravitation, or the 'provocations' which might impinge from the outside. This is the reverse of a conception – monadological again – which would only take account of 'internal' modifications in the structure of the personality.

not sharply outlined, nor easily predictable. On the other hand, the analyst's narcissism may risk blinding him, belittling the perspectives available outside for the pursuit of elaboration. Ultimately, the mastery of the analyst, at the end of the process as well as in its pursuit, is largely illusory; but a mastery which recognises its limits and acknowledges its own testimony is something different from one which strains itself and, in the end, fails.

Among the kinds of transference which exist 'before' analysis (before an individual analysis, and before the historical creation of analysis), we have accorded a privileged place to the multiple relations to the cultural, taken in the widest sense. Now, post-analytic transference will not be absolutely the same as pre-analytic transference, nor totally different from it. That is once again to say that the site of the cultural, as the site of an enigmatic interpellation, with many voices and ears, remains privileged in that it concerns the transference of transference.

To this must be added an essential factor: analysis cannot fail to take into account the fact that it is itself also present, in a privileged way, in that 'culture', which has been in-formed and transformed by its very intervention. I proposed, a few years ago,[26] the idea that, with psychoanalysis, sublimation *changed*: that not only our way of conceiving it, but the essence of sublimation itself changed. In other words, we could no longer speak of sublimation as an eternal and unchanging process: sublimation 'was no longer what it was', it had *drifted* because of the irreversible introduction of analysis into the culture, through all the modalities of analytic praxis, of which the practice of analytic treatment is the most eminent, without perhaps having the greatest impact. The analysand, having emerged from treatment to get involved in new gravitational forces, inevitably encounters, at the cultural sites of transference, the expanding presence of analysis. It is not necessary to think – as Lacan wished to – that the only analysis worthy of the name is that which leads to the practice of analytic treatment, in order to affirm that the analytic experience cannot be a simple parenthesis, which opens one day and closes another, in the human individual's destiny; and this is so even if he does not himself become a practising psychoanalyst.

Translated by Luke Thurston

---

26 *Problématiques III: La sublimation*, Paris: Presses Universitaires de France, 1980, part II, 'Faire dériver la sublimation' (especially the concluding pages).

9

Time and the Other

'I was in the habit', says Freud in *The Interpretation of Dreams*, 'of quoting this anecdote to explain the factor of "afterwardsness" [*Nachträglichkeit*][1] in the mechanism of the psychoneuroses'; 'A young man who was a great admirer of feminine beauty was talking once — so the story went — of the good-looking wet-nurse who had suckled him when he was a baby: "I'm sorry", he remarked, "that I didn't make a better use of my opportunity"'.[2]

In question is an association to the 'Three Fates' or *Knödel* dream,[3] introduced by the following remark: 'Love and hunger . . . meet at a woman's breast'. Indeed, in this dream Freud is concerned explicitly with sexual meanings; but, nevertheless, at a certain point he stops short, for reasons of discretion and decency. I will not go into the complexities of this dream, but only wish to take up the anecdote in the way it offers itself beyond this

---

1 [Laplanche's preferred translation into English of Freud's *Nachträglichkeit* (Fr. *après coup*) is the proposed neologism 'afterwardsness' rather than Strachey's 'deferred action' which suggests merely a delay or lapse of time between cause and effect. The specificity of the family of German terms formed from the stem 'nachträglich' is lost by translating them through a variety of English synonyms, e.g. afterwards, later, subsequently. For an extended discussion of the difficulties of the concept and its translation, see 'The Freud Museum Seminar' in *Jean Laplanche: Seduction, Translation and the Drives*, eds John Fletcher and Martin Stanton, London: Institute of Contemporary Arts, 1992, pp. 41–63; also 'Notes on Afterwardsness' in this volume, pp. 260–5. Editor's note.]
2 *GW* II–III, p. 211; *SE* IV–V, pp. 204–5.
3 The dream is given a detailed commentary by Didier Anzieu, in *Freud's Self-Analysis*, trans. Peter Graham, London: The Hogarth Press, 1986.

particular context: as an illustration of the *concept of afterwardsness*. There are grounds for believing that this illustration dates, like the dream, from 1898 – that is, right in the midst of the history of that concept, which extends from 1895 to 1917. I will not give the details of this complex history here, but I have followed it very precisely this year in my course at the university. Two points of view can be stated: Lacan locates the concept in the Wolf Man case-history, in other words in 1917; but he takes no account of the seduction theory. As if in symmetry, Georges-Arthur Goldschmidt thinks that Freud 'dropped this word' after 1898![4] Clearly, he could have been disabused by simply looking in 'Laplanche and Pontalis'. He also thinks that this word was a natural part of the flow of Freud's language; while in fact afterwardsness is a term plucked from everyday language, transformed into a noun (*Nachträglichkeit*) at a precise moment in the letters to Fliess, and valorised as a technical term by Freud himself. Everything points to this. The apotheosis of a concept, for Freud, was its quantification; and what expression could be more provoking in its scientistic ambition than this: 'The total amount of afterwardsness is thus greatly reduced'.[5]

Nevertheless, that afterwardsness in Freud is not always at the level of conceptual depth that we find in it . . . afterwards, is easily shown by the simple nature of the example chosen from *The Interpretation of Dreams*. Let us take our bearings, in a convenient manner, according to 'time's arrow' – past, present, future. The anecdote gives us two successive scenes, linked by this arrow: the child at the breast, then the adult lover of women thinking of his beautiful nurse's breast. A theory which reverses time's arrow would be that of retroactive interpretation, 'retrospective fantasising' (*Zurückphantasieren*). This is, after all, the position of the young man, who is not a Freudian and wants nothing to do with infantile sexuality. He simply puts himself back there: 'If only I'd known! If only I'd known about desire, been able to desire!' It is almost a joke, and moreover it causes a smile like one. A joke is often made at the expense of someone who is oblivious; here, the baby, who is unaware of his opportunity: sexuality is what is hidden from children, what they cannot even

---

4 G.-A. Goldschmidt, *Quand Freud voit la mer*, Paris: Buchet-Chastel, 1988, p. 87.
5 *GW* XII, p. 88. [I have translated this quotation from Laplanche's French, as the version Strachey gives – 'The period of time during which the effects were deferred is very greatly diminished' (*SE* XVII, p. 58) – illustrates rather well Laplanche's point (cf. two references fn. 1) about the interpretive 'choice' implied by the English translation. Its effect here is precisely to efface *Nachträglichkeit* as a substantive term. Translator's note.]

anticipate. But Freud's interpretation – practically all the texts bear witness to this – goes in the opposite direction; in other words, it does not reverse time's arrow, it is determinist. The English translation of *Nachträglichkeit* by Strachey as 'deferred action' certainly solidifies this choice, but it fits well enough with Freud's explicit doctrine. This doctrine, we know, is that of the 'double time' of the effect of excitation: a representation can cause a much greater excitation, and thus be much more traumatic, than the initial somatic irritation, but this is because an organic maturation has taken place in the intervening time.

It is remarkable that the context in which the concept of afterwardsness appears is the letter of 14 November 1897, which, after the abandonment of the seduction theory, marks a powerful return of the organic. This letter – where the concept first makes its appearance, five times, with the substantivised term *Nachträglichkeit* – immediately defines, like a sort of programme, what will be developed through the years as a succession of 'stages', linked to organic erogenous zones. Moreover, it subordinates this programme itself to a succession of phylogenetic epochs. I have shown how unacceptable I find this link.[6] This erogeneity conceived as purely physiological, organically determined and genetically predetermined, will pose too much of a challenge to Freud, who finds himself confronted with an aporia when it comes to *defining* infantile sexuality, in the enlarged sense he gives it. At least, he will maintain the requirement to do so, preferring not to 'give up the word' sexuality, rather than replacing it with more acceptable terms, like 'organ pleasure', 'interest', and so on.[7] Among his successors, the truth is that this aporia has even disappeared. If it is difficult to grasp infantile, non-

6 On several occasions, I have explicitly stated my absolute opposition to the phylogenetic hypothesis in *psychoanalysis*, whatever form it takes – the reproduction of phylogenesis in the ontogenesis of the drive, primal fantasies which are biologically transmitted, the genetic inheritance of the scenarios of the horde and Oedipus, the innateness of the id, etc.

My opposition is obviously not directed against the genetic transmission of psychophysiological aptitudes and functions acquired in the history of the living being and the species, which are intrinsically foreign to the field of psychoanalysis, even if they are presupposed by it. On the other hand, the problem of the transmission of sexuality (in the psychoanalytic sense) and also of its modes of binding (the Oedipus complex) *must be addressed with models relating to interhuman communication, and not to genetics.*

7 On this point, one should reread chapters XX and XXI of the *Introductory Lectures on Psychoanalysis* (1916–17), as well as the articles 'Sexuality' and 'Organ-pleasure' in *The Language of Psychoanalysis* (1967), trans. Donald Nicholson-Smith, London: The Hogarth Press, 1973.

genital sexuality – precisely as in our anecdote, where alimentary function and pleasure are not distinguished from oral sexuality, with its pleasure, its zone, its specific object – then it will be, purely and simply, abandoned. Reference will still be made to orality (anality) or to oral (anal) object relations, but practically no longer at all to oral or anal *sexuality*. Who, amongst the Kleinians, ever speaks now of infantile sexuality? Who is interested in pregenital erogenous pleasure?[8]

If I chose to start off with the little story of the lover of women, it is because it gives the simplest outline of a temporal sequence – but also because it opens onto two interpretations of *Nachträglichkeit*, which are equally impoverished, and in the end equally desexualising. The 'retrogressive' path, that of the so-called hermeneutical interpretation, completely dispenses with any postulation of infantile sexuality. But the 'progressive' path, that of a succession of stages, runs no less a risk of desexualisation. In today's conception of object relations, the infantile stages, even when they are still termed 'sexual', are only so metaphorically or by convention. We are no longer in the presence of meta-morphoses of sexuality, but of those of love and hate, rendering practically obsolete all reference to an object, to pleasure, to the zones of sexual excitation.

This discussion of time proposes *an elaboration of our thinking about time* which takes account of the advances of psychoanalysis. To be clear, there are two advances indicated by psychoanalysis, which are situated on entirely distinct levels of thinking about time: one of which is explicit, the other completely implicit. Concerning the latter everything, as it were, remains to be done, on the basis of brilliant or summary hints. As a preliminary clarification, I would like to introduce the following distinctions: thinking about time, whether philosophical or scientific, is to be developed on four levels,[9] at once sharply

---

8 It would be interesting to count the occurrence, in texts like those of Melanie Klein, of the terms 'sexuality' or 'erogeneity'. One would notice that they are completely disconnected from any relation to the erogenous zones: the tongue and the lips, the anus, let alone the breast, which is *never* conceived as the source of sexual *pleasure*. When one speaks of this in certain analytic *milieux*, one gets the surprising reply: 'It is you who are denying infantile sexuality; you ignore the baby's precocious erections'. The prepsychoanalytic reduction of sexuality to the genital is clearly at work.

9 During the discussion of this paper, Didier Anzieu reproached me for speaking of 'levels', preferring to this term that of 'fields'. I maintain the idea of levels, which is an explicit reference to a positivist hierarchy, just as much in the domain of reality as in that of the sciences. I see no reason to dispute the idea that life is constructed on an inanimate foundation, and the human being on life; only the relation between levels III and IV is more complex than the simple idea of superimposition would suggest.

distinct and clearly connected. What I call level I is that of cosmological time; let us say: the time of the world. Level II is perceptual time, that of immediate consciousness; this is also, as I will stress shortly, the time of the living being. Level III is the time of memory and of the individual project, the temporalisation of the human being. Level IV, finally, is that of history, the time of human societies, or even of humanity conceived as a whole. Each thinker occupies one or several of these levels. Usually, one level is taken as a privileged departure-point for moving on to a greater or lesser extent to the others. Here, we can peremptorily insert some names, if this is not, on occasion, provocative: at level I, we can situate Aristotle. At levels I and II, with an intimate and privileged relation between them, we situate Kant. At level II, recall, we place perceptual time, of which nothing allows one to say *a priori* that it is not the time of the animal in general. It is so much the more paradoxical to situate thinkers like Husserl and Saint Augustine there. I refer here to Ricoeur's analyses in *Time and Narrative* (1985). At level III are enthroned Heidegger and existentialism, and also hermeneutics. Level IV, the time of history, implies not only temporalisation like level III, but recapitulation. Without question historical societies may be defined as those whose archives exist, those who have their written memory and not just a memory incorporated into manners, customs, institutions, myths, etc. There can also, of course, be a history of individual temporalisation, in other words a recapitulation of the history of level III; this is precisely what we are discussing at today's conference: 'case-histories'.

What is Freud's place on this ladder? As you know, he makes many incursions onto the historical level (IV), but his principle site is double: a theory of time I call explicit is situated at level II; it is a theory formulated as such by Freud, as a psychological theory. As for the implicit thinking about time, implied by psychoanalysis but not developed by it, it is situated on the level of the temporalisation of existence, that is to say at level III.

The explicit theory, that of perceptual time, is presented at several points, but its principal presentation is the text on the 'Mystic Writing-Pad' (1925a, *SE* XIX). It is necessary to go back to it, for it is put forward as *the* Freudian theory of time, and thus as incontestable. But I wish to show that it is precisely right to contest it in order to elaborate a way of thinking about the time of human existence. Freud tells us, about this theory, that for a long time he kept it secret. In fact it emerges at very precise points in his speculations, and it probably originates partly in Breuer, or at least begins in the exchange between Breuer and Freud. This way of thinking links consciousness of time to consciousness of the working of the perceptual apparatus. This in turn is conceived, indeed, as periodical, rhythmical, made up of flashes and interruptions. I quote: 'It is as though the unconscious stretches out feelers, through the medium of the system *Pcpt.–Cs.*, towards the external world and hastily withdraws them as soon as they have sampled the excitations coming from it. . . . I further had a suspicion [Freud speaks in the past tense, as of something he has been thinking of for a very long time] that this discontinuous method of functioning of the system *Pcpt.–Cs.* lies at the bottom of the origin of the concept of time'.[10] It is not my wish to enter into the details here, as it is not my main object; I will limit myself to five remarks on this striking model. First, the consciousness of time is linked to a rhythm, which in a sense counters the seemingly obvious objection that the consciousness of time is being deduced from the consciousness of an apparatus's functioning in time. There has been no advance, since time has been deduced from time. In a sense, Freud escapes from this objection by linking the consciousness of time, as it were, to the time of time, in other words to rhythm. Linear time must be doubled in its 'derivative' (in the mathematical sense of the term), it must be reduplicated *materially* as rhythm – the rhythm precisely of interruption and connection, of light and dark – in order to become consciousness of time.

My second remark is that the being so described is from the beginning present to the world.[11] The perception of the world, far from being constituted by a *first not me*,[12] is on the contrary linked to the periodical extinction of excitation, to the periodical shutting-down that opposes the continuous action of the *not me*. The world is constituted in the living being by a retrenchment in reaction to an excess of world that, in the case of an inanimate being, could be said to be 'perception'. The stone has an excess of world, the living being cuts off from this excess of world precisely in order to establish a time for itself.[13]

10 'A Note upon the "Mystic Writing-Pad"', ibid., p. 231. [Laplanche's comments in square brackets.]
11 This runs counter to the image of the pseudopodia Freud advances. The model of the animalcule again carries the risk of conceiving the world as constituted on the basis of a narcissistic subject.
12 [Winnicott's phrase, in English in the original. Translator's note.]
13 [Laplanche is alluding here to the arguments of Bergson which contrast the exposure of any material entity to the influences of the surrounding world – 'la perception pure' – with the perception of the living being which is characterised by a limiting and diminution of incoming stimuli. For Freud, Laplanche adds, consciousness opposes to the continuous action of the 'not me' a periodic closure, which is a

There is no perception and no memory (even immediate) without something constituting itself as a separate organism, in active retrenchment from the world.

My third remark is that there is no reason at all to think that the model being advanced applies exclusively to the human being. The whole of the functioning described is that of a living being, albeit of the most rudimentary kind, since Freud takes the model (*Vorbild*) of the protoplasmic animalcule. The proto-plasmic animalcule is at once described in a real sense for itself and taken as an example of what happens, with some modifications, in a very complex creature. There is, one might say, at once metaphor, in other words a model for the living being, and metonymy, in other words continuity with the hierarchy of living beings. This clearly indicates that we are at level II and only at this level, which is that of a psychology of perception. It is moreover with some irony, but not with *impertinence*, that I place side by side here Freud, Husserl and Saint Augustine.[14] They all rely upon the link between perception and a rhythm. The examples most often put forward, those found in Husserl, in Saint Augustine, and no doubt also in Bergson, are those of the perception of a sound or of a musical sequence. I could also have invoked the authority of Merleau-Ponty, who never hesitated in his *Phenomenology of Perception* (1962), and already in his *Structure of Behaviour*, to re-establish the continuity between phenomenological analysis in the case of human beings and observation or experimentation in the case of animals.

My fourth contention is that this theory, whose truth remains to be tested but which in my opinion deserves to be, is situated in a way *outside psycho-analysis*. Not one of the major concepts of theory and practice can be found there: sexuality is absent, as are repression, defence and transference. As for time III, which is that of the history of a life, a case-history or history of a sick person, it is not clear how it would benefit from this theory of perception.[15]

My last point, finally, takes things further. This extra-psychoanalytic theory can become *anti-psychoanalytic* from the moment when one seeks to super-

form of self-defence. This rhythm of perception would give rise to a consciousness of time. See Émile Bergson, *Matter and Memory*, trans. Nancy Margaret Paul and W. Scott Palmer, London: Allen and Unwin, 1970. Editor's note.]

14 Cf. J. Lagrange, 'Problématiques du temps: phénoménologie et psychanalyse', in *Psychanalyse à l'Université*, 1988, vol. 13, no. 52, pp. 575–607.

15 This theory is not called upon for support in any of the case-histories.

impose it onto analysis. For me, testimony to this is given by the use of the term 'unconscious' in the text quoted: 'the unconscious stretches out feelers, through the medium of the system *Pcpt.–Cs.*, towards the external world'. Here Freud lapses back (as he does in many places, from the 'Formulations on the Two Principles of Mental Functioning' (1911c) to the notion of the id (1923b), etc.) into a conception of the human individual constructed around a primal kernel, which would be the unconscious – a necessarily innate, biological, instinctual kernel. The unconscious would thus be at the center of the individual, from where it would send out pseudopodia; the individual would resemble a Russian doll. Far from being an alien inside me, the unconscious would be my foundation, my starting-point.[16] One encounters here one of the many forms taken by the attempt to construct a psychology on the basis of psychoanalytic notions – with the latter thus losing all of their specificity, their extraneousness, their alienness.

Human time, time III, could be said to be proper to man. To be sure, there are many things 'proper to man': *erectus, habilis, sapiens,* or rather *sapiens sapiens*; laughter is proper to man, language is proper to man. For today's elaboration I am sticking to three attributes 'proper' to man: he temporalises himself;[17] he has an unconscious (with the fully scandalous nature of that expression: *having* an unconscious); he has an originary relation to the enigma of the other. I wish to show the conjunction of these three essential properties.

What more suitable terrain is there for this than that of loss: of the human being confronted with loss; to the extent that the dimension of loss is probably co-extensive with temporalisation itself? Mourning, then, is discussed by Freud well before 'Mourning and Melancholia' (1917e) and afterwards, too. It is mentioned in *Studies in Hysteria* (1895d) to indicate two elements which are directly linked to temporalisation: mourning is a kind of *work*, the work of memory (*Erinnerungsarbeit* in the case of Elisabeth); and it is an affect with a

---

16 In the text, from the same period as this one, 'Negation' (1925h), it is no longer the 'unconscious' but the 'ego' which puts out these pseudopodia: an indication, in our view, of the absolute wavering of Freud's thought at the moments when he reduces the psychoanalytic to the psychological. Cf., on all of this, J. Laplanche, *New Foundations for Psychoanalysis*, trans. Donald Macey (Oxford: Basil Blackwell, 1989, p. 54 ff.

17 [Laplanche is alluding to a conception of time current in Heideggerian and post-Heideggerian phenomenology in which human activity is conceived, not as taking place in time as a pregiven medium, but as giving rise to the process of time, as temporalisation. Editor's note.]

duration (*Daueraffekt*): it has a beginning and an end, it occupies a *lapse* of time. So I will once again speak of Freud, not to set out his theory, but to pick out from it, both as an indication and a lack, indeed precisely as an absence, that which is most important. Is it after all so surprising that, absence being in question, the most important elements announce themselves in the theory by their absence?

'Mourning and Melancholia' is thus not the only text on mourning, and it is framed by at least two other texts – *Totem and Taboo* (1912–13) and 'On Transience' (1916a). *Totem and Taboo* is nowadays not often read, even though Freud considered it his best book; something Jones reports, without for all that showing the least shame in classifying that work among the 'non-medical applications of psychoanalysis'.[18] In general, when it is referred to, it is for the great drama of the horde, the problem of the totem and the murder of the father. The murder of the father in *Totem and Taboo* overshadows everything, including our memory of the text; it overshadows notably chapter II, which is completely autonomous[19] and whose title is 'Taboo and Emotional Ambivalence'. From the beginning of this chapter let me pick out in passing the term 'enigma' (the enigma of the taboo),[20] which is never used, in Freud, to characterise merely minor problems needing to be resolved. The principal part of this second study is indisputably the 'taboo of the dead'. Other taboos than this, notably the 'taboo of enemies', are discussed, but it is quite remarkable to see how they are subordinated to it. The only taboo enemies are dead enemies. In other words, it is not enough to be an enemy to unleash a phobia about 'laying a hand on' or touching, one must, above all, be dead.

I am going to pick out some elements from this text, without going through it from beginning to end. A first interesting element is the notion of 'reserve'; the term is in French in Freud: 'something like the concept of a reserve is connected with the taboo';[21] for instance, in the sense in which the painter employs this term. *Spatial reserve*: there are, in the territory of the clan, zones one is not allowed to enter, spaces one cannot encroach upon, objects or

18 Ernest Jones, *The Life and Work of Sigmund Freud*, part 2, volume II, chapter XIV, 'The Non-medical Applications of Psychoanalysis', London: The Hogarth Press, 1955.
19 *Totem and Taboo* was published in a series of instalments; they are separate essays.
20 [Translated by Strachey as 'the riddle of the taboo' (see below, p. 254ff. and note 46); *SE* XIII, p. 22. Translator's note.]
21 [*Réserve* is translated inadequately by Strachey as 'something unapproachable' (*Totem and Taboo*, *SE* XIII, p. 18) Editor's note.].

persons one cannot touch. But it is also a *temporal reserve*, for there is a time of the taboo: those who have touched the dead are impure and untouchable but only for a determinate time, which moreover varies according to the honour and rank of the dead. One finds here, incidentally, something which evidently gives Freud pleasure, because of his fondness for quantification: there is a force of the taboo which is, as it were, quantitative, analogous to the forces of universal gravitation, attraction and repulsion; a force greater with a chief than with a deputy, greater with a father than with an uncle, etc. This empty space is thus not only constituted as a reserve zone, but also in time. The time of the taboo, however much it may be bound up with ritual, evokes no less irresistibly the time of mourning. Besides, mourning itself, even quite recently, was ritualised: one 'wore mourning' for a certain precise period, longer or shorter according to one's closeness to the person one was mourning.

A further very exciting aspect is a third kind of what Freud calls 'reserve', although he does not use the term here. This is what I would call a *linguistic* reserve. Here we reach the 'taboo of names'. Indeed, among the things which cannot be touched, there is the name of the dead person, which can no longer be pronounced. The best way to avoid the temptation of uttering the dead person's name is to change his name. Thus, the dead man's name is changed to take account of this prohibition, and to enable us still to speak of him. Little by little, all the names that relate to him are changed: those of persons, but also those of animals (especially totemic animals), familiar objects, etc. I quote a short passage with its air of folklore:

> Indeed, among the Guaycurus in Paraguay, when a death had taken place, the chief used to change the names of every member of the tribe; and 'from that moment everybody remembered his new name just as if he had borne it all his life'.[22] Moreover, if the name of the dead man happens to be the same as that of an animal or common object, some tribes think it necessary to give these animals or objects new names, so that the use of the former name shall not recall the dead man to memory. This usage leads to a perpetual change of vocabulary, which causes much difficulty to the missionaries, especially when such changes are permanent. . . . an important consequence of this process of suppression is that these peoples possess no

22 [Freud quoting an old Spanish observer (1733), from J. G. Fraser, *The Golden Bough*, part II, 3rd edn, London: Macmillan, 1911, p. 357. Editor's note.]

tradition and no historical memory, so that any research into their early history is faced by the greatest difficulties.

(*Totem and Taboo*, op. cit., p. 70)

This very obstacle to writing history is linked by Freud to this linguistic reserve, in other words to the wish to confuse matters, or more radically, to cover over the tracks, to prevent the establishing of any archive, something which the missionaries, who we know were elsewhere such great historians, evidently ran up against.

The problem of the changing of names is dealt with rather briskly in the course of Freud's elaboration, but it would open onto the immense question of the proper name, of its translatability, or even of the right to pronounce it. As you know, the Name *par excellence* – to the extent that today Chouraqui makes it into his principle war-horse in his translation of the Bible[23] – is the true name of Adonaï, which can be written, but which can be neither uttered nor, of course, translated. Names, says Freud, have, for certain people, the full 'meaning of a thing' or 'thing-meaning' (*volle Dingbedeutung*). 'For certain people', that is to say 'primitives and children'; and 'psychoanalysts', he adds; and I, too, would add by way of completion, for my part, translators. The proper name, like the dead person, is untranslatable: it could only be exchanged, in a rigorous sense, for the person himself.

What, then, does it mean to change all the names? It could be said that it draws the necessary consequences from the limitation of mourning. All the attributes of the dead person can be reworked: but his name is untouchable, impossible to *metabolise*. Thus the impossibility of doing a history of these societies. But is it not our tendency, we psychoanalysts, to wonder whether the *result* of a process is not its unconscious *goal*? I will thus propose the hypothesis that it is *in order to* prevent even the possibility of a history that this happens. *Post hoc ergo propter hoc*: this is one of our familiar arguments in psychoanalysis. Even if societies with a continual and absolute changing of names are at the extreme hardly conceivable, nonetheless, this lets us grasp how, through the taboo on using the name, a space of non-mourning is set up inside which

23 [For a discussion of Chouraqui's translational practice and its relevance to the theory of repression and the unconscious, see 'The Wall and the Arcade', *Jean Laplanche: Seduction, Translation and the Drives*, eds John Fletcher and Martin Stanton, London: Institute of Contemporary Arts, 1992, esp. pp. 207–8. Editor's note.]

mourning, *mourning for everything else,*[24] is possible. The taboo thus opens the much larger question: what is it, in loss, that can be metabolised, and what cannot?

For Freud, in his moments of all-conquering realism, everything can be metabolised. The taboo would be purely pathological, reducible without remainder to a purely subjective, internal, 'ipso-centric' mechanism.[25] Here, the two linked notions of ambivalence and projection are called to the rescue (I will pursue this question of the taboo slightly further). A dialogue with Wundt (an author completely forgotten today) comes in at this point, which might be thought confused, but which is nevertheless illuminating.[26] The initial ambivalence according to Wundt (as he can be reread through Freud's text) concerns the phenomenon itself, or even the word: the *word* 'taboo' would be ambivalent in itself – sacred and impure, to be venerated and to be loathed. One could even say, in a sense, pre-ambivalent. Wundt includes both aspects in an originary indistinct concept – the 'demonic' – which only later splits into veneration and loathing. On the other hand for Freud, and this is very important, the two sides – love and hate, veneration and loathing – are from the outset opposed, divided. The ambivalence of the signifier is secondary, for him, to an originary ambivalence of drives. In this there is a sort of prefiguration of the debate in which Benveniste will later come to discuss

24 [Laplanche comments: 'The simple changing of the name of the deceased defines an area of non-mourning: the name cannot be metabolised, it isn't worked over, it must be changed. By contrast this defines a much greater area of everything else (except the name) for which mourning is possible'. To change the name of the dead is paradoxically to preserve the original name as outside use, sacred, non-translatable, while the new name allows a continuing reference to the dead, and therefore a working through, a work of mourning. Editor's note.]

25 [A mental operation in which the subject is himself the agent of the mechanism as against an allocentric mechanism where the other is the agent of a mechanism directed at the subject. See the discussion of ipso-centric mechanisms on pp. 133ff. in this volume. Editor's note.]

26 Even if, at the very moment Freud claims in *Totem and Taboo* that he 'listens with attention' to Wundt, he lets out his rage in his letters: 'I . . . am furious about Wundt', he writes to Ferenczi on 17 October 1912: 'It is a harsh punishment to have to read this rubbish in the evening after eleven hours of work'. *The Complete Correspondence of Sigmund Freud and Sándor Ferenczi*, volume I: 1908–1914, eds E. Brabant, E. Falzeder and P. Gampieri-Deutsch, Cambridge, Mass.: The Belknap Press of Harvard University Press, 1993, p. 411.

Freud's text on 'The Antithetical Meaning of Primal Words'.[27] Primal words, Benveniste will say, do not have 'antithetical' meanings. They designate something prior to the splitting into two meanings. The Latin word *altus*, to recall the example shared by Benveniste and Freud, means 'high' *or* 'deep' to the translator. But in the original language, *altus* is pre-ambivalent: it indicates only the vertical dimension, prior to the moment when the observer takes up a fixed position, whether at the bottom of a well or at the top; and it is only from that moment that he can say, if he's at the bottom of the well, the well is high; and if he's at the top, the well is deep. Could it not be thought, I would ask for my part, that what is prefigured in Wundt, what Freud could have read there under the term 'demonic', was the original ambivalence – or rather 'pre-ambivalence' – of the message of the other? That which Freud rejects, in his disagreement with Wundt, and under the pretext of obscurity and irrationality, *is a conception in which the dead become demons, reveal themselves in their enigmatic aspect, and being henceforth absent give way entirely to their enigmatic message.*

Freud's objection is simple and profoundly rationalist: demons can in no way be considered to be final explanations, *letzte Dinge* ['last things']. Quite simply, we don't believe in demons! 'Neither fear nor demons can be regarded by psychology as "earliest" things, impervious to any attempt at discovering their antecedents. It would be another matter if demons really existed. But we know that, like gods, they are creations of the human mind'.[28]

By exploring the taboo in the case of the dead, Freud made things easy for himself. Demons already are quite clearly human creations. But neither do the dead – any more than demons – exist. In one sense, they too are a creation. They thus leave a space entirely open for projection. Projection which, in the last analysis, is that of a constitutional ambivalence of drives. This ambivalence, Freud tells us, is 'of greater or lesser strength according to predisposition'. Now, ambivalence – it is not very clear why – is particularly important in primitive peoples (just as in neurotics . . .).

This chapter of *Totem and Taboo* includes one of the most comprehensive discussions of projection. Comprehensive in that it presents us with a continuum, going from the projection or so-called projection of bodily sensa-

---

27 *SE* XI, pp. 155–61. Émile Benveniste, 'Remarks on the function of language in Freudian Theory', *Problems in General Linguistics* (1966), trans. Elizabeth Meek, Coral Gables: University of Miami Press, 1971, pp. 65–75.
28 *GW* IX, p. 34; *SE* XIII, p. 24. [Strachey translates Freud's *letzte Dinge* as 'earliest things'. Translator's note.]

tions, said to be what creates the external world, to paranoiac projection. There again, we see the psychoanalytic psychology (or even ontology) I was condemning a moment ago.

The dead are really dead. It is the limit case. But whether dead or not, the other is first constructed by projection. The path of projection will be the one taken by Melanie Klein, which will then engulf her totally. In her view, good and bad are qualities originally projected onto the other. I come back to the case of the enemy: even the enemy, however bad in reality, is not enough to elicit a taboo. His badness is not sufficient for him to be considered a bad object; for him to be a bad object, the projection of my hatred is necessary.

Is there, in Freud's elaboration around the taboo, anything which breaks this originary closure, from which the only way out is projection? I find two indications of this, one in *Totem and Taboo* itself, which is only an indirect testimony: the mention of an affinity between the taboo and the 'categorical imperative'. This indicates, for me, an opening towards the other, towards the message of the other. The superego is not yet present, but is announced; as we well know, the superego will be immediately connected to verbal traces, the traces of the parental 'word'. The other indication of an opening onto the originary dimension of the other is not in that text, but it can be found in 'The Taboo of Virginity' (1918a).[29] This is one of the few texts which breaks out of Freudian ipso-centrism. The fear of deflowering the woman, Freud tells us, is the fear of castration − but for once it is not entirely projected. The fine elaboration around projection is here partially invalidated. I quote: 'Wherever primitive man has set up a taboo he fears some danger and it cannot be disputed that a generalized dread of women is expressed in all these rules of avoidance. Perhaps this dread is based on the fact that woman is different from man (*anders ist als der Mann*), for ever incomprehensible and mysterious, strange and therefore apparently hostile' (*GW* XII, p. 168; *SE* XI, p. 198). A rare, and in every sense *extra*-ordinary, text. Not only is projection replaced by a centripetal movement, by an originary injection of fear, but the other term in the Freudian explication − that is, ambivalence, the ambivalence of love/hate − is relativised. Nor is hostility seen as a 'last thing', a final element; it is subordinated here to otherness: 'different and thus hostile'. Demons are not a last thing, Freud had objected to Wundt − what is final, what is originary is the ambivalence of love/

---

29 Cf. *Problématiques II: Castration-symbolisations*, Paris: Presses Universitaires de France, 1980, pp. 91−108, 175−8.

hate and the resulting projection. Here, in 'The Taboo of Virginity', one could say that in a way Wundt answers back. Ambivalence is not a 'last thing' – Wundt seems to say in Freud's voice – what is last, what is ultimate is the demonic, the hidden, the uncanny (*das Unheimliche*), that which is 'otherwise', which comes originarily *from* the other, in the mode of the other. It is only secondarily that it is split into good and bad.

Why does Freud not find in the relation to the dead person what he notices about the relation to the woman? It is my opinion that he lacks a category, which is neither external reality, real danger, nor the subjective, in other words the projected drives. As far as the relation to the woman is concerned, the lack of this category is not too evident. The woman is there, she is real: it is thus still possible for a real danger to be perceived, scented. Freud, it seems, can appeal from the category of fantasy to that of reality, with no need of a third domain of existence. But the dead person, for his part, is really dead. There is no danger, no otherness to be sensed, except by pure projection. A category is lacking here in Freud, but it is not that of the 'symbolic', it is that of the message or the signifier, which is something quite different. A way of approaching this category is to note that in it the difference between the living other and the dead other is relativised. A signifier remains a signifier, even if set down thousands of years ago, and found in the desert or in a pyramid. It could even be said thus to gain in otherness, as the other who emitted or wrote it is no longer there to support it, to be its guarantor or interpreter.

Mourning

To discuss mourning in Freud is to come up against this same lack, the lack of the category of the message, and in particular, of the enigmatic message. The point is not, for me, to re-examine 'Mourning and Melancholia' (1917e), but simply to mark its central aporia concerning mourning.

First, it is an extraordinary invention. Mourning, which seems so obvious, the pain, the time it takes, etc. – all that is only the manifest aspect of a kind of work; a work following the loss of the other and consisting in a *Lösung* or *Ablösung* (I will come back to these terms). But after this brilliant starting-point, the whole analysis will be turned towards the pathological: which is, I would say, in what is barely a play on words . . . quite normal. Mourning is described as the 'normal prototype' of melancholia – it is that which sheds light, and thus that on which there would be no light to be shed: how could light be illuminated? 'It never occurs to us', says Freud, '. . . to refer it to medical treatment'; thus no analysis is necessary, nor even desirable. 'We look upon any interference with it as useless or even harmful'. Or further: 'It is really only because we know so well how to explain it that this attitude (inhibition) does not seem to us pathological'. Finally, there is this extraordinary declaration: we relate 'melancholia . . . to an object-loss which is withdrawn from consciousness, in contradistinction to mourning, in which there is nothing about the loss that is unconscious' (*SE* XIV, p. 245). And we once again encounter the impressive psychopathological scaffolding of 'Mourning and Melancholia': a scaffolding operating on three ascending levels – that of simple loss, which is mourning; loss + ambivalence, producing obsessional mourning with guilt (already discussed in *Totem and Taboo*); and finally loss + ambivalence + narcissistic object-choice, which produces melancholia. This scaffolding, however, has a fragile base: mourning creaks beneath the burden of all that it is asked to support. Where are we to find mourning which would be only conscious, with no infantile reverberation, no ambivalence and no narcissistic consequences?

The creaking of mourning beneath the weight of the edifice of psychopathology and metapsychology can be heard from 'Mourning and Melancholia' onwards. The pain of mourning, Freud tells us at one point, 'is taken as a matter of course by us'. But then, several lines later: '[it] is not at all easy to explain in terms of economics'. If mourning, in fact, entails no narcissistic wound, no breaching of the ego, how can it be understood to be painful? Especially when pain, precisely, is conceived in Freudian thought above all as breaching. . . . Again, further on: 'We cannot even say how mourning achieves its task'.

I will leave behind these various creakings, to get to the point of the acknowledgement of failure, that the colossus has feet of clay: it is a year later, 'On Transience' (1916a). Let us read this lovely passage (lovely because of its anti-climax): 'Mourning over the loss of something that we have loved or admired seems so natural to the layman that he regards it as self-evident. But to psychologists mourning is a great riddle [this is the word that gives the game away],[30] one of those phenomena which cannot themselves be explained but to which other obscurities can be traced back'. And a little further on: 'But why it is that this detachment (*Ablösung*) of libido from its objects should be such a

---

30 [Laplanche's aside refers to the French translation of the German word *Rätsel* (in English, and in Strachey, 'riddle') as *énigme*, 'enigma'. For his comments on these riddles of translation, see below, pp. 254ff. and footnote 46. Translator's note.]

painful process is a mystery to us, and we have not hitherto been able to frame any hypothesis to account for it. We only see that libido clings to its objects and will not renounce those that are lost even when a substitute lies ready to hand'.

What a scandal for Freud! Why not change the object, as soon as the old one has gone and another is at hand? But despite the repetition of this enigma, the passage comes to a halt with an abrupt conclusion, as if impatient to finish: 'Such then is mourning' (*das also ist die Trauer*) (*GW* X, p. 360; *SE* XIV, pp. 306–7).

It is a scandal for a realist, for whom the dead are really dead. Why is all this work required to change object? Why so much palaver? Now this enigmatic block of mourning is to remain untouchable in what follows, and for posterity.[31] Abraham will seek for a moment to explore mourning, that is, to put Freud to work, but he will be promptly rebuffed.[32] Freud does not like being put to work. Very quickly, mourning will be buried, hidden beneath psychopathology, which little by little re-invests it. See Abraham, then Melanie Klein, even in the article where she analyses her own mourning;[33] and finally, Lagache, whose case entitled 'Pathological mourning'[34] perhaps did the most to re-open the question of mourning in its entirety.

There are many routes to re-open that question. Among others, there is one route that is both poetic and linguistic: a patient, when she came to consult me, straight away told me how she had seen her husband off to the war, some years previously. There had been no news! Searches in all the records, in all the camps, Russian or Nazi, proved in vain. It was said that he had escaped, but there was no proof, and already numerous young suitors were crowding round her, demanding that she change her object and remarry. And already . . . you have guessed that it's Penelope. You know of her ruse, the famous cloth. Let us, in turn, allow ourselves to be carried away by the ruse of some words:

31 [Laplanche is alluding to Mallarmé's poem, 'Le tombeau d'Edgar Poe': 'Calme bloc ici-bas chu d'un désastre obscur', *Mallarmé*, ed. with trans. by Anthony Hartley, Harmondsworth: Penguin Books, 1965, p. 90. Editor's note.]
32 Karl Abraham, 'A Short Study of the Development of the Libido' (1924), *Selected Papers*, London: The Hogarth Press, 1927.
33 Melanie Klein, 'Mourning and its relation to manic-depressive states' (1940), reprinted in *The Selected Melanie Klein*, ed. Juliet Mitchell, Harmondsworth: Penguin Books, 1986.
34 Daniel Lagache, 'Pathological Mourning' (1956), *Selected Writings*, trans. Elizabeth Holder, London: Karnac Books, 1993.

στησαμένη μέγαν ἱστὸν (94)[35]

having erected a huge mast.

This requires an explanation, because ἱστὸν [iston] will immediately mean, in the next line, a fabric. The link between the two meanings of the word is metonymic. On the weaving loom, as you know, the threads of the 'chain' are rolled onto a baton. Normally, we see a horizontal roll, but on the ancient looms the roll was vertical, the cloth was woven on a sort of mast, an erected baton, with all the associations you may wish.[36]

ἠματίη μὲν ὑφαίνεσκεν μέγαν ἱστόν (104)
By day she wove a great fabric
νύκτας δ᾽ ἀλλύεσκεν (105)
And by night, she analysed it.

(ἀλλύεσκεν [alluesken], the iterative imperfect of ἀναλύειν [analuein], that is to say undo, unweave, or . . . analyse).

The last line quoted describes the moment when the ruse is discovered by the suitors. Having begun to get suspicious about this work which never advances, they buy the complicity of a servant, break in one night and surprise Penelope at her work of unweaving:

καὶ τήν γ᾽ ἀλλύουσαν ἐφεύρομεν ἀγλαὸν ἱστόν (109)
and we found her in the midst of analysing her resplendent
fabric.

This, then, is Penelope's work; but what is it exactly? Is it weaving or unweaving? The analogy between 'analysing' and 'undoing' the fabric invites us to attempt to turn the whole process around. We are used to this kind of interpretation. We are told in the manifest tale: a faithful and wise spouse, she wishes to get rid of the suitors, and she weaves with the sole aim of unweaving, in other words to gain time until her Ulysses returns. One can equally well suppose, however, the reverse: that perhaps she only unweaves *in order* to weave, to be able to weave a new tapestry. It would thus be a case of *mourning*, mourning for Ulysses. But Penelope does not cut the threads, as in the Freudian

---

35 Homer, *The Odyssey*, ed. W. B. Stanford, London: Macmillan, 1967, Book II, p. 19.
36 A 'cloth' is thus named by the same word as the 'erected mast'. Furthermore, in the line quoted, στησαμένη [stesamene] (having erected) is from the same root as ἱστόν [iston] (erected mast).

theory of mourning; she patiently unpicks them, to be able to compose them again in a different way. Moreover, this work is nocturnal, far from the conscious lucidity with which, Freud claims, the threads are broken one by one. This work requires time, it is repetitive (thus the iterative verb form), it sets aside a reserve. One could say, to introduce at this point what has been established about the taboo: it sets aside the reserve of the *taboo of Ulysses*, the reserve of the *name of Ulysses*.[37] There is, however, a possible end. One can imagine that one evening the new cloth, for a while at least, will not be unwoven.

The route opened up with Homer takes us further on, then. Through the very words of the poet, it invites us to enter again into the text of 'Mourning and Melancholia'. The Greek verb – this point must be stressed – coincides exactly with the German *lösen*, 'to untie', 'resolve'. The *Lösung* of a problem is its 'solution' or its 'resolution'. From this, the German language develops a series of derivatives: *lösen, auflösen, ablösen, erlösen*. French has a series quite close to this, with words formed on the Latin root *solvere: solution* ('solution') (but no verb *soudre*, whence the rather ugly *solutionner*);[38] *résoudre* ('to resolve'), *dissoudre* ('to dissolve'), *absoudre* ('to absolve'); but the equivalences are not exact. Άναλύειν [analuein], at any rate, is very exactly *auf/lösen*, to dissolve, to ana/lyse: what it refers to is a resolution which operates by 'going back over' (*auf–άνα*), that is by drawing near the elementary or the originary. 'Psycho-analysis' could have been named by Freud, if he had not wished to choose a Greek term, *Seelen-Auflösung*: disentangling, dissolution or resolution of souls. Terms formed with *lösen* occur very often in Freud, and are moreover extremely difficult to translate, if one is trying to keep a certain continuity in the French. In 'Mourning and Melancholia' they appear in particular in the two forms *lösen* (*Lösung*) and *ablösen* (*Ablösung*). Thus, in the central passage, which is so well known, on mourning: 'Each single one of the memories and expectations in which the libido is bound to the object is brought up [*mis en position*] and hypercathected, and the *Lösung* of the libido is accomplished in respect of it'.[39]

---

37 The notion of a 'reserve of the name' would perhaps allow the famous question of the 'Name of the Father' to be put to work in a new way.

38 [English has 'to solve' as the solution of this French problem. Translator's note.]

39 *GW* X, p. 430; *SE* XIV, p. 245 [Strachey has 'detachment' for *Lösung*. Translator's note].

Two terms here deserve comment. First of all, '*mis en position*' [Strachey's 'brought up'], corresponding to the German '*einstellen*'. It is a question, very precisely, of the 'positioning' of a piece of cloth on a machine, in order to begin some work on it. In an old translation, we had proposed 'put on the loom', which was a more direct evocation of the 'weaving loom'.[40] One can only marvel to see Freud, who nowhere alludes to Penelope, coming close to the same image for the work of mourning.[41]

The term *Lösung* could also have taken us towards 'unweaving', the disentanglement of the libido; this nuance is certainly present in the German word, but, unfortunately, it is gradually effaced in the course of the article, in favour of *Ablösung*, which skews things towards detachment, the slipping of moorings, or rather the breaking of links. What prevails in Freud is clearly the detachment of the libido from the object or, more precisely, from the representation of the object. This does not surprise us as the object is constantly defined by him as 'what is most variable in the drive', so that the change of object, once the object has disappeared, seems to be a matter of course, save for any neurotic complications.[42] Whence, perhaps, the fact that Freud does not see that mourning as a work of unweaving, as much as it is the protoype of melancholy, can also be conceived as the very model of

40 And, of course, Boileau: 'Twenty times on the loom you begin again your work' (*Art Poétique*).

41 So much the more striking is Freud's other intuition, leading him to ascribe to woman the invention of weaving, seeing in it a sort of perfecting of the pubic hair which, according to him, masks the absence of the penis (in the *New Introductory Lectures*, *GW* XV, p. 142; *SE* XXII, p. 132).

Numerous paths open up from this starting-point:

That of Greek etymology, such as it is reflected in Homer's text, where ἱστόν [iston] is at once the penile mast of the loom and the cloth which is rolled onto it, veiling it. In the same way, the pubic tissue is at once what veils (*verhüllen*) and, symbolically, what is veiled (cf. 'Medusa's Head', *GW* XVII, pp. 45–8; *SE* XVIII, pp. 273–4).

A questioning of the privileged relation of woman to, at the same time, weaving-unweaving, mourning and melancholia.

The setting up of a relation between the lost object, in mourning and/or melancholia, and the lacking or lost penis.

42 Cf. on this point J. Laplanche and J.-B. Pontalis, *The Language of Psychoanalysis*, trans. Donald Nicholson-Smith (London: The Hogarth Press, 1973), the entry under 'Object'.

psychoanalysis: unweaving so that a new fabric can be woven, disentangling to *allow* the formation of new knots.[43]

What are the threads that are unwoven which this work of untying[44] bears upon? Freud spoke of 'memories' and 'expectations' attaching us to the other. What he doesn't take account of, but which is rarely absent – precisely in the fabric, the *context* of those memories and expectations – is the place for the *message* of the other. For the person in mourning, that message has never been adequately understood, never listened to enough. Mourning is hardly ever without the question: what would he be saying now? What would he have said? hardly ever without regret or remorse for not having been able to speak with the other enough, for not having heard what he had to say.

Éric Toubiana, in his work on 'the psychopathology of inheritance', shows this well.[45] The struggle for succession is not only a material struggle for the property of the deceased. The fury which breaks out around the will (that of Caesar, for instance) perpetuates a speech – enigmatic, traumatising, violent, or even deadly, the voice of the other. A voice no doubt related to the superego, but which is not entirely merged with it.

Enigma

When I hear talk of enigmas, I prick up my ears. .An enigma, despite the German term *Rätsel* we use it to translate, is not just a simple riddle [*devinette*] (from the verb *erraten*: *deviner*, 'to guess'). An enigma, as I understand it, is to be distinguished just as much from a riddle as from a problem to be resolved, or from a *mystery*.[46] When we hear enigmas talked of, I propose this procedure:

---

43 Freud gave a clear expression of the spontaneous character of 'psychosynthesis' in the patient in analysis in 'Lines of Advance in Psycho-Analytic Therapy' (1919a), *SE* XVII, pp. 160–1. The 'reconstruction' of the patient, at least in the analysis of neurotics, is not done by the analyst.

44 The French language brings together untying (Fr. *déliement*, Ger. *Lösung*) and unbinding (Fr. *déliaison*, Ger. *Entbindung*) in a way that German does not. At the same time, the relation between the unweaving of associative threads and the unbinding (unchaining) of libido should be stressed.

45 *L'héritage et sa psychopathologie*, Paris: Presses Universitaires de France, 1988.

46 One is entitled, to be sure, to equate these terms; for my part, I try to differentiate them. An enigma, like a riddle, is proposed to the subject by another subject. But the solution of a riddle in theory is completely in the conscious possession of the one who poses it, and thus it is entirely resolved by the answer. An enigma, on the contrary, can only be proposed by someone who does not master the answer, because his message

to move from the enigma *of*, to the enigma *in*, and then to the function of the enigma *in*.[47] Let me explain: when one speaks, to take up Freud's terms, of the enigma *of* femininity (what is woman?), I propose with Freud to move to the function of the enigma *in* femininity (what does a woman want?). In the same way (but Freud does not make this move), what he terms the enigma of the taboo takes us back to the function of the enigma in the taboo. And still more so, the enigma of mourning takes us to the function of the enigma in mourning: what does the dead person want? What does he want of me? What did he want to say to me?

The enigma leads back, then, to the otherness of the other; and the otherness of the other is his response to his unconscious, that is to say, to his otherness to himself. I put forward the title of this paper, 'Time and the Other', as a kind of approximation. On the one hand, it did not completely correspond to what I wanted to say; and on the other, I realised that it duplicated the title of a work by Levinas, of some years ago now.[48] A work which doubtless would not be the most adequate way to stage a debate between what I am arguing and the thought of that author. Unfortunately, the best title would have been rather too sophisticated: something like 'Time and the other(s)' [*Le temps et l'/les autre(s)*], in other words the different 'others'. In Freud, there are at least two domains of 'the other': *der Andere* and *das Andere*.

---

is a compromise-formation in which his unconscious takes part.

To speak of the 'enigma' of natural phenomena (the enigma of 'black holes') is, in our sense, incorrect, unless one supposes a demiurge with an unconscious. To say that the baby offers an enigma to the adult, just as much as the other way round (cf. D. Houzel, in *Journal de la psychanalyse de l'enfant*, 1990, vol. 8, p. 289) is to suppose that the psychical apparatus of the human infant is immediately split between 'unconscious' and 'preconscious-conscious', a constitutional split to my mind inadmissible.

As for mystery . . . let us leave to theologians the task of situating it in relation to the categories of the message and the signifier!

47 This 'in' has no topographical connotation here, and does not situate the enigma on the 'inside' of the psychical apparatus. If one had to situate the enigma, it would be on the contrary as a surface entity, first implanted in the skin of the body, then in the outer surface of the ego (cf. the schema for primal repression, *New Foundations for Psychoanalysis*, trans. David Macey, Oxford: Basil Blackwell, 1989, p. 135).

48 Emmanuel Levinas, *Time and the Other* (1948), trans. Richard A. Cohen, Pittsburgh: Duquesne University Press, 1987.

The other in the masculine we have to specify (in French) as the 'other person'; and *das Andere* or *das andere Psychische*, as the 'psychical other' or the 'other thing'. The 'other thing' is quite simply the unconscious. There is no reason to deny this 'other thing' the characteristics of timelessness and above all the absence of negation. The absence of negation, the absence of discursivity from the diachronic point of view, and the absence of 'value' (in the Saussurean sense of structural opposition) from the synchronic. On the other hand, as I indicated a moment ago in my criticism of a point in Freud's theory of perceptual time, the unconscious cannot in any way be considered the kernel of our being, the *Kern unseres Wesens*, in the sense of an *intimior intimo meo* ['something more inward than my inwardness']. Far from being my kernel, it is the other implanted in me, the metabolised product of the other in me: forever an 'internal foreign body'.

The Other Person

The other person is primal in relation to the construction of human subjectivity (level III of time), in other words, of sexual and temporal subjectivity. I would like this to be felt, for a moment, in relation to all the 'mechanisms' described by psychoanalysis. Take processes like introjection and projection, for instance: this pair has done well since Freud, and with Melanie Klein. Melanie Klein has been criticised, and in one sense not unjustly, for the primacy she accords to projection. I recalled this on the subject of the taboo: in Klein, but already in Freud too, the object is bad, primordially, through projection. Is it a question, for all that, of opposing to it an introjection which would be more originary? Are we not faced with the problem of the chicken and the egg: which comes first? Projection? Introjection? The only way not to get lost in this absurd quarrel over priority, this quest for a perpetual movement of self-engendering, is to *escape* from the dilemma. What I wish to say, fundamentally, is that introjection, just as much as projection (as well as repression, defence, identification, etc.), is a mechanism whose subject, the subject of the verb itself, is the individual in question: 'I introject'; but equally – for I am not setting in opposition mechanisms in the 1st, 2nd or 3rd person – 'you repress', 'Pierre or Sigmund identifies'. All these processes are 'conjugated' with the person in question; caught in the trap of ipso-centrism, psychoanalysis can only run after mechanisms in which the subject would still be active, all the while *pretending* to be passive.[49] Let us take the mechanism of disavowal, in which it is me without being me, who wishes to know nothing about it, yet all the same knows. Even Lacan's 'foreclosure' is caught in this trap: introduced following an admirable condemnation of the 'indestructible percipiens' underlying the whole conception of hallucination as purely projective, it constitutes, nonetheless, a veiled return to ipsocentrist positions which it was thought to have surpassed.[50] Foreclosure, refusal of entry to the symbolic, we are told . . . but *who* 'refuses entry', if not President Schreber as the 'indestructible' subject of the process? *Who* 'forecloses' the Name of the Father . . ., if not Daniel-Paul himself, *in person*? Can one not therefore propose a fundamental inversion: the originary mechanisms are not 'in person', but 'in otherness', to be formulated starting from the other: *he* implants, *he* intromits . . . into Pierre, Jacques or Sigmund?[51]

I will return now to my central theme, that of temporalisation; exactly that which Heidegger describes as stretched between its three *ekstases*: present, future and having-been. At this starting-point of the description I have no quarrel with this 'stretching out'. I indicated just now that my analysis is not located *in the wake of* Heidegger's, but certainly *on the same terrain* of being. My criticism does not therefore concern the tension between these *ekstases*, but the way they are linked together, and the priority to be established between them. My target here is not only Heidegger, but the whole of hermeneutics, including the vast hermeneutical movement which is nowadays invading psychoanalysis, and which we are not sufficiently aware of in France: not sufficiently present in the debate which is establishing itself, in the heart of the psychoanalytic movement, with hermeneutics. Heidegger and hermeneutics give priority to 'being for', as Ricoeur has recently restated: Heidegger asserts 'the primacy of the future in the [course] of the articulated structure of time'.[52] The originary

49 An exact reversal of, but also correlative to, Cocteau's famous formula: 'Since these mysteries are beyond me, let's pretend to be the one who organizes them' ('Les mariés de la Tour Eiffel', in *Théâtre de Cocteau*, tome I, Paris: Gallimard, 1949, p. 57). Clearly, I would say: 'Since this *enigma* . . .'.
50 Jacques Lacan, 'On a question preliminary to any possible treatment of psychosis' (1955–6), in *Écrits: A Selection*, London: Tavistock, 1977, p. 187.
51 For a rather fuller elaboration, cf. 'Implantation, Intromission' in this volume, pp. 133ff.
52 Paul Ricoeur, *Time and Narrative*, vol. 3, trans. Katherine Blamey and David Pellauer, University of Chicago Press, 1988. [Ricoeur's 'le parcours' is here translated as 'analysis' rather than 'course' as above. *Temps et Récit*, tome III, 'Le temps raconté', Paris: Seuil, 1985, p. 103. Editor's note.]

vector is the future, the 'to-come' [Fr. *l'à-venir*, Ger. *Zu-kunft*], the Orient[53] (*Woraufhin*) towards which the subject throws himself resolutely. One knows the Heideggerian term *Entschlossenheit*, translated either as 'decision', as 'resolution' or as 'resolute decision'. It is with the same resolute decision that Freud, for his part, goes towards the past. And here I have no argument, there is nothing I wish to reformulate on our part. Analysis is a movement towards the past, a going back over – the *Lösung* ['solution'] is an *Auflösung* ['dissolution'], a term which well indicates the movement. What should be added emphatically, however, is that it is a going back over which dissolves, which resolves, and not a going back to the so-called ultimate formula of my being. Beyond translations and past constructions, beyond the weavings it undoes, analysis goes back along the threads of the 'other': the other thing of our unconscious, the other person who has implanted his messages, with, as horizon, the other thing in the other person, that is, the unconscious of the other, which makes those messages enigmatic.

I speak of a fixed mover of temporalisation, repeating in a certain way the Aristotelian image. But rather than theorising on this subject, I would like to come back to the little story of the 'lover of women'. The anecdote is apparently limited to the relation between two scenes: the child at the breast, the adult in the presence of the breast. There are only two protagonists, the individual in question and his 'object', the breast. In this story of 1898, Freud, who has abandoned the theory of seduction, forgets or rather scotomises *the nurse*, in whom he refuses to see a new figure of the 'perverse adult' of the letters to Fliess. Here, she is hardly anything more than the support of an object without enigma, an object to be consumed. But what object, what consumption, is at issue here? Is it the milk which is to be ingested? Is it the breast which is to be . . . sucked . . .? Incorporated . . .? Caressed . . .? Stimulated . . . .? As for the nipple, precisely the erogenous part of the object, it is cruelly absent, as is any reference to the pleasure the other seeks there.

Here, then, is what is missed, in the imperfect, unfinished conceptualisation of afterwardsness, just as in the Freudian theory of infantile sexuality, and even in the theory of leaning-on:[54] beyond the movement which carries it to a so-called primal scene, 'the child at the breast', analysis (the unweaving of that

53 [In the wake of Hölderlin, Heidegger and Ricoeur, Laplanche comments that 'this term is a metaphor for the rising sun, towards which we are thrown'. Editor's note.]
54 Freud's *Anlehnung* translated by Strachey as 'anaclisis'.

scene) opens onto the activity, the implantation, the message and also the enigmatic sexual pleasure of the other. Thus, perhaps, there emerges a way out of the dilemma which troubles our practice, caught between pure determinism and the pure attribution of meaning. A primal 'to-be-translated', if it contained, like a seed, the whole of meaning, would be an 'open sesame' to be discovered, a master-key to open all doors. But, conversely, a primal 'to-be-translated', if it had the obtuseness of brute fact, would be open to all meanings, and from then on any attribution of meaning would be purely arbitrary. A primal 'to-be-translated', if it is a message unknown to itself, coming from the other and implanted by the other, first sets in motion the movement of translation-detranslation, which is that of human temporality.

Translated by Luke Thurston

10

Notes on Afterwardsness[1]

I want to stress first of all that the whole problematic of *Nachträglichkeit* (afterwardsness) also takes shape through a process of afterwardsness. It is due to the French reading and translation of Freud that the concept of afterwardsness has become important. If, for example, you take the indexes of the different volumes of Freud's *Gesammelte Werke*, you will find that neither *nachträglich* nor *Nachträglichkeit* are mentioned. The *Gesammtregister*, which dates from much later – 1968 in fact, so it comes after the publication of *The Language of Psychoanalysis* - actually has one or two entries under the adjective *nachträglich*, but these are not very significant examples. If you also look in the indexes of the work of Freud's main followers, you'll come to the same negative result. It's therefore in France, and in close relation to the problems of translation, that the importance of *Nachträglichkeit* has made itself felt. Its importance was first noted by Lacan who in 1953 drew attention to this term in a precise but restricted way, but he did not look at the broader implications of the concept for Freud's work. He focused only on its occurrence in the *Wolf Man* (1918b [1914]) case, and ignored its use in the period 1895–1900. It was left to Pontalis and myself to draw attention to the general importance of the concept – first, in 'Fantasy and the Origins of Sexuality' (1964), and then in *The Language of Psychoanalysis* (1967). I have continued this elaboration of the concept in my own work, in *Life and Death in Psychoanalysis* (1970) and in the *Problématiques* (1980–7) as well as in *New Foundations for Psychoanalysis* (1987b).

1 These 'notes' are based on a conversation between Jean Laplanche and Martin Stanton recorded in 1991. They appeared in *Jean Laplanche: Seduction, Translation and the Drives*, eds John Fletcher and Martin Stanton, London: Institute of Contemporary Arts, 1992, and have been added to and revised by Professor Laplanche for this volume (1998).

I am presently working on a larger paper on 'The Afterwardsness of *Nachträglichkeit*', which will eventually form a chapter in a book I am writing on time. In this, I give a detailed account of Freud's use of the term, and the way in which it differs from my conception, so here I will only present the outline of my argument. I'll develop my argument along three general lines: first, what happens to Freud's concept; second, the issue of its translation; and finally, my own conception of afterwardsness. Here again I must stress that one can examine carefully what Freud said without actually adhering to his thought and that is certainly my position!

First, Freud's view of afterwardsness. He used the terms *nachträglich* and *Nachträglichkeit* over a great period of his working life, in fact from the time of his correspondence with Fliess, through *The Interpretation of Dreams* (1900a), and *Little Hans* (1909b) to the *Wolf Man* (1918b [1914]), and indeed well beyond that. So it is possible to trace the development of these terms in the general context of his work. They never, however, became fully-fledged enough as concepts for Freud to dedicate a whole article to the concept of afterwardsness. We can see the early development of the term in Freud's correspondence with Fliess. Several things become apparent here. The adjective *nachträglich*, which is taken from current usage, is used by Freud in several ways. We can roughly distinguish three uses of the term by him: first, there's the sense of 'further' or 'secondary' – it relates secondary consciousness to a primary one. Strachey and Masson usually translate this by 'subsequently', so it assumes simply the temporal meaning of 'later'. The second usage follows the direction of time from the past to the future, and the third usage inverts it from the future towards the past. The second usage moving from past to the future is very much tied up with the seduction theory: it implies the deposit of something in the individual which will only be reactivated later, and so will only become active in a 'second time' – that's the seduction theory. One should point out that this seduction theory was very mechanical, because Freud never thought that one could reverse temporal direction. One can use the time-bomb example to illustrate this: the first memory is like a time-bomb which is triggered off by something outside it. There is no sense here of retroactivity. But there's a third usage which does convey the sense of retroactivity. There are a number of passages concerning things which are registered in a first time then understood retroactively. These are relatively rare in Freud.

I'll limit myself here to making a few contextual remarks about these three usages. In the choice between a determinist conception that proceeds from the past to the future and a retrospective or hermeneutic conception that proceeds from the present to the past, Freud always chooses the former. Indeed, he never even attempts to reconcile the two conceptions. I refer here to the letter to Fliess of 3 October 1897 in which he relates an episode of his self-analysis and comments: 'A harsh critic might say of all this that it was retrogressively fantasised instead of progressively determined. The *experimenta crucis* must decide against him'.[2] My other contextual point concerns the appearance of the substantive *Nachträglichkeit*. As you know, this word is relatively rare in German. It is remarkable that this substantive only appears in a relatively late letter to Fliess of 14 November 1897 (ibid., pp. 279–80). This letter comes after the so-called abandonment of the seduction theory, at a moment when Freud becomes even more 'determinist' – determinist in the sense that the future and the present are both determined by the past. This letter is entirely focused on the organic determinism of repression and therefore on the phylogenetic origin of ontogenetic development. It's on this level of the determinism of the development of individual sexual stages by phylogenetic stages that Freud poses 'afterwardsness', so there is no question of reversing temporal progression. Consequently things are not all that simple. Whereas we may wish to see a double and even contradictory use of *Nachträglichkeit*, we actually discover a use that is heavily determinist.

Now you could criticise this view for being too exclusively based on texts before 1898, so I'll give you some brief illustrations of Freud's consistent rejection of the reversibility of temporal direction in later texts. There are three important texts here: *The Interpretation of Dreams*, *Little Hans*, and the *Wolf Man*. In this progression, Freud becomes increasingly caught up in a theoretical exchange with Jung, defending his view that there is a real primal scene – 'real' in the sense of really experienced. Freud made some concessions but he never wavered in his conviction that what comes before determines what happens after. It seems to me therefore totally wrong to try to assimilate Freud's concept of *Nachträglichkeit* to Jung's notion of *Zurückphantasieren* (retrospective fantasizing).[3]

---

2 *The Complete Letters of Sigmund Freud to Wilhelm Fliess: 1887–1904*, trans. and ed. Jeffrey Moussaieff Masson, Cambridge, Mass.: The Belknap Press of Harvard University Press, 1985, p. 270.

3 Laplanche is here criticising recent attempts to assimilate Freud's use of *Nachträglichkeit* to the hermeneutic tradition, notably through parallels with Jung's notion of *Zurückphantasieren* ('Freud's *Nachträglichkeit* and Strachey's "Deferred Action": Trauma, Constructions and the Direction of Causality', Helmut Thomä and Neil Cheshire, *International Review of Psychoanalysis*, vol. 18, 1991, pp. 407–27).

Now to my second point: translation. Alternative translations are offered for this term as for many others. Either one decides that this term must be translated according to the context; in other words, it must be 'interpreted'. In this case, we could not have a single term in either English or French for *nachträglich/Nachträglichkeit*. This approach is well illustrated by Strachey who translates them by a whole series of terms according to the context: 'deferred action', 'subsequently', 'in a deferred fashion', 'subsequent', 'aftereffect', 'deferred effect', 'deferred nature of the effect', 'later', etc. As long as one wishes to 'interpret' in this way, and impose meaning on an essentially open text, a unitary translation is impossible. Let us now take the example of two translations of *Nachträglichkeit* which seem to be in competition: 'retrospective attribution' proposed by Helmut Thomä and 'deferred action' classically proposed by Strachey. Two examples will illustrate this: in the *Studies on Hysteria* (1895d), Freud talks of the 'nachträgliche Erledigung der Traumen' (*GW* I, p. 229), and, in the letters to Fliess, Freud writes 'Phantasien sind Dinge früh gehört erst nachträglich verstanden' ('Letter to Fliess, 6th April, 1897' in Masson (ed.), op. cit., p. 234). In the first example, it's totally impossible to translate *nachträglich* as 'by retroactive attribution', which would produce the absurd translation: 'the liquidation of the trauma by retrospective attribution'. It's equally absurd to translate the second sentence by: 'Fantasies are things which were heard previously and only understood by deferred action'. You can see in these two examples that interpretative translations fail to convey the whole context in which Freud employs the term *nachträglich*. So either one decides to split up and divide the term in translation, or one chooses a term that will allow the readers to stay with Freud's term and reinterpret it for themselves. That's why I propose a translation that is not interpretative: I suggest the term *après coup*, and 'afterwards' in English. In all cases in Freud it's possible to use either 'afterwards' or 'afterwardsness'.

I now want to talk about my own conception of *Nachträglichkeit*, and to stress that I differ from both the Freudian and the Jungian or hermeneutic conceptions. To introduce this, I would like to take a passage from *The Interpretation of Dreams* which has not been commented on by other critics: this is an association to the 'Knödel' (dumpling) dream:

In connection with the three women I thought of the three Fates who spin the destiny of man, and I knew that one of the three women – the inn-hostess in the dream – was the mother who gives life, and furthermore (as in my own case) gives the living creature its first nourishment. Love and hunger, I reflected, meet at a woman's breast. A young man who was a great admirer of feminine beauty was talking once – so the story went – of the good-looking wet-nurse who had suckled him when he was a baby: 'I'm sorry', he remarked, 'that I didn't make a better use of my opportunity'. I was in the habit of quoting this anecdote to explain the factor of after-wardsness in the mechanism of the psychoneuroses.[4]

This text is significant because it shows that in 1900 Freud still considered *Nachträglichkeit* an important concept that needed to be explained to his students. In this anecdote one finds reference to the two possible temporal directions involved in afterwardsness. The first direction is evoked when the adult man who sees the child at the wet-nurse's breast retrospectively imagines all that he could have drawn erotically from that situation if only he had known. So this is a true example of *Zurückphantasieren* (retrospective fantasizing) and of hermeneutics: he reinterprets the function of breast feeding in terms of his present situation. This is a totally Jungian conception. The other temporal direction is equally present, as one cannot forget that, according to Freud, oral sexuality is not purely invented by the adult. He thinks that the child at the breast enjoys sucking erotically, which he describes moreover in the *Three Essays on the Theory of Sexuality* (1905d) as the primary oral erotic experience. In this context, if the sexuality of the adult is awakened by the spectacle of the infant at the breast, it is because it has retained and preserved the traces of his own infantile sexuality. So two interpretations of this anecdote are possible, both progressive and retroactive, but they remain independent and isolated from each other.

Here I would like to intervene in Freud's account to give my own point of view, which is in no way a choice between these two options. It involves neither opting for the hermeneutic position nor for Freud's deterministic one. What Freud scotomises or does not wish to see in this example is simply . . . the wet-nurse. He only takes into account the two interlocutors equally centered on the subject: that is, the infantile subject, and the adult subject; the one sucks the breast, the other experiences erotic pleasure. Here Freud ignores the wet-nurse and her own sexuality. He has completely forgotten his seduction theory, and he does not take into account the pleasure of the seductive nurse or mother which will be central to the Leonardo study. He treats the breast as an *object* for

4 *The Interpretation of Dreams*, SE IV, p. 204–5. [Laplanche has substituted 'afterwards-ness' for Strachey's 'deferred action'. Editor's note.]

264

the infant, and not as an erotic zone for the nurse. So if one introduces a third term into this scene – that is, the nurse and her own sexuality, which is no doubt vaguely sensed by the baby – then it is no longer possible to consider afterwardsness as a combination of two opposed terms. The third term, then, is what is passed to the infant from the adult: the nurse's *message* to the infant.

The second element I would add to transform the concept of afterwardsness is the idea of translation. In my view, afterwardsness is inconceivable without a model of translation: that is, it presupposes that something is proffered by the other, and this is then afterwards retranslated and reinterpreted. On the one hand, there is my introduction of the notion of the *other*, and, on the other hand, there is the *translation* model. Even if we concentrate all our attention on the retroactive temporal direction, in the sense that someone reinterprets their past, this past cannot be a purely factual one, an unprocessed or raw 'given'. It contains rather in an immanent fashion something that comes before – a message from the other. It is impossible therefore to put forward a purely hermeneutic position on this – that is to say, that everyone interprets their past according to their present – because the past already has something deposited in it that demands to be deciphered, which is the message of the other person. But does not modern hermeneutics forget its very beginning, when it was – in the religious interpretation of sacred texts – a hermeneutic of the message?

To conclude, I would like to say that Freud's concept of afterwardsness contains both great richness and a certain ambiguity, combining a retrogressive and a progressive direction. I want to account for this problem of the different directions, to and fro, by arguing that, right at the start, there is something that goes in the direction of the past to the future, from the other to the individual in question, that is in the direction from the adult to the baby, which I call the implantation of the enigmatic message. This message is then retranslated, following a temporal direction which is, in an alternating fashion, by turns retrogressive and progressive (according to my general model of translation – detranslation – retranslation).

Select Bibliography

Abbreviations

SE The Standard Edition of the Complete Psychological Works of Sigmund Freud, ed. and trans. James Strachey, vols 1–24, London: The Hogarth Press, 1953–74. The references to Freud's works carry a lower-case letter after each date which follows the listing of works for each year as given in the Standard Edition.

GW Gesammelte Werke, eds Anna Freud with Marie Bonaparte (and others), vols 1–17, London: Imago Publishing Co., 1940–52; vol. 18, Frankfurt am Main: Fischer Verlag, 1968.

OCF Oeuvres Complètes de Freud (Psychanalyse), directeurs de publication: André Bourguignon and Pierre Cotet, directeur scientifique: Jean Laplanche, 21 vols (10 published), Paris: Presses Universitaires de France, 1988–.

Where more than one date appears within a given entry, the date immediately after the author's name is the date of the first publication, followed by the date of composition/delivery in square brackets where this is significantly different. The date of publication of the English translation is given at the end of the reference.

Abraham, Karl (1924), 'A Short Study of the Development of the Libido', *Selected Papers*, London: The Hogarth Press, 1927.

André, Jacques (1991), '*La sexualité féminine: retour aux sources*', *Psychanalyse à l'Université*, vol. 16, no. 62.

—— (1995), *Aux origines féminines de la sexualité*, Paris: Presses Universitaires de France.

Anzieu, Didier (1975), *Freud's Self-Analysis*, trans. Peter Graham, London: The Hogarth Press, 1986.

—— (1985), *The Skin Ego*, trans. Chris Turner, New Haven: Yale University Press, 1989.

Aron, Raymond (1938), *Introduction à la philosophie de l'histoire*, introd. Sylvie Mesure, Paris: Gallimard, 1986.

—— (1968), *La Révolution Introuvable*, Paris: Fayard.

Association Psychanalytique de France (1984), *La pulsion pour quoi faire?*, Paris.

Baudelaire, Charles (1859), *Selected Verse*, ed. with trans. Francis Scarfe, Harmondsworth: Penguin Books, 1961.

Benjamin, Andrew (1990), 'Translating Origins: Psychoanalysis and Philosophy', in *Rethinking Translation*, ed. Lawrence Venturi, London: Routledge.

—— (1992), 'The Unconscious: Structuring as a Translation', in *Jean Laplanche: Seduction, Translation and the Drives*, eds John Fletcher and Martin Stanton, London: Institute of Contemporary Arts.

Benveniste, Émile (1966), 'Remarks on the function of language in Freudian Theory', *Problems in General Linguistics*, trans. Elizabeth Meek, Coral Gables: University of Miami Press, 1971, pp. 65–75.

Bergson, Émile (1939), *Matter and Memory*, trans. Nancy Margaret Paul and W. Scott Palmer, London: Allen and Unwin, 1970.

Bernfeld, Suzanne (1951), 'Freud and Archaeology', *American Imago*, vol. 8, pp. 107–28.

Cocteau, Jean (1949), 'Les mariés de la Tour Eiffel', in *Théâtre de Cocteau*, tome I, Paris: Gallimard.

Cowie, Elizabeth (1992), 'The Seductive Theories of Jean Laplanche: a new view of the drive, passivity and femininity', in *Jean Laplanche: Seduction, Translation and the Drives*, eds John Fletcher and Martin Stanton, London: Institute of Contemporary Arts.

Crews, Frederick et al. (1995), *The Memory Wars*, London: Granta Books.

Dorey, Roger, Green, André, Rosolato, Guy et al. (1991), 'Psychanalyse hors les murs', *Psychanalyse à l'Université*, vol. 16, no. 64, pp. 3–28.

Duval, P. M. (1961), 'L'histoire et ses méthodes: Archéologie antique', *Encyclopédie Pléiade*, Paris: Gallimard.

Evans, Dylan (1996), *An Introductory Dictionary of Lacanian Psychoanalysis*, London: Routledge.

Fichte, J. G. (1792–3), *Attempt at a Critique of All Revelation*, trans. G. Green, Cambridge: Cambridge University Press, 1982.

Fletcher, John (1992), 'The Letter in the Unconscious: the enigmatic signifier in the work of Jean Laplanche', in *Jean Laplanche: Seduction, Translation and the Drives*, eds John Fletcher and Martin Stanton, London: Institute of Contemporary Arts, pp. 93–120.

Fletcher, John, and Stanton, Martin (eds) (1992), *Jean Laplanche: Seduction, Translation and the Drives*, London: Institute of Contemporary Arts.

Fraser, J. G. (1911), *The Golden Bough*, part II, 3rd edn, London: Macmillan.

Freud, Sigmund (1892–4), 'Preface and Footnotes to Charcot's *Tuesday Lectures*', *SE* I.

—— (1895), 'Letter 31 May, 1895 (Draft N)', in Freud (1985).

—— (1895d), *Studies on Hysteria*, *SE* II.

—— (1896c), 'The Aetiology of Hysteria', *SE* III.

—— (1897), 'Letter 21 September, 1897', in Freud (1985).

—— (1899a), 'Screen Memories', *SE* III.

—— (1900a), *The Interpretation of Dreams*, *SE* IV–V.

—— (1901b), *The Psychopathology of Everyday Life*, *SE* VI.

—— (1905d), *Three Essays on the Theory of Sexuality*, *SE* VII.

—— (1905e), 'Fragment of an Analysis of a Case of Hysteria' [Dora], *SE* VII.

—— (1906a), 'My Views on the Part Played by Sexuality in the Neuroses', *SE* VII.

—— (1908c), 'On the Sexual Theories of Children', *SE* IX.

—— (1908e), 'Creative Writers and Day-dreaming', *SE* IX.

—— (1909b), 'Analysis of a Phobia in a Five-Year-Old Boy' [Little Hans], *SE* X.

—— (1910c), *Leonardo da Vinci and a Memory of his Childhood*, *SE* XI.

—— (1910e), 'The Antithetical Meaning of Primal Words', *SE* XI.

—— (1911c), *Psycho-Analytic Notes on an Autobiographical Account of a Case of Paranoia (Dementia Paranoides)*, *SE* XII.

—— (1912b), 'The Dynamics of Transference', *SE* XII.

—— (1912–13), *Totem and Taboo*, *SE* XIII.

—— (1913j), 'The Claims of Psycho-Analysis to Scientific Interest', *SE* XIII.

—— (1914c), 'On Narcissism: An Introduction', *SE* XIV.

—— (1914d), 'On the History of the Psycho-Analytic Movement', *SE* XIV.

—— (1915a), 'Observations on Transference-Love (Further Recommendations on the Technique of Psycho-Analysis)', *SE* XII.

—— (1915b), 'Thoughts for the Times on War and Death', *SE* XIV.

—— (1915c), 'Instincts and their Vicissitudes', *SE* XIV.

—— (1915d), 'Repression', *SE* XIV.

—— (1915e), 'The Unconscious', *SE* XIV.

—— (1916a), 'On Transience', *SE* XIV.

—— (1916–17), *Introductory Lectures on Psycho-Analysis*, *SE* XV and XVI.

—— (1917a), 'A Difficulty in the Path of Psycho-Analysis', *SE* XVII.

—— (1917d), 'A Metapsychological Supplement to the Theory of Dreams', *SE* XIV.

—— (1917e), 'Mourning and Melancholia', *SE* XIV.

—— (1918a), 'The Taboo of Virginity (Contributions to the Psychology of Love III)', *SE* XI.

—— (1918b [1914]), *From the History of an Infantile Neurosis* [the Wolf Man], *SE* XVII.

—— (1919a), 'Lines of Advance in Psycho-Analytic Therapy', *SE* XVII.

—— (1919e), '"A Child is being Beaten": A Contribution to the Study of the Origin of Sexual Perversions', *SE* XVII.

—— (1919h), 'The Uncanny', *SE* XVII.

—— (1920g), *Beyond the Pleasure Principle*, *SE* XVIII.

—— (1922a), 'Dreams and Telepathy', *SE* XVIII.

—— (1922b), 'Some Neurotic Mechanisms in Jealousy, Paranoia and Homosexuality', *SE* XVIII.

—— (1923b), *The Ego and the Id*, *SE* XIX.

—— (1924b), 'Neurosis and Psychosis', *SE* XIX.

—— (1924c), 'The Economic Problem of Masochism', *SE* XIX.

—— (1924e), 'The Loss of Reality in Neurosis and Psychosis', *SE* XIX.

—— (1925a), 'A Note upon the "Mystic Writing-Pad"', *SE* XIX.

—— (1925d), *An Autobiographical Study*, *SE* XX.

—— (1925h), 'Negation', *SE* XIX.

—— (1926d), *Inhibitions, Symptoms and Anxiety*, *SE* XX.

—— (1927c), *The Future of an Illusion*, *SE* XXI.

—— (1928a), 'A Religious Experience', *SE* XXI.

—— (1930), Letter to Favez-Boutonier, 11 April 1930, *Bulletin Société Française de Philosophie*, janvier–mai, 1955.

—— (1930a), *Civilisation and its Discontents*, *SE* XXI.

—— (1933a), *New Introductory Lectures*, *SE* XXII.

—— (1935b), 'The Subtleties of a Faulty Action', *SE* XXII.

—— (1937c), 'Analysis Terminable and Interminable', *SE* XXIII.

—— (1937d), 'Constructions in Analysis', *SE* XXIII.

—— (1939a), *Moses and Monotheism: Three Essays*, *SE* XXIII.

—— (1940c), 'The Medusa's Head', *SE* XVIII.

—— (1950a [1895]), 'A Project for a Scientific Psychology', *SE* I.

—— (1954), *The Origins of Psycho-Analysis: Letters to Wilhelm Fliess, Drafts and Notes: 1887–1902*, London: Imago.

—— (1985), *The Complete Letters of Sigmund Freud to Wilhelm Fliess: 1887–1904*, trans. and ed. Jeffrey Moussaieff Masson, Cambridge, Mass.: The Belknap Press of Harvard University Press.

—— (1987 [1915]), *A Phylogenetic Fantasy: Overview of the Transference Neuroses*, ed. Ilse Gubrich-Simitis, Cambridge, Mass.: The Belknap Press of Harvard University Press.

—— (1993), *The Complete Correspondence of Sigmund Freud and Sándor Ferenczi, volume I: 1908–1914*, eds E. Brabant, E. Falzeder and P. Gampieri-Deutsch, Cambridge, Mass.: The Belknap Press of Harvard University Press.

Goldschmidt, G.-A. (1988), *Quand Freud voit la mer*, Paris: Buchet-Chastel.

Groddeck, Georg (1923), *The Book of the It*, London: C. W. Daniels, 1935.

Homer, *The Odyssey*, ed. W. B. Stanford, London: Macmillan, 1967.

Husserl, Edmund (1934), 'Foundational Investigations of the Phenomenological Origin of the Spatiality of Nature', trans. Fred Kersten, reprinted in *Husserl: Shorter Works*, eds Peter McCormick and Frederick A. Elliston, Indiana: University of Notre-Dame Press, 1981.

Imbert, Claude (1978), 'Pour une structure de la croyance: l'argument d'Anselme', *Nouvelle Revue de Psychanalyse*, vol. 18, pp. 43–54.

Isaacs, Susan (1948), 'Nature and Function of Phantasy', *International Journal of Psycho-analysis*, vol. 29, pp. 73–97, reprinted in *New Definitions in Psychoanalysis*, eds M. Klein, P. Heimann and R. Money-Kyrle, London: Maresfield, 1955.

Jones, Ernest (1955), *The Life and Work of Sigmund Freud*, London: The Hogarth Press.

Kant, Immanuel (1781), *The Critique of Pure Reason*, trans. J. M. D. Meiklejohn, London: J. M. Dent, 1934.

—— (1787), 'Preface' to 2nd edition of *The Critique of Pure Reason*, trans. Norman Kemp Smith, London: Macmillan, 1929/85.

Klein, Melanie (1940), 'Mourning and its relation to manic-depressive states', reprinted in *The Selected Melanie Klein*, ed. Juliet Mitchell, Harmondsworth: Penguin, 1986.

Lacan, Jacques (1966 [1953]), 'The function and field of speech and language in psychoanalysis', in Lacan (1977).

—— (1966 [1955–6]), 'On a question preliminary to any possible treatment of psychosis', in Lacan (1977).

—— (1966 [1957]), 'The agency of the letter in the unconscious or reason since Freud', in Lacan (1977).

—— (1966), *Écrits*, Paris: Seuil.

—— (1973 [1964]), *The Four Fundamental Concepts of Psychoanalysis*, ed. J.-A. Miller, trans. Alan Sheridan, Harmondsworth: Penguin Books, 1977.

—— (1977), *Écrits: A Selection*, trans. Alan Sheridan, London: Tavistock.

—— (1981), *The Psychoses: The Seminar of Jacques Lacan, Book III 1955–6*, ed. J.-A. Miller, trans. Russell Gigg, London: Routledge, 1993.

Lagache, Daniel (1956), 'Le problème du transfert', *Oeuvres III: Le transfert et autres travaux psychanalytiques*, Paris: Presses Universitaires de France, 1980.

—— (1956), 'Pathological Mourning', *Selected Writings*, trans. Elizabeth Holder, London: Karnac Books, 1993.

Lagrange, J. (1988), 'Problématiques du temps: phénoménologie et psychanalyse', in *Psychanalyse à l'Université*, vol. 13, no. 52, pp. 575–607.

Lanouzière, Jacqueline (1991), *Histoire secrète de la séduction sous la règne de Freud*, Paris: Presses Universitaires de France.

Laplanche, Jean (1961a), *Holderlin et la question du père*, Paris: Presses Universitaires de France.

—— (1961b), *La réalité dans la névrose et la psychose*, Paris: Société française de Psychanalyse.

—— (1968a), 'Interpréter [avec] Freud', reprinted in *La révolution copernicienne inachevée*, Paris: Aubier, 1992.

—— (1968b), 'La position originaire du masochisme dans le champ de la pulsion sexuelle', reprinted in *La révolution copernicienne inachevée*, Paris: Aubier, 1992.

—— (1969), 'Les principes du fonctionnement psychique', reprinted in *La révolution copernicienne inachevée*, Paris: Aubier, 1992.

—— (1970), *Life and Death in Psychoanalysis*, trans. Jeffrey Mehlman, Baltimore: The Johns Hopkins University Press, 1976.

—— (1971), 'Derivation of Psychoanalytic Entities', reprinted as an appendix to *Life and Death in Psychoanalysis*, trans. Jeffrey Mehlman, Baltimore: The Johns Hopkins University Press, 1976.

—— (1972), 'Le traitement psychanalytique des états psychotiques', reprinted in *La révolution copernicienne inachevée*, Paris: Aubier, 1992.

—— (1979), 'A Metapsychology put to the test of Anxiety', *International Journal of Psycho-Analysis*, vol. 62, 1981.

—— (1980a [1970–3]), *Problématiques I: L'angoisse*, Paris: Presses Universitaires de France.

—— (1980b [1973–5]), *Problématiques II: Castrations-symbolisations*, Paris: Presses Universitaires de France.

—— (1980c [1975–7]), *Problématiques III: La sublimation*, Paris: Presses Universitaires de France. (Part of this appeared as 'To situate sublimation', trans. Richard Miller, *October*, no. 28, Spring, 1984.)

—— (1981 [1977–9]), *Problématiques IV: L'inconscient et la ça*, Paris: Presses Universitaires de France, trans. Luke Thurston, *The Unconscious and the Id*, London: Rebus Press, 1999.

—— (1986), 'From the Restricted to the Generalised Theory of Seduction', in *Seduction, Suggestion, Psychoanalysis*, eds J. Corveleyn and Philippe van Haute, Pittsburgh: Leiven University Press and Duquesne University Press, 1998.

—— (1987a [1979–84]), *Problématiques V: Le baquet: transcendance du transfert*, Paris: Presses Universitaires de France.

—— (1987b), *New Foundations for Psychoanalysis*, trans. David Macey, Oxford: Basil Blackwell, 1989.

—— (1988), 'The Wall and the Arcade', trans. Martin Stanton in *Jean Laplanche: Seduction, Translation and the Drives*, eds John Fletcher and Martin Stanton, London: Institute of Contemporary Arts, 1992.

—— (1989a), 'Terminologie raisonnée', in *Traduire Freud*, eds André Bourguignon, Pierre Cotet, Jean Laplanche and François Robert, Paris: Presses Universitaires de France, trans. by Bertrand Vichyn in *Translating Freud*, ed. Darius Gray Ornston, New Haven: Yale University Press, 1992.

—— (1989b), 'Psychoanalysis, Time and Translation', in *Jean Laplanche: Seduction, Translation and the Drives*, eds John Fletcher and Martin Stanton, London: Institute of Contemporary Arts, 1992.

—— (1989c), 'Temporality and Translation', *Stanford Literary Review*, Autumn, 1989.

—— (1991a), 'Specificity of Terminological Problems in the Translation of Freud', *International Review of Psycho-Analysis*, vol. 18.

—— (1991b), 'Jean Laplanche talks to Martin Stanton: an Interview', *Free Associations*, vol. 2, no. 23.

—— (1992a), *La révolution copernicienne inachevée: travaux 1967–1992*, Paris: Aubier.

—— (1992b), 'The Freud Museum Seminar', in *Jean Laplanche: Seduction, Translation and the Drives*, eds John Fletcher and Martin Stanton, London: Institute of Contemporary Arts, 1992.

—— (1993), *Le fourvoiement biologisant de la sexualité chez Freud*, Paris: Synthélabo.

—— (1994), 'Psychoanalysis as Anti-hermeneutics', *Radical Philosophy*, no. 79, Sept./Oct. 1996.

—— (1996), 'Aims of the Psychoanalytic Process', *Journal of European Psychoanalysis*, vol. 5, Spring–Fall 1997, pp. 69–79.

—— (1997), 'The Theory of Seduction and the Problem of the Other', *International Journal of Psycho-Analysis*, vol. 78, no. 4.

Laplanche, Jean, and Leclaire, Serge (1966), 'The unconscious: A psychoanalytic study', trans. Patrick Coleman, *Yale French Studies*, no. 48, 1972, pp. 118–202.

Laplanche, Jean, and Pontalis, Jean-Bertrand (1964), 'Fantasy and the Origins of

Sexuality', in *International Journal of Psycho-Analysis*, vol. 49, 1968, reprinted in *Formations of Fantasy*, eds Victor Burgin, James Donald and Cora Kaplan, London: Methuen, 1986.

—— (1967), *The Language of Psychoanalysis*, trans. Donald Nicholson-Smith, London: The Hogarth Press, 1973.

Le Goff, J., and Nora, P. (1974), *Faire de l'Histoire*, Paris: Gallimard.

Levinas, Emmanuel (1948), *Time and the Other*, trans. Richard A. Cohen, Pittsburgh: Duquesne University Press, 1987.

Lyotard, J.-F. (1984), 'Figure foreclosed', trans. David Macey, in ed. Andrew Benjamin, *The Lyotard Reader*, Oxford: Basil Blackwell, 1989.

Macalpine, Ida (1950), 'The Development of the Transference', *Psychoanalytic Quarterly*, vol. XIX.

Maïdani-Gérard, J.-P. (1993), *Léonard da Vinci: mythologie ou théologie?*, Paris: Presses Universitaires de France.

Mallarmé, Stéphane (1965), *Mallarmé*, ed. with trans. Anthony Hartley, Harmondsworth: Penguin Books.

Malev, M. (1966), 'The Jewish orthodox circumcision ceremony', in *Journal of the American Psychoanalytic Association*, vol. 14, pp. 510–17.

Mannoni, Octave (1969), 'Je sais bien, mais quand même . . .', in *Clefs pour l'imaginaire de l'autre scène*, Paris: Seuil.

Masson, J. M. (1984), *The Assault on Truth: Freud's Suppression of the Seduction Theory* with new Preface and Afterword, Harmondsworth: Penguin Books, 1985.

Merleau-Ponty, Maurice (1945), *Phenomenology of Perception*, trans. Colin Smith, London: Routledge and Kegan Paul, 1962.

Moscovici, M. (1986), *Préface* to the French edition of Freud (1939a), Paris: Gallimard.

de M'Uzan, M. (1977), 'Un cas de masochisme pervers', *De l'art à la mort*, Paris: Gallimard.

Nouvelle Revue Psychanalytique (1993), 'L'inconscient mis à l'épreuve', no. 48.

Oppenheimer, Agnes (1984), 'Le meilleur des mondes possibles. A propos du projet de R. Schafer', in *Psychanalyse à l'Université*, vol. 9, no. 35, pp. 467–90.

Pascal, Blaise, (1669), *Pensées I*, ed. Zacharie Tourneur, Paris: Cluny, 1938.

Pasche, F., and Renard, M. (1956), 'Realité de l'objet et point de vue économique', in *Revue française de Psychanalyse*, XX, octobre–décembre, no. 4, pp. 517–24.

Plutarch, *Les Vies des Hommes Illustres Grecs et Romains: Vie de Demosthenes*, trans. Jacques Amyot (1559), Édition Critique par Jean Normand, Société des Textes Français Modernes, Paris: Librairie Hachette, 1924.

Pontalis, Jean-Bertrand (1978), 'Se fier à, sans croire en', introduction to *Nouvelle Revue Psychanalytique*, no. 18.

Ricoeur, Paul (1965), *Freud and Philosophy: An Essay on Interpretation*, New Haven: Yale University Press, 1970.

—— (1985), *Temps et Récit*, tome III, 'Le temps raconté', Paris: Seuil.

—— (1985), *Time and Narrative*, trans. Katherine Blamey and David Pellauer, University of Chicago Press, 1988.

Rosolato, Guy (1969), 'Paranoïa et scène primitive', in *Essais sur le symbolique*, Paris: Gallimard.

—— (1973), *Névrose, psychose et perversion*, Paris: Presses Universitaires de France.

—— (1978), *La Relation d'Inconnu*, Paris: Gallimard.

—— (1987), 'La pratique: son cadre, ses interdits', *Psychanalyse à l'Université*, vol. 12, no. 47, pp. 469–85.

—— (1991), *Le sacrifice*, Paris: Presses Universitaires de France.

—— (1992), 'Les fantasmes originaires et leurs mythes correspondants', *Nouvelle Revue de Psychanalyse*, vol. 46, pp. 223–46.

Roussillon, René (1992), *Du baquet de Mesmer au 'baquet' de S. Freud*, Paris: Presses Universitaires de France.

Rousso, Henri (1987), *Le Syndrome de Vichy de 1944 à nos Jours*, Paris: Seuil.

Sagan, Carl (1975), *Cosmic Connexion*, Paris: Seuil.

Scarfone, Dominique (1994), '"Ma mère, ce n'est pas elle". De la séduction à la négation', in Jean Laplanche et al., *Colloque internationale de psychanalyse: Montréal 3–5 juillet 1992*, Paris: Presses Universitaires de France.

Schafer, Roy (1976), *A New Language for Psychoanalysis*, New Haven: Yale University Press.

Société Psychanalytique de Paris (1974), 'Colloque: Constructions et reconstructions en psychanalyse', *Revue française de Psychanalyse*, vol. 38, pp. 171–384.

—— (1989), 'Colloque: Fonction dépressive et complexe d'Oedipe', *Revue française de psychanalyse*, vol. 53, mai–juin, no. 3.

Spence, Donald P. (1982), *Narrative Truth and Historical Truth*, New York and London: W. W. Norton.

Stalin (1973), 'On the question of Marxism in linguistics', in *The Essential Stalin: the Major Theoretical Writings 1905–1952*, ed. Bruce Franklin, London: Croom Helm.

Taton, René (ed.) (1966), *Histoire Générale des Sciences*, vol. I, Paris: Presses Universitaires de France.

Thomä, Helmut, and Cheshire, Neil (1991), 'Freud's *Nachträglichkeit* and Strachey's "Deferred Action": Trauma, Constructions and the Direction of Causality', *International Review of Psychoanalysis*, vol. 18, pp. 407–27.

Thomä, Helmut, and Kächele, H. *Lehrbuch der Psychanalytischen Therapie*, vol. I: 1985; vol. II: 1988, Berlin, Heidelberg and New York: Springer-Verlag.

Toubiana, Éric (1988), *L'héritage et sa psychopathologie*, Paris: Presses Universitaires de France.

Van Haute, Philippe (1995), 'Fatal Attraction: Jean Laplanche on Sexuality, Subjectivity and Singularity', *Radical Philosophy*, no. 73, Sept./Oct.

Viderman, Serge (1970), *La Construction de l'Espace Analytique*, Paris: Denoël.

—— (1974), 'La bouteille à la mer', *Revue française de psychanalyse*, vol. 38, pp. 323–84.

Widlöcher, Daniel (1993), 'Temps pour entendre, temps pour interpréter, temps pour comprendre', *Bulletin de la Fédération Européenne de Psychanalyse*, no. 40, pp. 24–5.

Index

274

Printed in Great Britain
by Amazon